THE
ROCKEFELLER
SYNDROME

BOOKS BY FERDINAND LUNDBERG
IMPERIAL HEARST
AMERICA'S SIXTY FAMILIES
MODERN WOMAN: THE LOST SEX (in collaboration)
THE TREASON OF THE PEOPLE
THE COMING WORLD TRANSFORMATION
SCOUNDRELS ALL
THE RICH AND THE SUPER-RICH
THE ROCKEFELLER SYNDROME

THE ROCKEFELLER SYNDROME

BY FERDINAND LUNDBERG

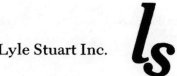

Lyle Stuart Inc.   Secaucus, New Jersey

First impression August, 1975

EDITED BY SANDRA LEE STUART
Published by Lyle Stuart Inc.

Library of Congress Catalog Number 75-23031
ISBN: 0-8184-0215-6

MANUFACTURED IN THE UNITED STATES OF AMERICA

Published simultaneously in Canada by George J. McLeod, Limited, Toronto, Ontario

Library of Congress Cataloging in Publication Data

Lundberg, Ferdinand, 1902–
  The Rockefeller syndrome.

  Bibliography: p. 394
  Includes index.
  1. Rockefeller family. 2. Capitalists and financiers—United States. I. Title.
HG172.R64L85   332'.092'2 [B]   75-23031
ISBN 0-8184-0215-6

To Sandy

Contents

One

Zeroing In On the Rockefellers

Amid excited predictions by media luminaries that the full extent of Rockefeller wealth was finally, at long last, to be unveiled for the public record, congressional hearings opened and sprawled over the final quarter of 1974 on Nelson Aldrich Rockefeller's nomination by unelected President Gerald Ford to be unelected vice-president of the United States. Alas for palpitant expectations! For what was disclosed had as much flashy form in it as solid substance.

Although many figures on Rockefeller wealth have been bruited about from time to time—from $600 million to $10 billion—there are on the public record positively no authentic, fully certified, standardly audited figures and inventory on the dimensions of the fortune at any given moment in time. The Washington hearings of 1974 produced no such credible figures. Moreover, what was presented was not subjected to the meticulous sifting mediamen had rashly forecast.

Actually, neither the House nor Senate committees charged with inquiring into the fitness of Nelson Rockefeller for the office had any official reason for conducting a rigorous financial analysis. It was enough, for their purposes, to establish in general for the record where the family interests radiated.

9

One often encounters the statement that the original John D. Rockefeller—John I—was personally worth $900 million in 1913 after having already funded foundations at approximately $500 million. The figure comes from the known market value in that year of the known amount of Standard Oil stock he owned at the time of the Supreme Court dissolution decree of 1911. But the figure does not include the value of his other undisclosed large holdings in United States Steel, of which he was the largest stockholder at its inception in 1901, International Harvester Company, in whose merger he participated, and many other companies and banks such as the National City Bank of New York. Nor did it reckon on the value of much real estate he held, various bond holdings governmental and corporate, and the like. Nor did it count in his cash. Or any gold, precious jewels, antiques, art work, and so on.

For John D. Rockefeller as of 1911-1913 owned much more than 25 percent of the Standard Oil Company of New Jersey—much, much more.

The fact is, from the very beginning to the present, there has been no properly audited and professionally certified *public* accounting of the Rockefeller fortune *in toto*. And what was presented at the congressional nomination hearings did not fill the bill. It was demonstrably a loophole affair, suitable for the occasion. Moreover, what was laid out was not given any public analysis by the backroom sharpshooters of the House and Senate committees. These withheld their fire.

What there was of disclosure in the hearings concerned instead certain aspects of the way the present generation of Rockefellers operates in politics. And while nothing felonious was brought to light, no smoking pistols or dead bodies (to the obvious disappointment of adversary individuals and groups), their fingerprints were turned up on poisoned pens and odd money transactions—enough in all to classify them as suspicious characters, to be carefully watched. Not the only suspicious characters in our fair realm, by any means. But among them.

Plenty of questions for electoral evaluation, a goodly measure of chicaneries and ambiguous stratagems, were laid on the record. As back-street philosophers often sagely observe, "That's politics." In brief, the sort of fakery fostered by the labyrinthine system itself. They didn't, in other words, emerge from the proceedings smelling like a bouquet of fresh-cut roses.

Politically the hearings accomplished this: they took away some of the edge Nelson enjoyed over other candidates for the presidency by reason of his wealth and the questionable high moral stance into which the family had been elevated by John D. II.

Nelson's appearance was related to two separate aspects of his background.

The first and official consideration bore on his personal fitness to be vice-president and possibly president of the superlatively marvelous United States of America. The next and unofficial but significant concern was the precise size and nature of his and his family's fortune, its banking and corporate control, and its corporate and general influence. As to control and influence—this last being vast—the hearings carefully abstained from inquiring although Nelson decried the "myth" of his family's power. If he really believes it is a myth, he can learn much by reading these pages.

The fundamental technical question posed for the record, providing the ostensible ground for the hearings and the summoning in of data, was whether there might be any conflict of interest involved in Nelson's filling either of the two high offices, one of them often orgulously described as the greatest gift within the power of the amazingly great American people. As was dourly observed by Congressman Wright Patman of Texas, for many years chairman of the House Banking and Currency Committee, the Rockefellers are "a family which has more conflicts of interest than any other in the world." So many, indeed, are these conflicts that in some cases they cancel each other. In the showdown in the corral of the OK Congress the redoubtable Patman voted against the confirmation and, naturally, bit the dust.

Quite a bit of unconscious irony was generated, though, in

the raising of the conflict-of-interest question. For both houses of Congress have been repeatedly and overwhelmingly
shown to be saturated with conflicts of interest, its dominant
members seldom scrupling to vote lucrative personal interests
rather than the fulsomely celebrated general interest. It
would, for a tiny example, be very much in the general interest to place strict control over private ownership of firearms.
Yet Congress, despite heavy public demand for it as shown by
polls, has repeatedly voted it down at the behest of the gun-
industry lobby with which many key congressmen enjoy
toothsome symbiotic connections. The consequence is there
are some fifty million private handguns scattered around the
country, giving rise to a fantastic quantity of civil carnage—
hardly a sign of quality government.

It's possible that as many people are shot to death out of
hand in the United States in a year—and stabbed, blud-
geoned, stomped, or otherwise rudely treated—as are now
done in by the often denounced Soviet KGB. In other words,
contrary to sturdy myth, it's easier to be slain by private parties in the sloppily run United States for nothing at all, not
even for money, right in one's bed, than to be hauled on the
carpet and tossed into Lubianka for failing to toe the political
line in the deplorable Soviet paradise.

One could cite hundreds of even more open-and-shut,
equally startling examples of stuff similar to the gun-control
fiasco, all defended by transparently casuistic arguments that
a child of twelve could demolish.

Naturally, Congress found there was no conflict of interest
involved in Rockefeller holding the office of vice-president—
no more qualitatively, at any rate, than in the cases of many of
its members. The clandestine partiality of government to special private interests with which its elected officials are gain-
fully allied is one of the elements that gives the United States
its distinctive high aroma.

The hearings dragged on for more than four months. Seventeen days were devoted to public sessions, others *in camera.*
Some three hundred FBI agents out of thirty-seven offices
staged 1,400 field interviews, an unusual scrutiny of an upper-

level candidate. Some observers became impatient and questioned the wisdom of the Twenty-fifth Amendment to the Constitution. This recent appendage provides for appointive interim vice-presidents in the event of unfortuitous vacancies.

While confirmatory procedures under the amendment turned out to be tedious for the impatient pro-Rockefeller people—at one point it seemed that the adverse pressures would force Rockefeller to withdraw—it is nevertheless a fact that through the congressional hearings on Ford and Rockefeller the country knows a great deal more about these two men and their *modus operandi* than about most who assume office. The incoming president can often be described, in truth, as The Unknown Man. Not that it makes much difference to most of the electorate, too addled in civic orientation to care.

Lyndon B. Johnson, Richard Nixon, and Spiro Agnew could hardly have survived such hearings, and certainly not Warren Gamaliel Harding. Whether the garrulous Coolidge or heavy-footed Hoover would have looked good under comparable inquiry and questioning, restrained though it was, is doubtful. Many others who have held the top offices, clinkers in one way or the other, would have made far worse showings than did Ford and Rockefeller. As I hint, the offices are seldom held by paragons, the presidential cult notwithstanding.

If, now, Ford and/or Rockefeller stand for election in 1976, the electorate, for whatever it is worth, will have a more penetrating perception of them than of any Democrat yet mentioned as a possible rival candidate. If all the candidates had to undergo the same sort of interrogation, which in the case of Rockefeller was not too searing, the effective field might be considerably reduced and the country at least slightly wiser if not better.

Confirmation came exactly 128 days after the nomination by Ford.

Why was Nelson Rockefeller, a nominal Republican, confirmed—by 90 to 7 in the Senate, 287 to 128 in the House of Representatives? Both bodies were overwhelmingly manned by members of the formally adversary Democratic party, dual arm of the collusive American bipartisan system that is, in effect, one party. The Senate Rules Committee had recommended the confirmation by 9 to 0, the House Judiciary Committee by 26 to 12.

In the first place, the country needed an interim vice-president under the Constitution and most members felt that the president was entitled to name whomever he wished. According to practice, almost anybody would do—provided he was not a man of independent ideas or genuine moral stature. If anything happened to Gerald Ford, such as an overzealous patriot gunning him down with one of thousands of readily available Colt .45s, the next person in the line of constitutional succession (pending the vice-presidential vacancy) was diminutive Speaker Carl Albert of the House of Representatives. He did not want the post and, anyhow, was not considered by anybody to conform to the image of a president. Albert, the fact is, lacked metaphysical as well as visual plausibility. The minimum informal requirement of the office is that one at least look the part; it was admirably met by Warren G. Harding, one of the worst presidents but nevertheless one whose low rating was quickly exceeded on the downside by Johnson and Nixon, two outstanding clinkers.

Short of showing that the nominee had been engaged in outlandishly gamy affairs, almost anyone named would have gained confirmation. The hearings on Ford and Rockefeller served, though, the prudent purpose for the political parties of avoiding later explosive surprises, as in the case of Spiro Agnew, whose bagmen secretly brought his graft to his vice-presidential office. Disclosure of this practice provided a thought-provoking scene for patriots at large.

Many of the freelance critics who showed up to bear witness against Rockefeller obviously labored under a serious fundamental misapprehension, viz., that in naming Rockefeller as vice-president something new and unusual, possibly sinister and underhanded, fascist or communist, was being proposed for the United States government. Yet Rockefeller represented no new or alien ingredient. He had zigzagged in and out of near-the-top federal appointive posts since 1940, was governor of the fabulous Empire State for fifteen years (three and three-quarters terms), and his family had been heavy funders, secret and open, of the Grand Old Party since the 1870s. For nearly thirty-five years he had hobnobbed on a first-name basis officially and unofficially with all the top dogs in government of both parties and had yak-yakked with nearly every foreign ruler and chief henchman thereof.

Furthermore, as vice-president he would have no more power than the president allowed him (except for casting the deciding vote in the rare event of a tie ballot in the Senate). As vice-president, then, he would have no more constitutional say-so than he had as a nominally plain citizen with thousands of devoted chums in key governmental posts, state and federal, many of them recipients of Rockefeller pecuniary awards, loans, and monetary gifts. He would, of course, be in more of a spotlight position than an ordinary citizen; but he could not make too obtrusive use of the spotlight without incurring presidential displeasure, tantamount politically for this office to exile in Siberia.

As later events showed, President Ford yielded him an unusually active role for a vice-president, almost enough to qualify as an assistant president or viceroy. He was first put in charge of the special commission to investigate the self-inculpated CIA, which amounted to the executive branch investigating itself. He was also made vice-chairman of the president's Domestic Council and allowed to organize it with some of his own people in charge, an important assignment that signaled to some observers the Ford presidency was now a duumvirate. The Rock unquestionably advises behind the scenes on many matters—that is, passes along the conclusions of his capable staff.

Although the final report in June, 1975, of his Commission on C.I.A. Activities abundantly confirmed that for more than two decades there had, as charged, been massive illegal domestic C.I.A. operations against critics and opponents of entrenched politicians or their policies, the Commission recoiled from probing into the charge that the agency had staged numerous assassinations abroad. The report said the Commission had found no "credible evidence" that the C.I.A. was involved

in the assassination of President John F. Kennedy. The resolution of all such explosive questions were left up to Congress.

That Rockefeller was to be no ordinary vice-president was
signalized right after his confirmation by the enplanement of
his entire large and very savvy New York staff for Washington.
An ordinary vice-president needs no such high-powered staff,
does not, in fact, need any staff at all.

If Rockefeller became president, of course, he would hold
the decisive voice for the executive department in thousands
of details, large and small, a supreme pontiff. Such a smashing
role would be something new for a Rockefeller, as indeed it is
for anyone who takes the office. Apart from George Washington, nobody who has stepped into the office has been clothed
prior to incumbency with plenary authority—moral, physical,
or occult.

But while neither Nelson nor any member of his family ever
had such a general final voice in national policy-making, both
he and his family for decades have made, usually through
their top lawyers, an extensive input of advice and recommendation to a generally receptive officialdom in all departments
of the government from bottom to top, including the White
House. The Rockefellers have never been helpless citizens
who, as politicos gambol and frolic, have nothing to say about
what goes on. With respect to almost every president since
Chester A. Arthur, they have had ground-floor entree and have
been respectfully listened to. Whenever they have been
turned down, under most presidents one may be sure the reasons were carefully explained to them. One may also be sure
they fully understood the hard necessities of each disappoint-
ing occasion. And although never White House incumbents,
they have, since the days of old John D., been closely associated with the president-makers.

In other words, not kings themselves, they have long been
among the ducal courtiers, palace advisors, and king-makers.

What objectors to his confirmation did not seem to understand fully was that if Nelson Aldrich Rockefeller ever entered the White House as the incumbent, it would not be at all
inappropriate if a banner were first placed over the front door

reading, "Welcome Home, Rocky." While such a prospect is out of harmony with political myth, it is imaginatively wholly in accord with reality.

Rockefeller, in other words, was no run-of-the-mill casual political bum to be shoved around by a bunch of congressmen and bearers of harsh witness. And Congress and its committees showed this by its restrained demeanor in his presence.

The exact size of his and his family's fortune, for one thing, was irrelevant to the proceedings although interesting for sociological reasons. For under no statutes or in the Constitution is there any barrier to a wealthy person entering the White House as suzerain. George Washington, the first president and one of the best if not *the* best, was one of the wealthiest men of his day. So here was a precedent right at the outset of the great American adventure (as school historians gaudily phrase it). Since that early time most presidents have been light-years away from pauperdom. Several current Democratic aspirants are multiple millionaires.

Under the Constitution a man may be a pauper or a multibillionaire ten times over, of any color or madcap belief, and still be eligible for the office. Or the president may be a woman, and wealthy to boot—a desirable combination. The basic formal requirement is that he or she be born in the United States, which rules out only Austrian house-painters, Corsican corporals, and such odd birds.

An assumption of many of the critics appeared to be that Rockefeller's wealth in and of itself was a disqualification. Such critics did not seem to be aware in the light either of the Constitution, its framers, or American history in general that the possession of wealth is not *ipso facto* a bad thing. Many of the founders and framers were wealthy, many born to wealth. Nor, contrary to the victims of public relations myth and fantasy, was the United States established as a haven for the poor, a roosting place for the wretched and oppressed of the earth. Nothing of the sort. Indeed, far from it.

Many of the Rockefeller critics, in other words, had implicitly in mind some system of government other than that of the United States or some system they would rather see in being.

The members of Congress who voted for the nomination, however, were under the spell of no such extraneous visions. They knew what the system of government really was. And they knew Nelson Rockefeller was no stranger to it, no outsider, no subversive.

Yet a few observers more subtly aware than the objectors marveled that a Rockefeller should seek the glittering office in view of the ability of the family to survive and thrive handsomely as, legally, ordinary garden-variety citizens. Most of the wealthy in the United States get their way through stooges in the government, onetime poor boys who are "succeeding" and surreptitiously building estates, *à la* Johnson and Nixon, while holding office, panting their way up the shaky ladder from oblivion to obscurity, selling the favors of the State under the table. By taking office themselves, especially prominent office, the wealthy run the risk of encountering an extra portion of public flak through assuming visible formal responsibility for seamy states of affairs as they bear disadvantageously on the lives of the *hoi polloi.* The avoidance of such flak is one of the prime objectives of the Rockefeller family as shown by their heavy reliance on astute public relations advisors. It is a self-contradiction, therefore, for one of them to place himself in a position to invite it.

Every president, of whatever caliber, no matter what decisions he makes, has to take a good deal of public flak. Washington, regarded by the best scholarship as the preeminent president because of his mastery of a very difficult situation, was literally sickened by the amount of criticism directed against him, most of it contrived by uncouth Jeffersonians for partisan reasons and ill grounded. Lincoln, regarded almost as highly, also was given the roughest sort of critical manhandling. And the third most competent president, Franklin D. Roosevelt, was raked over the coals almost as brutally as these two. No president, no matter how much of a pussycat, has totally escaped vicious below-the-belt jabs. It is all in the nature of the office and the society.

Rockefeller as president, even if he miraculously found the secret of eternal life for all, could hardly escape similar katzenjammer. And his family, no matter what he did short of making the tigers of the world suckle the lambs, could hardly escape being placed in the same basket. Its members would be regarded as coconspirators in whatever he did that the *hoi polloi* or captious critics found offensive.

As to why Rockefeller wants to be president, which it has long been clear he does, the reasons are not too evident. He certainly does not need the office to add to his wealth, which is blooming to high heaven anyhow. One reason advanced is that the office is without question a high public honor, and if he attains it, will conceivably shed luster on his family, which has not always been honored; but it also could, such is the nature of affairs, put it deep in the doghouse. Another explanation is that Nelson is a show-off and among other objectives wants the office in order to show that he has risen to greater heights even than gimlet-eyed John D. I, the patron saint of the family, regarded by it as the cat's whiskers.

Rockefeller himself says he seeks the office in order to be of vast public service and to aid the world with his unusual claimed abilities as a demon problem-solver. Even if he really believes this himself, nobody else in and around politics believes it. He's no savior, whatever else he may be.

My own rock-bottom analysis grounds itself at a deeper level. He unquestionably believes he is as capable as any other visible contender, which could be a fact, and he believes the office is attainable. But his motivation for setting the presidency as a goal to the inconvenience of his family stems, I believe, from simple sibling rivalry. The Rockefeller boys, like the Kennedy boys, were reared with the understanding that they were to be active and were to distinguish themselves in some way in the world, not to be merely ornamental. Rivalry developed among them in showing what each could do, with Nelson the most drivingly competitive. The rivalry was not as overt, not as open to display, as among the pugnacious Kennedys, where all four boys in succession were bitten by the presidential bug, implanted by their demonic father. But it was nevertheless apparent and insensibly nurtured itself in a household that esteemed performance, put a prize on achievement, and offered concrete special rewards.

While none of the Rockefeller boys other than Nelson conceived such a vaunting ambition, they all developed some sort of more-than-ordinary ambition. And one who was not able for a long time to measure up to the family expectations felt it keenly and became a painful family problem until, after a fashion, he straightened himself out and scored.

The fundamental unconscious reason, then, that exuberant Nelson Aldrich Rockefeller is ambitious to be president is that it will show him to be the prize man vis-à-vis his brothers, the one worthiest of parental approbation, teacher's pet. Aware that such valuable psychological *aperçus* are looked at askance by the incognoscenti, I simply put forth the idea for the consideration of any who want a rock-bottom explanation. Let who will supply a better one.

The oppressively massive and extensively deployed Albany Mall is one clear illustration that Nelson Rockefeller is a man of imperial, possibly zany, ambition, one whose dreams take him far beyond the mere possession of a large fortune. Nobody else asked for the Mall, which cost $1 to $1.5 billion of public money, and which was built without legislative or popular approval. So busy have commentators been trying to cut it down to human proportions by means of comic epithets —Instant Stonehenge, Neo-Stalinesque, Late Nuremberg and Pharaonic—that nobody seems to have troubled to ask what the five towering, grim architectural slabs mean, subjectively and objectively.

These ultraimperial slabs certainly express something. What and for whom? The affair makes the Washington Monument and the Lincoln and Jefferson Memorials look, by comparison, like trivial toys. No government structure in Washington compares with it, and certainly not the modest White House nor the Supreme Court Building nor even the Roman-type Capitol nor the United Nations Building in New York. It out-Pentagons the Pentagon.

Could the gigantic Mall be taken to express the Spirit of New York State? That is hardly possible; for New York State is only a small fraction of the Union and neither the nation itself nor any other nation possesses so forbidding and grandiloquent architectural symbolization. Does it represent some sort of superimperial dream for the United States? That, too, is hardly possible; for then it would not be located in obscure Albany, one of fifty minor state capitals. Albany itself is a pimple of a city, the Kabul of the Hudson.

Totalitarian, Babylonian, Assyrian, Byzantine—the Mall simply must be taken as representing some inner urge to overweening dominance or preeminence by its sole patron, the one who alone called it into being. Although Wallace K. Harrison, a longtime family associate, was the chief architect, Nelson was assiduous in supplying sketches for the project. It was elaborated out of the heads of the two men, with Nelson supplying the demiurgic propulsion.

It can hardly be taken as expressing the American spirit. If it did that, protest against it would not be so vehement. It plainly goes straight against the American grain—too rigid, too inflexible, too corporately bureaucratic.

Massively overpowering in appearance against the sky, the soaring tusks one sees rising overhead and spread out are, one might say, the least part of it. It consists of eleven buildings set deep on ninety-eight acres: there are five high-rise office buildings of trapezoidal shape standing in rank, one a forty-four-story office tower (tallest building in the state outside Manhattan) and four narrow twenty-three-story office buildings; three lower but wider office buildings; and the other buildings comprising a meeting and cultural center, library, and museum. All are faced with Vermont and Georgia marble —ultraposh. The Meeting Center is bowl shaped. The buildings stand, with the space underneath a clear esplanade, on giant rounded steel arches, clawing into the ground like strange, soulless monsters.

The five high-risers and the Meeting Center stand over a construction dubbed the Main Platform, which is 1,440 feet long and 600 feet wide. This consists of five levels, with three below ground holding mechanical and storage areas, a huge fallout shelter, a medical center, a garage for 3,300 cars, and a tunnel for a four-lane highway. On the fourth level are offices, cafeterias, boutiques, meeting halls, exhibition areas, and a bus terminal. On the upper level are landscaped plazas with fountains, pools, and walkways.

By comparison the entire Rube Goldberg affair writ large

makes the hanging gardens of Babylon by contrast look like a
midget's toy. Had Hitler won the big war, he and Albert Speer
might have worked out something similar by way of commemorating victory. "Sieg heil" one feels forced to cry as one
contemplates it.

As Nelson Rockefeller was the idea-man for the creation, as
there is no external *raison d'être* for it, I take it, lacking any
other explanation, to be a projection on the world of Nelson
Rockefeller's self-conception, his personal apotheosis in
stone, steel, cement, and marble—a massive, towering, and
overpowering presence: El Supremo, the pharaoh of pharaohs, the shah of shahs, the Caesar of Caesars, the emperor of
emperors. It is his statement and his alone. The Mall, clearly,
is a fantasy in stone and metal expressing a delusion or aspira-
tion of intense grandeur and superiority. Some would call it
megalomania. Or *is* it a delusion? Perhaps Nelson Rockefeller
really is El Supremo or feels himself destined to be—in
dreams, at least.

The most revealing aspect of the Mall, however, and the one
which shows most clearly the cool arrogance of its creator, is
not its architectural massivity but the way it was sneaked into
being at oppressive public expense. A genuine sneak-play of
big dimensions which added to the already great Rockefeller-
induced public tax burden. Here we get into a big variation
and fugue on the theme of what David Hapgood calls "the
screwing of the average man."[1] The legislature did not author-
ize this construction, had nothing to do with the plans or the
method of handling although it was obviously aware and
winked an eye. Rockefeller could never have obtained on-the-
record legislative approval for it. There was no due process.

Here is how the deal was swung.

Governor Rockefeller, acting autonomously for the state,
entered into an agreement with Mayor Erastus Corning of
Albany, acting for Albany County. This was set forth in a
lease-purchase contract under which the state "consented" to

---

1. See David Hapgood, *The Screwing of the Average Man.* Gorgeous examples are
given in profusion.

become the county's agent for erecting the Mall. So the state did not, legally, erect the building; Albany County did that. But the state, oddly, acted as the county's agent, an act of *noblesse oblige,* the dog obliging the tail. The legislature, however, appropriated start-up operating expenses, known as first-instance funds. However, the county now sold to banks, insurance companies, and big investors tax-exempt bonds and reimbursed the state each quarter for the first-instance funds. So the county, apparently, was really financing the whole thing. The state was not paying.

So to suppose, however, is a delusion. For the state by the terms of the agreement of governor and mayor was committed to pay an annual rental, *whatever was needed,* equal to the principal and interest due on the county bonds, *whatever this was,* and also to make supplementary payments to the county for its services. The whole price, ostensibly rent, was open-ended. At the point where all the principal and interest on the county bonds has been paid off with state rent money, the state takes title to the Mall. All this was subterfuge of the first water, impenetrable by the average mind.

The huge amount of money the state pays to the county, $1 to $1.5 billion dollars (the latter figure including the interest), comes out of state taxes. So, in the end, the state taxpayers pay for it all, not the county taxpayers. Here is where the taxpayers get screwed. And screwed and screwed.

This sort of financial legerdemain clearly shows that tricky minds were at work on this project in order to avoid legislative consideration for it all and public review and understanding. Nelson called the tricky shots all the way. The idea behind all the hocus-pocus was to conceal what was being done and to enable Nelson to stage a huge rip-off of the public for his self-aggrandizement. If there is any other interpretation, let someone bring it forward.

The Mall is, too, an outgrowth of sibling rivalry.

For while Nelson was devising the imperial slabs of the Mall in Albany, his younger brother David was busily arranging with the Rockefeller-packed Port Authority of New York and New Jersey to have built with public money, no legislative approval needed, the $750-million twin 110-story towers of the eye-crushing, soul-shattering World Trade Center on Lower Manhattan. It is tax-exempt.

The country, then, or New York State, therefore possesses two architectural monstrosities single-handedly produced by rivalrous Rockefeller brothers at taxpayers' expense. For at the end of the line the taxpayer in both these cases foots the bill, as he does for everything else financial politicos devise. The two structures therefore represent a double screwing.

The two oppressive structures stand, one in New York City, the other in Albany, like giant bookends of the gods, with Rockefellerland-on-the-Hudson stretching in between, the home domain. In the meantime, ordinary citizens crawl along in the overpowering structural shadows like bugs, reduced in physical proportion to their true spiritual proportions in the established scheme of things: nothings, serfs. Neither structure is anything the psyche can humanly absorb. Each repels.

Symbolisms such as these, conscious and unconscious, stud the Rockefeller history. The internal symbol of Rockefeller Center, for example, is a huge gilded Prometheus, the Greek god of light, firebringer to the world, tortured and held prisoner by Zeus for his good deeds on behalf of man. Nearby is the god Atlas, supporter of the lost continent of Atlantis, the Atlantic world. Both of these were overpowering characters in Greek mythology. As self-chosen, conscious symbols, they are spectacularly revealing of astounding pretensions. Further attention to Rockefeller symbolism is left to the final chapter.

The presidential office, according to the expressed belief of the constitutional framers, would naturally gravitate to one of the "first characters" in the nation, men such as Washington, Adams, Jefferson, and Madison as it turned out. But in the long run the framers reckoned without the populace and the politicians; it was not long before the character of the incumbents slid to a mediocre politician-molded level, interspersed at long intervals by miraculously competent men. Most of the presidents have been quite mediocre, some obviously scared of the office, far from "first characters." That the quality of the presidents has not been uniformly high is clearly demonstrated in a key work, *Presidential Greatness,* by historian Thomas Andrew Bailey (1966). In some it has been shockingly low and crude.

The idea, which has been expressed, that Nelson Rockefeller as president would show unusual favor to the Standard Oil group or to Chase Manhattan Bank of New York may be dismissed out of hand. Even if he wanted to, he could not do it as he would be too closely watched. Anyhow, those entities are too solidly established and integral to the system to need any special assistance. The Rockefellers have other fish to fry.

Just how good a president would Nelson Rockefeller make?

Any answer is necessarily speculative. But, confining our scrutiny merely to this century, it is difficult to see him being as ineffective as Harding, Coolidge, or Hoover, or worse than Taft or Kennedy, as inept as Lyndon B. Johnson or Richard Nixon, or as gullible in the sphere of foreign relations as was Wilson. On the other hand, he surely would not be as effective as either of the Roosevelts, Truman, or Eisenhower. It is at least plausible, however, to imagine him in the office, his megalomania not apparent to most observers.

As Franklin D. Roosevelt showed, in this century, with high-powered pressure-groups breathing in through every nook and cranny of the White House, a president, in addition to a constructive vision of what he wants, needs an ability to manipulate all the sharks, vultures, buzzards, and barracudas hemming him in in order to nullify their potency for mischief and put that potency to work in the common effort to survive. He needs to know, in other words, how to pull the fangs of a large number of rattlesnakes, blunt the teeth of sharks. Could Rockefeller do this? Would he want to? He never did in New York. There he often played ball for the benefit of the Interests.

While Rockefeller is old enough—born in 1908—not to be as adventuristic as his form to date portends, he is, for one thing, more committed to currently detested points of view than was Roosevelt, who took office at age fifty-one and was comparatively an unknown quantity. And Rockefeller is an eager beaver, a show-off anxious to hit the long ball, be a star.

He is, too, a foreign-policy hawk, and a hard-liner. Roosevelt had served two two-year routine terms as governor of New York and had during World War I been assistant secretary of the Navy. In the fateful years between 1920 and 1932 he had no connection at all with the federal government, which was through and through Old Guard Republican and was run like a third-class bordello.

He was, therefore, not implicated in the bankrupt national policy of the Republicans and could start, especially owing to the emergency of the Depression, with a relatively clean slate. Rockefeller, however, much older, is deeply implicated in the much disputed—some would say discredited—national policies of the past twenty to thirty years, and was tied in with all the latter downhill presidents in one way or the other. The question then is: could he nevertheless make a fresh start, set up some new perspectives? Or would an administration under him be only the mixture as before, a warmed-over version of Johnsonian, Nixonian, and Fordist policies cast in heroic Nelsonian proportions?

Just how much of a corporation man is he? Does he, in brief, regard the corporation as a means, which would be proper, or the corporation as an end in itself? The distinction is crucial. Clues to his orientation are to be found in his superheated governorship and his corporate-state architecture. Contrary to what some say, neither Franklin Roosevelt nor Truman was hostile to the corporation, even the very big corporation. But they certainly did not regard it as the end, the darling of policy. They could smack it on the snout when they thought it needful.

Most politicians, and most presidential aspirants, whatever they say to the contrary, regard the corporation, particularly the big corporation, as the Holy Grail. Even Eisenhower did to a considerable extent, and Johnson and Nixon regarded it as sacrosanct. Harding, Coolidge, and Hoover were corporation venerators, believed at bottom that the polity existed for the corporation and not vice versa. Government regulatory bureaus are especially imbued with this credo.

If Rockefeller achieves the top spot, at any rate, he would be the first president who had been born with corporations and city blocks as his potential playtoys. Could such a man transcend his heritage and look with detachment at the corporation, see it in relation to other and deeper requirements of the polity? The corporation when properly harnessed can be a useful instrumentality. But when it runs amok, as it has often done in American history, it can be a disaster. Would he, furthermore, intervene in the screwing of the average man, try to moderate it? Or even stop it?

Speculation that visualizes Nelson Rockefeller as the Republican candidate for 1976 is far from idle. For there is much informed discussion predicated on the belief that Gerald Ford, no matter what he says to the contrary, does not intend to run, that Rockefeller has indeed been picked for the Number One spot by Republican insiders. Ford, in this view, is merely holding the office as a trustee. In any event, Rockefeller is his big backup man, entrusted with important White House duties.

The theoretical ticket-makers, moreover, see Edward M. Kennedy of Massachusetts, brother of the martyred president, as the logical Democratic candidate against Rockefeller. On opposing tickets both men would be carrying comparable disabilities in the eyes of large sections of the voters—Kennedy with Chappaquiddick and other incubi on his back and Rockefeller with a variety of stuff as set forth in this chapter and Chapter Four. Much of this could be worked up to scandalous proportions, enough to scare the pants off the booboisie.

Neither Gerald Ford nor a large number of possible Democratic candidates who have thus far been mentioned, especially including Henry Jackson of Washington, are regarded by the ticket-makers as having "oomph." Whatever it is, both Kennedy and Rockefeller are conceded on every hand to have this quality that excites the electorate, pro or con.

Both wealthy men, their political disabilities are thought to be complementary and reciprocally nullifying, leaving the choice up to the electorate about which is O.K., which not O.K. One would prefer George Washington, or even Harry Truman.

As campaigners, both are far and away the best of anyone who has yet been mentioned. Both come on strong.

Whether these men will head the respective tickets, of course, lies in the capacious laps of the gods or, rather, the controllers of the state delegations to the conventions. So many twistings and turnings, wheelings and dealings, go into the shaping of final tickets that nobody in his right mind would attempt to predict the outcome far in advance of the event. The campaign of 1976, at any rate, commemorating the stupendous year 1776, the bicentennial of the miraculous founding, appears pretty sure to be a regular Pier Six brawl, no matter who heads the tickets. Too much loot is at stake, too much dynamite is lying around, for it to be a tranquil affair. It could be an unusually dirty affair.

Both Rockefeller and Kennedy are considered to be the choice of the smart money for the 1976 scene, at least at this long range. "First characters" such as Elliott Richardson, Judge John Sirica, George W. Ball, Kingman Brewster, and other such true blues are dismissed by prognosticators as having little chance of getting the nod from the hard-faced, tight-lipped "boys in the backroom," the American Politburo of shadowy operators.

In any event, if Nelson Rockefeller is not the choice of the Republican convention to be its standard-bearer in the magic year 1976, he will, one may be sure, have a great deal to say about who the choice is. He won't be one of the boys in the backroom, but he'll be in close telephonic touch with them, "on the blower."

2.

The step-by-step stripteasing way the congressional committees elicited their highest figures on the extent of Nelson's and his family's wealth suggests that the Rockefellers were testing the water as the hearings went on and were trying to minimize the total revealed as much as possible. This, of course, is the strategy of the super-rich at all times. The strate-

gy of the moderately rich is, *per contra,* to leave the impression they are richer than they really are, thereby lubricating their dealings all along the line.

What guides here are canons of good public relations. For to be super-rich, especially in mass-beguiling politics, is not a winning stance. It is especially not acceptable to simple minds who believe that virtue resides in being without money, as were Hitler, Lenin, Stalin, and Mussolini. In general, the super-rich in the years since the Bolshevik Revolution find it expedient to deny they are as wealthy as they really are. The news attracts gnats and flies.

The first figure given out on the extent of Nelson's wealth occasioned a guffaw all around. It was $33 million. Nelson hastened to state that committee people had "leaked" a very preliminary figure, without explaining why such a preliminary figure had been submitted. A misunderstanding?

The next figure to come up was $62,581,225, which also soon fell by the wayside, going to $69 million and then $73 million and finally more than $100 million. As it turned out, he was also the beneficiary of two trusts worth, as of August 23, 1974, the extremely depressed market value of $116,-503,758. By reason of abnormally high money rates imposed by the Federal Reserve Board throughout the year, both the stock and bond markets had slipped and slithered to the lowest levels in many years, a fortunate twist for Rockefeller from the viewpoint of public relations—the idea always being to keep such figures minimal in order to soothe the *hoi polloi.* High money rates had depressed the securities markets by inducing much liquidation and the transfer of funds to short-term high-yield instrumentalities. "Nervous money" had temporarily flown the coop, to roost over greener pastures.

Under sedate questioning by Chairman Howard W. Cannon of the transcendent Senate Rules Committee, Rockefeller reluctantly admitted that the trust funds were wholly subject to his order as to principal and income. In other words, they were so much money in pocket, not subject to the control of others. Under this arrangement, though, they are separately taxed.

In addition his wife holds securities and is the beneficiary of trusts aggregating $3.8 million, and his children hold assets, in trust or directly, totaling $35.7 million. All this comes to $218.584 million for his own nuclear family, at very depressed market prices—and is understated even so.

If one assumes that each of his brothers and his sister have similar holdings, the holdings of the family come to $1.3 billion, a figure approximate to one later submitted by the Rockefeller family manager.

It should always be remembered, though, that the valuations were at the depressed levels for both stocks and bonds in the summer of 1974. As schedules were submitted for the holdings, with each one named except for much real estate and other stuff that was not specifically valued, one can at any time under different market conditions figure out the values.

As will appear in a moment, for reasons given, I do not accept these totals even apart from the issue of depressed market prices. They are far too low. The Rockefellers have always placed a minimal valuation on what they own. John D. Rockefeller did this throughout with Standard Oil. As he once said in a famous statement: "We never deceived ourselves." Not, at least, in the area of money.

In the ten years up to 1974, Nelson Rockefeller received total income of $46.8 million, of which about $1 million each year came from tax-exempt securities. This alone was equivalent to an impressive fortune. Combined, the liquid incomes of the family exceed $30 million per year. Deferred income puts the total above $50 million.

During his lifetime, he testified, he has paid $69 million in taxes of all kinds but in 1970 paid no federal income tax owing to the interaction of trust funds manipulations and personal holdings with respect to capital-gain operations. However, he had some $2.5 million income for the year. His federal tax payments have been steadily at the level of 25 percent of income, near the low end of the tax schedule.

In an effort to minimize his and his family's presence in the Standard Oil companies, he pointed out that he, personally, owns no more than 2/10ths of 1 percent of the shares of any oil company and his family no more than 2.06 percent. This leaves for explanation precisely how the Standard Oil companies are controlled. He also said he owned no stock in the Chase Manhattan Bank, but one of the trusts he benefits from held 325,000 shares of such stock—which means that he really did own stock in Chase Manhattan!

In explanation of the original $33-million figure and the revised figure of $69 million, then $73 million, then much higher, Rockefeller said the first figure did not include, through inadvertence, $20.5 million of art and the rest in real estate which he has pledged to leave at death to "public use and enjoyment." (Soft music plays here.) As all these totals were stated to be market values, the only market value one can take for the art and realty is the acquisition cost. And since acquisition, the presumptive value of these holdings has increased. All the art the Rockefellers buy is go-go stuff in the market, sure to increase in value under the pressure of expert valuations and worldwide museum demand. Visual art, in brief, is a modern form of self-enhancing currency, even more so than rare postage stamps. And in donating it at fully appraised values, there is capital realization in the form of tax write-offs. For example, by giving away $10 million of appraised art acquired years earlier for $1 million cash, one offsets $9 million of cash income, leaving it tax-exempt instead of having to pay some $7 million tax. The deal therefore nets close to $6 million, less insurance.

The congressional committees, however, did not step into this thorny thicket, which is enough in any computation to drive an Einstein to drink.

What Rockefeller held specifically consisted of diversified stocks in leading corporations, certificates of deposit and bonds, state and municipal bonds, corporate bonds, and U.S. Treasury bills. Corporation stocks held included Aluminum Company of America, AT&T, Archer Daniels Midland, Capitol Hill Associates, Caterpillar Tractor, Coherent Radiation Laboratories, Continental Oil Company, Corporate Property Investors, Corning Glass Works, Daniel International, Dow Chemical, Eastman Kodak, Exxon, General Electric, Hewlett

Packard, C. A. Industria Lactea de Carabobo, Intel, International Basic Economy Corporation, IBM, International Paper, Itek, Malnar Ltd., Marathon Oil, Merchants, Inc., Merck Company, Mobil Oil, Monte Sacro, S.A., Pan Ocean Oil, Polaroid, Reliance Electric, Rockefeller Brothers, Inc., Standard Oil Company of California, Standard Oil Company of Indiana, Teledyne, Inc., Texaco, Inc., Urban National Corporation, Warner Lambert Corporation, and Westinghouse. Some of these stocks were at the time of valuation selling at 50 percent or more below valuations of the year before and have since in some cases risen spectacularly in value.

In the trust funds there were also holdings of Du Pont, General Electric, Caterpillar Tractor, Minnesota Mining and Manufacturing, Monsanto, IT&T, Motorola, Upjohn, and S.S. Kresge.

As to holdings of the major Standard Oil companies by descendants of John D. Rockefeller, Jr., they were given as follows:

	Shares	*%*
Standard Oil Company of California	3,506,954	2.05
Exxon	2,355,613	1.07
Mobil Oil	1,778,719	1.75
Marathon Oil	205,224	0.68
Standard Oil Company of Indiana	154,652	0.23

Holdings in Chase Manhattan Bank amounted to 429,959 shares, 1.34 percent of all outstanding, mostly held by individuals. The holdings were worth $12 million as of October 31, 1974, way down from previous levels as were all bank stocks at the time.

As none of this by itself is sufficient to "control" any of these companies, how control is achieved will need to be discussed. An alternative thought is that the companies aren't controlled by the Rockefellers, are floating free and clear. If that were true in this age of corporate take-overs, one may be sure they would be gobbled up. Any Swiss-Dutch-Arab syndicate with plenty of money is at liberty to try taking over. The simple reason no extraneous group, no conglomerate, would dream of reaching for any of these companies is that they know or strongly suspect they are completely controlled—and by the Rockefellers.

In the upshot appeared J. Richardson Dilworth, general manager of Rockefeller Family & Associates. In addition to family members, his office, he said, "consists of 154 staff people who provide accounting, investment, legal, philanthropic, public relations, and tax services to these multiple employers. The office also maintains a library, files, messenger and travel services, and has a cafeteria as well as a small purchasing and maintenance group to service its requirements. In addition, individual members of the family employ other people both within the office and elsewhere."

The family members, he said, are not interested in controlling anything. "The family members are simply investors"—that is, rentiers, income-poops.

Investments over a wide corporate range owned outright by eighty-four members of the family totaled $244,220,000 and similar investments held by them in personal trust came to $51,168,000. Investments held in trust for his descendants created by John D. Rockefeller, Jr. were as follows: 1934 trusts—$640,000,000; 1952 trusts—$98,600,000. There was also a total of $224,599,000 allotted to charities, of which 90 percent related to Rockefeller University and Colonial Williamsburg, Inc., and not to the extensive array of other Rockefeller foundations nor to the Rockefeller Brothers Fund nor the Rockefeller Family Fund. These, big affairs, are under other management.

In brief, only the foundation funds over which Dilworth's office has supervision were included in this list submitted to Congress.

The figures submitted by Dilworth took market values as of October 31, 1974, for everything. However, a big question mark is raised by the valuation of only $98.3 million for trust-held Rockefeller Center, Inc., which is 100 percent owned and held in the trusts left by Rockefeller Junior. First, shares of Rockefeller Center are not traded, are wholly owned by the trusts, and hence have no current "market value." The assigned market value of $98.3 million for the Center, furthermore, is ridiculous unless 9/10ths of the Center is mortgaged to others—which no one believes. The assessed valuation of the Center for tax purposes was given as $133 million. Assessed valuations in New York City are only a fraction of true values. The lower the assessment, the lower the taxes.

Leading real estate experts in New York appraise Rockefeller Center as worth, overall, at least $1 billion, or ten times more than the value assigned to it in Dilworth's statement. Only if the place is heavily mortgaged, which is doubtful and was not claimed, could such a figure be assigned as the value of the stock. What appears to be the case is that Rockefeller Center is carried on the books at original 1934 cost.

Early in 1975 the very old Plaza Hotel seven blocks north of the Center on Fifth Avenue sold for $25 million. A few years ago the solitary Empire State Building at Thirty-fourth Street and Fifth sold for $100 million. If those nearby values are any guide, the multibuildinged Rockefeller Center is certainly worth $1 billion. In the extension of Rockefeller Center west of Sixth Avenue, four leading companies—Celanese, Exxon, McGraw-Hill, Time-Life—own percentages of the buildings; but reports in the press have always stressed that the Center owns a heavily predominant portion.

If, then, merely the original section of Rockefeller Center is wholly owned by Rockefeller Center, Inc., Dilworth's figures are too light by some value running up toward $900 million. As put forth, the figures are at least ambiguous. In view of the Rockefeller propensity toward minimization of values rather than exaggeration, it seems to me one should take the valuation of $98.3 million on Rockefeller Center among $640-million 1934 trust assets as a resounding understatement.

Omitted entirely from Dilworth's accounting was Laurance Rockefeller's known holdings in Eastern Airlines. He owned approximately 125,000 shares of the common and the entire issue of 216,836 shares of $100 par $3.75 convertible preferred; it is convertible into common at $63 a share. Chase

Manhattan Bank is also known to own or control a large batch of Eastern Airlines. In October, 1974, the bid and asked for Eastern Airlines common was 4 1/4 to 5 1/8. The market price range in 1960-1973 was 5 1/4 to 61 5/8. As of March 7, 1975, the closing market on the common was 5 7/8. At $5 a share, the common is worth $625,000. Assigning the preferred an arbitrary market value of $20 (as it is not traded), Laurance's holding in this issue is worth $4,336,720. At its peak it was worth $29,386,725.

Furthermore, Dilworth's list excluded anything the Rockefellers owned that was worth less than $1.3 million per item. They own a large range of low-priced high technology companies, few of which he mentioned but which come up later in this account. Depending on how many of these they own, such a list of below-$1.3 million holdings could amount to a good deal. All such high technology issues are held by the Rockefellers owing to their belief that they will be worth much more. Such holdings, worth $500,000 today, could be worth $50 million in a few years, per issue.

Such omissions and low valuation as for Rockefeller Center certainly signal to the intelligent analyst that the Dilworth parade of figures should be taken *cum grano salis.* There is, in other words, a large X factor involved in his presentation.

The lean total given by Dilworth aggregated $1,278,587,000 ($1.278 billion), including $244,599,000 for Rockefeller University and Colonial Williamsburg, Inc., but not including the Rockefeller Brothers Fund or the Rockefeller Family Fund or any of the major foundations.

If the figure for the Center is short by $900 million, then the total should have stood at $2,178,587,000 ($2.178 billion), not including the Rockefeller Brothers Fund or the Rockefeller Family Fund. At the very least the valuation given for the Center is questionable. The congressional committees did not question it nor dwell on possible omissions.

The separately operated Rockefeller Brothers Fund as of December 31, 1969 (the latest date available in *The Foundation Directory,* 4th edition, 1971), had total assets of $198,-175,471; these had their base in much higher market prices, it should be noted. At the same time the Rockefeller Family Fund had assets of $232,587. Each of these funds is in receipt of additional capital funds from time to time.

Not touched upon at all in Dilworth's presentation was the Rockefeller Foundation, which at the end of 1969 had assets of $757,088,188, or the Martha Baird Rockefeller Fund for Music, set up by Junior's second wife, with assets of $983,-459. Discussion of the various foundations, extant and discontinued, is left to Chapter Five.

There are, it is evident, grounds other than the ambiguity about Rockefeller Center and the abnormally low market, in which prime stocks were selling at an absurd four and five times earnings and AAA bonds at discounts of 25 to 35 percent, for considering Dilworth's figures too low. And this, too, after taking in Dilworth's explanation that perhaps $200 million additional was located in miscellaneous unlisted real estate.

Market shrinkage alone would not account for the discrepancy between these figures and those I presented in the pages of *The Rich and the Super-Rich* (1968). There, taking only major stockholdings of the Rockefellers as ascertained by a joint Senate-Securities and Exchange Commission study *Investigation of Concentration of Economic Power,* 76th Congress, 3rd session, (Monograph 29, Temporary National Economic Committee, 1940-41), one is able to obtain some concrete data. In this study it was shown that the Rockefellers were among the twenty largest stockholders of twenty-one corporations; the study did not inquire into their bond, realty, or bank holdings.

These holdings were ascertained as of 1937. Assuming they held precisely these same holdings through the years, although conceding that they may have been changed (as they were), I computed their values at closing prices for 1964. Their then-indicated market value was $4,741,515,014 ($4.741 billion). At the end of 1962 the market values of the then-existent foundations came to $823,485,972.

The TNEC study, resting ultimately on subpoenas calling for the data (so there was little likelihood of foolery with the rampaging New Deal under way), found that the family's holdings consisted of 30 percent in foundations, 30 percent in trust funds, and 40 percent in individual holdings, mostly held by John D. Jr. Taking this as a basis for developing another figure, I took the actual 1962 market-value figure of the foundations and allotted it 30 percent, set down the same figure for the trust funds, and arrived at $2,724,953,240 for the 40 percent of individual holdings. So somewhere between this figure and $4.741 billion was the projected value of the Rockefeller fortune, its possible high and low. Actually it had to be higher owing to items not included.

From time to time within an entity like the Rockefellers, there are unannounced changes in holdings and alterations in the location of holdings as between holdings for self, tax-serving donations and holdings in foundations. Since the time of the TNEC study, the holdings have not been substantially invaded by inheritance taxes although in *intra vivos* transfers there have been imposed gift taxes. Rockefeller Jr. paid no federal inheritance tax as he left his retained estate of approximately $150 million—half to his wife (tax exempt) and half to the Rockefeller Brothers Fund (tax exempt). So the holdings in the intervening years have not been hit by capital taxes other than relatively light capital gains and gift taxes.

After considering various other possibilities, I concluded that the total Rockefeller financial worth as of 1964 was around $5 billion, this figure including foundations, trust funds, and personal holdings. Between this figure and Mr. Dilworth's $1,278,587,000, his additional $200 million for realty and miscellaneous, plus the Rockefeller Foundation of $757,088,188, there is a considerable discrepancy. These immediately preceding figures give a total of $2,235,675,188 ($2.236 billion).

The temporary shrinkage in market values would account for some of it—but not all. In the early months of 1975 the financial markets made considerable recoveries owing to a sharp reduction in interest rates all around, but not enough recovery to make up the gap. If, however, the value of Rockefeller Center is understated in the Dilworth report, as it veritably appears to be, it would account for a large portion of the gap.

Something one will be able to do from time to time as the markets recover is to compute the new market values of the Dilworth schedules, which should show that the Rockefellers are worth considerably more than the $1 billion naively assigned to them by the newspapers (*New York Times*, December 4, 1974, 1:1). The writers of such reports are not financial analysts. Unless Rockefeller Center and other realty is sometime sold, one will not know precisely what their market value is.

According to Dilworth, the present generation of Rockefellers has given $235 million to charity, a word that covers a multitude of affairs. He did not specify, though, how much of this came out of income, how much out of capital, or what was subsumed under the ever-blessed word "charity."

I conclude, then, that in the present situation, values on much the Rockefellers own are concealed in temporary market depreciation, omitted holdings, and in nonlisted real estate (nonlisted on any exchange). Real estate is not considered a liquid asset, as are listed stocks and bonds. The liquidating value of these latter is the latest market price, which is their "true" *present* value. But the price-values of stocks and bonds, as anyone can see by tracing them individually or collectively, are on a roller coaster through time.

That the markets were down to very low levels at the time the Dilworth figures were presented is shown by the stock indices. The Dow-Jones average of industrial stocks for October, 1974, stood at a high of 673.0, a low of 584.6; a year before it was 987.1-948.8. There had been a decline of about one-third in a year. It held in the 900-range in 1972 and 1971. At the close for 1964 it was 874.1-857.5.

For October, 1974, the market price for all listed stocks, according to the New York Stock Exchange computation, was $549.7 billion compared with $808.7 billion for October, 1973, and $824.9 billion for October, 1972. The bond list showed similar declines. What is more to the point, however, is that the declines were temporary, depending upon money-rate and fiscal and other manipulations by Washington. One may be sure, unless everything is heading for the bow-wows, that the markets will move higher. Indeed, they already have as of March 1, 1975. The Dow-Jones average advanced more than 100 points within the first two months of 1975.

So, what the Rockefellers are *really* worth, depends at what point on the market roller-coaster one reads off the figures, how complete an inventory is submitted, and also what their art, real estate, and *unstated* assets are *really* worth. Perhaps the safest conclusion is that they own a tremendous lot of revenue-producing property, which gives them leverage over even larger expanses of property and public events. One must always remember that from the point of view of "public relations," it is to their advantage to understate net worth.

While more details of specific holdings are given in the schedules Dilworth presented, it would be somewhat idle to reproduce it all here as all are subject to change without notice in the course of making portfolio changes. A year from now they may own none of the stuff Dilworth reported but may be into something altogether different.

The size of the Rockefeller fortune has always excited a good deal of speculation and calculation. Jules Abels, in *The Rockefeller Billions* (1965), after very careful estimations, figures the Rockefeller fortune then as worth $4 billion. In 1921 H. H. Klein put it at $2.5 billions and B. C. Forbes at $1.2 billions. The lowest figure ever set for it, and one demonstrably wrong, was stated in 1927 by Stuart Chase; he placed it at $600 million in an article in the *New York Times* (February 13) that represented the Fords as the then-richest family in the nation. He did this even though publicized income-tax figures for 1923 showed that Rockefeller Jr. paid a tax 50 percent greater than Henry and Edsel Ford combined. Stewart Alsop in the 1960s estimated the fortune at $10 billion, which is obviously too high even if one reckons in what went to the families of John D. Rockefeller's other children—Bessie (Mrs. Charles A. Strong), Alta (Mrs. E. Parmalee Prentice), and Edith (Mrs. Harold F. McCormick)—and throws in the holdings of the descendants of William Rockefeller, brother of the immortal John.

The surest method, it seems to me, is to take data submitted under oath or subpoena and to extrapolate from them. If one extrapolates backward on the data submitted by Dilworth, one arrives at a much higher level for the value of the stocks and bonds than the one for October 31, 1974. The value of the real estate is not as precisely ascertainable.

3.

Despite the fascination of the press with Dilworth's figures and the general lack of critical evaluation of them, the congressional committees did not come to grips at all with the actual mechanism of the Rockefeller power. For this we must turn to other sources, far away from Congress.

There exists a very thorough, recent, and eye-opening study by Dr. James C. Knowles of the University of Southern California that shows very exactly just what the Rockefeller power consists of. The study is titled *The Rockefeller Financial Group* (Warner Modular Publications, Inc., Module 343, 1973, Andover, Massachusetts, Library of Congress Catalog Card Number 73-3873).

Research for this study was carried out in 1970, and the findings were submitted for criticism and revision to a battery of professors at Stanford University, the University of Wisconsin, Cornell, Dartmouth, Brandeis, the University of Michigan, Harvard, and Princeton—a standard procedure with academic research of this kind.

Not only is the study sprinkled liberally with nuggets of significant specific information, but it contains much minute discussion of the perspectives—none of which can be reproduced here simply out of considerations of space. Students of corporation control should refer to it.

In the United States, as the study truly observes, there are ten or more major financial "interest groups" consisting of wealthy corporate families allied with other wealthy families, the leading ones owning stocks in major banks or groups of banks and many sitting on their boards. The banks are the core of a credit-supplying fount for their respective corporations and are allied with enormous pools of capital in major insurance companies and investment entities. Around this insurance-bank nucleus is usually gathered "a set of law firms, investment banking firms, foundations, universities, and other institutions of power and influence associated with the group." All true—the McCoy, the lowdown.

The Rockefeller Group, or Syndicate, is the largest and most important of all, now exceeding the Morgan Group gathered around the Morgan Guaranty Trust Company and Morgan, Stanley and Company. There are similar groups in Boston, Cleveland, Philadelphia, San Francisco, Connecticut, Chicago, Texas, and Pittsburgh (Mellon), but these are essentially local or regional as opposed to the national and international scope of the Rockefeller and Morgan Groups.

The financial core of the Rockefeller Syndicate consists of the Chase Manhattan Bank, the First National City Bank of New York (Citicorp), the Chemical Bank of New York, and the First National Bank of Chicago. These rank second, third, sixth, and tenth nationally as of 1969 assets. Closely allied with them are the three "mutual" life insurance companies— Metropolitan, Equitable, and New York Life. These rank nationally second, third, and fourth. "Mutual" means they have no stockholders, are run as personal preserves (under law) by trustees who in turn are named to the posts by well-placed money-market people. Ownership vests, atomistically, in the policyholders. They have no more say-so, though, than they have over the Kremlin. One might even say, less.

As of 1969 total assets of these seven institutions amounted to $113 billion, or about 25 percent of the assets of the fifty largest commercial banks of the country and 30 percent of the assets of the fifty largest life insurance companies. This sentence gives some preliminary idea of the size of the Syndicate, although there is much more to it than this. For the tally of assets does not include the trust holdings of the four banks, which amounted to $35 billion and brought up to $148 billion the total of merely basic assets under Syndicate sway. If one does not want to stay with the 1969 computation, one is at liberty to update it from public records at any time, obtaining ever-enlarging figures. The secular trend for these institutions is for assets to increase. For they are always acquiring new subinstitutions, and book values increase through earnings retained in part.

Among these core financial institutions, the directorates are tightly interlocked—that is, directors of one entity sit on the board of another entity, producing a common policy and one big happy family for seven giant institutions. Subject to these are scores of major corporations and lesser banks, all interlocked.

In the overarching Rockefeller Syndicate, Doctor Knowles traced twenty-three ordinary functional interlocks plus five additional wherein two members of the same family sit on the boards of two different financial institutions of the group.

Knowles now took for comparison four non-Rockefeller banks—Manufacturers Hanover, Morgan Guaranty Trust, Bankers Trust, and the Continental Illinois National Bank of Chicago, their deposits in 1969 only $40.7 billion compared with $62.1 billion for the four Rockefeller banks—and showed that there were only five director interlocks between them and the three "Rockefeller" insurance companies. The non-Rockefeller Chicago bank had no ties at all with the New York financial institutions. These non-Rockefeller banks ranked fourth, fifth, seventh, and eighth in deposits.

The Rockefeller Syndicate also heavily dominated the board of the Consolidated Edison Company, second largest utility company, and until 1969 all six of the Rockefeller entities in New York had directors on its board. Other large Wall Street financial institutions had no directors on the Con Ed Board. It similarly dominated the Anaconda Copper Company and provided eight of nineteen directors of AT & T, in which it shares influence with the Morgan Group.

The First National City Bank (Citicorp) is the headquarters of the William Rockefeller branch of the family. At one time John D. Rockefeller held stock in it, but he transferred to Chase National Bank, now Chase Manhattan. In Chapter Four material is presented on the William Rockefeller branch and William appears from time to time in this account. William and John always operated in close harmony.

The Rockefellers alone do not own any of these institutions, or single-handedly "control" them, just as John D. Rockefeller neither owned nor controlled the original Standard Oil Company. His interest in it ranged at different times between 25 and 30 percent. His associates together owned more than he did; one of these associates was his brother William who at one time owned about 12.5 percent. The associates could have outvoted John D. at any time. The point is: they did not want to. The general staff does not vote down a field marshal who is winning battles, conquering the world.

In the same way David Rockefeller, as chairman of Chase Manhattan, is the spokesman or head man for this group, functioning much as John D. did in Standard Oil subject to suggestions and criticisms from his associates, but having much more pervasive power. Within the group he is by no means a dictator. Nor was John D. in Standard Oil. But, as with old John D., anyone who wishes to gainsay him had better be prepared with bone-crunching arguments. He isn't subject to veto out of hand, arbitrarily. David, it must be said, almost certainly depends more on the thinking of others than did strongly self-willed John D. He is also more *simpatico.* He is, too. far subtler, more sophisticated, than old John D. ever was.

The family interlocks at the top of the Rockefeller network, apart from those purely functional, are as follows: David Rockefeller (CM) and James Stillman Rockefeller (FNCB), Hulbert S. Aldrich (CB) and Malcolm Aldrich (E), Amory Houghton (FNCB) and Arthur K. Houghton, Jr., (NYL), Amory Houghton, Jr. (FNCB) and Arthur K. Houghton, Jr. (NYL), and Amory Houghton (M) and Arthur K. Houghton, Jr. (NYL).

Chemical Bank of New York is the outgrowth of a merger in 1955 between the Chemical Corn Exchange Bank and the New York Trust Company. In this latter, the dominant family was that of Edward S. Harkness, descendant of Stephen V. Harkness, chief Standard Oil associate of Rockefeller in early days, the largest S. O. stockholder after the Founding Father. Malcolm and Hulbert Aldrich were for many years partners and advisors of Edward S. Harkness. Hulbert started his career with the New York Trust Company, of which he became chairman. Malcolm is chairman of the Commonwealth Fund, a huge foundation set up by the Harkness family. Hulbert finally became chairman of the board and chairman of the trust committee of the Chemical Bank.

The ties of the group to the First National Bank of Chicago come about through two companies—Standard Oil of Indiana and the International Harvester Company—and the Rockefeller link by marriage to the McCormick family of International Harvester. The bank manages the employee pension fund of Standard of Indiana, which holds around 7.7 percent of the company's common stock—a big voting position. Brooks McCormick is president of International Harvester and a director of First National of Chicago.

The leading directors of all the Syndicate banks, as Knowles points out, all represent large inherited fortunes.

First, as to Chase: C. Douglas Dillon is the heir of Clarence Dillon of the big investment banking house of Dillon, Read and Company, ambassador to France (1953-1957), undersecretary of state (1959-1960), and secretary of the treasury, (1960-1965). The party holding the White House made no difference. Jeremiah Milbank, Jr., is the principal heir of the Milbank fortune, originating in the Borden Company (dairy products) and ramifying into Corn Products Refining Company, the Southern Railway, and Commercial Solvents Company.

There is, too, William Hewlettt, board chairman of the Hewlett-Packard Company and in the super-rich class; Whitney Stone, board chairman of Stone and Webster Company, founded by his father and a partner, and now a principal holder of stock in Transcontinental Gas Pipeline and huge Tenneco, Inc.; Ralph Lazarus, chairman of the immense Federated Department Store chain, ninth largest national retailer and one in which his family is a heavy stockholder; Robert O. Anderson, chairman of the Atlantic Richfield Company (Standard Oil), in which he held $70 million of stock as of 1968.

On the board of First National City Bank sit the Houghtons, owners of 30 percent of Corning Glass Works. Also present is the Milliken family through Roger Milliken, big holder of Deering-Milliken Company and controlling owner of the Mercantile Stores chain. There is, too, the Grace-Phipps family represented by J. Peter Grace and John Phipps, major holders in the Ingersoll-Rand Corporation and the International Paper Company. John Phipps is a descendant of Henry Phipps, partner of Andrew Carnegie and the second largest stockholder in Carnegie Steel at the time of its merger into US Steel. The Graces trace back to the founder of W. R. Grace and Company, fiftieth largest industrial company in 1969; J. Peter Grace is its chairman. Two Phipps are directors of the Grace enterprise.

George F. Baker, III, a member of FNCB board, principally manages his family's trust funds and is a heavy holder of FNCB stock. He, too, got his money the easy way, by inheritance. His father was George F. Baker, II, closely associated with J. P. Morgan and for many years the dominant owner of the First National Bank of New York, which merged in 1955 with National City Bank. Baker and Baker II, the latter married to a Schiff daughter of Kuhn Loeb & Co., for many years had heavy holdings in many large corporations, including especially US Steel and AT & T.

Other wealthy families with places on the board of FNCB include the Stillman-Rockefellers (James Stillman Rockefeller, retired chairman); the Kimberly-Clark Company (John R. Kimberly, chairman); the Winthrops, onetime bankers now headquartered in the law firm of Shearman and Sterling, and the investment house of Wood, Struthers and Winthrop (Robert Winthrop); and the Chubb family of Chubb Corporation, insurance holding company of $900 million assets (Percy Chubb, chairman).

As Knowles points out, the situation is the same at Chemical Bank and First National of Chicago. Directors present at Chemical other than any already mentioned are Lammot du Pont Copeland, board chairman of E. I. du Pont de Nemours at the time of the study; Henry Hillman of the Pittsburgh

National Bank, the Wheeling Pittsburgh Steel Company, the Pittsburgh Coke and Chemical Company, and Texas Gas Transmission, worth at least $300 million in 1968; J. Irwin Miller, chairman and heavy owner of Cummins Engine Company; Robert Goelet, heir of one of the very old New York real estate fortunes and a descendant of participating founders of Chemical Bank; and Henry Upham Harris, board chairman of the investment banking firm of Harris, Upham & Company.

One finds the same sort of wealthy family-inheritor grouping at the First National Bank of Chicago. Directors there consist of Marshall Field, IV, of the Marshall Field department store fortune of vast magnitude and Field Enterprises, publisher of the *Chicago Sun Times,* an around-the-clock newspaper (morning, afternoon, and evening); Brooks McCormick of International Harvester and the McCormick-Deering family; Gaylord Donnelly, board chairman of the huge R. R. Donnelly Company, large-scale printers; R. Douglas Stuart, Jr., president of the Quaker Oats Company which his family founded; William Woods Prince, heir to Frederick Prince who controlled Armour and Company, later acquired by Greyhound; Joseph Block, chairman of the Inland Steel Company in which his family has long been dominant; and Charles Walgreen, Jr., board chairman of the Walgreen Drug Stores chain, thirty-third largest retail chain as of 1969.

"The wealthy families who are represented among the directors of these banks," as Knowles remarks, "do not function as individual centers of power in competition with one another. Instead, they have formed alliances with other wealthy families not only within the same bank but also, in some instances, between banks."

In other words, the wagons are drawn up in a tight circle, scouts out among the redskins. All these people are heirs. None is a Horatio Alger success. Moreover, they make up a significant slice of the American *haut bourgeoisie,* the managing elite. They are the counterparts on the American scene of the upper managing strata of the Communist party, USSR.

The directorships mentioned by no means exhaust the list of the connections of these thirteen very wealthy families.

Actually they hold (among many others) directorships in ten of the fifty largest commerical banks of the country, with 1969 assets of $96 billion or 40 percent of the fifty largest commercial banks; eleven of the thirty largest bank trust departments which in 1967 held $77 billion in trust assets or 31 percent of all in the country; and in eight of the fifty largest life insurance companies with 1969 assets of $73 billions or 44 percent of the assets of the fifty largest life insurance companies.

Exactly how much of the stock in the top banks do they own? That is a carefully guarded secret. But it is pretty obvious that all together the holdings of these families, starting with those of the Rockefellers, add up to a pretty large block of stock, giving at least working control, possibly absolute control. It has been shown in Patman congressional inquiries that the trust funds of the various banks also own stock in a trustee bank and in other banks, which by interbank courtesy adds strength to the management voting position. In almost any possible showdown, these same people would emerge as the controlling force. They can't lose.

What was shown in the Dilworth list of Rockefeller holdings, then, relates to the actual Rockefeller financial power as no more than personal reserves, separate and apart from their external control and financial influence by other positional means. The power lies in unchallengeable and stupefying control and influence over what Louis D. Brandeis once called "other people's money." And over public policy.

Just what is control? Some discussion of the meaning of corporate control appears to be necessary as a good many professors have shown confusion about it and consequently people in general are confused.

Banks and corporations are chartered under law and operate under their own bylaws, which may not contradict the law but are extensions and extrapolations of it. In nearly all cases a majority of the common stock gives absolute control (unless something in the bylaws stipulates that senior securities have voting privileges either absolutely or under certain conditions). Thus, 51 percent of the common stock will give control, whether held by one person or by several acting together.

Below 51 percent, blocks of different magnitudes will yield what is known as practical control or working control. If much stock is disseminated widely in small quantities, as little as 10 percent ownership in one person or family, or even 5 percent, will give "working control." But safe practical control usually resides in an individual or joint holding of 25 percent or thereabouts.

The question remains: What is control? When one has control of a company it means that one is able, singly or jointly, to name a majority of the board of directors and set general company policy (such as who one banks with). As a majority of the board under the bylaws names the chief officers of the company, and they command the company operations on a day-to-day basis, this is where the control factor mainly lodges. Non-alliance interests may also name some members to the board; but they are outsiders—observers, advisors. They watch the controllers control, may offer tentative suggestions. They are along only for the ride and dividends.

In discussions at the Rockefeller hearings in Washington, the word "control" seemed to bother many people, including the Rockefellers. Mr. Dilworth said the Rockefellers were not "interested" in controlling anything and did not control anything. One could, though, be uninterested in controlling and still be in control. That apart, he was demonstrably factually wrong in one obvious instance, that of Rockefeller Center, Inc., which is 100 percent Rockefeller-owned. They simply *have* to control that, for they are the whole thing. This error revealed that he was really carrying on a veiled hyperbolic polemic, against people worried about "control."

Actually the Rockefellers control, and influence, much more—much, much more. But they do not do it alone, never did.

Before entering into this, however, the word "control" at the hearings appeared to many to connote having somebody by the throat or in a straitjacket, a common misconception. Corporate control isn't like that at all. It is a very quiet affair—*until it is challenged.* At that point all hell may break loose, and often does in the infrequent cases where it is challenged.

Dead cats and brickbats may fly through the air amid ugly accusations.

There is a general stockholders' meeting held every year in the companies and banks "controlled" by the banks, insurance companies, and scores of corporations of a group like the Rockefeller Syndicate. Anyone who owns stock (and stock can usually be freely bought in the open market) is allowed to attend or send in a proxy for the number of shares he owns. Usually there is only one slate in the field—the management slate. Each share of stock gets one vote. A million shares get a million votes. Simple. If a rival slate is fielded, one may send one's proxy to it. Usually only if there is great discontent among the general stockholders is there a rival slate, and often not then, for nobody volunteers to carry the challenge.

Major holders, associated with the existing board of directors, send their proxies in to the existing managers. In the case of Chase National Bank, First National City Bank, and, in fact, any bank or corporation, holdings of leading families such as those named go to the management—at Chase Manhattan to David Rockefeller and his colleagues. Also going to the management are proxies for any stock in the trust funds and, as it happens, as a matter of reciprocal courtesy the trust fund holdings for the stock held in the trust funds of other banks. Also, the stocks of various foundations and private trust funds of which the principal directors are founders or managers, plus the stocks held in a wide range of endowments, as for private universities, a big repository of voting power. On top of this usually comes stock in "street" names— that is, stock held by brokers for the accounts of customers. Brokers usually vote with the existing management.

The system works like this in all major companies, and in the companies of all these financial syndicates. In general the members of the Syndicate do not participate in the voting of all the companies, only in the companies of particular interest to one family. Where they have any influence over stock, however, they exert it in favor of the people with whom they are associated in the larger arena.

As to the Syndicate core itself of banks and insurance companies, somebody simply must have the voice of last instance. This will be the chairmen of the respective entities—in the case of the Rockefeller Syndicate, as perceived by Knowles, the chairmen of four banks and three insurance companies. No one of these tells the others where to head in. They talk things over and come to a consensus. All are cooperative people, with common goals. For this consensus there must be a spokesman. In the case of the Rockefeller Syndicate the spokesman is, as the public record clearly indicates, David Rockefeller. We know this because it is he who speaks. Simple: the spokesman speaks, the others keep pretty quiet once policy is set.

How are the Standard Oil companies controlled? In the manner I have outlined. Some people will deny they are so controlled, and, as the record shows, the Rockefellers for reasons of their own do. If they don't control, then nobody controls. Or, as some professors fatuously believe, the nonowning top executives in charge of the companies, who also sit on the boards of directors, are the controllers—a ridiculous contention.

The thesis was laid down in 1932 (A. A. Berle and Gardiner C. Means, *The Modern Corporation and Private Property*) that corporations are no longer in control of stockholders, owners, who are scattered and have only small holdings (a contention that is in instance after instance demonstrably false) and that corporations are actually controlled by executive officers who own little or no stock. Many academicians, and some journalists, followed blindly after Berle and Means, and wound up with a lot of egg on their faces. Corporations are controlled, in fact, by owners or owning trustees of big blocks of stock, the holdings sometimes parceled out to different family members or to entities under family control, like foundations. This holds in every case and is readily demonstrable on the basis of monthly reports by the Securities and Exchange Commission.

There is nothing at all to the Berle-Means fantasy. Large owners control; property is in the saddle, always and forever —Hurrah! Indeed, large owners control and significantly influence a great deal more than they actually own by means of these pooling and trustee alliances.

Now, if nobody in particular controls the Standard Oil companies they are, in this day of take-over bids, open to being taken over by somebody. As fine properties, it would be desirable to have them and to manage them. It will be noticed, however, that none of the big take-over outfits goes near them. Indeed, they avoid them as though they were rattlesnakes or plague-ridden.

What happens if someone challenges for control? As it used to be said in the days of the Old West, in such a case one had better be "carrying a lot of iron." Actually, it has already happened with one of the Standard Oil companies. In 1929 the chairman of the Standard Oil Company of Indiana, "Col." Robert W. Stewart, decided to take control of the company away from the Rockefellers. John D. Rockefeller, Jr., had become displeased with Stewart because he was secretly involved in the Teapot Dome imbroglio and had lied that he was not and, furthermore, because he had "milked" the company to some extent—an unpardonable offense. Rockefeller called upon him to resign. Stewart refused, and in a bid for general stockholder support declared a 50 percent stock dividend.

I was then a financial writer for the *New York Herald Tribune* and covered the stockholders' meeting, was a witness, as it were, at the OK Corral as Ike Clanton and his gang faced the Earp brothers and Doc Holliday in deadly combat. Before the showdown newspapers gave excited imaginative previews of the coming colossal struggle, of which the outcome hung in suspense. Doubtful, I inquired among the customary unimpeachable sources in Wall Street to which I had access about the chances of the Rockefellers being ousted.

It was explained to me that there was no chance at all because on the Rockefeller side would be (1) whatever stock they owned, (2) the stock in Standard of Indiana owned by Standard of New Jersey, (3) all the stock of Indiana owned by various Rockefeller foundations, (4) endowment stock of Indiana owned by the University of Chicago, (5) stock in "Street" names, (6) stock in Chase National Bank trust funds, (7) stock in other bank trust funds, (8) stock still owned by members of all the old-line Standard Oil families, etc. My report appeared on the front page of the *Herald Tribune,* January 17, 1929, nearly two months before the stockholders' meeting on March 7. In other words, it was demonstrably possible to predict such outcomes far in advance.

The meeting, held in a company hall at Whiting, Indiana, was sparsely attended, no more than two hundred or so persons present, many of them from the press. Winthrop Aldrich of Chase led the Rockefeller contingent of lawyers and clerks. There were no Rockefellers present; there never are at such public showdowns. Aldrich was pale and tense as the affair opened, no doubt suspecting some sort of trick by Stewart.

There was no trick. Proxies were submitted to vote tellers, were counted, and the results announced. The Rockefellers won with close to 65 percent of the stock, a walkaway. Small pro-Stewart stockholders were flattened. The direct family interest in the company at the time was 4.5 percent of stock in the name of Rockefeller Jr. and close to 5 percent in trust funds for two sisters. Standard Oil of New Jersey, however, held a substantial minority interest. The whole scene played as easily, and as smoothly, as the Soviet army taking over Czechoslovakia many years later. The true bosses were showing their hand—all aces.

Apart from initial tenseness the meeting was about the quietest affair I have ever seen—in fact, boring. For excitement any parent-teacher association school meeting would top it. Stewart, in the chair, was completely civil and correct, knowing in advance that he was beaten. Had he pulled some sort of delaying tactic, the issue would have been resolved in court, the result the same. Stewart was graciously allowed to retire on a pension—the end of the line for him. Financially he was a midget, deluded by the resonance of his own voice.

What if someone decides to take over a Syndicate bank? There is an illustration of this also of record.

The idea of taking over the Chemical Bank of New York, no less, was recently conceived by youthful Saul P. Steinberg, one of an endless procession of Wall Street wizards, boy wonders, founder in 1965 of Leasco Data Processing Equipment Corporation, a computer-leasing company, and successful in many take-over bids, notably of the old-line Reliance Insurance Company of Philadelphia, a coup. Leasco has since been transformed into the Reliance Group, Inc.

As incredulous word got around that the boy wizard had his eyes on Chemical Bank, a pillar of the Syndicate, events took place as reported in *Business Week,* July 25, 1970: "Leasco's stock plunged from 140 to 106 in two weeks. Though even Leasco's Saul P. Steinberg would never admit it publicly, it appeared that bank trust departments and perhaps other institutions dumped their shares to protect Chemical. 'I always knew there was an Establishment,' said Steinberg at the time. 'I just used to think I was part of it.' "

In so thinking he was like many similar others—wrong. Just because one thinks like the Establishment, harmonizes with it, doesn't make one part of it.

The decline in market value of Leasco was fatal to the looming take-over proposal because such transactions are contrived through an exchange of stock at market values. With Leasco's market-value undermined, and still sinking, a take-over attempt was impossible. In this case there was no showdown. The foe was simply disarmed in advance, scuttled before the battle began.

In an aggregation like that of the Rockefellers or the Rockefeller Syndicate, precisely how much stock an individual or a family owns in a company is a matter of slight importance. In some cases a great deal is owned, in others very little. In the case of the Standard Oil companies, much of the stock is now spread through foundations. Still other stock is spread in greater or smaller amounts through all the old Standard Oil families and their foundations, universities, investment trusts, insurance companies. Much, too, is in the trust funds of the leading banks. Exxon is one of the most heavily owned stocks among institutional investors, all of which, in any showdown, would come out on the side of the Rockefellers.

Again, in any looming showdown over control, more stock can be acquired, if necessary, in the open market. Holdings in other quarters can be liquidated to get funds for showdown stock.

Anyone, therefore, would be very foolish to reach for control of any of the Standard Oil companies without first asking David Rockefeller if it was permissible. The answer would probably be No. If so, forget about it or prepare to take an expensive beating.

Why is control desirable to retain?—a question seldom raised. The Rockefeller Syndicate controls scores, even hundreds of companies. Where it doesn't control, it influences. Why do this? What is the percentage?

The sort of capitalism practiced by this and other syndicates is known as finance capitalism as distinguished from industrial capitalism. Finance capitalism is banking intermeshed with captive industrial companies—not straight banking. John D. Rockefeller was an industrial capitalist, but he was already making the transition to being a finance capitalist in his postmature years, when he took a position in National City Bank and then in Chase National Bank. The Mellons started out as finance capitalists, their fingers in many companies.

The following thirteen completely controlled family corporations, as Professor Knowles shows, are the first tier of the Rockefeller Syndicate industrial companies with the numbers in parenthesis their rank on the 1969 *Fortune* magazine list (*Fortune,* May, 1970).*

E. I. du Pont de Nemours (15), W. R. Grace Inc., (50), Corning Glass Works (210), Owens Corning Fiberglass (220), Cummins Engine (245), Hewlett-Packard (293), R. R. Donnelly and Sons (304), International Basic Economy Corporation (Rockefeller) (N.R.), Pittsburgh Coke and Chemical (711), Commercial Solvents (674), Deering-Milliken (N.R.), Field Enterprises (N.R.), and Mercantile Stores (N.R.). To this one might well add as a fourteenth, Rockefeller Center, Inc., a billion-dollar affair but not rated as an industrial.

In a second tier there are twenty-three mammoth industrial corporations over which the group individually and collectively exerts undisputed working control:

---

*Knowles states these as asset rank but cites *Fortune* ranks by sales. The asset ranks are, however, very nearly similar.

Standard Oil of New Jersey, now Exxon (2) (Rockefeller) (in assets it is #1); Mobil Oil (7), formerly Standard Oil of New York and Vacuum Oil (Rockefeller); Standard Oil Company of California (13) (Rockefeller); Standard Oil Company of Indiana (18) (Rockefeller); International Harvester (31) (Mc-Cormick); Inland Steel (93) (Block); Marathon Oil (126), formerly Ohio Oil (S.O.) (Rockefeller); Quaker Oats (195) (Stuart); Wheeling-Pittsburgh Steel (213) (Hillman); Freeport Sulphur (462) (Rockefeller, Stillman-Rockefeller, and Whitney); Itek (521) (Rockefeller); Copeland Refrigeration (639) (Hillman); Global Marine (N.R.) (Hillman-Whitney); Marquardt Corporation (671) (Rockefeller); GCA (N.R.) (Rockefeller); Shakespeare Corporation (N.R.) (Hillman); Stone and Webster (N.R.) (Stone, Webster); Federated Department Stores, ninth largest retailer, (Lazarus); Walgreen Stores, thirty-third largest retailer, (Walgreen); Marshall Field, forty-fifth largest retailer, (Field); Transcontinental Gas Pipeline, twenty-eighth largest utility, (Stone, Webster); Texas Gas Transmission (N.R.) (Hillman).

Among companies under firm control of the Syndicate, Knowles isolated Consolidated Edison, second largest utility, and Anaconda Copper Company, seventy-sixth largest industrial.

Under coalition control with other syndicates, mainly Morgan, he found American Telephone and Telegraph, largest utility or company of any class in the world; U.S. Steel (12); Monsanto Chemical (43); and General Foods (46). Under joint control with several groups was Chrysler (6); Olin Corporation (99); Pan American World Airways, eighth largest transportation company; Colgate Palmolive (103); Borg-Warner (108); and the Home Insurance Company. In the firmly controlled group the Rockefellers had 50 percent or more of the directors, in the coalition group 40 to 42 percent, and in the joint control group 22 to 36 percent.

Bondholdings of the three insurance companies in leading corporations were huge, ranging from 13 percent of all issued for RCA (21) up to 39 percent for International Paper (52).

All these various dominant owners and controllers are also

into a wide variety of other companies to a lesser extent, as we saw by the Dilworth report the Rockefellers were. They aren't in only one or two companies. Nor when it can be shown precisely what they own in a company do they necessarily retain this exact position forever; they increase or decrease holdings as it suits them, like a musician going from pianissimo to fortissimo and back to pianissimo, from legato to staccato, and so on.

Just what is the advantage of this sort of syndicate operation to the participants? What is the payoff? Profit, of course, is among the objectives. But any one of several millions of people can buy shares in any or all of these companies and draw dividends without controlling. What advantage have the controllers?

The syndicate operation as a part of finance capitalism has the advantage of offering all the leading participants—that is, the chief stockholders and directors of the banks—broad flexibility and many options, neither of which they would enjoy if they concentrated all their holdings in one or a few companies. Furthermore, their risks would then be greater as they would be tied to the fluctuating fortunes of one enterprise or industry.

As it is, with the syndicate operation they can draw down their holdings if they wish (some do, some don't) in their major company and diversify them elsewhere, participate in broader control. And at the same time they retain control over their main company through acting in concert with others. Wide control's the thing with which to catch the puissance of the king (or State).

The transition from industrial to finance capitalism has the advantages shown by this simple model: A man (or his family) owns 51 percent of one big company, all the eggs in one basket, subject to the vicissitudes of one industry. This amount of ownership gives control. If he gradually reduces his ownership, meanwhile retaining control because nobody challenges it, he is able to diversify into other industries, thus gaining defensive diversification, income from many sources. If he takes a moderately substantial position in the ownership of a bank, he gains reciprocal financial advantages as between the bank and his major company and any minor companies he may be interested in. And if other industrialists, all noncompetitive, do the same thing, they come to form a powerful alliance or insiders' club around the bank, then in and around several banks. Along the way they pick up by infiltration dominance in one or several large insurance companies, pools of capital waiting to be tapped, requiring investment outlets. Mutually trusted people are placed at the top.

The stock ownership in the major family company, control of which is retained all along, can be drawn down to 20 percent, 10 percent, even less, without impairing control, which remains in place until challenged. If it is ever challenged, the entire alliance then will spring into action to mobilize the stock necessary to retain control, repel invaders.

Among other things, one can move one's stockholdings around and into companies where the earnings are at the moment greater than elsewhere. The whole operation becomes a turkey shoot.

It is a clear case all along of eating one's cake and having it too—always recognized as a desirable consummation. Even better than that, it is a case of eating one's cake and possessing an ever-enlarging cake. The public, meanwhile, knows nothing of all this going on, too busy eating hot dogs, watching TV, engaging in *amour,* or just goofing along.

Now along come some professors and conveniently say, due to simple outsider ignorance, that the original company is now in control of its hired executive officers, that ownership does not control. Property has been separated from control, nonowners are controlling property, which is floating about like soap bubbles—a pipe dream. They also say that all the companies operate separately, in competitive, arms'-length relationships. They are in fact all in the same bed, supporting and patronizing each other.

The value of control in conjunction with a base in an alliance of big money-market banks is concretely twofold.

First, the banks benefit by enjoying a great deal of lucrative captive wholesale business: deposits of the corporations;

bank services for the giant corporations as paying and transfer agents, payroll supervisors, trustees for employees' pension funds, and so on; similar services, especially trust accounts, for members of the owning families, etc., etc., etc.

Secondly, the corporations benefit by having always readily available large pools of bank-insurance company capital for (1) short-term loans, (2) syndicate sales of new stock, bonds, and debentures, (3) quick assistance for the owning families in maintaining control vis-à-vis take-over outfits, (4) allied corporations functioning as captive suppliers or customers, etc.

A great deal of reciprocal leverage is generated by the arrangement.

As to where one banks, the executive officers of the respective corporations, unless they are also big owners (as some of them are), have nothing to say. Nor do they determine dividend policy and much else. Only operations are in their sphere. They execute policy, do not make it.

The executive officers, for their part, are chosen by their respective boards of directors to run their companies in a purely businesslike way and not make an undue amount of waves. What the executives do is subject to periodic review by the boards of directors. Officers who do not come up to the mark are retired, fired, transferred, or given indefinite leaves of absence. It happens all the time.

The ease with which top management can be turned out by controllers was illustrated in Anaconda Copper in 1971. J. B. M. Place, vice-chairman of the Chase Manhattan Bank, completely inexperienced in mining, was suddenly sent out to Butte, Montana, to become chairman, president, general manager, and chief executive officer. The entire top echelon of officers, with the company for decades, was swept away, and lower officers also abruptly walked the plank.

What had happened?

Anaconda had fallen on evil days. Its net income in 1966 had reached $131.2 million, and it sold soon thereafter at $66 a share. In 1970 the net was down to $63.8 million, and the stock sold at $19 a share. When Place took over, earnings were running at a low rate of $16 million annually.

In 1969 the government of Chile had decided to take over by purchase the lucrative properties of Anaconda and other mining companies such as Kennecott. An arrangement was reached to have the nationalized properties paid for over a period of many years. But in 1971 the new, semirevolutionary government of Salvador Allende, since deposed in a blood-bath during which he was killed, expropriated the properties and retained the option to pay whatever price, if any, that the government set. Other properties of American companies were similarly abruptly gobbled up.

The Allende forces preened themselves on how "democratic" they were, by which they meant they had "taken power" in an election and continued to tolerate an opposition. But when one confiscates the properties of powerful outsiders—or even domestic owners—one must consider the possibility that they will collaborate just as ruthlessly with internal oppositionists. The American constitutional founders were very alert to the possibility of interference in American affairs by Great Britain, France, and Spain, discussed it at the constitutional convention, and set up roadblocks against it in the Constitution. Even so there was in fact surreptitious intervention by Great Britain, France, and Spain in American affairs, including mass agitation against the government through oppositionists. It was squelched. But other subtle interventions reached into the cabinet and army command, all coming to naught for a variety of reasons including exposure. Governments have so comported themselves for centuries.

After the confiscation decrees of 1971, the anti-Allende opposition grew stronger and stronger. It has since been disclosed that the Central Intelligence Agency of the United States took a hand by furnishing funds for anti-Allende newspapers and opposition groups. Very possibly the anti-Allende movement could not have gathered momentum without such timely assistance. And while the CIA's Chilean caper was under way, Nelson Rockefeller was a member of the Foreign Intelligence Advisory Board, supervising the CIA, certainly in a strategic spot and a party of explicit interest.

Had Allende consulted anyone acquainted with the realities about confiscating Anaconda, Kennecott, IT&T and others, he'd have been told, "Don't do it." For he was biting off more than he could chew, internally as well as externally. It is easy for half-baked leftists to read in Lenin, "Expropriate the expropriators, rob the robbers," but these are fighting words, meaning that thousands, even millions must die to replace one set of tricksters with another possibly worse set of tricksters. In Russia millions died through the application of the easy formula, with plenty of assistance being given the opposition from outside. In the process, one set of czars was exchanged for another.

One certainly can't take a juicy piece of meat away from a lion bare-handed. One needs for such exploits in politics a preponderance of armed force or must stand ready to sacrifice the whole populace (which street-corner revolutionaries are always ready to do). Allende, as events showed, didn't have the army with him.

In Chile, now, the government, Anaconda, and other American companies are again discussing reinstituting the method of purchase. Things look distinctly better for Anaconda and the others.

The fact, then, as shown in the Dilworth statement, that the Rockefeller family owns only a little more than 2 percent of oil company stock proves nothing, it is clear, with respect to control. For at any moment the Rockefellers felt it necessary, readying for a showdown, to vote more stock, they could come up—again and again—with something like 65 percent. Rival syndicates know this—and keep hands off.

Even in companies merely under the influence of one of these finance-capital syndicates, where none of the syndicate individuals or their families own any stock to speak of, the displeasure of the syndicate is to be avoided by the company executives. For, once the word gets out that the executives are engaging in disapproved practices (as they sometimes do), punishment is swift. Starting as a trickle, there is soon observable a deluge of selling of the stock and bonds of the offending company, the selling coming seemingly from all quarters. What is happening is that trust funds, captive investment trusts, and insurance companies are unloading. Newspapers report opaquely that "big institutional sellers" are behind it all. Now frightened small holders join in, and there ensues a cataclysmic collapse of prices. Wayward company executives and maverick owners understand. They are being scuttled.

On the other hand, companies within the sphere of influence of one of these syndicates, if they get into trouble, through no fault of their own, have a friend to turn to in the form of the syndicate. They can get help, perhaps at a price; but help at a price is better than no help at all.

So it pays to "play ball," do what is expected of one. Mavericks are not welcome.

Anyone who plays the syndicate false, plays it for a sucker, will almost certainly not get away with it. There will be a day of reckoning, hard on the pocketbook, sometimes fatal. In other words, be meek. Stand at attention. Salute.

The various syndicates, moreover, are careful not to come into confrontation with each other, which would be mutually expensive. Here it is, in a smaller theater, much like confrontation between the United States and the Soviet Union, something to be avoided by both sides. Poaching on each others' turf may be permitted, a bit of nibbling here and there, some fast footwork. But no confrontation. Detente prevails all around.

Control, then, over a wide area, is valuable, giving syndicate members much extra ground for aggressive and defensive lucrative maneuver, not tied in to a single situation and isolated in the capitalist jungle. One can be cut down there. Many have been. Control, over a wide area, finally, is steadily profitable, not erratically so.

Although Professor Knowles's report is confined to sixty large pages, it covers far too much to do full justice to by way of reportage without going into many ancillary matters in exhaustive detail. Knowles tried to get the exact position of all the big bank stockholders but ran into a stone wall of obvious aliases as uncovered by Congressman Wright Patman, chairman of the House Banking and Currency Committee, in *Chain Banking: Stockholder and Loan Links of 200 Largest Member Banks,* Washington, 1963.

Knowles also presents a list of thirty large corporations, none heretofore mentioned, in which the trust departments of Chase Manhattan and First National City hold various percentages of stock up to 10.8 percent. Such holdings give a trustee bank some voice in the determination of management. It isn't that the bank attempts to dictate to the corporate management or its dominant controllers; but it certainly has a voice in the company. Displeased about the way anything is handled, unappeased, the bank trustee will simply sell its trusteed stock, thereby putting market pressure on the price, depressing its value. Corporate managers don't like that to happen as it makes future financing difficult, so they toe the line, whatever it is.

As Professor Knowles shows, all the directorial elements of the Rockefeller Syndicate hold or have held reciprocal dominating positions in many foundations, many of the leading private universities, corporation directorships outside the leading companies of the group, the federal government up to the cabinet level, in important newspaper, magazine, and publishing houses (idea dissemination), and comprise additionally a widespread network of interlocking corporate directorships apart from the top interlocks of banks and insurance companies. The lists are too long to reproduce here. Seekers after complete light are referred to the study.

Among thirty-one leading Rockefeller Syndicate people, three had been secretary of state (Professor Knowles omitted Christian Herter, married into the Pratt Standard Oil family), eight had been other Cabinet officers, two had been head of the World Bank, one High Commissioner to Germany (actually two), six had been major ambassadors, one was the original long-term head of the Central Intelligence Agency, three were top armed service officers, two were governors, and one a United States senator.

Thirty-four Rockefeller people, leading directors of their banks, insurance companies, and corporations, or otherwise connected, held dominant posts in idea-developing institutions. Five were presidents of leading private universities. Many more were university trustees. Influence, influence, influence. . . .

Professor Knowles discusses what he terms the "misuse" of political power by agencies, governmental and private, under the control of the group in Iran, Peru, India, and Greece and shows that the Syndicate effectively threw its weight with "inside men" against eliminating the oil-import quotas under President Nixon, costly to American consumers, an embarrassment to the country in general.

Whether one agrees in detail or not with the general thesis of Professor Knowles, the candid reader must agree that he at least makes a very strong case that this is a group, one of a number not as large, that imposes its independent decisions in the form of wide-ranging policy and extrapolates public policy for its own benefit. This is power, in the *Hobbesian sense of the term*, the veiled power of the State. (See Thomas Hobbes, *Leviathan*, 1651.) Myself a modified Hobbesian, not a group radical, group liberal, or pseudoconservative, American-style, I think I at least know what power is and when it is being exerted. The Rockefellers have it, to a high degree.

With respect to coming events, Professor Knowles believes the "likely directions in which Rockefeller Group political power will be exercised in the future may both threaten world peace and impose economic burdens on the domestic front. The principal international threat stems from the continued position of the oil industry as the Group's industrial mainstay. The two areas in the world which pose the greatest potential danger to peace—the Middle East and Southeast Asia—are also (or soon will be, in the case of Southeast Asia) the two major oil-producing areas of the world. The Middle East's position as the leading oil-producing area is, of course, well known. Less well known is the rapid emergence of Southeast Asia as a major oil-producing area."

In conclusion, Professor Knowles holds "that the structure and exercise of vast economic and political power on the part of the Rockefeller Financial Group stems ultimately from the enormous repositories of inherited wealth represented by the Group's leading families. No set of reforms or controls short of breaking down the immense concentration of so much personal wealth would have any lasting effect in altering the present distribution of power in this country. As long as concentrations of inherited wealth remain intact, it will be possible [a misprint for "impossible"?] for new structures of power to be devised in the economic sphere. And as long as the corporate world continues to exercise a dominant role in the financing of elections and in the administration of government, a hierarchical power structure in the economic sphere will continue to have its political counterpart."

Now, two of the interesting side aspects of this study, a genuine cruncher, are that it was not brought into the congressional hearings on the nomination of Nelson Rockefeller to be vice-president and was not reproduced at the time of its publication or later by any leading newspaper. As far as the panorama unfolded by Professor Knowles is concerned, the general public, even usually informed persons, are as much in the dark about what is going on in the United States as in the center of Tibet.

The study leaves it clear, at any rate, that the numbers game of how little stock the Rockefeller family controls under the management of Mr. Dilworth's office has little relevancy to the power and authority of the family. The fact that key Rockefellers are the top dogs among the top dogs of the Syndicate reveals clearly the guiding role conceded to them by the associated brass-tacks Syndicate participants. They are members of what writers get their knuckles rapped by Syndicate professors for calling a Ruling Class.

There appeared before the Senate Rules Committee, however, Prof. G. William Domhoff, social psychologist, and Prof. Charles L. Schwartz, physicist, of the University of California, to present a dual study of their own titled *Probing the Rockefeller Fortune.* This effort showed Rockefeller family connections ramifying in many directions other than those shown by Knowles. The labyrinth is endless.

How a physicist came to be involved in the nomination hearings of a vice-president of the United States is itself interesting. Professor Schwartz explained in his statement, "As a professional scientist and someone who has become interested in exploring the ways in which science is tied into other aspects of American life, I recently started looking at some of the business corporations which are known as leaders in advanced technology. I quickly discovered two representatives of RF&A who sat on the boards of directors of a few such companies. Looking up the listing for these two men in *Who's Who* I was able to collect a sizeable list of corporations they directed."

He continued his inquiries and found out a lot, most of it of little interest to congressmen because no electoral "oomph" was attached to any of it. One thing he discovered, and discovered it being flatly stated, was that the scientific enterprise is conducted in all its phases in a quest for mundane power and profit. Leave those out and science has no more interest to the corporation crowd than Hindu mythology. In other words, there are far more things under heaven and on earth than are dreamed of in the average scientist's philosophy. As far as comprehending the politico-economic-social picture, most scientists, in fact, are *shmos,* don't really know what goes on. Few seem to care. Perhaps too many variables are involved for the scientific mentality to deal with.

Professor Schwartz, for example, found that Charles B. Smith, with the Rockefeller office since 1962 and director of nine high-technology Rockefeller companies, made the following remarks in a lecture titled "Venture Capital and Management," reported in the Proceedings of the Second Annual Management Seminar, Boston College, May 28-29, 1970:

"We are a relatively loosely organized group of a few people who attempt to invest some of the personal funds of a wealthy family in high risk and potentially high reward companies ordinarily included within the loose, current meaning of venture capital. We concentrate on advanced technologies, generally in the early life of the companies, including start-ups. We are primarily equity investors. . . .

"Our goal like everybody else's [?], is to make wads and wads of money for the family. . . .

"We are known, I guess, as relatively hard dealers for our dollars *in that we don't like to give them away* [emphasis added]. We feel that it is not only cheating our employers but is also unfair to the entrepreneur. When we invest, we really think our money is the cheapest, no strings, generally. Afterwards, we are generous with the management's incentives."

Up to 1960, he pointed out, one could finance a technological company on the basis of government research and development contracts. Through those one could build up one's capital equipment portfolio. But since 1960, alas, no more.

This isn't the sort of image of the Rockefellers put forth by the public relations staff. In the hands of the PR boys, all is sweetness and light, centered on charity, humanitarianism, philanthropy, and good will toward all men.

The Domhoff-Schwartz presentation revealed that fifteen employees of the family office hold directorships in nearly 100 corporations, almost none of which were even mentioned in the Knowles study or by Dilworth. These corporations include many in advanced technology ventures under the eye of Laurance Rockefeller. The combined assets of these companies came to $70 billion. In a few instances there were overlappings with the Knowles lists.

In reply, the Rockefeller office asserted that these employees held these directorships on their own, unconnected with the Rockefellers—something no seasoned financial observer could believe. Mr. Dilworth himself was a director in sixteen corporations, including the Chase Manhattan Bank, Rockefeller Center, and the International Basic Economy Corporation; these alone stamp him a Rockefeller man, all wool and a yard wide. Robert W. Purcell, a consultant to Rockefeller Family and Associates since the late 1950s, was a director of twenty-one companies, including several that are 100 percent Rockefeller such as Caneel Bay Plantations, International Basic Economy Corporation, Mauna Kea Beach Hotel Corporation, and others less than 100 percent owned.

Reginald G. Coombe was a director through 1966 of the National Bank of Westchester, in which the Rockefellers had a position, since relinquished, and two other companies. Carl E. Siegesmund was also a director of the National Bank of Westchester and two other companies. Theodore F. Walkowicz, with the Rockefeller office since 1952, was a director in all of twenty companies, including several known to be under the direct sponsorship of Laurance Rockefeller: Itek, CCI-Marquardt, Airborne Instruments Laboratory, Pocantico Oil and Gas, Cryonetics, etc.

Harper Woodward, in the Rockefeller family office since 1946, was a director of fifteen companies, including known Rockefeller outfits like Eastern Air Lines, Itek, CCI-Marquardt, Flight Refueling, Nuclear Development, Dorado Beach Hotel, Airborne Instruments, and so on.

Reginald B. Smith of the family office was a director of nine companies, M. Frederik Smith of six, Warren T. Lindquist of one, Peter O. Crisp of four, and Louise A. Boyer of one, the International Basic Economy Corporation founded by Nelson Rockefeller.

In addition many of these employee-directors were trustees of private colleges, universities, foundations, and other "nonprofit" entities in which the Rockefellers are interested, sometimes also personally present.

To claim that these employees are acting "on their own" as directors and trustees, are not functioning as the Rockefeller "presence," simply stretches credulity past the breaking point. What really appears to be the case is that these operations out of the Rockefeller family office are simply separate from the big syndicate presided over by David and his cousins in the First National City Bank (Citicorp). They are part of the Rockefeller personal reserve operation, the home reservation.

The Domhoff-Schwartz presentation concluded by listing major corporations with multiple interlocks with the Rockefeller family, in some cases including or excluding corporations mentioned by Professor Knowles. This list consisted of fifty-nine industrial corporations, seventeen commercial banks, eight life insurance companies, four diversified financial companies, three utilities, seven retail chains, and two big airlines, Eastern and Pan Am.

Is there anything immoral, illegal, or subversive about all this? Nothing whatever. All is in harmony with the system. What makes some people take it amiss, however, is that they are imbued with American myths. Through school, newspa-

per, and politicians' patriotic propaganda, they have been instilled with a different vision of what is the prevailing state of
affairs in the United States. The real, actual, genuine United
States is to all such of the illusioned *terra incognita.* Among
other things such myth-inspired people continuously misread
the Constitution.

What is the issue about all this? The issue is, simply, are the
Rockefellers merely a wealthy family in reduced circumstances, quietly going their own ways, or are they a concentrated
entity with managerial fingers extended into a thousand political and economic areas on the American scene?

Each wayfarer on life's way, examining the data, must make
up his own mind and decide for himself whether Nelson was
right in saying that it was a "myth and misconception" that
the family wields enormous power. To my way of looking at
the situation, it seems that the Rockefeller Syndicate, with
each member of it having a full coalitional say, controls or
influences possibly $500 billion (or more) of income-produc-
ing assets, is an integral part along with other similar syndicates of the United States government and exercises a
pervasive authority over the managements of cultural institutions such as foundations, museums, libraries, research centers, bird sanctuaries, and private universities and colleges.
Many persons of standing in Wall Street share this opinion,
which is not derived through Marxist or any other ideological
fantasies. The opinion, in other words, is empirically based,
fact-anchored.

4.

The big surprises of the Rockefeller hearings before the
Senate Rules Committee and the House Judiciary Committee
detonated around the disclosures of how Nelson interrelated
pecuniarily with his political henchmen and peers, his tax
maneuvers, campaign funding, and the ways he and at least
one brother functioned surreptitiously and deviously to mold
public opinion in aid of the advancement of their schemes.

Rocky, it turned out, was a pecuniary Machiavelli. The Rockefeller trail, it developed, was lavishly strewn with money, all the way, all the time: money, the universal solvent, the modern-style philosophers' stone. Without money, of course, the Rockefellers would be on all fours with everybody else, for they give no evidence of being magically talented unless as virtuosi of pecuniary proclivity. If Nobel prizes were given away for pecuniary expertise they would, concededly, be laureates.

There was much education made available through the hearings for the myth-ridden American people. Of prime interest was how rich people use their money, not (as popularly supposed) for living *la dolce vita,* indulging in wine, women, and song and related shenanigans—except perhaps on rare occasions. The money is used, prudently, for the retention and expansion of power and authority. Rich people, for the most part, are too seriously self-oriented to engage to any great extent in the nip-ups popularly fantasied.

Compressed, the hearings showed the following:*

1. Nelson Rockefeller over a period of seventeen years made personal loans and gifts to friends, relatives, and political associates of more than $2 million plus $840,000 state and federal gift taxes. More than 75 percent of it went to political associates in New York with most of this lion's share ultimately converted into gifts. A political Santa Claus was clearly on a rampage. All of this, however, was so much small change to Rocky, who was a bit nonplused by the fuss. He had a reason to feel baffled because he didn't, apparently, realize the extent to which the public mentality is myth ridden and the extent to which politicians and captive publicists cater to the myth-ridden peasantry. One of the myths is that governmental affairs, by and large, are on the up-and-up. Not so; they are, often as not, plain crooked in a system full of holes.

---

* The sources for what follows are the televised hearings of the Senate Rules Committee, the House Judiciary Committee, the news columns of the *New York Times,* staff commentators in the *New York Times,* and such other sources as are mentioned in the text. The printed records of the hearings and investigations were not yet available for this disquisition.

New York statutes sternly forbid, under penalty, etc., making a gift to any state employee even if it is not a bribe, even if it is as innocent as an infant's kiss. That the statute was kept well in mind was shown by the fact that the noninterest and in some cases low-interest loans were not converted into gifts until the official was severed, usually temporarily, from the state payroll. Although the law was not broken in letter, it was clearly sidestepped, delicately. If one could prove the loans were made intentionally as disguised compensation, one might sustain a legal process. In some cases outright gifts were made prior to assumption of state office. In other cases loan-gifts were made to outside people, mainly on the edges of politics.

Many of the loan-gifts or straight loans were substantial. The largest amount, $625,000, went to Dr. William J. Ronan, New York University professor who was, first, Nelson's executive secretary and, displaying competence, was advanced by stages through important jobs to become, finally, chairman of heavily funded Port Authority of New York and New Jersey. Prior to this appointment by Rockefeller, he was head of the Metropolitan Transportation Authority. He also became the $100,000-a-year advisor to the Rockefeller family—a fount of practical knowledge.

Ronan converted his loan-gifts into lucrative investments, just what he was expected to do. These made him an independently wealthy man of the lower orders of wealth, the general prime objective of a multitude of once poor boys in American politics. For there is much slush in the land of opportunity.

Other big loan-gift transactions were the following:

Gift to Rockefeller-sponsored United States Secretary of State Henry A. Kissinger, $50,000 in 1969 when he became national security advisor to President-elect Nixon. Legal clearance for the gift was obtained, via letter, from Edward L. Morgan and Egil Krogh, Jr., at the time deputy counsel to the president-elect. Krogh later went to jail after pleading guilty to helping mastermind the White House-sponsored burglary of the office of a physician treating Daniel Ellsberg, discloser of the celebrated Pentagon Papers. The idea was to obtain bad-sounding information (and/or misinformation) to be used in boiling up public opinion against Ellsberg. The whole Nixon crew, as it came out in the Watergate Affair, was awash in illicit money (the always-magic substance) and ultragamy operations, as ultimately shown in scores of open-court convictions of corporations and high officials up to the cabinet level. The entire administration was "on the take," bought, with the president even manipulating the price of milk upward in orchestration with a big milk-industry slush fund.

Loan-gift of $101,900 to L. Judson Morhouse, state Republican chairman who was later convicted in open court of accepting a $100,000 fee from the Playboy Club to bribe and procure for a separate $50,000 a State Liquor Authority chairman, who in turn was duly and securely bribed. With his gift Morhouse made highly lucrative investments on Long Island, as detailed by the *New York Post,* under the guidance of Rockefeller family connections, netting him some $600,000. Rockefeller also commuted the jail sentence of Morhouse, who never served a day, and set all his aides to work justifying the commutation to the ever-trustful public. It was Morhouse who initially guided Rockefeller into the governor's chair like a trained seeing-eye dog.

A year after Nelson Rockefeller took office as governor of New York, Laurance Rockefeller made a loan of $49,000 to Morhouse, a general magnet for dubious money.

A preappointment gift of $31,389 and a loan of $145,000 were made to Edward J. Logue, head of Rockefeller's pet, the giant Urban Development Corporation, later in vast financial distress at, naturally, public expense.

A gift in 1970 of $155,000 to Emmet John Hughes, author, journalist, columnist, and former speech writer for President Eisenhower. Hughes for many years engaged in columnar political punditry for the benefit of the *hoi polloi,* giving no word that he was a Rockefeller librettist. Hughes at first responded by saying the money was pay for consulting services rendered in 1968, which would make it a gem among consultations; this, as it was noted, made the money subject to retroactive income taxes. Rockefeller spokesmen, however, made it clear the money was a flat gift on which Rockefeller had paid 57 percent taxes, nontaxable to the recipient. Hughes finally conceded this was so.

To Alton G. Marshall, Rockefeller's executive secretary in Albany and later president of Rockefeller Center, gift of $306,867.

To James W. Gaynor, state commissioner of housing and community renewal, gift of $107,000.

To Henry L. Diamond, head of the Department of Environmental Conservation and then executive director of Rockefeller's Commission on Critical Choices for Americans, a heavily funded springboard for Rockefeller to the presidency in 1976, gift of $100,000.

To Victor Borella, special assistant on labor issues under Governor Rockefeller, gift of $100,000.

To Hugh Morrow, Rockefeller's press secretary for fifteen years, gift of $135,000.

To Mrs. Anne Whitman, secretary to President Eisenhower and assistant to Rockefeller, $48,000 in loans and gifts.

To Meade Esposito, Brooklyn Democratic chieftain, gift of a $2,000 Picasso lithograph.

To Robert B. Anderson, onetime secretary of the navy and secretary of the treasury, a loan of $84,000 during the interim between these two jobs.

To George A. Dudley, chief executive officer of the New York State Council on Architecture, an out-of-office loan of $6,000.

To John J. Gilhooley, former federal subcabinet officer and City Transit Authority member, an out-of-office loan of $6,000.

To Wallace K. Harrison, former director of the Office of Inter-American affairs and architect of record of the Albany South Mall, an out-of-office loan of $60,000.

To Francis A. Jamieson, in the United States Office of the Coordinator of Inter-American Affairs under Rockefeller, an out-of-office loan of $12,000.

To Dr. W. Kenneth Riland, member of the State Public

Health Council and of the Commission on the Uses and Regulation of Acupuncture, an out-of-office loan of $6,000.

To Theodore C. Streibert, director of the United States Information Agency in the 1940s and later an employee in the Rockefeller family office, an out-of-office loan of $6,000.

To Anna M. Rosenberg, Democrat and assistant secretary of defense under President Truman, an out-of-office loan of $6,000 for the purchase of stock in the Rockefeller International Basic Economy Corporation.

Various State Constitutional Convention employees, $6,600 in-advance-of-salary loans in 1958 during a legislative recess. Nelson was chairman of this commission and through it received the statewide identity that helped him snare the 1958 gubernatorial nomination.

To Joan Braden, wife of political columnist Thomas W. Braden, loan of $6,000, of which $4,283 was still outstanding.

To Washington columnist and former member of the Clandestine Services Division of the CIA Thomas Braden of the Los Angeles Times Syndicate, financing in the amount of $160,000 in 1954 to purchase the Oceanside (Cal.) *Blade-Tribune,* nearly one-third the purchase price. It was a loan converted into a gift, and Rockefeller was a secret stockholder. The Rockefeller presence in this deal was kept secret although newspapers are required by law to show participating interests. At one point in the transaction a "nonprofit" Rockefeller corporation established to promote self-development among substandard people of the world, perhaps convert them to wholesome American ways, was utilized to handle the transaction. This kept Rockefeller's name off the public record, showing how easily unpoliced "nonprofit" outfits can be secretly used for extracurricular deviations. Just how much of this undercover work is done by thousands of "nonprofit" outfits is not known as the point has never been investigated. "Nonprofit," in any event, is no guarantee of virginity; the KGB is nonprofit, a point to be pondered in Peoria and Walla Walla. Other nonprofit outfits may be similarly dubious.

One could hardly call this Oceanside deal an attempt at press control or influence, however; the Rockefellers have much more direct access to such—as through the front door with bands playing, publishers and editors saluting—if they care to exercise it. Oceanside, though, could possibly have been a "cover." Opinion-makers by the hundreds are ready, willing, and able, as the incused record shows, to accommodate Rockefellers at any time, and for no direct *quid pro quo.* Taken all together the opinion-molding panegyrics to the Rockefellers are enough to sink a continent.

Gift of $83,200 to Victor Andrade, Bolivian politician and high officeholder whom Rockefeller described as a "close personal friend." But all these recipients were friends; they certainly were not enemies or persons indifferent to Rockefeller fortunes.

During 1974 the CBS television network did a one-hour soft-focus, rose-tinted documentary entitled "The Rockefellers," and William Safire in the *New York Times* several times contended that 12 percent of CBS stock was in Chase bank trust holdings, that the documentary was inspired. He implied undue influence. CBS in rebuttal claimed that Chase bank had sway over less than 1 percent of CBS stock and that Federal Communications Commission figures supporting Safire's charges were all wrong. Even if in error on this specific point, Safire's nose was at least pointed in the right general direction.

Gift of fourteen $2,500 Steuben glass vases for Christmas, 1973, to each of fourteen political fellow members, five of them United States senators, of the Commission on Water Quality. Some of the senators kept the objects, others passed them on to public institutions. This sort of exuberance in golf is known as pressing. It induces slicing into the rough.

To Fred Young, successor to Morhouse as New York State Republican party chairman, gift of $15,000.

It was also brought out that New York State Republican national committeeman George L. Hinman went on the Rockefeller family payroll in 1960, less than a year after he took the party post. Hinman said, however, that there was no conflict of interest here as the interests of the Republican party and the Rockefellers are identical. On this point he was surely right.

"Overlooked" at first, later "recollected," was a strategic loan of $30,000 made in 1961, eve of the '64 presidential election, to former Congressman William E. Miller, Republican national chairman then and in 1964 Goldwater's running mate for vice-president. At the time Rockefeller was angling for the Republican presidential nomination, was repelled the next year by the wrathful Goldwater forces; and Miller was in the same key position nationally as Morhouse had been statewide in 1958.

The tardy disclosure of the Miller loan after all the other careful listings was explained by Rocky and his brother as attributable to inadvertent oversight, which could well be the case as the Rockefellers and their staffs are into so many things—far too many to explore in less than multivolume bulk with the labor of a full-scale research staff. One demon researcher couldn't cover all the ground even in twenty years. There could also have been a temptation to overlook that the Republican national chairman had been the object of their solicitude—a Freudian failure of computer memory!

Rockefeller contended, in response, that the basis of the no-interest or low-interest no-collateral loans and outright gifts was friendship and a desire to be personally helpful. Undaunted, he quoted Scripture, citing the injunction to "forgive us our debtors"—a maudlin tip for the banks. Here was true Nelsonian *chutzpah.* Obviously he was not unfriendly to any of these people; but what caught the attention of normally detached observers, not career anti-Rockefellerites, was the fact that nearly all these individuals were of past, present, or future official standing, in positions of influence. Without being churlish or at least *infra dig.,* such persons could hardly avoid being reciprocally friendly when called upon. The question here arose of conflict of interest, not directly on Rockefeller's part but on theirs.

In any showdown, whose side would they be on, Rockefeller's or the deathlessly grand government of laws, not men? To hardened political observers the loans and gifts looked exactly like an extra form of patronage or bonus that only a wealthy man could dispense, to the frustration of all the putative Lincolns striving to attain the same high office. To such observers all these people looked bought and paid for. To many nonpartisan people Rockefeller's explanations sounded disingenuous, childish.

Just how bad do I think all this was? On the level of politics as it is played in the United States, not very bad, almost but not quite Sunday Schoolish. Compared with the prepresidential capers of such as Johnson and Nixon, it was little more than par for the course. And as Rockefeller and his people said, there was nothing illegal about it. Whether it was immoral, which they also denied, depends upon one's view of morality, especially political morality. Against the background of rampant mythic misconceptions about government and politics in the United States, however, it all looked highly suspicious, even sinister, possibly lethal.

Alexis de Tocqueville, in his classic *Democracy in America* (1835), after noting the proclivity of American officeholders to receive money surreptitiously, marvels that the wealthy had, yet, not used their riches to smooth their own way to high office. Had he lived long enough he would have been able to see this logical possibility of reenacting a European theme realized in the career of rambunctious Nelson Rockefeller. For certainly none of these money gifts, until disclosed, did anything but lubricate his progress upward toward the American Pantheon.

Americans have long since ceased to be surprised at disclosures that officeholders are taking money, including campaign "contributions," in exchange for the favors of the State. Many average citizens, however, were confused by the novelty of the implication that somebody might be spreading money around to obtain personal access to the most strategic levers of the State. For hitherto the political role of the wealthy in these respects has been to allow simon-pure hymn-singing plebians the job of operating the levers while they ponied up the money in order to call the shots. Nixons, Johnsons, and such *canaille* have long been a dime a dozen.

2. The biggest blow to the Rockefeller image and swollen pretensions came with the disclosure through the FBI investigation that the Rockefellers had called into being and fi-

nanced a lumpish derogatory biography of Arthur Goldberg, former United States Supreme Court justice who was Nelson's Democratic opponent for the governorship in 1970. The disclosure aroused consternation even among editorial writers usually quick to explain away cracks in the Establishment as only skin deep. Rockefeller at the time was running for his fourth term.

As Goldberg was not considered by anybody at all to have the slightest chance of winning, the need for the book was put down to inner feelings of Rockefeller insecurity and the desire for ultimate insurance in case electoral fate should prove capricious. What made Goldberg to fine-tuned observers less than a shining light, pompously impressed with his own self-importance as a poor Jewish boy who had made it to the High Court from the steamy West Side of Chicago, was the fact that he had shown himself to be a Lyndon B. Johnson puppet, at the request of Johnson stepping off the Court to which Kennedy had appointed him when Johnson had a different, and minor errand for him to run. Certainly John Marshall and a long line of austere justices would have taken a scowling view of such ready flexibility.

At any rate, the Goldberg affair, a "dirty trick"*à la* Nixon in the eyes of many senators and others despite Rocky's vehement denial that it was, turned into a contretemps for Rockefeller. For Goldberg was certainly not a communist or enemy of the CIA. At first Rockefeller flatly denied he had anything to do with it, asserted he had nothing to do with it, no knowledge of it. The ball was in his brother Laurance's court. Two days later Rockefeller in a quick about-face took full responsibility, one of several such quick changes of script at the hearings in Washington.

This turn surprised Chairman Cannon of the Senate Committee who said he need not have done it. But had Rockefeller not done it, the heat would have been on his brother. Many of the situations that turned up at the hearings were in this way double-edged for Rockefeller. He got cut whichever way he turned.

The bottom-line story, as finally stated, was this: A Rockefeller lawyer came to Rocky's office to suggest that a hatchet job be written by one Victor Lasky, an acquaintance in the business of turning out rightist hack jobs. He had done one on Robert Kennedy, a more plausible target, and one on John F. Kennedy. The lawyer was referred by Rockefeller to another lawyer, who turned to Laurance to find some "investors" in such a book. Laurance now authorized "his people" to underwrite the project with $60,000 while other "investors" were being sought. Laurance insisted to the end, "stonewalling," that the deal was launched purely as a money-making investment, a notion widely hooted down. The book was inherently, intrinsically and extrinsically a market loser, a dog, about a man of limited reader-interest whom Norman Mailer characterized in 1970 as a "dunce."

A secret dummy corporation—secrecy, secrecy all the way —was now set up to "launder" the money. The stealth observed indicates full awareness of the impropriety of the project. Contact was made on behalf of the dummy corporation with Arlington House, which issued the book ostensibly as a bona-fide spontaneous literary enterprise in the dear public interest to warn the ever-deserving electorate about how slippery a character Goldberg really was. Termed scurrilous by some, derogatory by others, it was not complimentary; it was in fact an upside-down snide version of the usual campaign biography in which the candidate is spotlighted as potentially another Lincoln, perhaps better. Nelson has had several of these Lincolnesque tracts written about him, unquestionably financed in one way or the other out of the Rockefeller coffers. Arlington House is owned by Starr Broadcasting, whose chairman is the languidly ineffable William F. Buckley, Jr., editor of the rightist *National Review* and, according to E. Howard Hunt, a former CIA agent in Mexico. Hunt is the career CIA officer who led the Watergate burglars.* (CIA elements, it would seem, as readily pitch in against domestic dissenters and political challengers as against foreign foot-

---

*Hunt makes his disclosures in *Undercover: Memoirs of an American Secret Agent,* Berkley Publishing Corporation, N.Y., 1974.

draggers and foes of the United States. What they want is for everybody to shape up with the correct outlook.)

Buckley himself, who apparently did not know anything about the book, could well and characteristically have described himself as in a state of complete nescience about it. He said it would be "naive" to suppose the book constituted "a business-like approach" to publishing. With $10,000 going to the author, the front money involved was much too much to launch a slight book expected to sell. It was a subsidy to all hands. To cover the costs of a market "turkey," however, the sum was about right. Rockefeller forces around the state distributed the book like a Gideon Society gone mad.

Rockefeller, pressed, and never at a loss for words, called the book a "mistake." It was not, however, a mistake of inadvertence or carelessness, but a mistake of practical judgment and perspective that backfired. It was the kind of mistake Napoleon made at Waterloo. Moral or immoral, the book was just not necessary to holding the office. He apologized to Goldberg who, stung, disdained accepting the apology in a cold fury.

Investigators were now stirred to inquire into the mechanisms behind recent derogatory biographies of Barry Goldwater and John Connally, both ultrapatriots but past and present obstacles to Rockefeller on the glory road to the White House. These, too, were books about men who needed no voluminous literary diminution. The question that actuated suspicious observers was: *cui bono?* Nothing turned up to sustain these natural suspicions although it was noticed that nontrade elements took spontaneous interest in distributing the books gratis.

Of equal or even greater significance (but working the other side of the street and not made as much of by commentators as the literary bushwacking of Goldberg) was a recent "gift" of $89,952 by Rockefeller to the American Academy of Political Science in Philadelphia. Striking about this figure was its unevenness, as though it were payment of an account. Concomitantly and subsequently there was rushed to press by the academy a book spreading unguents, frankincense, and myrrh over Rockefeller's governorship. The title of the opus was *Governing New York State: The Rockefeller Years*. Published early in 1974, the book was edited by Prof. Robert H. Connery of Columbia University, who is also president of the academy, and Prof. Gerald Benjamin of the State University College, New Paltz, New York.

The opus is a potpourri of essays by twenty degree-bedizened academicians, impressive to the laity, *shnooks* to sophisticates. Although Professor Benjamin was reported by the *New York Times* as saying the editors and authors had not consulted with Rockefeller people, implying that the book was an immaculate conception, this was forthrightly disputed by Hugh Morrow, Rockefeller's press secretary, who said flatly there had been preliminary discussions and data checks and that the book mentors and Rockefeller people had together rummaged over the state programs that might be piquant to peek into, titillating to the uninformed.

As Martin Tolchin pointed out in the *Times,* Professor Connery's presidential *festschrift* is the most flattering in the book. About Rockefeller's use of patronage, Connery wrote "although he came to understand and value the use of patronage, Rockefeller insisted that his appointments secretary and the Republican state chairman realize that high professional competence was the underlying consideration in making appointments." Whoops! Tolchin went on to point out mordantly that the governor's first state chairman, of several years standing, a typical political hack, was convicted of procuring bribery; much in the way of nice discrimination could hardly have been reasonably expected of him. Morhouse, like many politicians, always looked the part. In him as in many others, any intelligent person could always sense what he was up to in general. At least, nothing good.

Although Rockefeller made use of public opinion polls, Professor Connery said, "he ignored them as often as he heeded them, for he saw it as his responsibility to lead as well as to respond to public opinion." In other words, reading between the lines, he was a stalwart for the ages, a man of unshakable resolution. What Rockefeller usually did as governor was more often to defer outwardly to public opinion but to go indirectly counter to it in very large and expensive (to the public) matters. He was a master of covert and indirect operations, an excellent CIA supervisor.

As to charges that Rockefeller was inaccessible to the press, Professor Connery defended him because "he felt that open controversy with the Legislature in the press was not the way to succeed in getting his program approved." This amounts to a change of subject because the issue was not exclusively tied to legislative matters but to general inaccessibility.

Not only did Rockefeller keep himself inaccessible, said major Albany newsmen in a late 1974 television interview over New York's Channel 13, but when he did see the press he invariably fobbed it off no matter what the subject with non-responsive badinage and persiflage, the old dummy-up technique. None of the Albany news people had the least foreknowledge of all the steamy stuff brought out in the Washington hearings and during earthshaking post-Rockefeller state governmental crises involving his own agencies. They had been "had" in a big way, given the usual soft-soaping.

Nearly a year before the Washington hearings, writing in *the Christian Century,* January 30, 1974, Richard J. Neuhaus pointed out how Rockefeller largesse—a euphemistic term of description widely employed during the hearings—can serve peculiar ends from A to Z. There had just been set up by Rockefeller the Commission on Critical Choices for America. The members included fifteen tame politicians, eleven business tycoons, and thirteen trained-seal academicians and educators—not a bite in a carload. Budgeted at the mind-boggling figure of $20 million, of which $3 million was obtained from governmental and private agencies and $1 million apiece from Nelson and Laurance Rockefeller (with more expected from foundations and such), the outfit was generally interpreted as a vehicle for Rocky's fourth attempt to snare the presidency, designed to get around the new restrictive campaign financing law. Rockefeller asked Congress for $1 million for the self-promoting affair, an example of outstanding *chutzpah.* He didn't get the money.

"The thirteen academics who are commission members are

but the tip of the iceberg," Neuhaus noted. "Reportedly several hundred of America's academic elite have been invited to 'consult' with the commission or to write papers for its projected publications. The sum of $5,000 for tossing off a 25-page paper is not an insignificant sum. Others may be offered more or less. New York University's Irving Kristol, whose last great political contribution was lining up academics for Nixon in 1972, is active in dispensing the favors." In political circles this practice is considered *sub rosa* patronage.

So here is a bit of insight for the uninstructed on how things really work: through liberal application of purchased verbal axle grease, slapped on by degree-bearers.

As Neuhaus remarked, "I am not so cynical as to believe distinguished academics can be bought off for $5,000. Some demand at least five times that much, and others are people of unquestionable integrity who would be appalled at the suggestion that Rockefeller is purchasing their political support. Even they, however, may be badly compromised. How can I publicly declare the commission to be a political ploy wrapped in intellectual fraud if its reports bear *my* name?"

At the very least the academics' exercise of the critical function with respect to Rockefeller is quelled. At most some are pressed into service as propagandists—press agents, public relations men, ad men, publicity roustabouts. In between these extremes, others function as verbose window dressing, dazzling and benumbing the public with a string of recondite degrees and awards.

But one thing this method of employing hundreds of paid "consultants" does, unquestionably, is to still their tongues for the future, keep them from writing detached analyses for periodicals and reviews. One can hardly take a stiff fee from a Rockefeller or anyone else as a consultant and then sit down and do a critical or even mildly thoughtful analysis of the man or project, which would be a proper mission of a man of knowledge and presumed wisdom. All such academic consultants and contributors all along the line invariably present their patron or his project either without the warts or with the warts suitably cosmeticized. And so we get another chapter in the unending "American Adventure," a historical soap opera, no lowdown on the higher-ups. Few if any of such contributors, however, come from the hard sciences or the humanities. They are all creatures of the so-called "policy sciences," a mishmash of pretentious subjectivity.

As the record shows, all writers who produce laudatory or tinted soft-focus compositions about the Rockefellers and their projects run openly or under scarcely veiled camouflage out of Rockefeller stables. And few writers, hardly any, who adopt a skeptical stance toward them are institutionally connected. Free-lancers alone seem uninhibited enough to forthrightly grapple with many open-and-shut facts. It is very rare for any university-based writer to find the least blemish on their affairs; and certainly not on balance. Despite academic strictures against "mere journalism," leading metropolitan newspaper commentators such as Tom Wicker, Anthony Lewis, Russell Baker, Nicholas von Hoffman, Eileen Shanahan, and several others do far, far better. They do, in fact, bolster one's failing faith in the human mentality, a faith undermined by the performance of wayward professors. Money, one is forced to conclude, has damped down critical ardor in academia which, however, often springs into fierce flame with the appearance of free-lance dissident testaments of outsiders. Disbelievers in the benignity of the nobly born and well connected are apt to get from grant-laden academics sharp reproof or even open-and-shut falsifications for the least show of *lèse majesté* toward high-riding establishmentarians. *Le roi le veut.*

3. Also brought under scrutiny—among many other matters too numerous to mention—was a Rockefeller campaign contribution of $200,000 in 1972 to Richard Nixon in juxtaposition with a telegram from Laurance Rockefeller, largest Eastern Airlines stockholder, to President Nixon requesting a review of two adverse rulings by the Civil Aeronautics Board. The board had refused an Eastern request to acquire Carib Air from Caribbean-Atlantic Airlines, Inc. Nixon reversed the ruling four months after receiving the contribution. Eastern got Carib Air. The big unresolved question was whether there

was undue, even illegal influence at work here. Knowing Nixon as we now do, what would one say? Steamy stuff—a witches' brew.

A television series was produced during Rockefeller's governorship titled "Executive Chamber." The cost of it, $274,704, was defrayed by Rockefeller and was deducted on his tax return as a *gift to the state*. This deduction was approved by the Internal Revenue Service. The series showed the workings of the executive branch, was presumably educational; but at the same time it enhanced the image of the incumbent, gave him extra publicity, glorified him in the eyes of the numerous ignorant. Was it really a gift? If so, there was no referendum allowing the people of the state to say they accepted it. As a citizen of the state in question it doesn't resemble a gift to me.

As to gifts in general, United States courts have held that they are not necessarily gifts as understood by the tax laws. In the view of the courts each gift needs to be examined on its merits. A similar sort of ambiguity may attach to a loan. In the case of the Rockefeller loans to officeholders, there was a transfer of often large amounts of money to a man who continued to retain office for many years, the loan meanwhile outstanding, a reminder over his head. Finally the man left public office, sometimes for a day while shifting jobs, and on that day the long-standing loan is suddenly designated a gift. The question arises: Was it a gift, in contravention of law, from the very beginning, merely the definition being arbitrarily shifted? Again, were the loan-gifts extra compensation for personal service? If so, they would be taxable as income. Or, a darker question, were they indirect bribes? Congress did not pursue these issues although they were discussed in some publications. To many hard-nosed observers, the loan-gifts looked distinctly fishy, so much slush.

4. A blizzard of figures concerning campaign contributions, by Rockefeller and by his extended family, and tax payments and nonpayments was produced by the congressional inquiries. Before looking at a few of the tax figures—not all, for to do

so would require hundreds of pages of analysis and explanation—let me set down what conclusions were drawn by expert observers, with whom I concur. First, however, it should be remembered that the tax returns submitted were for Rockefeller personally and did not include those for his trust funds, which are a separate affair.

a. On an annual income generally running at a level of around $5 million (some $25 to $30 million for all the brothers and a sister), Nelson Rockefeller paid taxes in the 25-percent bracket or at about the level of someone with income of $12,000 to $16,000. (Over the same ten-year period, as will be shown in Chapter Four, his brother John D. Rockefeller 3 was liable to no federal income taxes at all but voluntarily threw into the pot 5 to 10 percent—not being more precise in his revelation of the arrangement).

b. Nelson got himself into the low-tax bracket by means of deductions and in many cases by means of overstated deductions disallowed by the Internal Revenue Service for the five-year period 1969-1973 in a suddenly sprung tax audit. For 1964-1968 it had found him short by only $8,500 of taxes. These deductions were stated by Nelson as for "charity" but IRS, suddenly as alert as the air force on the outer atmospheric frontiers, found for 1969-1973 many large items classified as charity that could hardly be sustained as charity—a point for everyone to note. In other words, what is called charity and philanthropy ain't necessarily so. In earlier audits IRS had not, it came out, found as much amiss.

Now, the IRS is a collection of technicians. I haven't the slightest doubt that, all the time, it can do its job to perfection, dotting every "i", crossing every "t," with respect to everybody. However, these technicians are under the direct eye of the politicians in the executive branch, the White House, and it is now known that both Presidents Nixon and Johnson, and possibly earlier presidents, have at times ordered IRS to perform dirty tricks of omission and commission. This time, though, all this material was going to be laid before a preponderantly Democratic Congress, at least some members of

which were known to look with a bilious eye on tax shenanigans. IRS, therefore, now performed like a crack Phantom jet
drill team before flabbergasted visiting foreign potentates.

Something few Americans seem to realize is that the tax
rates as stated mean nothing. The so-called graduated income-
tax rates up to 70 percent don't mean that anyone pays 70
percent. What brings the actual payments down are the deductions. And, as to deductions, what matters is what one is
allowed to *count* as a deduction.

In the matter of deductions for "charity," the amounts stated do not necessarily mean, usually do not, that any money or
money-equivalent has gone into the hands of the lame, the
halt, the blind, or the needy, which is what the average dope
believes is the case. What Nelson Rockefeller did in the way
of claiming deductions, it was shown, was to throw in just
about everything except the kitchen sink as a deductible item.

Early in the hearings it developed that for 1970, when Nelson had income of $2,443,703, he incurred no tax liability
owing to "technical" offsetting deductions. In general, this
news was given downplay all over, which led Safire in the
New York Times to contrast it with the news barrage two years
earlier about similar legerdemain on the part of Richard M.
Nixon. Here was illustrated the difference between news
downplay and up-play, pianissimo and fortissimo.

The disclosure led the *Times* (September 27, 1974) to edito-
rialize melancholily that it was incongruous that Rockefeller
should have income of $2.5 million for 1970, entitling him to
a basic personal exemption of $2,500, and still not owe any
taxes for the year. And it was even more depressed to note that
Nelson's returns over a ten-year period showed him paying
less taxes percentage-wise than ordinary middle-class citizens.

But this wasn't all by any means. For 1966 his tax was $685!

A large number of citizens are up in metaphoric arms over
large sums being spent by the government for social amelioration—welfare, home relief, aid to needy families, unemployment insurance, Medicare, and the like—and another large
number are opposed to the enormous sums devoted to arma-

ments: defense. Persons calling themselves liberals castigate the former as inhuman; persons calling themselves conservatives castigate the latter as deficienctly patriotic.

Many persons who are wealthy join in the castigation, mostly against those opposing big defense-spending.

What few people realize is that most of the big-income big proponents of high and higher-cost defense either pay no taxes at all, sometimes year after year, or pay taxes at exceptionally low rates owing to their use of deductions, often dubiously. And some wealthy liberals are in the same position, clamoring for more and more aid to the poor while they pay sketchy or no taxes. The Rockefellers, for their part, are conspicuous supporters both of heavy defense-spending and sustained high-cost so-called welfare programs. One might call them premier exponents of the Warfare-Welfare State, which generates much lucrative economic activity. In general, the most voluble patriots are the most economical taxpayers.

But—and here is the big joker in the deck—most of the tax money taken to sustain all this comes from the *employed labor force*, as the annual tax statistics put out by IRS clearly show. Both the superpatriots and the superliberals, howling for more defense, more welfare, are enjoying either a free tax ride or a bargain-counter tax ride. They are not, as official figures clearly show, sharing in the cost, which is borne by jobholders who may any day be out of work for a variety of purely extraneous reasons—such as "technological advance."

Nelson Rockefeller has been, at least until recently, a liberal in the sense that he has been liberal with other people's money, as is shown in Chapter Four in the way he ran up the tax and debt-burden in New York State. But he is not a liberal taxpayer.

For the period of ten years under scrutiny up to 1974, Rockefeller, the figures showed, reported total income of $46.9 million that was flatly subject to federal income tax but that for the same period he claimed deductions of $30.1 million. Rockefeller's personal deductions for "office, investment and other expenses" from 1964 through 1973 totaled $6.4 million while his personal income, excluding trust income, was $8.5

million; the trusts brought $38.5 million in the same period (*New York Times*, October 15, 1974; 29:2).

The tax audit suddenly instituted when he was nominated vice-president covered the previous five years. IRS now found he must pay $820,718 additional federal income taxes and $83,000 more in gift taxes, a total of $903,718. Interest at 6 percent will add about $125,000 to this bill. This was about one hundred times more added tax than in the preceding five years.

What the significant story is here, though, is not what was found he must pay, but how he had underpaid. His deductions for office and investment expenses were reduced by IRS in the amount of $824,598 and his deductions for "charity" were reduced by $420,649.

As Rockefeller presented the figures it appeared that he had underpaid by only 1/20th or 5 percent but under analysis it developed that he had underpaid by more than 1/5th or a shade more than 21 percent. What he had already paid for five years was $4,212,974; what he had to pay additionally was $896,173.

Among the charitable contributions Rockefeller carried the item of $420,649 disallowed as above. What charity was this for? It consisted of his out-of-pocket expenses while on a tumultuous Latin American trip for President Nixon in 1969 during which leftist splinter groups stirred up enormously destructive riots in nearly every country visited. What Rockefeller had done was bring along a large personal staff for which he footed the bills. His own expenses were paid by the United States government—that is, the American taxpayers. Under a much earlier ruling by IRS relating to former vice-president Hubert H. Humphrey, out-of-pocket government expenses on official trips may not be taken as a "contribution" in excess of 20 percent of the taxpayer's income (*New York Times*, October 20, 1974; 1:6).

As an offset to all the peculiar tax stuff, the Rockefeller forces laid down a barrage to the committee on the heavy Rockefeller "philanthropies," a subject I tackle *au fond* in

Chapter Five. But for the benefit of Congress, Nelson stated that over the period of the previous seventeen years he had made $24,712,245 in charitable donations to 193 organizations. The gifts ranged from $10 for Phillips Academy to nearly $6.6 million to the Museum of Primitive Art; $6,500 to the United States government and $656,393 to New York State, mainly consisting of an unwanted television broadcast previously adverted to here.

None of this included anything from more than six extant family foundations. Recipients included, it was stated, forty-one universities, eighteen secondary schools, seventeen churches and church organizations, twelve museums, nine hospitals, and two symphony orchestras.

As to the nature of these gifts, his press secretary, Mr. Morrow, said they included cash, stocks, and bonds but also art objects, paintings, sculpture, furniture, "almost anything you can think of to give away." The gift to the US government, said Morrow, was probably an art object. No personal papers were included, reassuring to those who might have thought ghosted speeches and letters *à la* Nixon were included. Included, though, was $760,481 for the Latin American Mission of which about $400,000 was whittled away by IRS.

But $1,874,996 went to Dartmouth College; $251,766 to Memorial Hospital for Cancer and Allied Diseases; $2,-653,420 to the Museum of Modern Art; $959,721 to Jackson Hole Preserve; $132,312 to Ebenezer Baptist Church in Atlanta (black); $5,000 to Sixteenth St. Baptist Church in Birmingham, Ala. (black); $29,596 to Union Church of Pocantico Hills, the family church; $1,626,751 to American International Association for Economic and Social Development; $1,-026,180 to Government Affairs Foundation; more than $1 million each to the Museum of Modern Art and the 3d Century Corporation; $880,510 to Rockefeller Brothers Fund; and $13,463 to Rockefeller University.

The reason Morrow stressed that things other than money were given away was to show Nelson spread around not only money. But this raised a point that is too subtle for the average man: for a wealthy person can retain more money in-pocket, very often, by giving something away. In other words, by giving one may retain more money-wise.

The reason for this lies in the crazy tax laws, which none of the Rockefellers, professed reformers though they are, has ever gone on record as opposing. Indeed, they explicitly defend them, as shown in Chapter Four.

In giving stocks, even bonds, land, and anything else such as art objects, furniture, automobiles (Nelson gave an automobile to New York State), or anything whatever, one counts the value at the time of making the gift. On a stock or bond one is guided by ascertainable market value, impersonal. Anything else, including land, is given at estimated value, as set by an appraiser. And appraisers, like accountants (and even professors and judges), are flexible.

The value of the gift is not taken as the original acquisition-cost but the present value, as shown either by the market or by an appraisal. The appraiser is hired by the donor. In court contests different sides bring their own appraisers, who often differ widely, in accordance with what is advantageous to their client.

Let us say stocks are given, worth $100,000 at the market. An inquiry might show they were acquired for $10,000. If sold they'd show a capital profit of $90,000 subject to 35 percent capital gains tax, or $31,500. This would leave the seller with a profit of $58,500.

If given away by someone in the 70 percent tax bracket, however, the $90,000 of value would be worth to the donor 70 percent or $73,000. By giving instead of selling, then, the donor benefits by an extra $14,500. Multiply this one item, now, by many donative items, and one runs into a very considerable sum of advantage, proving in cold figures that it is more blessed to give than to sell at a profit. It's open and shut, like shooting fish in a barrel.

To big income-receivers, it is definitely and distinctly more advantageous to give up to a certain point—the point being to get into a much lower tax bracket—than to retain or to sell at a profit.

It works the same with art objects. A painting bought for

$1,000 and held for ten or twenty years until it can be given an appraisal value of $10,000 produces the same result. Do it with hundreds of paintings and one gets the beneficial results hundreds of times over.

May not the paintings decline in value? Hardly. They are bought with the advice of experts. The world network of museums supported by the wealthy provides an outlet for them. Are the donors art lovers? Perhaps. First they acquire the stuff; this must show love. But why, now, give it away? Does one give away a love-object? The answer: It is given out of love for humanity, to let others share in the joy. But why, now, not merely buy it and give it away instantly? If one did that, though, one wouldn't get the benefit of the capital gain and the tax deduction.

Most of the wealthy who go in for art collecting are no more lovers of art than philatelists are lovers of stamps or collectors of rare books lovers of literature. What they are lovers of are—market value. It is all a money game, with a cash advantage for the skilled players. Nelson Rockefeller, by all reports, is a skilled player in the art market.

In any event, giving a work of art to a museum of art or other institution isn't an act of charity, may not even be philanthropic. Let the reader judge if I know the meaning of these words. If a valuable painting is given to a museum or other institution for retention and display, I say that isn't charity. If, however, one has such a painting, puts it up for public auction, and allows the proceeds to go to an orphan asylum, a home for the blind, or a sagging hospital for crippled children, I call that charity. But if one gains tax-wise by the deal, if one bought the painting for $50,000 and it auctions for $1 million, and one claims the last as a tax deduction, I say the act of charity is qualified by that much. I say one gave $50,000, less by whatever one gained tax-wise on the deal. It may turn out that one gave nothing up, instead gained monetarily.

The same holds for philanthropy. I don't deny that Nelson Rockefeller and the other Rockefellers love humanity. Arithmetically, dollar-wise, they apparently love humanity about a trillion times more than I do, but make huge personal gains out of it. Love pays.

Eileen Shanahan in the *New York Times* (October 27, 1974; IV, 6:3) did an excellent roundup analysis of the way Nelson Rockefeller over a period of ten years brought himself down into the 25 percent tax bracket, a very low bracket indeed for a man with his income.

In the upshot of the hearings and investigations and Congressional Joint Committee on Internal Revenue and Taxation and the Internal Revenue Service had run Nelson Rockefeller's personal net worth far above the original figure of $33 million or his revised figure of $62 million. It found, in fact, that his personal net worth is $107,658,000 as of the low market values of 1974 by figuring in his lifetime beneficial interest in the trust funds. In other words, potential trust income is part of his net worth, a concept Rockefeller said he did not dispute. (*New York Times*, November 14, 1974; 38:1).

In conclusion, Rockefeller promised that if confirmed as vice-president, he will not continue his gift-giving among officialdom. As to his personal fortune, he said he was placing it in a "blind trust." When President Johnson did this, it was widely commented that the gesture meant nothing; such comment came from impeccably moderate-conservative publications. What such a trust means is that the owner turns all his holdings over to one or more trustees to supervise, without his knowledge, until he leaves office. Naturally he does not turn it over to anyone who might convert it all into Russian rubles or Turkish piasters. Now, as a public official, he does not know what he owns, cannot favor certain holdings by his decisions. But he knows, in general, that he is the owner of a lot of property and that the trustees will do as well by his holdings as he would, or better. They won't take them all out to Las Vegas and lose them.

Rockefeller came through the hearings, it can be said, very definitely, diminished in stature, both personally and politically. If he runs for office nationally in 1976, a lot of this material is going to be replayed unless the opposing Democratic National Committee meanwhile falls under the Rocke-feller money-spell, which is not impossible.

All the hullabaloo, however, was quite a bit of a surprise for all hands as the nomination of Rockefeller by Ford was at first thought to be noncontroversial. Rockefeller was regarded as a shoo-in. It was a distinct surprise that midway, because of the revelations, it seemed he might be turned down or forced to withdraw. Actually, on the basis of the material as laid out, unsifted to the ultimate cipher, reasons could have been found by Congress for rejecting him. In which case the vice-presidency would have remained vacant. And constitutional-ists, like Nature, abhor a vacuum.

In the beginning, for a while, with *Time* magazine and *Newsweek* leading the way nationally, it seemed as though President Ford, the pardoner of Nixon, Ford the Pardoner, might have scored a triumph in naming Rockefeller for the sacred spot.

"Only rarely since the days of John Adams and Thomas Jefferson has a man with the stature of Nelson Rockefeller risen to the U. S. vice presidency," *Time* rhapsodized, September 2, 1974. "Indeed, Rockefeller brings to this new job an unprecedented portfolio of assets . . . the country was plainly relieved and approving. . . . To restore national confidence it was necessary to pick the best man for the vice presidency and few would deny that Rockefeller fitted that description. . . . Ford's selection of Rockefeller is an indication of his own political maturity . . . the Rockefeller style will at last have national scope."

Newsweek came in with close but muted harmony, refer-ring to "this symbol of national unity," this "omni-talented aristocrat" who has "brought Ford's homespun Presidency a dash of glamor, a dollop of high style, and a direct line to the Rockefeller lode of cash, connections and brain power."

Returning to its symphonic task, *Time* said "He is of extra-ordinary breadth . . . the political equivalent of a natural force . . . exuberant lifestyle . . . ebullient . . . tender social con-science . . . humanitarian instincts . . . enormously capable,

ambitious, idealistic—and also arrogant . . . a patron of ideas .
. . effusive . . . gallant . . . wears the mantle of his heritage with
easy grace."

Newsweek chimed in with "well-qualified heir designate . .
. his thousand-watt incandescence . . . characteristic take-
charge air . . . his awesome energy, his polished political skills
and his broad experience . . . charismatic . . . Nelson Rockefeller has been the golden boy with the common touch."

Nicholas von Hoffman, the nationally syndicated columnist
of the *Washington Post,* in reviewing these exudations noted
that the publications made no mention of Rockefeller's having served on the Foreign Intelligence Advisory Board under
Nixon, of his disastrous South American tour for Nixon in
1969, or of various other thought-provoking matters.

In von Hoffman's view, "The man is a nuke freak, always
has been one, and in the mid-1950s, operating through the
instrumentality of the tax-exempt Rockefeller Brothers Fund,
he hired Henry Kissinger to direct one of those famous studies
of his on the general topic of our defenselessness. Hundreds
of thousands of dollars were spent disseminating this docu-
ment called *International Security: The Military Aspect.*"

One thing that became very clear as a result of the hearings
is that Nelson Rockefeller is very much of an operator, a hus-
tler, a wheeler-dealer. When one examines his entire career, it
becomes plain that he is an upward striver, willing to cut
corners to his own advantage at the expense of others. In this
he may be no worse than many others. But he is no better.

Has Rockefeller peaked politically? Has he met his Waterloo in the form of various committees of Congress, the FBI,
the IRS, and assorted free-swinging newspaper commentators, the hounds of hell let loose? Time alone will tell whether
he will come crashing back carrying a big electoral victory, a
knockout punch in either hand.

Unless I'm losing my wits, which is not impossible for anyone, it seems to me he is as a national figure now highly
vulnerable, a contender with a glass jaw. At the very least, he's
beatable.

Ford the Pardoner and Rockefeller the Tax-Chiseler will
make an odd pair of Bicentennial Minutemen of 1976.

Two

John D. Rockefeller:
The Enigma Solved

John D. Rockefeller was a deeply religious, punctilious, home-loving, family man who for more than thirty years presided over the most extensive and lucrative outlaw operation in the history of the United States—the Standard Oil Trust. Whatever else Rockefeller was—and he had several divergent facets—he was a successful outlaw and owes his position in history chiefly to this single fact. All treacle to the contrary may be disregarded. He emerged the wealthiest single commoner in the world up until his time, worth approximately $900 million in Standard Oil stocks alone in 1913 after already having bestowed some $500 or more millions to his own foundations. He had many other large investments besides. And his was only one of a dozen huge Standard Oil fortunes credited to associates.

The Standard Oil fortunes were like a flotilla of battleships rising suddenly over the horizon, a haze of dollar signs rising from their smokestacks.

Controversy, sacred and profane, theological and political, judicial and extrajudicial, was stirred up early in Rockefeller's career and echoes around his descendants today. Except among their many boosters, suspicion dogs the footsteps of the Rockefellers whatever they do, as was soon shown after the naming of Nelson A. Rockefeller as a United States vice-president designate. It is precisely true to say that old John D. was, largely by reason of a series of chance events, the most controversial figure in the entire history of the United States.

As a consequence of the controversy, there are three broad public images of Rockefeller for each wayfarer on life's way to choose as he wishes. All are demonstrably erroneous. There is, first, Rockefeller as a uniquely conspiratorial devil and archfiend. This he was definitely not. There is, next, Rockefeller as a saint—a modern Francis of Assisi—and this version is equally absurd. And there is, finally, a potpourri Rockefeller, a haphazard mixture of unpatterned and inexplicable extreme good and extreme bad.

In this last view, the prevalent one today and the one with most appeal for those who try to read innocuous "balance" into all situations, Rockefeller is seen as a rather eccentric super-Robin Hood who, oddly, set himself to wrest vast sums from the world economy by illicit and high-handed processes and then quixotically set about establishing a series of colossal and generally laudable charitable institutions. In the minds of many observers, these institutions overbalance any culpability in the devious and unsanctioned means by which the money was obtained. And such observers often cite the disarming quotation, a favorite of Rockefeller's, "There is so much good in the worst of us, and so much bad in the best of us, that it hardly behooves any of us to talk about the rest of us"—thought to be the handiwork of Gov. Edward Wallis Hoch of Kansas (1849-1925). At this rate, all personal evaluation should be discarded, a prospect no doubt pleasing to many politicians and tycoons.

The founding Rockefeller has been so extensively investigated, observed, written about, and wrangled over that a great deal is known about details of his life, even intimate personal details. It would seem, then, that there is little more to be said, especially something fresh for the record. But anyone who supposes this is very wrong, as I believe I can show.

In discussing John D. as the originating point in the running Rockefeller controversy while seeking to throw new light on the whole affair, I rely mainly on what I consider by all odds the two best books on the man and his fortune. These are *God's Gold* by John T. Flynn, a somewhat soft-focus study, (Harcourt Brace & Co., N.Y., 1932) and *The Rockefeller Billions* by Jules Abels (The Macmillan Company, 1965), a sharper appraisal. Anyone seeking further gory details is referred to these books and their copious bibliographies.

But although both these writers set down just about everything significant known about Rockefeller, pro and con, the man and what made him tick remains pretty much a mystery even to his closest observers. Indeed, he becomes even more elusive as more raw facts accumulate on the record.

Those who read all the materials on Rockefeller—abusive, commendatory, and neutral—in the end begin to feel pretty much like one of Pavlov's hapless laboratory dogs after having the Pavlovian signals repeatedly crossed. And in this they are pretty much like the American rank and file on most issues. Not knowing how to react finally, such readers either sink into an intellectual stupor or decide arbitrarily to go with one set of signals or another. But on doing so, how does one account for all the credible countervailing testimony?

To solve this veritable mystery, in place of doing a whole new biography in which the known facts are placed in a new perspective, it is only necessary to take the extant writings and treat them in the light of applicable modern knowledge the way one treats a basic map with transparent overlays. One may, for example, possess an automobile road map or a war map showing the movement of troops in battles. Much about the windings of roads and the operations of troops seems inexplicable or even stupid. Now one places over the first map a transparent topographical and climatic map that shows hills, mountains, valleys, rainfall, seasonal temperatures, swamps, and deserts, and much about the reasons for the placement of the roads and the movement of troops becomes crystal clear. The general result is a much more coherent and understandable picture.

What is lacking in the two books mentioned and, indeed, in

all books on Rockefeller, is the psychic topographical map, a clue to what made the man act as he did. True, here and there some psychological touches are ventured. But nothing very penetrating and, usually, not particularly enlightening. As a result, all is either mystery or false simplicity.

But anyone with a grasp of modern depth-psychology as applied in psychiatry has little difficulty, upon reading Flynn's very full account and Abels's supplementation, in discerning that in the case of Rockefeller one is dealing with a full-fledged obsessive-compulsive character. And if one takes the known clinical characteristics of this particular type as delineated by authoritative specialists and applies them as an overlay to the Flynn and Abels books, one sees at once that just about everything in Rockefeller's life corresponds with it. Everything becomes clear.

These kinds of characters are described by a prominent psychiatrist, quite aptly, as "living machines." And this is precisely what John D. Rockefeller was, all his life and in every aspect of his life—a machine.[1] There is wide agreement among psychiatrists with this description, which is mentioned in a book useful here for a general description of the obsessive-compulsive personality.[2]

According to doctors Franz Alexander and Louis B. Shapiro,

"Full-blown cases of obsessive-compulsive states present a dynamic equilibrium in which obsessive preoccupation with ego-alien fantasies (incestuous, coprophilic, sadistic-homicidal ideas) are precariously balanced by rituals representing an exaggeration of social standards, such as cleanliness, punctuality, consideration for others. The obsessive ideas are mostly asocial in nature, whereas the compulsive rituals are caricatures of morality. The dynamic formula is similar to bookkeep-

---

1. Wilhelm Reich, *Character Analysis*, p. 199. Although Reich became highly controversial among psychiatrists owing to later theorizing, this particular book is well regarded and widely accepted as a basic contribution to the subject of its title.
2. David Shapiro, M.D., *Neurotic Styles*. It is number 5 in the Austen Riggs Center Monograph series. The immediately relevant section is the whole of chapter Two.

ing, in which on the one side of the ledger are the asocial tendencies which the patient tries to balance precisely on the other side with moralistic and social attitudes. The 50-50 ratio is characteristic of these patients and explains their central characteristic: doubt, indecision and ambivalence. Every asocial move must be undone by an opposing one . . . the left hand must undo the sin committed by the right hand. . . .

In the compulsive-obsessive states the repression is not successful—the ego-alien ideas appear in consciousness sometimes without any distortion whatever. The defense consists in allaying anxiety and resolving the conflict by compensating measures (overly moralistic rituals), by which the asocial tendencies are undone, and by isolation of the ego-alien tendencies from the rest of the mental content. The objectionable ideas are de-emotionalized; they appear disconnected and almost like abstractions, like foreign bodies for which the patient does not feel responsible. Displacement, too, may play an important part in obsessive-compulsive symptomatology. . . .

The preponderance of anal-sadistic impulses is well established in compulsive states. The defensive measures employed are particularly suited for dealing with the conflicts aroused by hostility."[3]

The psychiatric expression "ego-alien" refers to material consciously repugnant to the person experiencing some fantasy. The victim doesn't like it, feels either guilty, anxious, or both about the material. In the case of the obsessive-compulsive, the dominant feeling is one of anxiety, and ritual behavior—habitual doing or not doing something—is resorted to in order to escape the anxiety, which the victim may feel to be overwhelming. Performing that ritual temporarily dispels the anxiety. If ever there was a man of ritual, John D. Rockefeller

---

3. Franz Alexander and Louis B. Shapiro, "Neuroses, Behavior Disorders, and Perversions," in *Dynamic Psychiatry*, eds. Franz Alexander and Helen Ross (Chicago and London: The University of Chicago Press, 1952), pp. 127-28.

was one—from his compulsive bookkeeping to his playing golf no matter what the weather.

> An obsession may be a single thought (e.g. a line of verse that the patient cannot stop repeating to himself; an obscene word that keeps coming into his mind, perhaps at any time, or perhaps only when he is attending church or in social settings in which it would be highly inappropriate). Another type of obsession is obsessive rumination; instead of a single thought the patient keeps thinking of a subject, a personal problem or an abstract philosophical topic. The thoughts on the subject are repetitive and stereotyped and no conclusions are reached. A variant of this is obsessive doubting or indecision in which one ruminates over a decision or choice without being able to come to a conclusion; this may involve a relatively important decision (e.g. changing jobs) or a minor one (e.g. selecting a necktie to wear). . . .
>
> If an obsessive thought is foolish, the patient recognizes its absurdity. If it is unreasonable he knows this and will readily acknowledge it. In some instances this may be helpful in distinguishing an obsession from a delusion.
>
> An inhibiting obsession is a recurring thought, or fear, that one may do something that he does not want to do (the most common is the fear of harming some member of the family).[4] And so on.

In the obsessive-compulsive person "underlying conflicts often relate to feelings about authority and external control, to hostile or sadistic impulses, and to matters related to neatness, cleanliness and orderliness. A connection between the symptom and these conflicts is often readily apparent."[5]

Obsessives, among other things, "resent being questioned," are generally resentful of authority. Part of this "is feeling that

---

4. Merril T. Eaton, and Margaret H. Peterson, *Psychiatry*, (New York: Medical Examination Publishing Company, 1969), p. 164.

5. Ibid., p. 166.

thoughts and experiences are personal possessions which the patient is parsimoniously unwilling to share with another. . . . Most obsessionals have a narrow range of interests. Their emotional range also appears limited sometimes to a degree approaching the apparent flatness of affect of the schizophrenic."[6] John D., as I will show later in this chapter, was the dourest of men. His features seemingly had only one expression. Emotion, except when he made a large business coup, was not part of his makeup.

As they grow older obsessive-compulsives tend to grow worse although all of them aren't clinical cases. And in many mild subclinical cases they can't be readily distinguished from normal people who have transient bouts of obsessiveness.

"The compulsive personality is conforming, hardworking and tends to defer pleasure."[7]

As to obsessive-compulsive personalities, distinguished from persons who have gone over the line into a full-blown neurosis,

> They are conscientious, hardworking, conforming, and adhere rigidly to social customs and moral codes. Though they may appear to have a number of friends, their interpersonal relations lack closeness. They do a great deal for others, but the services are rendered out of a sense of duty, without spontaneity, enthusiasm, or affection. They have few recreations, and get little enjoyment out of living. Their energies are directed toward attaining security, not satisfaction [and security here refers to inner feelings of security, not life station—F.L.]. There is a tendency to resent authority, but the resentment is rarely expressed overtly. Occasionally there is a trace of passive-aggressive behavior, but this is outweighed by the overall pattern of conformity.[8]

---

6. Ibid., p. 167.

7. Ibid., p. 187.

8. Ibid., p. 127.

"Disability is usually slight" in the obsessive-compulsive personality.

> Many jobs are open to the hardworking, meticulous, conscientious person. However, the compulsive personality is not likely to achieve positions of leadership. He lacks imagination and originality. His preoccupation with detail makes him a slow worker; this is a handicap unless the job requires that each "i" be dotted and each "t" be crossed with meticulous accuracy. Preoccupation with minor details leads to neglect of major problems; these are not people who "fail to see the forest for the trees;" they fail to see the tree while counting leaves. . . .
>
> Compulsivity is relative; so is the lack of *joie de vivre* that accompanies it. At worst, one rarely sees suffering, or a life of quiet desperation, but, more often, dull, meaningless and pleasureless existence, relieved only by hope that virtue will someday be rewarded, or that the next life will be better.[9]

An outstanding trait of obsessionals, as many psychiatrists note, is their intense power of concentration, either on trifles or on objects of more recognized interest. They make good chess-players. Rockefeller had this trait to a high degree.

Psychiatry has traced the origin of the obsessive-compulsive personality (and neurosis) to the bowel-training stage of child raising. As put in the *American Handbook of Psychiatry,* a standard medical manual, the infant strives "to retain *control* over the evacuation of the bowels and over the pleasure associated with expulsion and retention. The struggle includes the mother's attempt to institute toilet training; she attempts to impose her will as to where and when the evacuations will occur. When toilet training has been harsh, rigid, and carried out in an atmosphere of fear and threats, the child will submit out of fear and will manifest an apparent compliance while concealing profound rage, resentment, and the

---

9. Ibid., p. 128.

need to find opportunities for disguised defiance. The proto-type of all later disciplinary, conforming experiences is estab-lished here."[10]

On the basis of what we know of Rockefeller's outward character and of his mother, we may be sure that the scenario of stringency in training was followed scrupulously in his early life.

What develops now as derivatives from this early experi-ence, the *Handbook* continues, are the following phenomena:

1. *Reaction formation,* in which impulses are turned into their opposite. Rage and resentment are expresssed as exag-gerated kindness and considerateness. Upon scores of public occasions different observers reported that Rockefeller seemed extremely kind, considerate, and soft-spoken, even on the witness stand in response to very rough handling by pros-ecutors and investigators. He was always extremely polite. And until late life he was always extremely well dressed to the point of fastidiousness.

2. *Undoing,* a technique that allows defiance, rage, and neg-ativism to be expresssed in some areas with less disguise than in reaction formation, but only if a severe penalty, punish-ment, or compensatory corrective action is contrived to undo the original destructive action. Rockefeller engaged in such undoing. His destructive illegal actions toward business ri-vals, most of which were secret and unknown until much later by these rivals, and toward the legal system, were balanced early by corrective donations to churches and individuals, later to foundations and the like.

3. *Isolation* of feelings. Rockefeller seemed to all who knew him devoid of feelings, his face frozen (a characteristic of obsessionals), seldom if ever laughing. There was no joy in the man. This isolation of feelings is necessary to obsessionals so that feelings do not become involved with their own de-structive obsessional fantasies. Feelings are separated from actions and fantasies, machinelike.

---

10. *American Handbook of Psychiatry,* 2nd ed., Vol. I pp. 760–61.

The compulsions in turn serve as a defense against anxiety by channeling aggressive impulses into socially approved, nonguilt-producing harmless activities, usually rituals. Rockefeller all his life from the teens onward kept himself involved in one ritual after the other. He was extremely ritualistic, and most of his known rituals (unlike the case with many compulsives) "made sense" to the public. Many were widely approved such as his steady churchgoing and mechanical money giving and obsessive late-life golfing.

The obsessive-compulsive is fully aware of his intense inner rage but can't account for it. He strongly feels required never to lose control of himself lest some shadowy nemesis engulf him. It was one of Rockefeller's marked characteristics, noted by many observers, that no matter what the provocation or how dire a situation seemed, he was always icily in control of himself. And in the case of the obsessive-compulsive "Freedom, spontaneity, and impulsive behavior are associated with loss of control of oneself and the unleashing of one's wide-ranging murderousness and destructiveness."[11]

All of this, and a great deal more, fits the case of John D. Rockefeller the way a latex glove fits a surgeon's hand—perfectly, tightly, and with nothing uncovered or covered too much and always allowing for the *mutatis mutandis* of individual instances.

What were Rockefeller's fearful fantasies?

This, of course, we don't know, and he probably discussed them with no one. We can, however, make an educated guess, based on the known circumstances of his early life. My surmise is that, unbidden and unwelcome as the thought was, he often imagined killing his father, with whom he always maintained an outwardly dutiful but increasingly troubled relationship. He had good human reason, as we shall see, for such a feeling of murderous hate. Perhaps his mother, too, figured in this unbidden death-wish, enough to make him constantly oversolicitous of her. Other horrendous material, possibly of

---

11. Ibid., 761.

an obscene nature, may well have also figured, distastefully of course, in his private thoughts, a reflex to an extreme puritanical upbringing.

In passing, one may note that the obsessive-compulsive personality is perhaps the distortion of self that is most highly approved socially, even lauded. Such a personality makes a very good worker and organization man, especially as a technician. Rockefeller was always basically a technican, a bookkeeper, and Flynn finds this role central in his life. He was, in modern terms, a human computer at the core of Standard Oil.

As to calling on medical depth-psychology for an explanation of what I call the Rockefeller Syndrome—which by historical circumstance extends far beyond Rockefeller to include a wide pro-and-con public and much of American culture—I know one heads into great public resistance, on many grounds. For one thing, most people fear the very idea of psychiatric analysis, fear that they may themselves be subject to it. They also fear anyone stigmatized as a clear-cut object of it, just as many persons fear the very *words* cancer and syphilis. Use the word, or hear it, and you'll catch it yourself, seems to be the feeling.

This last attitude was nationally displayed, dramatically, in the 1972 presidential election. Sen. Thomas F. Eagleton of Missouri was suddenly yanked off the Democratic ticket after it was disclosed he had been treated for depressions, about the mildest and most prevalent psychiatric disorder. Depression is almost as common as the common cold in the United States and usually untreated. The public was not aware, apparently, that Abraham Lincoln was a depressive. Nor was the public aware that Richard M. Nixon, the incumbent president, was far, far more disordered psychiatrically than Eagleton, and obviously had been for many years. Nixon was a full-blown sociopath, his finger firmly on the magic button as millions cheered and felt unwarrantably safe.

Just as everyone now and then has physical aches and pains without becoming what a doctor would term diseased, so nearly everyone experiences, at least transiently, some of the emotional disorders that, bunched together, serve to produce a well-marked psychiatric case. Nobody, in other words, is totally immune; everyone lives potentially in the glass house of psychiatric as well as physiological science. As to the difference between a neurosis and a personality disorder such as Rockefeller obviously had—his closest business associates had other disorders, and worse ones from a social point of view—the mental doctors point out that "Neuroses have an identifiable onset whereas the Personality Disorders are lifelong processes."[12]

And now let us see briefly how the known facts of Rockefeller's life fit into all this.

2.

John Davison Rockefeller (1839-1937) was born in south central New York State on the outskirts of the small town of Richford and lived on farms in the general region with his mother, brothers, and sisters until going away to school in Cleveland at the age of fourteen.

His father, William, was a gusty quack medicine salesman, a braggadocio spellbinder who dispensed his dubious wares to gaping crowds of yokels. He was the descendant of a prolific, many-branched German family, possibly remotely French, that had come to the United States in the early eighteenth century.

The mother, obviously the key figure in the formation of John's character (as the father was usually absent for months on end with nobody knowing his whereabouts), was Eliza Davison, daughter of a local farmer. Hers was an ultra-austere religious family, originated among the early English and Scottish settlers of seventeenth-century New England.

Rockefeller, in point of fact, was the product of what today would be classified as a troubled home and what in 1855 became literally a broken home when the father abandoned his wife in Cleveland to contract a long-secret bigamous mar-

---

12. Eaton and Peterson, *Psychiatry,* p. 174.

riage with a twenty-year-old Canadian girl with whom he spent the rest of his life. All of this was a carefully guarded family skeleton of the Rockefellers for more than fifty years until the *New York World,* on September 2, 1908, told with great circumstantiality and public-source citation of the doings of William Avery Rockefeller, sire to the oil king. The profligate father died May 11, 1906, in Freeport, Illinois, at the age of ninety-six. Most writers, including Flynn, pass lightly over the father, but in doing this, they miss much of the point about John D.

During Rockefeller's entire childhood, his father would be absent for long periods peddling his nostrums to the hinds, whom he freely boasted of cheating. The family was never in material want, was never poor, although the outlook for it at times seemed uncertain. But any financial uncertainty was dispelled whenever the wanderer came home because he was always flush with money, which he liked to flourish triumphantly. During his absences he had credit arrangements with local stores so that his family was always provided with ample food and clothing. They lived in houses on different farms he owned from time to time, and a man was usually hired to work the farm. The household usually had a servant.

Wild Bill Rockefeller did not drink spirits, but he did just about everything else forbidden in the puritan lexicon, including respond with vigorous affirmation to the charms of women. By all accounts he was a rapt and dedicated student of the Mount of Venus. And in the New York region where he lived, there was finally issued a warrant for his arrest for ravishing a young woman, one of his domestics. As the warrant was issued fifteen months after the alleged event, it may well be true, as claimed, that it was sworn out from spite, with or without basis, on the part of persons engaged in horse thievery with whom Wild Bill had fallen out. In one version of this story Bill was one of the horse thieves. In another he deflected blame for horse thievery from himself to others. In any event, his accusers cast him true to ripsnorting type. The existence of the warrant, however, is a fact, and its issuance induced him to move to another county. He never risked appearing in court to defend himself. His father-in-law compensated the alleged victim.

What brought Wild Bill and Eliza Davison, the local farmer's daughter together, is the usual mystery. For while he was wholly uninhibited and heedless of anyone's opinion, she was a prissy little Puritan who under the impact of domestic adversity became more harshly puritanical and fault finding with the years. Perhaps it was precisely the promise of freedom that a free spirit like Bill offered that fatally attracted her. At any rate, she married him in 1837 and bore him six children, one of whom died in infancy. In the order of their arrival they were Lucy, John D., Mary Ann, William, Frank, and Frances (a twin who died).

While lusty Bill supplied the money for the family, with some periods of uncertainty, Eliza was certainly its backbone and emotional mainstay. Without her it surely would have foundered. As it was, she gave all her children a tight upbringing according to strict Old Testament precept, and she unquestionably was most zealous about John D. because he was the first boy and she was still new to the game. She was certainly less stringent with the others, as their characters showed, and least stringent with Frank, who was all his life the most spontaneous and unpredictable of the brood.

If, the uninstructed layman asks, character formation takes place along the lines psychiatrists say, why didn't all the children turn out the same, as from a cookie cutter? The simple reason for this is that the parent, under different stresses and vicissitudes, gives different emphasis, at different times, to each child. Every one of a group of siblings is brought up in a different family, has his emotions aroused in different ways at different times, undergoes a different set of frustrations, differently imposed. Eliza Davison, in the course of years, just became less zealous, or had less time for superintending the new arrivals as closely as she did John. There is, too, constitutional variation among siblings.

Details of the family's life are supplied by Flynn, but he goes astray, I believe, in trying to locate the germ of John D's money-making proclivities. As Flynn found, young John was taught to be "sharp" about money by his father, who purposely cheated him with this end in view and led him to save money and lend it at interest. But the money-saving routine Rockefeller was taught, including the precept to be careful about money, was quite common in white, lower middle-class Protestant American households. It doesn't necessarily produce Rockefellers. Nor does cheating children.

In the meantime, in the absence of Wild Bill, Eliza Davison ran a tight ship, never sparing the rod whenever the boys got out of line. Her household was always in apple-pie order, and the children were always neatly and decently dressed. Outwardly everything was serene. A very religious woman, Eliza looked with distaste on the roistering, semifrontier communities in which she lived, in which drinking, the bane of the Davison's, was always a prime order of business. Bill's family were heavy drinkers. The United States, in point of fact, could never have been settled as it was without the aid of whiskey, the great frontier anodyne. Whiskey and the rifle had as much to do with settling the country as the Bible and the ax.

But Rockefeller's basic character, formed as in the case of everyone else by the time he was six, showed itself in a number of anecdotes. In the matter of games with other boys, for example, Rockefeller would never play unless he was allowed to *choose the game.* This anecdote dovetails neatly with another one from later, when Standard Oil was moving upward.

During an altercation with an associate in the course of some of the early turmoil beginning to envelop Standard Oil, Rockefeller suddenly said: "You can abuse me, you can strike me, if you will only let me have my own way."

This could well be the motto of the Rockefeller family escutcheon.

In both cases one sees clearly the stamp of the obsessive-compulsive.

As to Rockefeller's boyhood, people reported as follows to Ida Tarbell, pioneer among Rockefeller students: "He never mixed much with the rest of us," "He seemed always to be thinking," "He was different from his brothers and the rest of us." Rockefeller, indeed, was a loner and would be a loner all his life. He was the sort of person who was alone in a crowd, concentrating on his own thoughts.

A former neighbor recalled that "He was just an ordinary well-behaved boy plodding along with his lessons. There was nothing about him to make anybody pay especial attention to him or speculate about his future. He used to walk slowly along, and often seemed to be thinking as he went." A local boy recalled later that "most of the time he seemed to be going along quietly thinking things over."

His detached concentration was noted by many, and in playing something like checkers, he carefully pondered each move before he made it. Later, in business, associates were to notice that Rockefeller always intensely concentrated on all the immediate consequences of any proposed move. He could always see further ahead than his associates. Concentration, persistence, thriftiness, neatness, orderliness, cleanliness, promptness, punctilio, economy of speech were all observed early in Rockefeller, and stayed with him all his life. And all, especially in combination, are hallmarks of the obsessive-compulsive.

As with all people, Rockefeller's personality lay on two planes, the conscious and the unconscious. While his mother unquestionably was the major influence in the shaping of his unconscious, his father with his purposely sharp dealings and secrecy about his operations unquestionably shaped his consciousness.

As Jules Abels writes, "While Rockefeller seemed to be his mother's son in personality, the habits of thinking of his father sprang out in his business life—William's acquisitiveness, his cunning, his self-assurance, and his boldness. And make no mistake about it—this young Rockefeller, though secret and dour, was bold and daring. He was to be much more so than his associates and his rivals. He had in his veins the boldness of the Spanish conquistador in quest of gold, like Hernando Cortez who burned his ships behind him so that his small band could only march forward toward the gold of Montezuma."

Rockefeller and his brothers were far from distinguished scholars in the local schools he attended, but he was attracted to arithmetic with its system, its order, its precision. Here was the beginning of one of his ritualistic attachments, which carried over into his bookkeeping and love of office routine.

In 1853, with John now thirteen, the family gave up New York and settled near Cleveland. There Wild Bill installed them in the best house they had ever lived in, and all had been decent to very good. But the next year his father arranged for John to board in Cleveland so that he could attend Central High School. With him he brought his small savings, gleaned from doing odd jobs in and out of the household in the customary manner of American youths of the lower classes of an earlier day. Rockefeller's boyhood experiences with money, chores, or odd jobs weren't in any way unusual, apart from his father's tricks.

At Central High he made two connections that were to be momentous in his life. In the class ahead of his was Mark Hanna, who was later to become the big Republican political boss and president-maker. Back in Owego, New York, Rockefeller had gone to school with Tom Platt, future boss of New York State. Another person at Central High was Laura Celestia Spelman, of a locally affluent family, who was later to become his wife. She was the first and, we may be sure, the only girl in Rockefeller's life. And she was very much like his mother in outlook and temperament, far from a happy augury for their children.

Perhaps as momentous both for Rockefeller and for world history was an old gardener named Alexander Sked who lived near where young Rockefeller boarded. How they met, perhaps by chance, is not known. But Deacon Sked introduced the solemn-faced youth to the nearby Erie Street Baptist Church, a new congregation later to become the Euclid Avenue Baptist Church, famed as the Rockefeller spiritual center. There Rockefeller was baptized in 1854. And it was there that he found one of his abiding homes.

The church had a Sunday School of about three hundred young people. In it Rockefeller met many enduring acquaintances and future employees. He never had any close friends, not even one.

Rockefeller soon became a high-school dropout, transferring to a local business college where he concentrated on a three-month course in bookkeeping, the lifelong love. He was graduated in 1855 and went jobhunting, landing his first clerical job in a commission house where he earned $350 a year.

Meanwhile he attended church regularly and happily. He had found his Rock of Ages, to which he would forever cling. The little congregation, however, was soon in financial difficulties, with a mortgage of $2,000 due. Unpaid, the mortgage holder would foreclose. Hearing this news from the pulpit, young Rockefeller was shocked and decided to do something to protect his newfound sanctuary. He posted himself at the door as the congregation emerged and began persuading members to pledge something to the lifting of the mortgage. He visited laggards at their homes. So successful was he after several months that he had the $2,000, a goodly sum for the times, and the church was finally saved.

In gratitude for this initiative, the congregation elected the persistent teen-ager first as secretary and then, at twenty-one, a church trustee, an unusual position of local dignity for one so young but quite in harmony with Rockefeller's solemn mien. It is here, I believe, as Jules Abels observes with unquestionably accurate insight, that the foundation of Rockefeller's financial proclivities was laid—in the church. Rockefeller at the time was a youth who, in the jargon of today, was reaching out for an "identity." To the question "Who am I?" —which he probably never asked—he could only say, "A struggling commission clerk and a Baptist." But with the acclaim he received, and the trusteeship, he could now say, "I'm a church trustee." And to this he wanted to add the distinction of being a successful—that is, rich—businessman, which would soon come.

Rockefeller himself was to say later in life, "My first ambition to earn more money was aroused by this and similar undertakings." So, if one wishes to emulate Rockefeller in becoming rich—go to church, raise money for it, become a trustee. Tomorrow the world . . .

Raising money, quite evidently, gave one status and acclaim, and Rockefeller for many years was to be a demon money-raiser in a rapidly growing business. And he and the Rockefellers after him were to be philanthropic money-raisers on a grand scale, offering to match the contributions of others. All this conferred status, prestige—and power. It gave one command over people, built up valuable associations extending over wide areas.

After serving his low-paid clerical apprenticeship, Rockefeller was ready to go into business for himself. He needed $2,000, however, to match an equal amount of a ready partner, but he had only $800, his lifetime savings. He was able to borrow $1,000 from his wayward father—at 10 percent interest! The partnership was launched as a produce commission house, and in a rapidly expanding local economy, it prospered from the start. In its first year it grossed $450,000, with a net of $4,400 or better than 100 percent on invested capital.

The business soon took on another partner and prospered through the Civil War boom, but by 1865 Rockefeller decided to concentrate on handling only the recently discovered oil from the nearby Pennsylvania fields, refining and selling it.

The first firm was Clark and Rockefeller and the next year became Clark, Gardner and Company. In 1863 he invested as a partner $4,000 in another firm—Andrews, Clark and Company—which operated a small oil refinery.

By 1865, as indicated above, he had decided to concentrate on oil, give up the produce business, but he did not want Clark along because he felt he was too timorous. Clark, in fact, was merely normal, undemonic. As neither man would sell out, they decided to bid against each other for their shares in Andrews, Clark and Company, and Rockefeller finally won out with a bid of $72,500. Clark would go no higher. Rockefeller paid at once, so we see that he was worth at least this much at age twenty-five. He was, in fact, worth a great deal more. Clark also took as a consolation prize Rockefeller's share of the produce business, not at all bad from his purely live-and-let-live point of view. The new firm was called Rockefeller and Andrews. And Clark soon went into the oil business with others, again selling out advantageously to Rockefeller.

Rockefeller now persuaded his brother William, also in the oil business, to go to New York and establish there William Rockefeller and Company, the germ of the Standard Oil Company of New York, later Socony, then Socony-Vacuum, and now Mobil Oil. He would function as an exporter for Rockefeller and Andrews. All the while the new business was prospering under the diligent eye of the senior partner, who took no time off then or ever for amusements or distractions other than churchgoing and conducting Bible classes. Rockefeller disapproved both for himself and others of drinking, smoking (his mother smoked a pipe), dancing, card playing, wenching, theater going, concert going, banqueting, idling, general socializing, and "good fellowship." He often lectured against the last to his Bible classes. Sitting around chatting, dining, and sipping drinks was, to him, merely time wasting in a world where a well-organized man had to economize on time, save money and "get ahead" on his pilgrimage to the grave.

In 1867 Rockefeller invited into the partnership a slightly older businessman who occupied the same office building, Henry M. Flagler, who had married the niece of Stephen V. Harkness, a wealthy whiskey distiller. Rockefeller, a desk general, needed field officers and was constantly in need of new capital for expansion. He constantly borrowed heavily from the banks, where he was increasingly welcome as he always paid back on the dot. Soon he was able, through hard-driving, ambitious, and imaginative Flagler, to get Harkness to put $70,000 (whiskey money!) into the business, a big stake for the times. In business matters Flagler and Rockefeller were thereafter as Siamese twins, although Flagler was a ready talker and bon vivant whereas Rockefeller was usually tight lipped.

Anyone who put in with Rockefeller—rather, was selected by him—and stayed with him was to become incredibly rich, in the astromillions, and was later to be ecstasized over by economic historians—professors, naturally—as an industrial statesman. But Rockefeller chose his field lieutenants carefully.

When they speak of Rockefeller power, most people don't

have the slightest glimmering of what they are talking about. What they mean, of course, is concentrated money, and money—or, better, properties—is at the core of it. But hundreds of American families own vast properties, larger than, equal to, or almost equal to the Rockefeller properties without having the power punch of the Rockefellers. The secret relates to people. For in addition to collecting money, properties, works of art, and the general run of investments, the Rockefellers also carefully collect people, key people, some of them brilliant. And it is the people they collect that is one of the major sources of their pervading power.

As to the associates he gradually collected in setting the course for Standard Oil, Rockefeller himself later remarked: "The ability to deal with people is as purchasable a commodity as sugar or coffee, and I pay more for that ability than for any other under the sun."

His grandsons learned that lesson well, and the public record shows clearly that Nelson is trying to emulate the old man and his own father. Eliminate about five people, non-Rockefellers, from the Rockefeller entourage and the whole script would fall apart. Everything would be different.

And the people (many of them Nobel laureates) brought in to the Rockefeller projects, whether commercial or noncommercial are persons interchangeable, as the record shows, with the highest posts in government, scientific and international affairs. From time to time, and often continuously, Rockefeller philanthropic managers head the leading departments and top echelons of government, their lawyers move into leading judgeships, their advisors into advanced posts. Would any of these be apt to turn on their sponsors?

3.

In 1870 the business, now gushing like an oil well (although few outsiders knew it), was reorganized with a capital of $1,000,000 as the Standard Oil Company of Ohio. The name came from one of its refineries, known as the Standard

Works; the other one was the Excelsior Works. In this new company Rockefeller took 2,667 shares; Flagler, Samuel Andrews, and William Rockefeller 1,333 shares each; Harkness, 1,334 shares; and O. B. Jennings, progenitor of the Jennings fortune of many members, 1,000 shares. The firm of Rockefeller, Flagler and Andrews got 1,000 shares in return for plant and business valued at $400,000 and these shares, presumably, were distributed to the partners in proportion to their individual stakes, most going no doubt to Rockefeller. So Rockefeller and his brother held 40 percent of the stock plus presumably at least 40 percent of what went to the old firm or at least 44 percent in all. This wasn't an unfair division as Rockefeller was giving his whole life and thought to the business, except for detours to church two or three times a week, and the others were living it up in off hours, or, like Harkness, were not active in the business.

To his original partners Rockefeller soon added more from among able competitors whom he bought out with stock at full value and brought into his circle: Henry Huddleston Rogers, John D. Archbold, Oliver H. Payne, J. N. Camden, Charles H. Pratt, Jabez Bostwick, and others. The various associates made up what later came to be referred to as "the Standard Oil gang."

All these men were very different from the rigid, inscrutable, tight-lipped, machinelike Rockefeller. In dealing with people Rockefeller was able only to outline clear-cut propositions in which advantage could be shown for acceding to the proposition. At this Rockefeller was very good. But in the "handling" of people in the sense of manipulating and soft-soaping them, acting the parts of diplomats, politicians, and fixers, Rockefeller knew he was no good and depended here first on Flagler, then on Archbold, Rogers, Camden, and others.

All the active partners of Standard Oil apart from Rockefeller corresponded to what were known as "confidence men." They harmonized completely, from beginning to end, including their early life histories, with what psychiatrists call delinquents, psychopaths, or sociopaths. They would literally stick at nothing, legal or illegal, and this observation applies especially to Flagler, Archbold, and Rogers. Brother William in time took after them.[13] Without them Standard Oil could not have operated with the serpentine facility that it did.

All this came under the heading of freedom, American-style.

Writing by way of reassurance to his wife in 1870 at the time of the launching of Standard Oil, Rockefeller said: "You know we are independently rich outside investments in oil." Rockefeller was now thirty-one years old. Actually, he had been moderately rich at twenty-two and could have retired in comfort at age twenty-five. Rockefeller was never a speculator or a gambler, although as side issues, on a relatively small scale, he was to do some speculating, was even to make some bad investments of a minor nature. Rockefeller was a sure-thing player, never risking much. And as far as competitors were concerned, he always went for the jugular.

As of 1870 the oil industry was regarded in the main as speculative, and it was indeed speculative for most of its participants. For one thing, nobody knew if and when the flow of oil might cease. But Rockefeller, as his letter to his wife shows, was prepared for that. If Standard Oil of Ohio proved to be a flop, they would be rich anyhow, on the basis of other properties he owned—real estate, participations in banks, government bonds.

And when Standard Oil was solidly established, no longer speculative, he could afford to take gambles with investments. One of these side investments was the acquisition for a song of the rich Mesabi Range of iron ore in northern Minnesota, which he sold with some nearby properties to J. P. Morgan's United States Steel Corporation for $80 million, half in common stock, half in preferred. An additional $8.5 million in cash was paid for the Great Lakes ore-carrying fleet. The deal left Rockefeller the largest single stockholder in heavily watered U.S. Steel. Rockefeller probably sold out here very early, realizing on his investment. From a Rockefeller point of view, the U.S. Steel setup would not look good.

---

[13] For an outline of this personality type see Prof. Robert A. Woodruff, M.D., Prof. Donald W. Goodwin, M.D., and Prof. Samuel B. Guze, M.D., *Psychiatric Diagnosis*, Pp. 143-53.

The Standard Oil operation, then, appears to have been under the direction of a highly moral, God-fearing, churchgoing man who had collaborating with him a set of utterly unscrupulous operators. Was this a paradox? It was indeed no more paradoxical than in the more familiar case of a godly, Bible-reading field marshal who has under him field generals noted for their general cruelty, sadism, and heedlessness of human life. All the marshal does is turn a deaf ear to stories of their butcheries and concentrate on the fact that they carry out his plans at whatever cost and win battles. That is the thing to do: win battles.

Without these field lieutenants and their temperaments, Standard Oil could not have succeeded. Nor could it have succeeded without Rockefeller, the demonic Calvinistic planner and organizer in the back room.

4.

In order to understand the Standard Oil Company in all its permutations and combinations from 1870 to 1911, it is necessary to note that it operated on two levels: legal and illegal. It was also increasingly worldwide. In its illegal aspects it was like some famous revolutionary parties of history. Had it been *only* a complex of illegality, it certainly could not have survived. In such a case it would have been like any common organized underworld enterprise, doomed to self-destruction.

Standard Oil was a company legally chartered under Ohio laws at its inception and it did a legal business. And its wholly legal business, thanks largely to Rockefeller, it carried out better than any competitor, more efficiently. Whereas many of the competing oil companies were small, dirty, and disorderly, it was noticed that all the premises and equipment of Standard Oil were scrupulously clean at all times—refineries, storage depots, horses, wagons, barrels, containers. One could have picnicked on the floors. And everything was orderly. Efficiency ruled. Nothing was wasted. Nobody other than Rockefeller had invoked knife-edge efficiency. But he, the obsessive-compulsive, insisted upon it at all times.

Again, Standard Oil took upon itself, always at a saving, the provision of all intermediary services. Instead of buying crude oil from jobbers, Standard bought direct from the fields. Instead of buying barrels, Standard set up its own cooperage works. Instead of depending upon outside draymen and wagons and on the flat cars of railroads to haul barrels, it had built its own tank cars, its own wagons. It did not pay to store oil. It built its own storage tanks.

Even had Standard not applied unfair and illegal pressures upon them, many of its competitors all along the line would have gone out of business owing to sheer inefficiency, profligacy, and the oscillations of the business cycle. For most of the people in the business, from producing to refining and delivering, were quick-profit adventurers.

But Standard also had secret weapons, many of them, and was to develop more. And none of these was originated at any point by Rockefeller, who was never an originator, always just an organizer (period). One of these weapons was the rebate, a percentage of the cost of transportation that the railroads returned secretly to certain favored businesses. The rebate, illegal for common carriers to bestow, was already well established at the time Rockefeller first went into business. Anyone who knew anything at all knew the arrogant railroads gave rebates. Other oil shippers than Rockefeller also got rebates.

But Standard Oil stepped in and induced the competing railroads to deny rebates to some, even raise the rates, and to give it larger rebates on the higher rates. Rockefeller said later that this came about because Standard was able to guarantee larger and more regular shipments by reason of his take-overs and to supply extra facilities. But analysis shows that Standard got larger rebates than even some efficient, large-shipment early competitors. Apologists for Standard point out that it was not the perpetrator of the rebates; the railroads were. It was, however, the beneficiary, either as an accessory after the fact or as a receiver of stolen goods. It did not report to the authorities that the railroads were violating the common law. In failing so to report, Standard Oil was not acting the often extolled role of the law-abiding citizen.

Standard was able to persuade the railroads to give it un-usually heavy and often exclusive rebates, thus setting up a hidden source of fresh capital that enabled it to grow rapidly. What caused most of its competitors to fail was, precisely, lack of capital that would ensure growth. Just why Standard was able to get heavier rebates than other large-scale refiners has been made into something of a mystery although there is really no mystery about it.

What the game really was was given away by Frank Rocke-feller, a former Standard Oil vice-president, himself now a business competitor of Standard Oil and long hostile thereaf-er to his brother, in testimony as early as 1876 before a con-gressional committee. Standard Oil simply paid a good old American "kickback" to railroad officials, some of them lead-ing stockholders of the roads. Here was ample motivation to give one shipper a more advantageous rebate.

Not only did Standard Oil get big rebates enabling it to grow while competitors stood still, but it apparently invented the "drawback," which was a secret rebate given to it on the transportation charges paid *by its competitors!* In other words, Standard Oil secretly profited on the shipments of its rivals, a neat way of succeeding in business without trying.

What, other than a system of kickbacks, would induce rail-road officials to reach over into the money paid to the railroad by shippers and turn part of that money over to a rival shipper?

Now, it is clear, in paying out rebates and drawbacks the railroad officials, some of whom were leading stockholders of the roads, were certainly depriving their own companies of money, a peculiar and traitorous thing to do. Why would they do this? The kickback, which went into their own pockets, was the obvious inducement. While railroad profits were unquestionably adversely affected by rebates and drawbacks, more profit was bypassed into the pockets of the corrupt rail officials and leading railroad stockholders. The loss went to the generality of the railroad stockholders who were not recip-ients of the kickbacks.

Leading railroad people like William H. Vanderbilt became

stockholders of Standard Oil without any record of their having contributed capital. So it may be that the kickbacks took the form of stock rather than money, or of stock and money. Leading bankers, too, who lent money freely to Standard Oil, also turned up as Standard stockholders without having contributed any capital to the company. No doubt the stock gifts led to an easier special loan policy.

Standard Oil stock at the time was closely held. One could not go out in the open market and buy any quantity of it although here and there stock changed hands in small amounts among lesser holders who had acquired it by means other than purchase. Most of the small refiners who sold out to Rockefeller insisted upon being paid in cash (as they needed funds to live on), although the larger ones like Rogers, Archbold, and Bostwick took stock and became part of the management. No doubt these had had the inner workings of the illegal portion of Standard Oil fully explained to them.

The bulk of the capital that enabled Standard Oil to grow so rapidly came not from efficiency but unquestionably from the flood of rebates and drawbacks. Here was the hidden spring, a gusher.

Simply between the years 1872 and 1879 the portion of total United States refining capacity held by Standard Oil catapulted from 25 percent to 95 percent, giving it an almost total monopoly before either the name of the company or of Rockefeller was publicly very well known. Shortly prior to 1872 Standard had less than 10 percent of capacity.

The way the railroad officials allowed Standard Oil to operate in time enabled the company to gain a whip hand in the matter of oil shipments. Standard, finally, was able to dictate rates, for itself as well as for others. It played one road off against the other, varying shipments as leverage. With the advent of pipelines, which Standard went in for heavily even as it opposed down to the use of brute force with paid thugs the building of pipelines by others, Standard could name its own railroad rates from its shipping points. But others, dependent on the railroads and without pipelines of their own, found railroad rates from their shipping points very high. As a result their costs were higher, their profit margins lower, their competitive positions vis-à-vis Standard very weak. They were as though paralyzed by an invisible force.

Apologists for Rockefeller, and they have been many, in order to place him in a better light, have depicted everyone in the oil business as a rascal. But this was not wholly true. Some were merely plodding businessmen, naively taking stated rules and laws at face value. This Rockefeller and his associates never did.

While smaller companies were absorbed at cut rates by Standard Oil, usually under the pressure of local price-cutting competition or the threat thereof as well as bad business conditions, larger companies were bought out at full value, usually with the payment of stock. And in most cases nobody knew these companies had been bought out. For a long time nobody knew the companies belonged to Standard Oil, not even the railroads.

Standard Oil acquisitions outside of Ohio, in Philadelphia, Baltimore, and New York, were illegal under Ohio law, which forbade an Ohio corporation to own out-of-state companies without special legislative dispensation. This Standard never had. Standard originally took title to these companies in return for stock but left the original owners in charge. This made for a cumbersome operation.

It was to overcome this cumbersomeness that the trust device, thought up by Rockefeller's attorney, Samuel C. T. Dodd, was developed. In April, 1879, the trust was born, secretly. Under it the individual trustees of companies that had been taken over, the thirty-seven Standard Oil stockholders, and the Standard Oil Company of Ohio conveyed all stock of out-of-state subsidiaries to three trustees, who were clerks of Standard Oil, "dummies." The untenable theory behind this was that the subsidiaries now no longer belonged, in defiance of law, to Standard Oil of Ohio but to the trustees. But trustees never own that for which they act as trustees.

As this arrangement also proved unsatisfactory, because it did not include the stock of Standard of Ohio, it was superseded in 1882 with another. Now the three dummy trustees, forty-two present S.O. stockholders and Standard Oil of Ohio conveyed all the stock to nine trustees. These included Rockefeller, William Rockefeller, Payne, Flagler, and Archbold. Rockefeller was president of the combine. The trust had no name, was what is known as a common-law trust. For each share of stock, each stockholder received twenty trust certificates. The trust was capitalized now, modestly, at $70 million. Its average annual earnings were around $10 million. Rockefeller personally held 25 percent of the shares, which was to be his approximate stake in Standard Oil up to the Supreme Court dissolution decree of 1911 although at one time he held 30 percent. By 1890 the trust earned $19,131,000 per annum, with the end of the rainbow still far out of sight up in the sky. All along Rockefeller's salary was relatively modest—$12,000 in 1875, $30,000 by 1900.

It was not until 1888 that the full text of the trust agreement became publicly known although prior to this time it had been copied, via the lawyers' grapevine, in other industries.

What Rockefeller and his associates had done was to establish a secret cartel. And cartels, secret or open, were and are forbidden in the United States although the United States is unquestionaly heavily cartelized at this very moment. In Europe, however, much to the disdain of patriotic Americans, cartels exist openly and are legal. But in wicked Europe, governments have participation in the cartels, often to the direct benefit of the public treasury. In the United States the public treasury draws no benefits from the cartels or artificial monopolies. The ones who draw the reciprocal benefits, under the table, are politicians and political parties.

Under the American antitrust laws, prosecutions for monopoly, trustification, or cartelization are wholly optional with the attorney general—that is, the president, whose absolute creature the attorney general is. And heavy political contributions are made, by the cartels, precisely to those candidates and parties that give sub-rosa assurance the antitrust laws, among others, will be enforced only delicately. Without such benign assurances, no heavy campaign contributions. . . .

Now and then, as economic conditions turn sour, unemployment increases, and public tempers rise, the politicians need scapegoats to appease the now restive electorate. For when it comes, rarely, to a showdown between votes or campaign money, the votes will win; without them there can be no offices for the nimble politicos. At such occasional moments, much to the bewilderment of Europeans, leading gilt-edged American corporations are brusquely summoned into court and their sins publicly probed. No heavy penalties are imposed, however. Only a rearrangement is required, arrived at usually through a "consent decree." In brief, the company consents to the government's case and is in effect put on unsupervised probation.

And soon everything is back approximately where it was. The only clear beneficiaries of the process are the defense lawyers, who draw big fees, and competitive newspapers which get revelatory copy—who got what, when, where, and why. Noncompetitive newspapers practically ignore the entire gaudy proceedings.

As to criticisms of Rockefeller and his associates, these are generally thought to emanate solely from defeated competitors, soreheads, radicals, and muckrakers. But many of the men who became his associates in Standard Oil in the course of its expansion had, prior to the association, said harsh things about him. If one gathers together only the remarks of such as a general commentary, Rockefeller does not come out smelling like a rose. But Rockefeller bore no hard feelings against the former antagonists.

Apologists, usually well paid, directly or indirectly, have taken note of many false allegations made against Rockefeller. And it is correct that falsehood was sometimes mingled with truth. But as for weeping for Rockefeller on this account, as the apologists invite one to do, this is much like weeping for a conquering general who is wounded in battle by a sneakily placed enemy sharpshooter using dumdum bullets. Falsehood entered the campaign against Standard Oil in the effort to enlist support among simpler people. It took the form, invariably, of tear-jerking tales of widows and children cheated out of their properties, men driven to suicide, or of rival refineries burned out on orders of Rockefeller. The larger and more serious charges of corporate wrongdoing were not readily understood by the man in the street. It was all too complicated.

Just how illegal, immoral, or generally odious was Standard Oil?

From the beginning, and increasingly, the company violated laws right and left and engaged in snide practices. It was not, of course, the only rising company to so conduct itself. Indeed, many reliable observers are of the opinion that Standard Oil was the best of a bad lot. As to this, I couldn't say. Although it gouged on prices, stifled competition, charged all the traffic would bear as it reduced production costs to a minimum, Standard Oil at least did not issue watered stock to the ever-gullible investing public, overstate its capitalization, or fob off inferior products on the consumer. Many other companies did all that. But Standard Oil did just about everything else and was finally found guilty after protracted legal processes of general illegality by two high courts.

As early as March, 1892, the Supreme Court of Ohio ordered Standard Oil of Ohio to withdraw from the trust, which was held illegal. Owing to the statute of limitations, which made the prosecution too late, it could not revoke the company charter, a bit of Rockefeller luck. In effect, the company simply ignored this judgment, holding it impossible to comply with because it could not force the return of the trust certificates of small holders. Rockefeller remained as president of Standard of Ohio. Brother William was made president of Standard of New York, Flagler of Standard Oil of New Jersey, James Moffett of Standard of Indiana. All the presidents had their offices at 26 Broadway, New York City, the Standard Oil building. The boards of directors of each company were identical. And the trustees kept performing the same functions as before the liquidation order. So much for court orders and the law.

But in the same year Rockefeller's health began to suffer. He developed a stomach disorder that alarmed him. He went on a simple milk and cereal diet; he may well have had ulcers. Somewhat later he developed alopecia, a generalized nervous disorder, often psychosomatic, in which he lost all his hair permanently. After this he was to wear a wig. But now, increasingly, he began to stay away from his beloved office, expressing his wishes to Archbold over the phone. As he admitted later, he was now very worried and often sleepless.

But even worse days were coming although by this time many leading newspapers, not yet harnessed to the rising national corporations, had for a considerable period been in full cry against the company and its chief executive.

The first of these blows was a book by a sharp-witted Chicago journalist who had long been investigating the Rockefeller enterprise. He was Henry Demarest Lloyd and the book, a masterly polemic, was *Wealth Against Commonwealth* (1894). Lloyd had somewhat earlier written critically of the company and its head man in *The Atlantic Monthly,* attracting international attention.

Just about when the furor aroused by Lloyd had begun to die down, dynamite was dumped on the embers with the appearance of Ida M. Tarbell's heavily documented *The History of the Standard Oil Company* (1905), a classic of American exposé literature, a really creamy job. The book was heavily researched from the public record, drawing upon court proceedings, legislative investigations, congressional hearings, talks with witnesses, newspaper analyses, and industry statistics. The public effect of it was devastating, irrefutable. It remains the basic point of departure for any book on Rockefeller and Standard Oil, a Gibraltar of granitic fact. Not to have read it is not to know the old Standard Oil.

An inevitable and unconscious distortion wrought by the book was that it necessarily concentrated on Standard Oil and the oil industry, without taking in the whole sweep of business practices of the era. In consequence it made Rockefeller and his associates in Standard Oil stand out as unique villains in an otherwise idyllic world. Rockefeller apologists have repeatedly made this point. As a consequence they have directed attention to the business practices of others, which were far from wholesome. And by reason of this zeal to exculpate Rockefeller, more knowledge and insight has been gained of the entire American social system, of the system of law and, indeed, of the constitutional system. In order to get Rockefeller off the hook, the apologists, in effect, successfully impugned the whole system in a way to give joy to the ghost of Karl Marx. Rockefeller, the apologists point out, was only one of many. And even captious critics agree that he was definitely not the worst.

But how guiltless is anyone because others commit the same crime? The mental balance of a lawyer would be seriously questioned by any English or American judge who heard the lawyer argue on behalf of a client accused of burglary that the offense was inconsequential because burglary was an old crime committed down through history by millions and that thousands were presently committing the crime as shown by government statistics. Most of the Rockefeller apologetics have this same strained quality.

With all this material now out in the open and being publicly discussed, there was little the government could do, whatever it might have wanted to do or not do, but bring suit under the feeble Sherman Anti-Trust Act of 1890. Suit was filed November 15, 1906, by, ironically, Atty. Gen. Charles Joseph Bonaparte, grandson of Jerome, brother of *the* Bonaparte. The very name of the complaining official boded ill for the pious bookkeeper of Richford, New York. The suit prayed for a dissolution of the combine. At the end of this year there were twenty-one suits pending in state courts against Standard Oil, eight in Ohio and the balance in nine other states. There were also seven other suits in the federal courts.

Another general blow against Standard Oil fell in May, 1906, when the newly formed Bureau of Corporations issued its report on oil transportation. The main point was that Standard was still getting secret rebates and was being openly favored through the regularly posted rates. In a supplemental report the Bureau of Corporations showered the country with figures to prove that Standard Oil was gouging on prices. In the meantime the volatile President Theodore Roosevelt fulminated regularly against Standard Oil, thereby getting the undeserved reputation of being a terrible giant-killer. There was fakery all around in the Standard Oil case, pro and con.

In one of the suits brought by the government, Rockefeller, often lucky, was to be especially lucky. This action involved rebates allegedly paid by the Chicago and Alton Railroad to Standard Oil. It was tried in Chicago before Judge Kenesaw Mountain Landis, a grandstand player and self-promoter of the first water. The government prosecutors did not want to call Rockefeller, whose testimony was not necessary anyhow, because by forcing him to testify, thereby possibly incriminating himself, they would have to give him personal immunity for the more important case under the Sherman Act.

All this was carefully explained to Landis who, however, was miffed because Rockefeller was evading his process server. By this time Rockefeller had for years evaded process servers in suits civil and criminal, often hiding out like a gangster on the run. "I'm going to bring him before this court to vindicate its dignity," Landis thundered. He did this. Rockefeller testified with the newspapers making much brouhaha about his appearance. His testimony added nothing vital to the case. And by this appearance he gained immunity from criminal prosecution later. He was now personally free and clear, thanks to Landis.

Landis wound up the case by fining Standard Oil a spectacular $29.24 million to great public acclaim. The fine was $20,000 for each of 1,462 carloads whereas, legally, if the case had been proven, it should have been $20,000 for each trainload. On appeal the case was reversed by a competent judge. On retrial it was unceremoniously thrown out of court. But Landis, having punched Rockefeller square on the nose (as the public thought), went on to become the high-paid "czar" or internal arbiter of the corrupt baseball industry (for there was corruption all around, coast to coast and Gulf to Canada, and neck deep, and the public needed some reassurance that a ball game at least was on the level). Landis is one person Rockefeller owed a handsome unpaid award.

But the suit for dissolution, among others, was pressed. No less than four hundred witnesses testified and twelve thousand pages of testimony filling twelve volumes were taken. The case ground on over four and a half years and special counsel for the government was Frank B. Kellogg of St. Paul, who came into favorable public notice with the litigation and was later a secretary of state.

The United States Circuit Court of Appeals on November 20, 1909, gave its decision, entirely sustaining the government's case. It ordered the Standard Oil Company of New Jersey, parent holding company, to divest itself of all subsidiaries in thirty days. Standard Oil appealed to the American forum of last resort, the Supreme Court, which heard the case argued in March, 1910, and reargued in January, 1911. The decision was issued on May 15, 1911. Chief Justice White read the twenty-thousand-word opinion to the always hushed courtroom. The decision, sustaining the lower court, was unanimous except for a concurrent opinion by Justice John Marshall Harlan taking exception to a crucial point of the majority. Standard Oil was a monopoly in violation of the law, precisely what Henry Demarest Lloyd had originally contended.

Public denunciation of Rockefeller was now at its most virulent. It greatly exceeded, indeed, the denunciation later of General Tojo after Pearl Harbor or Adolf Hitler after anything he did. Judging simply by the weight of outcry, Rockefeller was a far worse enemy of the country than either Tojo or Hitler, a manifest absurdity. But right here, amid all this hullabaloo and furor, Rockefeller was inadvertently performing the greatest service anyone ever performed for laissez-faire American capitalism. For he was, like a lightning rod, deflecting discontent with the system and the conditions it had bred away from the system itself to himself. He was being crucified, if that is the word, largely for the sins of others, who would go scot-free as the furor subsided. And so would he.

There was no foot dragging now by Standard Oil in complying with the court order as in the case of the order of 1892 by the Ohio court. For had Standard Oil now procrastinated, its officers would surely have faced chilling jail sentences for contempt of the highest court in the land.

Yet the incident was nevertheless to be trammeled by the

court itself in an act called "self-wounding" by lawyers, one
of several such in the history of the court. The majority opinion called for adherence to what became known as "the rule of
reason" in enforcing the trust laws—that is, "reasonable"
trusts were to be allowed, "unreasonable" ones disallowed.
And Standard Oil was an unreasonable trust. In brief, all
trusts were not henceforth subject to the antitrust laws, as the
Sherman Act was merely designed "to prevent *undue* re-
straints of every kind and nature." In his partial dissent Justice Harlan vehemently objected to this interpretation,
holding that the prohibitions of the Sherman Act were absolute and that the court was in effect unconstitutionally legislating, embroidering upon an act of Congress. This the court
has done several times in its history, sometimes provoking
violent reactions as in the Dred Scott case.

What the court mainly objected to was that the Standard Oil
Trust had had the intent from the beginning to establish a
monopoly and "to drive others from the field and exclude
them from their right to trade." Now it was to become the
American cartel idea that if one allowed *some* competitors to
survive, cartelization was OK. Token competition was to be
the rule.

The combine was broken down into thirty-eight separate
companies, the shares of the subsidiaries distributed to stockholders *pro rata.* The various companies were to have separate
boards of directors and separate officers. Rockefeller resigned
as president of Standard Oil of New Jersey, was succeeded by
Archbold, his alter ego. William Rockefeller resigned as vice-
president and his son, William G. Rockefeller, as assistant
treasurer. H. H. Rogers had died. Flagler, now deep in developing the Florida East Coast on his own, gave up his directorship. All the original Standard Oil gang was out, although
they retained their huge stockholdings, a nice, nice point.

As it turned out, Rockefeller himself held 244,500 of 983,-
383 shares, and ten members of the Standard Oil clique held
more than 50 percent of the stock. Rockefeller's share of nearly 25 percent was below his earlier approximate 30 percent of
holdings because for some years now, as his published letters

show, he had been distributing stock to his children and grandchildren. He was to continue doing this, and on a larger scale, and at his death he would own very little.

As it also turned out, the stock had been greatly undervalued. But stock traders, having now had a peek inside the lush empire, soon took care of that in a great Standard Oil bull movement. From January to October, 1912, the stocks doubled and trebled in market value. New Jersey moved from 360 to 595, New York from 260 to 580, Atlantic Refining from 260 to 620, Galena-Signal from 215 to 245, South Penn Oil from 350 to 825, and Standard of Indiana from 3,500 to 9,500. Rockefeller was becoming richer!

And what is more, unusual in such furious bull movements, the stocks were fully worth their newfound market prices. Standard of New Jersey had paid dividends of 48 percent in 1900 and 1901 and in subsequent years paid in the range of 36 to 45 percent up to dissolution. But in the first eleven months of 1912, twenty-six of the thirty-four companies to come out of the combination paid dividends amounting to 53 percent on the old stock!

Dividends at this rate clearly indicate that the company every two years was returning the full paid-in stated capital to the stockholders, the managing officers holding about 4/7ths of the stock at all times. Nor did the company by any means pay out all its earnings in dividends. It retained large portions for further expansion. All these figures are taken from an extremely friendly, pro-Rockefeller source—Allan Nevins, *Study in Power: John D. Rockefeller, Industrialist and Philanthropist* (Charles Scribner's Sons, N.Y., 1953).

From 1891 to 1899 earnings increased from $27,367,000 to $64,457,000 yearly. In 1907 they were $131,291,000 and in 1908 they were $116,460,000. For the automobile was just coming to the fore. Of these earnings Rockefeller's portion was always between 25 and 30 percent and of him and his management group nearly 60 percent. In all this time the vast majority of persons in the United States labor force was paid less than $1,000 per year in wages and salaries. As of 1914 a corporation bookkeeper in Chicago was paid $17 per week with no vacations, no pension, no sick leave, no severance pay.

Apologists for Standard Oil claim the company was especially kind to its sixty-five thousand employees, never having had "labor troubles." The company actually paid all along the line a shade more than the going market rate for similar work, thus getting good employees for steady jobs (the last being much desired then as now in a cyclical economy). Standard Oil, it is true, was early in installing a bona fide retirement plan; but this worked two ways. It retained for the company reliable workers, not always easy to find.

And in the course of time it was to achieve "labor troubles."

But as Jules Abels points out, dividends of nearly $40 million per year in the early 1900s compared with a wage bill of $65,000,000 or about $1,000 for each employee. In 1963 Standard Oil of New Jersey paid wages and salaries, including officers' salaries, of $1,011,278,000 compared with dividends of $592.5 million. Wages and salaries the same year at General Motors were approximately four times the dividends and at United States Steel wages and salaries were ten times the dividends.

What is of relevance here is the relative reward for labor and capital. The oil industry, of course, is highly automated, is less labor-intensive than either steel or motors. But it wasn't as automated in the early years of this century.

In the ten years leading up to 1911 the *earnings* of the combine exceeded $1 *billion.*

Just what proportion of this is traceable to illegality is impossible to measure. One can, however, say that without general and particular illegality from its very inception, the operation would not have been nearly as impressive.

Now, all these figures, although large, tend to leave very little impression on the common man today when there is daily talk of gross national product exceeding $1 trillion annually and national budgets of $300 billion. Such figures benumb the average mind, sound like talk of stars hundreds of millions of light-years away.

A difference, though, between the figures for matters like gross national product and national budgets and private fortunes is that the former represent aggregate flow-through money and the latter represent diverted hold-on-to money that also produces income. The flow-through money is much like the waters of the Mississippi coursing to the sea—it's an awful lot of money in circulation. The money of the fortunes is more like water retained for private use in private lakes, large and small, adjoining the mighty Mississippi. The water of the Mississippi, massive in quantity, is nobody's or everybody's. The less massive waters in the private lakes is *somebody's* money, representing personal power in reserve.

Perhaps a better figure of speech would be to liken the sums for gross national product and national income to free-flowing air, which is all around us, and private capital sums to the compressed air held in tanks—compressed power. The funds of the fortunes are much like this compressed air, deployable anywhere, at will. While the air around us is valuable, in fact indispensable, it is certainly not as dynamic as the tank-held compressed air, which can be mobilized with startling effects at given points.

Another way of getting perspective is to notice that the median line for per person net worth in the United States *today* is $800. In other words, half the populace is worth less than this truly modest figure. The other half is worth more, but most of it not very much more.

But constant talk about the flow-through money, running into large aggregates, tends to diminish in people's minds the actual dimensions of private fortunes, Rockefeller's included. Merely $1 million of capital is, for the individual, an awful lot of money, inflation or no inflation.

5.

How, in a nutshell, cutting through volumes of apologetics, did the original Standard Oil operate? It operated in such a way as to be a model for any secret service operation such as the CIA or the GPU and KGB. Standard Oil had nothing whatever to learn from them.

In the first place, a large portion of Standard Oil's operations was illegal, as ascertained by the courts. And its illegal operations were invariably secret. The rule of secrecy was one constantly enjoined upon his associates by Rockefeller himself. As many of these were men of expansive temperament, they would have been, unless carefully coached, apt to tell anyone with pride what they were doing, thus showing what clever fellows they were.

Standard Oil, as we have noted, illegally took rebates and drawbacks, thereby profiting at a great rate, and paid out kickbacks. But it went beyond this: it secretly established ownership in presumably competing companies. And when such ownership became known, it secretly established or bought "independent" companies in order to deceive the growing number of persons who did not wish to do business with Standard Oil. With its secretly controlled "independents," it waged phony price wars, driving true independents to the wall. Then it raised prices.

And when someone would nevertheless refuse to do business either with Standard or one of its satellites, the buyer would be threatened with commercial extinction. There was a wide range of petroleum products, but kerosene was the major one until gasoline took over with the rise of the automobile, motorboat, and airplane. The principal outlet for kerosene was locally owned small grocery stores. To the recalcitrant owners of some such, the Standard representative would threaten to establish a competing store nearby, which could be done easily for less than $10,000. In the face of such a menace the hapless grocer would capitulate and buy Standard.

In addition to using the aliases and disguises of satellite companies, Standard Oil operated with a secret code and ciphers, lest anyone know what it was doing. It also had an efficient internal and external espionage system. It not only knew what everyone in its employ was doing (and internal pilferers and loafers were dropped at once), but it knew about the internal operations of those trying to compete. It not only had its paid informants planted in other companies, but through the handling of the shipments of others through apparently independent Standard-owned shipping agencies, it learned who rivals' customers were, the quantities being shipped, and the prices paid. It used this information to the detriment of the competitor.

Early in the business Rockefeller at the end of every day used to compute ritualistically the exact financial position of the company—cash, receivables, payables, loans, inventories, goods in transit, etc. As the business developed he had subordinates do this for him so that at the end of every day he got a full report. Soon in its development the management of Standard Oil was broken down into committees, each committee in charge of an associate who reported to the board of trustees, the politburo of the outfit.

And Rockefeller, the head of the board, had all relevant information funneled upward to where he and all his associates could scrutinize, analyze, and discuss it. The information was such that he and his associates not only knew the exact position of Standard Oil at the end of each day, but they were able to estimate with X-ray accuracy what the position was of every remaining competitor either in refining, transportation, jobbing, storage, or exporting.

Beyond this Standard Oil early in the game began paying money to many newspapers and magazines in order to influence what they said and to keep hostile analyses out. Rockefeller's policy from the beginning had been not to comment on anything whatever that was said against him. Later he was to attribute much of the company's troubles to the fact that the public had not been given "our story." But had Standard come anywhere near explaining what it was doing it would, manifestly, have put the fat in the fire much sooner than Ida Tarbell did. Standard simply could not have operated with an open policy of public relations.

And when investigations began to get near inner secrets, papers would be mysteriously burned, books would disappear, witnesses would become tongue-tied, confused. Everything pertaining to romantic conspiracies was present in the Standard Oil scenario, as a fact, except the cloaks, daggers, false whiskers, rope ladders, and beautiful women. Rockefeller scolded associates who made public display of affluence, as by buying yachts. He advised living on a modest scale so as not to attract attention.

Nor is this all, by any means.

While Standard Oil was operating in secret conspiratorial illegality, one must not suppose that everyone outside the oil business was so stupid as not to be aware of this. Investigations began very early in its history. In every county of the United States (and there are now more than three thousand counties) and in every state, of which there are now fifty, there are at least two cohesive political groups or parties which are known to the irreverent as "the courthouse gang." They are the career officeholders and contenders and their appointees. And the courthouse gang in every jurisdiction, up to the national courthouse gang, knows just about everything going on in its jurisdiction, including the identity and operating scope of those conducting organized illegal operations. Of these latter there are always many, native and foreign-born.

The groups get the name "courthouse gang" because in the nonurban counties, which once held most of the population, officeholders, aspirants, and their minions were always clustered in or around the local county courthouse. All land deals, probates, and litigations were known to the courthouse denizens, and all contractors interested in the work of public improvements eventually had to go there. The county courthouse was the narrow funnel for all public business, after which came the state capital and then the national capital.

For Standard Oil to operate as it did, and get its way, it needed political help, in legislatures and executive chambers. And it got this help by paying money, as always. Standard Oil knew what made the people it dealt with tick. It was money, money, money—all along the line.

The political payoff men for Standard Oil were, first, J.N. Camden and then John D. Archbold. The public got a close look at how this operation worked because two minor office employees of Standard Oil at 26 Broadway, New York, in 1904 and 1905 surreptitiously took sheaves of letters from the files in Archbold's office to the offices of William Randolph Hearst's *New York American* newspaper where they were photographed, bought, and paid for. Hearst did not make them public until the 1908 presidential campaign, during which he supported an improbable candidate named Thomas L. Hisgen. Hearst himself, incidentally, was as much of a sociopath as anyone in the Standard Oil crowd.

What the letters showed was leading elements of the United States House of Representatives and the Senate receiving steady large payments from Archbold in return for general and specific support of measures and obstructions beneficial to Standard Oil. One of these recipients of large sums was Senator Joseph B. Foraker of Ohio, who at the time was widely regarded as a possible future Republican president. Among other recipients of large *sub-rosa* funds were Senators Mark Hanna of Ohio, Matthew Quay and Bois Penrose of Pennsylvania, Joseph Bailey of Texas (Democrat); Congressmen Joseph Sibley of Pennsylvania, a Democrat and widely hailed "reformer"; Republican leader Cornelius Bliss; Senators Nathan B. Scott and Stephen B. Elkins of West Virginia; Congressman W.C. Stone, former lieutenant governor of Pennsylvania; Senator McLaurin of South Carolina; and various others in both parties. Many of these did not have to be sought out but appealed to Standard Oil for funds. President McKinley, through his mentor Mark Hanna, was always deep in the pocket of Standard Oil and the other trusts, a willing puppet.

Various critics of Standard Oil charge that the company was a corrupting influence, that it corrupted people who would otherwise have been virginal. One thing is certain: Standard Oil never corrupted anybody. The people it dealt with in this way were already long since corrupted, were self-dedicated to corruption, former poor boys democratically "on the make." It was corruption, in fact, that made politics attractive to them, an opportunity to build estates while preening before a gullible public. Without the opportunity for corruption they would have sought some other field, preferably in the line of racketeering.

And this was true, too, of newspapers that were "corrupted"

by Standard Oil. As Abels remarks, "let it be noted that the records of Standard Oil show that there was a flood of requests from publications of all kinds, newspapers and newspapermen, to be corrupted with Standard Oil funds." And the Archbold files as made public show that it was the same with politicians. Many were begging for money.

As to such national scandals as stem from revelations like the Archbold letters, the ordinary man thinks of them as single episodes. Rather is it the chance lifting of the curtain on a continous performance—the scandals of the Grant administration, the Crédit Mobilier, the Archbold letters, Teapot Dome, the Alien Property Custodian after World War II, and Watergate. All these seeming separate episodes, and others, simply amount to accidental disclosures of something that is going on all the time, a continuous performance. The idea that Richard M. Nixon was unique will simply not stand examination. Actually, Lyndon B. Johnson was far worse for a longer period but was far more adroit. Johnson was the big shadowy figure in the Bobby Baker case. Baker was, simply, Johnson's bagman. But the investigation of Baker by the Senate did not proceed to Johnson because senatorial "courtesy" required that senators not investigate senators, more especially the majority leader of the Senate. Baker, as the saying goes, "took the fall," went to jail—but kept the money. Dr. Martin Sweig, House Speaker John MacCormack's bagman, soon after did the same for MacCormack. What tripped the Nixonites was not wrongdoing but wanton arrogance and insolence, *hubris.* Nixon and his adjutants felt they were so safe in the high office that they could do anything, and carelessly. Here was their heel of Achilles. One should be adroit in this game. Johnson was.

As early as 1882 J. N. Camden wrote to Rockefeller: "I have arranged to kill two bills in the Maryland legislature at comparatively small expense." Standard Oil, at the time, was operating in the state legislatures, as indeed were many others. It was widely known for a long period after the Civil War that the Pennsylvania legislature was completely under the thumb of the Pennsylvania Railroad, bought and paid for.

Hardly anybody in business or politics is ever corrupted by someone else. The corruptee is invariably more than willing to be corrupted by the corrupter. Indeed, he is yearning for it.

Is, then, everybody in business and politics corrupt?

Not at all. In a preliminary approach, one can apply to the relevant people en masse the law of large numbers, there being about 1,500,000 elected officeholders and career contenders in the United States—the ins and the outs. At least 25 percent is corrupt from the word go, soliciting payoffs. Another 25 percent is about as incorruptible as anyone can be, anywhere, always granting that everybody has his vulnerabilities and that the political arena does not attract virgins. In between is the 50 percent that is more or less corruptible, off and on, depending upon circumstance, sheer opportunists. While these percentages may not hold absolutely on the empirical level, they no doubt come close within small percentage spreads. And skewness in the figures would be toward corruption rather than toward adamantine rectitude.

If anyone supposes that Standard Oil was alone in this period in dishing out gratuities to public officers, he is very mistaken. The record shows it to have been a general game. And the record also shows, from time to time, that the game continues, is booming today. But the fact that others were operating in the same way does not exculpate Standard or Rockefeller. Nonetheless someone is bound to say, what else could Rockefeller do in such an atmosphere? The answer is: if he was as high minded as some claim, he could have become a Trappist monk. Simple.

Rockefeller apologists, and Rockefeller himself, claim that so much went on in such a large operation as Standard Oil that he could not be blamed for the overzealousness of underlings. And this is simple nonsense. While Rockefeller unquestionably did not know everything that went on in Standard Oil's worldwide operations, he certainly knew more than anyone else, made it his business to know. He knew more about all the ins and outs, as an obsessive-compulsive, than any other person.

As Abels states, "there is no instance where Rockefeller

chastised or rebuked an employee for 'overzeal' in behalf of
Standard Oil, no matter what the employee resorted to—
which implies his condoning their acts." After the news of the
Archbold letters spilled out, Rockefeller made no move
against Archbold. In fact, Archbold succeeded Rockefeller as
president of Standard of New Jersey when the combine was
dissolved, with no demur from Rockefeller.

Why didn't Rockefeller, if he was as high minded as his
apologists paint him, at least dump Archbold? The fact is that
even had Rockefeller wanted to do so—and he certainly didn't
—he could not have because he was himself caught in the
dialectic of the operation with his associates. Archbold, a real
tough hombre, was nobody anyone, including Rockefeller,
could step on like a bug and throw aside. Nor were any of the
top Standard Oil associates. In any fight they were all very
mean gents—really mean.

The situation throughout its history was such that the
Standard Oil junta of different characters had to hang together
or hang separately. Had Rockefeller tried to apply pressure on
Archbold to leave, having known all along precisely what
Archbold was doing as he knew back in 1882 what Camden
was doing, Archbold, a man of fiery temperament, would certainly have retaliated by spilling his guts about the whole
Standard Oil operation. And then many remaining dark corners would have been lighted. Archbold wasn't one to be
thrown to the wolves by anyone.

But Rockefeller unquestionably never had the remotest
thought of doing anything of the kind either to Archbold or
any other pro-Standard transgressor. He just wasn't operating
on this level of moral high-mindedness except in the fantasies
of apologists. Archbold may have been a louse, and a dangerous one, but Rockefeller knew he was his very own self-select-
ed louse. To suppose anything else is to insult Rockefeller's
intelligence. Rockefeller was as guilty as anyone of anything.

Something to take serious note of, as to Ohio especially, is
that no public official who gave Standard Oil serious trouble
had much of a political career left to him. Those who brought
the suit that led to the 1892 court decision are especially cases

in point. They disappeared without trace. And this holds true in general in American politics of anyone who gives the corporations or other entrenched interests a hard time. The reason is that those of the vast electorate who applaud corporate foes cannot be counted upon for future support. But the regular party organizations, which always cater in return for money to the larger interests, can be counted upon to deliver their patronage-fed supporters on election day.

The "good guys" lose in the long run, just the reverse of a Hollywood movie. Or, rather, it turns out on the historical script as written by corporation-subsidized historians that the good guys, the critics, are really the bad guys—muckrakers, scavengers, defamers. The critics are stigmatized as hysterical demagogues, or worse. The sound men, the true patriots, are— surprise, surprise!—the corporate operators, Rockefeller and his associates and their imitators in the corporate world. And Lyndon Johnson, Richard M. Nixon et al.

Much is heard in the United States, constantly, about "due process of law." Everybody is for it. "Due process" means that decisions, whatever they are, are made according to prescribed laws by duly prescribed governmental agencies. Yet, strangely, most decisions in the United States that affect the public interest are not made according to "due process" at all. They are, rather, made by the boards of corporations whose self-serving decisions constantly affect the whole texture of life, often adversely. "Due process" covers a relatively small area, and is usually very late in getting into the areas affected by unilateral, self-serving corporate decisions.

6.

A lesson that is never drawn from the history of Standard Oil is that that operation would never have been possible without the conscious and unconscious assistance of an extremely loose, even rickety, political and legal system, about which eulogies are continually delivered. Nor would the rise of innumerable large similar operations be possible without the continuance of such a system. In the corporate world this is what is known as the "opportunity" provided by the land of the free—Penn Central Railroad, I. T. & T., Equity Funding Corporation, United States National Bank of San Diego, Franklin National Bank of New York, Four Seasons Nursing Homes, and so on through literally thousands of cases.

But the sort of inherent, freely operating corruption that is revealed in the history of Standard Oil up to 1911 as well as of other big American corporations is not nearly so serious, in my opinion, as the intellectual corruption that was revealed. And this corruption came to light in the numerous attempts by certified academicians to whitewash Standard Oil and other corporations.

"The United States has always been a corrupt society," Gore Vidal writes. "Periodically, 'good' citizens band together and elect to office political opportunists who are presented to the public as *non*-politicians. Briefly, things appear to be clean. But of course bribes are still given; taken. Nothing ever changes nor is there ever going to be any change until we summon up the courage to ask ourselves a simple if potentially dangerous question: is the man who gives a bribe as guilty as the man who takes a bribe?"[14]

Standard Oil not only ladled out money to politicians, in and out of office, and to newspapers, and quickly hired for itself any especially bright young lawyers it found acting for its competitors or hostile government agencies, but it had vast success in enlisting the aid of certified academicians. And here, in my opinion, was the worst subversion of all—the trammeling of the very citadel of truth.

Both Flynn and Abels take note of the ease with which Standard Oil lined up intellectuals. "An attempt has been made to explain the reasonableness of the drawback and the inevitable professor is found to do it," says Flynn (p. 268). "In the *Bibliotheca Sacra*, one of the most dignified of religious journals, one writer called rebates quite proper and even de-

---

14. Gore Vidal, *New York Review of Books,* 17 October 1974, p. 3.

fended the ethical character of drawbacks," (p. 407). Prof. George Gunton, an early Rockefeller stooge, "was at least the first of that merry band of college professors who write 'studies' and 'surveys' and 'books' and what not for wealthy but undisclosed patrons and seek to give to otherwise dishonest and unimportant creeds the respectability which flows from their titles as professors of economics," (p. 329). Here the word is not "bribes," it is "grants." As Abel remarks, "The intellectual who hires his reputation to industry or any other buyer infested the woods then [early this century] as he does now," (p. 267). Both Flynn and Abels cite many examples; yet they treat only glancingly what is really a very big target.

The man who has written most voluminously about Rockefeller and Standard Oil is the late Prof. Allan Nevins of Columbia University. Nevins had made a reputation as a sound, prolific, rather routine American historian when in 1940 he published a two-volume work, *John D. Rockefeller: The Heroic Age of American Enterprise.* This work was undertaken at the request of the Rockefeller family, which in itself guaranteed its wide distribution. For the Flynn book of 1932, although softly focused in many respects, showed Rockefeller as less than heroic.

Of the Nevins work Norman Cousins in the *Saturday Review* wrote that "If it had appeared a quarter of a century ago it might have been called 'inspired whitewashing' at worst or 'warmly sympathetic' at best." And this just about epitomizes the volume although most major reviews gushed over it as great and "definitive."

Apparently not satisfied with the impact of the first two volumes, Nevins returned to the charge in 1953 with another double-decker: *Study in Power: John D. Rockefeller, Industrialist and Philanthropist.* It reworked the same material somewhat more plausibly. A few years later an edited one-volume edition of this work was issued for readers allergic to two-volume prolixities.

Reviewers also hailed *Study in Power* as "definitive" on Rockefeller. It is in fact no more definitive than Mata Hari was the reincarnation of Joan of Arc. The definitive book is yet to be written. But this one is stocked in libraries coast to coast whereas Abels is hard to come by and is not today even catalogued in the great New York Public Library. However, five other books by Abels are catalogued.

Study in Power has some value, though, for the student of Rockefeller. It has the advantage, like its predecessor by Nevins, of containing the Rockefeller papers. But it is not difficult to discern the pattern of pro-Rockefeller bias in Nevins. He is intent, first, on impugning Rockefeller critics, especially Lloyd and Tarbell, and more especially Lloyd. Both of these were pioneers in the field, working without aid, and did in some minor respects leave themselves open to correction. Both, however, were much more firmly on target than Nevins makes out and have been so certified by high academicians.

Nevins's next ploy is to plead an alibi for Rockefeller on many matters in which he was in fact deeply involved. His general verdict about some of the worst charges is that Rockefeller wasn't there, had no part in it, can't be shown holding the smoking pistol over the corpse. But while Rockefeller, the theoretician of the entire operation, comes off relatively well, everybody else fares badly: Standard Oil, the Rockefeller associates, Rockefeller competitors, politicians, and so on. Perjury by Rockefeller in open court, and evasiveness under investigatory questioning, are passed over as minor foibles, "taradiddles." Rockefeller lied, in court or out, whenever necessary to protect Standard Oil, which is precisely what, in the circumstances, one would expect any chief corporate officer to do.

One of the alibis Nevins presents for Rockefeller is that he "retired" from Standard Oil in 1899. And if he was retired he surely cannot be held responsible for anything that happened after that. But Rockefeller's was a peculiar retirement. He told no one of it, not even his closest associates, and made no personal record of it. Actually, Rockefeller did not retire until 1911 when he gave up the presidency of Standard Oil. What had happened was that, like many tycoons, he simply gave up going to the office every day. Instead he kept in daily touch by phone with Archbold.

And during the period of his supposed retirement, he was subpoenaed many times to give public testimony, never stating that he was out of the picture, retired.

The Nevins opus is subject to many similar observations and, except for cold documentation, must be used with extreme caution by anyone interested in the truth. Nevins's interpretations, particularly as they bear on Rockefeller, are naively dubious.

It was in the course of doing the work for the five Rockefeller books that Nevins developed the interesting thesis that the American corporation adventurers to whom Matthew Josephson gave the enduring name of "The Robber Barons" were in fact American heroes, builders of American civilization and democracy. He invited other historians to follow in his footsteps in this thesis, but so far nobody has conspicuously accepted. And if anyone does, one will be able to see the American intellectual horizon further muddled.

I have given writers like Nevins the soubriquet of "counter-savants." A savant, or man of learning, is devoted to increasing knowledge. And knowledge has the function of deepening understanding. A counter-savant, however, is a man of knowledge who uses his knowledge, for reasons known only to himself, to obfuscate understanding, to confuse readers. The fact is that Nevins's corrective portrait of Rockefeller is not only false with respect to the central character, but frustrates understanding in the unsophisticated reader.

What makes such work especially bad is that professors are in fact highly regarded by Americans even though they may uneasily make defensive jokes about them and refer to a barber, bartender, or bordello pianist as "professor." At the same time Americans commonly deride Germans for their supposed overdeference toward professors and other authoritarian figures; it is a common American notion that Germans even click their heels and salute uniformed hotel doormen. Yet it is Americans, more than Germans, who are apt to take just about anything as gospel that a professor—or colonel—says, without analyzing the proposition on its merits. The United States, incidentally, has more "honorary" colonels than all the rest of the world. And the title is seriously used as though the man addressed were the commander of the toughest battle-hardened paratroop unit in the world.

7.

Was Rockefeller a genius?

Many people claim he was. The historian James Ford Rhodes compared him to Napoleon. Bertrand Russell compared him to Bismarck. James MacNeil Whistler saw in him another Francis of Assisi. No doubt someone has even likened him to Einstein—the Einstein of the modern corporation.

Rockefeller, in fact, was no genius, not even an evil one, but a simple and quite simpleminded man, a bookkeeper with a very narrow outlook. He was meagerly educated; never read anything except newspapers, business reports, and the Bible; never engaged in intellectual or even theological discussions; had little spirit of inquiry or wonder about him. With one exception—Oliver Payne—his associates were no different.

How, then, did he come to officiate in the building of so complicated a mechanism as Standard Oil, which gave birth to the various complicated mechanisms that are now the world-premier Standard Oil companies? Had Standard Oil been constructed according to an original plan devised by Rockefeller one would, in truth, have to concede he was a genius. For Standard Oil at the end was as complicated and smoothly working as a Bach fugue.

But Rockefeller did nothing of the sort. He played everything "by ear," one step leading to another. From the very beginning Standard Oil developed by a series of gradual steps, improvisations, one annex laid next to the other. Each step was taken as opportunity offered, obstacle by obstacle removed, addition by addition supplied.

Nevins pontificated tautologically that Standard Oil was an "historical accident," and was quoted before Congress to this effect by Nelson Rockefeller as though the statement had significance. But all history is no more than a series of accidents.

The United States, France, the Soviet Union, and other states are accidents, from inception to fruition. The British Empire was an accident; so was its disintegration. Historical event is always accidental, that is to say, in the sense that it is not logically necessary, not ordained, not inevitable. There might have been no Standard Oil, without Rockefeller, without surrounding conditions, without the purely accidental discovery of oil. True. But without an analogous concatenation of events there might not have been a United States. Merely without a single bullheaded British cabinet there would almost surely never have been a United States but, rather, a later Dominion of North America. And then, today, we might enjoy more frequent visits of the queen (or king), drink more tea, play more cricket and soccer, and have a more self-assured gentry.

It was Rockefeller, of course, who was compulsively committed to incessant growth, expansion, from the very beginning. It was this commitment to incessant growth that brought him to loggerheads with his first partner, Clark.

And whatever impeded Standard Oil's growth had, in Rockefeller's demonic view, to be removed, no matter what the consequences were to anyone else.

For Rockefeller, through Standard Oil, was not engaging in competition. He was engaging in secret economic warfare. Those who limn Rockefeller as a stiff competitor know not of what they speak. Rockefeller was hostile to competition *per se*, wanted nothing to do with it.

As he had no mission in life beyond building Standard Oil, all his pent-up energies and inner hostilities went into this task.

Yet—and here we get the Pavlovian effect, the crossing of the neurological signals—Rockefeller was a man who gave away money, a lot of money, and gave much of it, most of it, without any strings attached. How is that? How can anyone who gives away money, valuable money, be bad? There must be some good in such a man, the ordinary person concludes, baffled by anything to the contrary.

If a person steals, society agrees, that is bad and he should be jailed. But, say the psychiatrists, some persons have an inner compulsion to steal. Kleptomaniacs, they cannot help themselves. They steal not in order to profit but to relieve some inner tension. Such persons, the courts agree, are sick and need treatment. And it is so ordered.

While a compulsion to steal is not looked upon favorably, a compulsion to give money is. A giver, it is commonly reasoned, must be a compassionate, sympathetic, empathic person, one devoted to the welfare of his fellow man. But Rockefeller, as the most superficial reading of his life shows, was none of these.

As to giving, it was in my opinion one of his compulsions, part of his personality disorder, an amiable part from the point of view of the world. Such compulsive giving constitutes *didomania,* to coin a companion word for kleptomania from the Greek.

8.

Rockefeller began giving money very early, in his teens, and kept it up, unfailingly, regularly, all his life. He also, compulsively, obsessively, made a record in his famous Ledger A of each gift. Thus in 1855, when he was sixteen years old, he gave $2.77 of his meager earnings, the next year $19.31, the next year $28.37, and then $43.85, $72.22, $107.35, $259.97, and so on, every year, on an ascending scale. Here was growth in giving. In 1865 his gifts crossed $1,000, in 1869 $5,000, in 1879 $29,000, and in 1884 $119,000. He gave more than half a million in 1891 and nearly a million and a half in 1892 and was thereafter to give more than a million or even two million every year for many years. Certain years the giving was especially heavy—in 1907 it was $39,170,480.52; in 1909 it was $71,453,231.15; in 1913 it was $45,499.367.63; in 1914 it ran to $67,627,095.87; and in 1919 it went to the stupendous total of $138,624,574.61 with several big years still to come. (These figures are tabulated year by year by Nevins, *Study in Power.*)

One theory advanced for all this was that Rockefeller gave

to gain public favor. But he was already giving madly before he was ever known so this couldn't be entirely true. Nor was it true that he gave out of inherent generosity; for Rockefeller wasn't a generous man. Nor did Rockefeller's gifts for a long time always make sense.

Until he began endowing the University of Chicago in the 1890s—this on the advice of a newly found brilliant advisor, Frederick T. Gates—Rockefeller's gifts had been quite helter-skelter. He gave mainly to the Baptist Church and to Baptist foreign missions but also, now and then, to some other churches. Rockefeller, too, gave money directly to individuals. Early in his life at the Euclid Avenue Baptist Church he would unostentatiously press money into the palms of various parishioners he deemed needy and worthy. He would not, however, give money to organizations that served holiday dinners to down-and-outers, about the only charity he ever turned his back on.

Word had got out, though, that there was this man who was giving away gobs of money—and long before the wily Andrew Carnegie had been heard of as a giver—with the consequence that Rockefeller was besieged for largesse. He was, indeed, driven to distraction by the appeals, mostly from obvious cranks and freeloaders. He finally delegated Gates to handle the giving, inquire into the value of it. It was Gates, himself a clergyman, who reported that the missionary giving, which was the largest part, amounted to practically throwing the money away as most of the missionaries were incompetent people, accomplishing little of value. And for years the money of Rockefeller and others had sustained them in an international invasion of other long-vital cultures where they presumed to instruct chieftains and kings. Gates called a halt to that sort of mindless giving. Most of the Rockefeller giving up to this point, Gates found, was of doubtful value.

The high quality of the enterprises for which Rockefeller money thereafter went (apart from money that went to the Republican party and Republican candidates which to date amounts on the record to a visible $100 million and may run to $250 million), is attributable entirely to Gates, who became a Rockefeller window on the world as were Flagler, Rogers, and Archbold. Rockefeller had an uncanny ability to settle on the right man once he saw him. And Gates it was who literally badgered Rockefeller into increasing the size of gifts on the ground that he was accumulating so much money it would destroy his family.

All in all Rockefeller dispensed on the nonpolitical circuit a clearly visible $486,719,371.22—and the 22 cents is important as showing how meticulously the record was kept. On top of this the son, John D. Rockefeller, Jr., in turn gave $473 million, all of which, and more, he had been given by his father long before the father died. Between the two more than $1 billion was given. Nothing like this had been seen before, anywhere. Nor has it been seen since. And, best of all, an awful lot was left.

A great deal of this was given, it should be noted, before any tax benefits accrued from the giving. It was only with the inauguration of income, inheritance, and gift taxes in 1913 that one was able to offset taxable income with timely gifts. The massive Ford Foundation was established in lieu of paying a 90 percent inheritance tax, at the same time helping retain control of Ford Motor for the Ford family. Had it not been established, the money would have been vacuumed up in taxes, and no doubt then squandered by the Pentagon.

The main gifts by Rockefeller were as follows:

Rockefeller Foundation	$182,851,480.90
General Education Board	129,209,167.10
Laura Spelman Rockefeller Memorial Fund	73,985,313.77
Rockefeller Institute for Medical Research (now Rockefeller University, a purely high-quality graduate school)	60,673,409.45
University of Chicago	40,000,000.00
Total	$486,719,371.22

As Rockefeller was neither a lover of mankind (as proven by the depredations of Standard Oil) nor a person of a generous temperament nor visibly sympathetic toward strangers nor a giver purely to earn public esteem or tax economies, there is, on the surface, considerable mystery about this steady giving, just the reverse of kleptomania. And the only rational explanation in the light of available learning is that it was a ritual affair that relieved his constant upwelling unconscious anxiety. Giving, and taking too, made him feel better, relieved inner tensions.

Most people, worldwide, are more inclined to take than to give. The outstretched hand is familiar the world over. And thievery is common. Taking, one must conclude, is more normal than giving, especially compulsive, more or less blind, giving. Rockefeller's taking presents no mystery to anyone. Of course, many people before Rockefeller gave for centuries to favorite churches, hospitals, asylums, colleges, monasteries, and the like. But nearly always they gave to something specific for which they had a sentimental personal attachment. Giving for the sake of giving was seldom seen, and certainly not on a large scale.

But Rockefeller, before Gates came on the scene, gave quite randomly. Most that he gave in the pre-Gates period could be considered wasted. Here was Rockefeller, the keen moneyman, nevertheless ladling out heavy money like candy bars at a children's party. Such giving had to be part of a compulsive pattern, a ritual.

And Rockefeller gained something from it, a lifting of the heavy anxiety postulated here for his behavior. But this aberrant giving was precisely what gave many people pause in passing adverse judgment on him.

All such rituals, according to our friends the psychiatrists, have as their purpose the lifting or quelling of anxiety. And Rockefeller's rituals were many, and most of them in the eyes of observers "made sense", unlike the rituals of many obsessive-compulsives. They weren't "crazy" rituals as in the case of many compulsions. Arithmetic and bookkeeping were rituals. Standard Oil was itself a ritual but one favorably received at first by the world because it was, after all, a business. That made sense. Constant going to church and teaching Bible classes was a ritual and also made sense to millions.

For many years critics contended that Rockefeller's church-going was a hypocritical blind, a cover for nefarious operations. But this it was not. Rockefeller needed the church as a ritual as well as a sanctuary. And he went to church regularly long before anyone criticized his business behavior and he continued going to church long after. And he required that his children be regular churchgoers and Bible-class teachers. He must have felt that going to church produced concrete personal benefits.

Indeed, everything that Rockefeller did was ritualized. He got up at the same hour every day, appeared at the office at the same hour every day and when he had settled in New York he always took the Sixth Avenue "El" downtown, paying his nickel to ride. About the only variation in his office routine was that he often stayed late in the evening. But on Sundays he never worked or discussed business. Sunday observance was a routine, a ritual. Variations in Rockefeller's routine were rare.

And when he took up golf late in life, he made of it an invariable routine, a ritual. For Rockefeller golfed in all weathers, rain or shine, every day, metronomically. Nothing, seemingly, could keep him off the golf course, of which he maintained four, one for every season—in Maine, New York, southern New Jersey, and Florida. He also maintained homes adjacent to each, all on a comfortable but not monumental scale. Rockefeller never believed in ostentatious display, unlike his contemporary tycoons who built palazzos that rivaled some of the most elaborate European structures.

And it was a happy inspiration of his public relations impresario, Ivy Lee, to start him, late in life, handing out dimes to all and sundry. For here was another ritual, and one that seemed to put everyone in a good humor. One wonders if he ever asked in his thrifty soul whether it might not have been better, and more profitable, if he had started early to give out only dimes. Would it, internally and externally, have done him as much good?

9.

Most of the writings on Rockefeller that are at all critical suggest that he was a very shrewd, crafty, and realistic fellow. And in a business way no doubt he was.But actually Rockefeller was not realistic, or was realistic in a limited way only. In a broad sense Rockefeller didn't know what everything was all about—a very strange statement to make I must admit. He was, in truth, a very ignorant, limited man.

The obsessive-compulsive, as the psychiatrists report, is not out of touch with reality but his attention is always focused on a narrow segment of it, as though he were looking at the world through a narrow slit. The narrow slit comes about through the constant narrowing of attention, the focusing of it on purely technical or circumstantial details.

"The obsessive-compulsive's experience can be compared in this way to the experience of a pilot who flies at night or in a fog with accurate and well-functioning instruments. He can fly his plane, he can fly *as if* he were seeing clearly, but nothing in his situation is experienced directly; only indicators are experienced, things that signify other things."[15]

Rockefeller was more like the commander of a battleship, Standard Oil. Its mission: search and destroy distant targets. The commander consults instruments, takes readings, as Rockefeller consulted his books and data about the opposition. Orders are given in terms of the readings. "Fire" is the order on the battleship, "Go" in Standard Oil. What happens now? Nothing except more readings. Nobody is near anybody getting hurt, nobody sees anything sinking, anyone dying. The seas are now clear. The indicators show everything is well. Full steam ahead.

The obsessive-compulsive is not only filled with doubt, but the doubt is balanced with dogma. He is dogmatic. Rockefeller belonged to a dogmatic religious sect, and its dogmatism no doubt gave him strength. He was dogmatic in other re-

---

15. David Shapiro, *Neurotic Styles*, pp. 48–50.

spects as well. Among other things he believed nobody at all, constituted authorities or whatever, had any right to inquire into whatever business agreements he made with others. These were purely private arrangements. But here a tidal wave of history was against him, the history of government and law. To suppose for even a fleeting instant that the operations of a publicly chartered company, doing a large public business, are entitled to be free of scrutiny is surely unrealistic. It was this larger unrealism that got Standard Oil into trouble, very much surprising Rockefeller. All criticism, indeed surprised him, seemed undue.

"Both doubt and dogma rely in an essential way on the narrowed attention and the technical-indicator style of thinking and apprehension of the world characteristic of the obsessive-compulsive. In the case of dogma, this is more obvious. The narrow, rigid attention of the obsessive-compulsive allows him to avoid new information; he regards it not as potentially interesting, but only as potentially distracting. At the same time, his narrow interest in technical indicators allows the dogmatic person to feel completely satisfied with his solutions or, rather, completely satisfied so easily."[16]

As Dr. Shapiro goes on to point out, the restricted interest of the obsessive-compulsive in technical signs and indicators keeps him from seeing things in their true proportions, from absorbing shadings or "recognizing the real substance of the world." He lives with blinkers on. And this Rockefeller did in a very big way.

Hence, too, the obsessive-compulsive's addiction to ritual. For "Ritualistic *interest* depends on a narrowly focused, indicator style of cognition and impairment of the sense of substantial reality."

Thus, if asked whether or not he were a generous man or not, Rockefeller would not be likely to say "I am very definitely a generous man." He would be, along with most of the world, inclined to say: "I *must* be a generous man or I

---

16. Ibid., p. 51.

wouldn't be giving away all this money." In other words, he would assay the act of giving not for what it was, whatever it was, but as an indicator of something else.

Rockefeller's general position was that he was OK but that his critics were not, were mistaken or worse. And he sincerely believed this, an example of the narrowness of his cognition. Many times he said that he had a completely clear conscience. And he undoubtedly did.

Flynn (p. 266) says, "Rockefeller has always found complete shelter for his conscience in legal and business fictions which he has set up to cover the real character of his acts." While it is true that Rockefeller did cite legal and business fictions, and theological ones as well, he did not do this consciously, with intent to deceive as lawyers would say. He did it because he did not believe he could do anything wrong or that anyone could validly evaluate anything he did as wrong legally, morally, or esthetically. It was simply inconceivable to Rockefeller that anything he did could be wrong. For wasn't he a moral man by definition? He could not understand the true character of his acts.

"Whatever I do is right," was his basic position throughout. And in taking and holding to this position, and transmitting it to his family and confidants, Rockefeller just shows how divorced he was from reality.

Or should we say, as Rockefeller probably felt, that the United States Supreme Court in its decision of 1911 was divorced from reality?

Was Rockefeller a bad man, though, in the sense of one planning to do harm and actually doing harm?

Upon a careful reading of the record I think the answer has to be "No." But he was a distorted man, a twisted man, who certainly did a lot of harmful things and eventually balanced them more or less by doing good things and things generally regarded as good. And what is harmful and what is good I take here to be according to standards imposed by the world. People know what they like and don't like although they don't always know why.

10.

The larger significance of this section does not lie in its being a capsuled reprise of the Rockefeller story with a psychiatric interpretation laid on although it is that, too. Everything in this section is significant for this book as showing the origin of the Rockefeller style of operations, the continuing Rockefeller scenario.

Rockefeller gave his descendants more than money and an ambiguous reputation to deal with. He also gave them a *modus operandi*, much of it running into pure serendipity. It is this *modus operandi* or scenario more than the money that keeps the Rockefellers to the fore, and flourishing.

Although, let us never forget, the money helps.

Three

Dynastic Vistas

The Rockefeller scenario unfolds like a Shakespearean or Greek drama depicting men and women tangled in a global web of power—a strong first act projecting the smashing rise and ascendancy of the Standard Oil Trust, an equally strong change-of-pace second act showing the consolidation and exfoliation of that power around the children of the founder (along with their tribulations and triumphs), and a soaring third act tracing the extension of the family power worldwide under the pianissimo touch of grandson David. The fourth and fifth acts are still to come with generations already in the wings. The family is a modern version of the Medici, who in many ways conducted themselves similarly in the fourteenth, fifteenth, and sixteenth centuries. The papacy was then the goal as the presidency is now.

The main characters of the second act are the founder's only son, John Jr.—"Mr. John" as the father tenderly called him— and John's wife, Abby Aldrich, daughter of United States Senator Nelson Aldrich, of 110 Benevolent Street, Providence, Rhode Island. She was schooled on nearby Benefit Street. Abby brought new life—no, life itself—and, perhaps, salva-

157

tion of the spirit, into what until then was a heavily gloomy
Gothic ménage which concentrated on sin, prayers, spoils,
and stratagems although, happily, not treasons. She was quite
literally providential both to her husband and children, a
much needed ray of sunshine in the encircling terror of hell-
fire baptism and psychic dissonance.

The Standard Oil tycoon also had three daughters who survived infancy; another, Alice, died in the cradle. The survi-
vors were Bessie (1866-1906), Alta (1871-1926), Edith
(1872-1932) and, of course, John D. Jr. (1874-1960).

Alta acquired defective hearing through an infection, probably something of a blessing to her as it served to mute the
incessant barrage of elevated precepts that flowed like water
from her mother. In 1901 she married E. Parmalee Prentice, a
high-toned New York corporation lawyer, legal writer, publisher, and gentleman cattle breeder. By him she had three
children—John Rockefeller Prentice, Mary Adaline, and
Spelman.

Bessie, the only daughter to go to college (Vassar), in 1889
married Dr. Charles A. Strong, a professor of psychology. She
died on the Côte d'Azur after a long illness and a stroke.
Newspapers pounced like famished ghouls on the tidbit that
she suffered deathbed delusions of dying poor, a neat "human
interest" twist to news editors of the day. She had a daughter,
Margaret S., born in 1897. So, Strongs and Prentices are num-
bered among The Cousins.

Edith was the only daughter to become enmeshed in dynastic affairs. In 1895 she married Harold Fowler McCormick,
principal heir to the International Harvester Company of Chicago, which the elder Rockefeller had helped form as a trusti-
fied merger of leading companies and in which he had a large
investment, one of his many side bets. A stormy petrel of the
Rockefeller clan, widely regarded as kooky, a trial to her father, she and Harold divorced in 1921 but not before she bore
five children, three of whom survived infancy—Harold Fowler McCormick (1898), Muriel McCormick Hubbard (1902)
and Mathilde McCormick Oser (1905). According to postmor-
tem news reports, her father settled $40 million on her, which

under the speculative ministrations of self-chosen advisors largely, except for trust funds, went down the drain. Her children, of course, are among The Cousins.

Upon the death in 1918 of Mrs. Potter (Bertha Honoré) Palmer, who had been the imperious leader of Chicago High Society, Edith succeeded her as the undisputed queen of the corn-belt *haut monde*. Naturally, like most of the wealthy, Edith traveled about a good deal on the usual deluxe circuit and had come to make Switzerland her foreign headquarters. Somewhere along the line something about her tight Baptist conditioning began to become unraveled, and during World War I she became a patient of Dr. Carl Jung of Zurich, one of the pioneer psychoanalysts who broke away from Freud to set up shop with minor variations on the Freudian themes. Both Jung and Freud treated many distraught American millionaires, who at least could afford the expensive therapy.

Just how much good Jung did Edith is hard to judge. My pure guess is that he at least relieved her of some inner tensions. But, returned to the United States, she seemed more eccentric than ever. What Jung probably accomplished was to open her up, free her of some of the crushing weight of her extremely repressive upbringing. Newspapers in reporting gingerly on this episode said she "studied" under Jung. But the psychoanalyst never had nonprofessional students. She was plainly a patient, and Jung probably learned more than anyone else ever knew about the inner currents in the Rockefeller household.

Edith, as her subsequent conduct showed, saw herself as something other than a dutiful *materfamilias*. A deserving heiress in her own right (as she no doubt saw it), married to the scion of a big Chicago fortune, she proceeded to dominate Chicago "society" functions. She became the chief patroness of the opera and similar affairs—charity balls, parties, art displays, the familiar circuit—and was suitably caparisoned and bejeweled. She always styled herself Edith *Rockefeller* McCormick, not merely Mrs. Harold F. McCormick or Edith McCormick. She wasn't here, she seemed to be saying, simply because a local midget tycoon had married her; she was here as the representative princess of a distant powerful chieftain. As a counterweight to her unquestionably battered ego, she seemed to entertain delusions of intense gentility.

In time, the more she showed herself, newspapers came to hinting that she might be "eccentric," and, finally, that in fact she was eccentric, very eccentric. And this she was. Local gossips dwelt on her quirks. She and her husband obviously didn't hit it off, as the post-Jungian divorce showed. To external observers she was merely a prima donna of money, a spoiled darling of wealth, possibly wacky, but to all who saw advantage in her patronage, her word was as divine law. Among her minor eccentricities was her proclivity for inviting people to a luncheon or dinner and then, at the eleventh hour, canceling the affair. Yet, many were happy to pay her obeisance.

She came to engage in public wrangles with members of her family, notably with her daughter Mathilde, who had fallen in love with a Swiss riding master, Max Oser, and soon married him over her mother's strenuous objections. Edith also dabbled in astrology, wrote song lyrics, and claimed to have cured people of unspecified ailments by means of "synthetic psychology."

The final stanza in one offering of her post-Jungian "Love Song Cycle" was as follows:

The fairest dew of God-made morn
Is frail enough to be the tears
That fall from my eyes, dearest,
Because I cannot see.

Another line ran, "We know through the trust born of love." No Sappho she.

The "Love Song Cycle" was accompanied by rumors that she might marry Edwin Krenn, her Swiss real estate advisor of the Chicago firm of Krenn and Dato, heavily financed by her. Newspaper reporters hotly pursued her for confirmation of these momentous tidings. She eluded them and had a high fence built around her Lake Forest estate where she spent such time as she did not put in at her mansion at 1000 Lake

Shore Drive. She left Krenn 5/12ths of her estate in her will, but, the family opposing this spontaneous flourish with batteries of cold-eyed counsel, Krenn settled for a modest life annuity of $24,000.

But before all this a Swiss newspaper retrospectively accused her of having violated Swiss hospitality back in 1917 by helping an interned French aviator escape. A number of times she was accused of trying to smuggle goods into the United States without paying duty but these slips, understandable in a grande dame, were soon ironed out.

She set up a fund with which to speculate in Chicago real estate, eventually lost money there with the onset of the Depression, and had to be bailed out by her brother, who came to Chicago to reorganize her sadly tangled affairs. Before this denouement, however, she was challenged in a lawsuit by her husband, children, and brother in the matter of having Standard Oil stock dividends from her trust taken as income. Their contention was that they should be treated as capital, which guaranteed their retention.

Mathilde was later reconciled with her mother. Edith's son Fowler, however, provided another field day for the newspapers by marrying Anne Urquhart "Fifi" Stillman, twenty-one years senior to his age of thirty-two, the mother of several children, and a central figure in one of many rousing New York "society" divorce scandals of the 1920s. Fifi's husband, James Stillman, son of the original National City Bank tycoon and himself president of the big bank, accused her on gossamer grounds of fobbing off on him a child fathered in *crim. con.* by a Canadian Indian guide. By all appearances Stillman labored under a delusion. After losing his divorce action he was for a time reconciled with his wife, who then divorced him and immediately, in 1931, married Fowler. And Fowler went on to become a managing officer of International Harvester, of which he became a big stockholder by inheritence.

Edith is the only one of the early-generation Rockefellers I have found who came under the point-blank scrutiny of the psychiatric brethren although her brother John, and her father and mother too, could unquestionably have been greatly relieved of inner tensions by the newly developing techniques of the mental doctors. In the fourth generation there has been freer recourse to the mind doctors.

2.

But the jewel of the oil baron's children was his son—next to, equal to, or superior in his estimation to Standard Oil itself. And Standard Oil was indeed such a darling of his that he almost daily, and publicly, ritualistically invoked the blessing of heaven on it. A favorite crackpot salutation of his to all and sundry on the street in later years was: "God bless you, and God bless Standard Oil."

"Mr. John," however, was one of his few genuine enthusiasms. The only times of which witnesses report any display of emotion in him was whenever he put over a big business deal and when his only son was born. At the latter event he was rhapsodic, beside himself with joy as dynastic vistas opened. In the case of successful business deals, he would smack his hands together, skip a step, and show great elation much as Hitler did upon surveying prostrate Paris for the first time. Otherwise, everybody reports, in public he was usually pretty dour and tight-lipped. At home, with his grandchildren, he often acted the waggish clown, giving some of his family the idea that he had a great sense of humor. He was in fact, despite such intramural foolery, as humorless as a guillotine.

His children, and especially his son, were always closely superintended, monitored, watched over like vault-jewels, tenderly but constantly admonished to assure perfection and, in general, never given the least chance to develop any spontaneity. In consequence Junior was as stiff as a board most of his life and inwardly troubled until advanced in years. As put in his insider's account by Raymond Fosdick, long a trustee of the Rockefeller Foundation and eventually President of Rockefeller's General Education Board, the elder Rockefeller gave his wife "complete credit for the children's training." And trained they were, like a group of performing seals.

She put John Jr. through the same wringer that her husband had been through, but much more thoroughly. For the elder Rockefeller was at least able to cope with the world on its own terms and master it in a big way; his son wasn't.

Mrs. Rockefeller, the mother of John Jr., was directly responsible for the children on a full-time basis, like one of her husband's subordinate officers in charge of a department at Standard Oil. The family head was away most of the time engineering ever-enlarging deals in the multimillions and disputing with investigatory commissions and courts. And Mrs. Rockefeller would not leave anything as important as the children to nurses and governesses.

"She organized their activities and scrutinized their interests, making certain at all times that religion might have the preeminence. And while her goal was clear her methods were not overbearing or dictatorial. 'Never have I heard my mother speak a sharp or petulant word to her husband, her children, or any of her household. Small in stature, frail in body, she had a wonderful will and perfect self-control.' recalled JDR Jr. 'She never coerced; it was not necessary.' As Lucy Spelman [her sister] said, 'There was a persuasion in her touch as she laid her fingers ever so gently on your arm.' Unobtrusively but effectively, she was able to carry out her plans."[1]

In brief, she ran a tender-loving psychic concentration camp for the children, who bore the scars the rest of their lives. And everything she did, let it be fully understood, would have been fully approved by every respectable upper middle-class family head of nineteenth-century United States, and especially by the clergy (although perhaps not by the children of clergy). Fundamentalist morality, self-defined duty, the law as the family lawyers stated it, the Bible and God were all on her side in full force. With such an armament, all wrapped in affection, how could any child defend himself?

Morning began with long-winded prayers. Anyone who came late paid a fine of one cent, and John Jr. at age ten was

---

1. Raymond B. Fosdick, *John D. Rockefeller Jr.: A Portrait*, p. 18-19.

delegated to keep written tabs on recreants, like a recording angel. Money, incidentally (the paternal touch), was always used freely in the household by way of fines and rewards, the carrot and the stick, and in such circumstances inevitably came to have about it a magic quality. Pennies, for example, were doled out to the children for doing household chores (which were insisted upon), practicing musical instruments, and performing in various other presumably edifying ways; nothing, apparently, was ever done by anyone for its own sake, nor was such performance apparently expected. Fines and payments were written down in special ledgers, and also time worked or practice hours put in, money contributed at church and Sunday School, etc., etc., etc. In other words, John D. through his wife was passing on his bookkeeping and control manias to his children, and both parents were putting the finishing touches on much the same sort of obsessiveness that gripped the sire.

As to this, psychiatrists hold that families transmit through generations similar characters to their children. It is not, as commonly supposed, a matter of similar genes; it is a matter of similar conditioning. Feeling more or less satisfied about their own upbringing, knowing nothing else, parents tend to give the same sort of upbringing to their children they themselves experienced.

All this routine in the Rockefeller household was supposed to "build character"; teach the value of money, or work, and of application; and teach that they were all, despite ever-blessed wealth, common people in the eyes of the Lord. It was all pretty much a repeat, although more efficiently done and amid luxurious cushioned surroundings, of the elder's boyhood in upper New York, part of the enduring Rockefeller scenario. As a foundation of the prevailing Rockefeller family self-appraisal that boyhood itself has magic properties for all time; many unsophisticated people agree in view of the fact that it led to a solid gold rainbow of several billions of dollars.

The Rockefellers, in short, are themselves impressed by the presumed moral validity of the founder's formative experience and impressed by themselves, as impressed as any of their admirers! While insisting they are simple people, so much bottle glass in a Cartier setting, all their words and actions of familial self-veneration—and this stood out several times in Nelson Rockefeller's testimony before a Senate committee bemused over Nelson's nomination to be vice-president of the remarkable United States—strongly imply "How wonderful we really are in our deeply cushioned humility and how well and truly our forebears wrought." One could almost see Nelson gravely genuflecting to the reflected image of his family as he referred to it several times as an especially lofty affair, its judgments to be feared by its members.

On Sunday evenings Mrs. Rockefeller, always busy, busy, busy at being a model Christian mother (working the other side of the street from her husband out in the corporate world), gave her children solemn home talks, usually "quietly exhortative, more practical than theological" as Fosdick informs us in his authorized biography of John the Second. But she did not skip theology by any means. She always had the Bible handy to back up her remarks. And one may be sure she did not misquote that tome which contains, no less, the direct word of God.

"The condition of her children's souls was obviously as important to Mrs. Rockefeller as their physical well-being," says Fosdick. "For her, a 'besetting sin' could arouse as much anxiety as a high fever and required the same amount of patient attention." And, children being as they are, loaded with original sin, one may be sure she found in them many besetting sins that required careful and firm extirpation. Christian perfection was her goal. Nothing was too good for a Rockefeller.

"This was the environment by which the younger Rockefeller was enveloped in his early years," Fosdick, an intimate of JDR Jr., vouches. "That it did not suffocate or estrange him, that it sowed no seeds of later repulsion or rebellion, speaks well both for the spirit of independence which his parents instilled in him and for his own growing acceptance of personal responsibility and self-direction."

And in this formulation Fosdick goes straight off the rails, and subjects informed readers to the Pavlov effect—the crossing of signals that induces something akin to a minor nervous breakdown for anyone seriously following the script.

For on the evidence Fosdick himself presents further along, young Rockefeller was in fact if not thoroughly suffocated at least left in a half-strangled, half-drowning condition—certainly crippled. He was not, indeed, estranged, nor were there ever any signs in him of repulsion or rebellion; his natural resources were too sapped by overprotection and zealous overcare for anything like that to happen. But as for any spirit of independence in him, it was slow in showing itself, became only clearly evident, and then modestly, when he reached his fifties. Most of his life he was a good deal like a semirobot directed by remote wireless control, not (to all appearances) even unconsciously striving to free himself of invisible fetters. He was not at all unlike a fly caught on sticky flypaper, hemmed in by corporations and foundations. "In money we trust."

3.

Rockefeller Jr. was born in Cleveland but at an early age was brought to New York City, first living with his family in hotel suites and then in the heavily gloomy longtime family residence on West Fifty-fourth Street, just off Fifth Avenue, the thoroughfare then lorded over by the Vanderbilts and other spendthrift butterflies. Family summers were spent on the Cleveland estate, in a large Victorian gingerbread mansion; now and then the family took extended trips, all together.

Young Rockefeller sporadically and briefly attended three nondescript private schools in New York (he never went to public school) but was finally put under an old-fashioned tutor named John A. Browning. Also brought in for tutoring were his cousin Percy, son of John D.'s brother, William, Harold and Stanley McCormick of the McCormick Reaper family, and other young gentlemen. Out of these home-tutoring sessions grew the Browning School, initially set up right on the next block, an adjunct to the Rockefeller home and financed by Rockefeller and his brother. That enterprise became a highly respected standard nonresidential college preparatory school, patronized by the Rockefellers into the next generation. It still exists on East Sixty-second Street.

Among his many compulsions the senior Rockefeller always kept members of his family close by and carefully selected the associates of his children. There were no Huckleberry Finns in Junior's life, no Nigger Jims or Indian Joes, nobody at all to sound a non-Rockefeller note. Various of the parents' in-laws were shepherded into the ultra-Victorian household and also a Rockefeller sister, as family pensioners. As the old man's children married, he kept them either in his household or set them up in separate houses nearby, except for ill-starred Edith, exiled to roaring Chicago. When the oil magnate traveled, everybody went with him, by private railway car in the United States, by suites on ships to hotel suites in Europe. Servants, children, in-laws, relatives—all went along with the always humble and polite *grand seigneur.* The home usually harbored coveys of clergymen, and when Rockefeller traveled he often had along his personal physician and a clergyman. A direct line to God was maintained at all times.

The region of West Fifty-fourth and West Fifty-fifth Streets between Fifth and Sixth Avenues, just north of where Rockefeller Center now towers, in time became very much of an open Rockefeller compound, the homes of relatives and servitors right at hand. And soon the tycoon was to carve out a vast domain of thousands of acres near Tarryton, New York— Pocantico Hills on the Hudson—that remains today a forty-five-hundred-plus acres compound of woods, meadows, and large family houses. It is a perfect billionaire's retreat which today is alone worth a substantial fortune, at least $100 million (and, incidentally, is lightly taxed according to competent researchers of record). It is a princely affair. To this was to be added big houses and vast tracts in Maine, New Jersey, Florida, and elsewhere inside and outside the United States, so as to catch each season precisely in its most agreeable mood. Money, in other words, flowed like Coca-Cola at a Sunday School picnic.

Junior was always a moderately able and concientious student, always got high grades in school and addressed himself at Brown University to solid subject-matter, concentrating mainly in languages and the humanities. But, as many who knew him later testified, he was extremely inhibited, stiff, and was well aware that he felt ill at ease with others, abnormally so. He chose to go to Brown because some of his family-picked familiars at the Browning School were going there. He was indeed very self-conscious and shy, insecure internally, and always would be, unquestionably the consequence of his having been constantly corrected and admonished by his mother. Junior, one would say today, had an enormous inferiority complex, and would never get rid of it. All his life he wore his self-consciousness like a hair shirt. It always bothered him.

As to similarities and differences between him and his father, both were obsessive-compulsives. Whereas Rockefeller senior received very close attention from his mother because he was the first boy, Junior came in for much the same overtreatment because he was the only boy, the jewel beyond price, the being who was to be guided at once toward instant perfection. But whereas there were wide later gaps in the maternal overzealousness that the elder experienced, Junior was subject without letup to maternal overzeal. The elder could develop his own form of aggressiveness along with his compulsiveness, but the younger was forced by always tender pressure into complete submissiveness. The younger would accept some of his father's compulsive rituals but not the acquisitive ritual. We see here then, from what is known on other grounds, that while one can readily create an obsessive-compulsive, one cannot as easily determine just what rituals he will feel comfortable with.

Junior met Abby Aldrich in his second year at college, from which he was graduated in 1897 with the Phi Beta Kappa award for scholarship. This last may have come to him in part, as with Nelson later at Dartmouth, because of the family's wealth. At any rate, that year some other students at Brown refused the award on the ground that its value had been lowered by giving it undeservedly to Junior. Big universities, always money-hungry, then as now weren't always squeamish about what they did to blandish potential donors. But it was not until 1901, after seeing Abby off and on many times and traveling to Europe with her and her family, that he got around to proposing marriage, which took place the same year. He proposed, though, only after long hesitation and painful soul-searching and finally—naturally—seeking the advice of his mother about it.

"I remember the situation as if it were yesterday," he told Fosdick. "She laughed and said, 'Of course you love Miss Aldrich. Why don't you go at once and tell her so?' "

And, like a good little boy, he did, and he and Abby were married in a gala affair with champagne served although he had prissily asked that the dangerous substance not be offered. Happy about it all, eight months later he nevertheless anxiously wrote to his mother: "And now, Mother dear, you who saw so clearly and even before I did [*sic*] what was right and best for me to do, who helped me so sweetly and lovingly with my doubts and uncertainties, is your judgment corroborated and do you feel that Abby is the best wife for me imaginable? Do you know you have never really told me what you thought of her."

In her reassuring reply his mother said, among other things, "You have made no mistake." She might well have said, "I have made no mistake." Nor had she. Abby had passed the Rockefeller test! Junior's lingering doubts were resolved.

Young Rockefeller, always markedly shy, self-effacing and unself-assertive, induced in everybody he came into direct contact with (who has left a record) the feeling that he was just splendid, a wonderful person. For a person like that poses no personal threat to anybody, raises no hackles. He concedes at once to what in ordinary encounters a more normal person might legitimately dispute or attempt to modify. Junior constantly deferred to his wife as to his mother—indeed, to everyone.

Many stories are told on the record, always admiringly, of how "democratically" unassertive he was, but the prize concerns a visit he paid to Versailles in his mature years, in 1927.

Junior had put up heavy money to restore the then-crumbling French monuments of Versailles, Fontainebleau, and Rheims Cathedral, and in 1927 paid a visit to inspect the renovated Versailles, as Fosdick narrates. But he arrived just at 4 P.M., as the gates were closing. Upon being told by a guard that it was too late to be admitted, he at once, without a word, returned to his car and motored back to Paris. But someone had recognized him from a distance, and soon frantic officials were after him at his hotel to apologize, and newspapers blazed headlines with the story. The idea of an American multimillionaire allowing himself to be turned away like a nobody, without protest, when he had given more than $2 million for the restoration, staggered people, brought an avalanche of commendation for such saintly humility, such a show of democratic equality.

But the story can be interpreted in quite another way, as an exercise in undue self-abnegation, hardly normal. Commendable as it may be to demand no special treatment because of one's position, the issue in this case was trivial; it injured nobody in the world if he or anybody else had talked his way in after hours—no harm done. And the avoidance of harm to others is what morality is all about. But, brought up on moral absolutes, Rockefeller did not see it this way. Beyond this, if it was his idea to seek no special privileges over others, he already existed in a special position of overprivilege, based on large-scale illegal overreaching of which he was the prime beneficiary. To be consistent with his act of self-denial about entering Versailles after hours, he should have joined millions of others in the lines at employment offices. And something that is overlooked by the gratified tellers of this tale is that Junior may have obtained satisfaction, a touch of masochistic pleasure, out of denying himself entrance. Far from seeing it as a commendable act, I, on the basis of the story as commonly presented, think he was just being silly, playing a little game with himself. Of course, while seeing not the slightest merit in the act, democratic or otherwise, I see no harm in it.

A similar story from some years later, over which the newspapers also tore their hair in ecstasies, concerned the building of Rockefeller Center. As the deep placements for the foundations were being dug out of solid rock, boardings were placed at sidewalk level around the excavations. Junior one day stopped to peer through a crack at the work in progress and a nearby workman said something like, "Move along, Jack; you can't stand there." Instead of turning to the man with a smile and saying, "Look, Buster, this is my project, and I'm sure you won't mind if I have a peek," Junior meekly turned without a word and trotted off. Such simple confrontations were too much for him.

But the Rockefeller dander was now up, and the world was going to hear about all this. On returning to his office and possibly discussing the subject thoroughly with a staff member, Rockefeller ordered that windows be placed at intervals on the boardings so that passers-by might stop and have an unimpeded look. The name of Sidewalk Superintendents Club was given by some inspired wag to such watchers. The newspapers reported heavily on this new wrinkle, this bold defiance of invisible powers-that-be who brutally decree that people may not watch excavations through cracks. Junior had struck a clear blow for freedom! And although the idea was copied here and there, it has since gradually fallen into disuse. The public obviously finds it more fun to peer furtively through cracks. There are, in the opinion of pundits, profound psychological reasons for this.

Junior was like this all his life. On the one hand he acted, mostly in minor matters, according to a set of stultifying moral absolutes derived from a highly dogmatic religion and on the other hand he had zero self-esteem, as is clear from his wife's letters to their children away at school as reported by Mary Ellen Chase in her *Abby Aldrich Rockefeller* (1950). She wrote to one: "Your father is so modest, so unassuming, and often so doubtful of his own ability that I wonder if you always realize what a tower of strength he is to me and to us all." In another letter she wrote: "Your father is so wonderfully thoughtful himself and so considerate of all the people with whom he comes in contact that I am sure he must occasionally find the rest of us somewhat difficult." Abby all her life was one of her husband's biggest fans.

So low, indeed, was Junior's sense of self-esteem, as low or lower than that of competitors who had been battered out of existence by Standard Oil, that it was noticeable to all who knew him. Fosdick records a letter written to Junior by a college chum in 1898 in which the writer carefully analyzed the oil scion with a view to stressing his various personal strengths. The writer found he had good judgment, capacity, industry, but that he was "altogether too grumpy, too morose and gloomy . . . you are thinking too much of yourself not *selfishly,* you understand, but introspectively. . . . I truly think if would do you good, for instance, to take up smoking an occasional cigarette, or something of that sort. I am not joking. Just try being a shade more reckless, or careless as to whether or not you reach perfection within five years, and see if you don't find more happiness." The correspondent went on to say that the "fault is that you are comparing yourself with your father and Mr. Gates all the time instead of with those of within five or ten years of your age."[2]

Well meant though the advice was, it was ventured on the basis of inadequate knowledge of psychic operations. What ailed young Rockefeller was not something easily removed by minor rearrangements of his life. If he was to transcend his conditioning, he was as much in need of expert psychotherapy as his sister Edith.

Later that same year Junior wrote to Harold McCormick, now Edith's husband, and referred to "my own incompetency," which he always felt keenly—and mistakenly. For he was far from incompetent. But Junior, the envy of the world because of the money he was heir to, always felt like a midget among giants, always measured himself and found himself wanting. But this sort of constant self-measurement is in itself neurotic. One is whatever one is, and if one happens to be a genius, certainly little credit for it devolves upon oneself.

One doesn't know as much, or from as many different sources, about the junior Rockefeller and others of the money-heavy clan as about the old man. But on the basis of what is

---

2. Fosdick, *op. cit.,* pp. 88-89.

reported by intimates, much of it set down naively without understanding its inward meaning, it is clear that Junior, unlike his father, was completely subservient to all authority, a trait derivative from his childhood vassalage to his mother. And from her, of course, he derived the unshakable conviction that his father was a very great man. And not only had she instilled in him a harsh Calvinistic conscience but also, in the jargon of the psychiatrists, a dictatorial super-ego. Between the demands of his strict super-ego (autonomic conscience) and his normal animal inclinations, his ego, the autonomic executive of the conscious personality, was inevitably battered. Rather than being twisted like his father's, his personality was instead flattened. Neither of the Rockefellers, it would seem, did anything they did, whatever it was, on the basis of autonomous rational choice. They acted as they did because of unconscious and irresistible motivations although their actions were very different. They were, as much as anyone can well be, robots.

At the root of young Rockefeller's actions was a constant low-grade fear—fear of people, fear of himself, fear of his own judgment, fear of his parents, fear of public opinon. Although not so intense as to paralyze him completely, his fear was intense enough to keep him functioning in as much of a pattern as his father functioned in. Both men, looked upon by the world as bold planners and kings of the jungle, men who knew precisely what they were doing at all times, were really confused, bewildered, and groping their way in the world—always, of course, with a lot of wealth ready at hand. Neither one really knew, from moment to moment, where he was headed or, as some might say today, what it was all about. Both, though, knew they were on a giant roller coaster which they could not get off nor stop even had they wanted to. Hence the need at every step for advisors, and more advisors, who were more farseeing and who knew the answers to simple as well as knotty questions.

One of Junior's concrete difficulties, in the light of his instilled claim to unusually high moral rectitude, was the family fortune and the increasingly known shady ways in which it had been acquired. What he came to do about this in time, never relinquishing the high principles, was a compromise. He diminished the fortune somewhat by "gifts," which turned out anyhow, whether foreseen or not, to be self-serving; and he trimmed demonstrably on the lofty principles. He did not choose resolutely to go in one direction—to follow the "public be damned" attitude of the other tycoons or to turn his back on the fortune, enter a monastery, and spend the rest of his life on his knees in prayer. He wanted, as most people do, to have his cake and eat it too, proving only that he was not an exceptional individual, not in any sense "bad" or a hypocrite.

4.

Immediately after his graduation from Brown University, Junior's father introduced his beloved only son to an office at 26 Broadway, headquarters of the trust, where he was put under the tutelage of the hardheaded and imaginative Frederick T. Gates, one of the few people to whom the now sorely beset trust-builder had learned to defer without serious question. There had never been any question of the son's having any choice in the matter of vocation. He was, in fact, conscripted into the family enterprise. A year later Junior, the recent undergraduate, was made a trustee of the University of Chicago. He was soon also made a director of a long string of huge corporations: the Missouri Pacific Railroad, the Standard Oil Company of New Jersey (later he was a vice-president), the National City Bank of New York, the Manhattan Railway Company, the Colorado Fuel and Iron Company, the American Linseed Company, the United States Steel Corporation, the Delaware, Lackawanna and Western Railroad, and others. There can be no doubt the old man intended him to step into his own corporate shoes.

In time, also, he was brought on to the boards of the emerging Rockefeller philanthropic enterprises—the Rockefeller Institute for Medical Research (now a graduate university aimed pretty much at producing prospective Nobel laureates), the General Education Board, the Rockefeller Foundation, and others.

As to the corporate boards, putting apparently unbriefed young Rockefeller—who most enjoyed being a conventional Sunday School teacher at the Fifth Avenue Baptist Church— among the directors was much like installing with instant high rank a particularly callow novice Boy Scout on a first-class military high command, and in time of war to boot or, if one prefers, like putting a convent-bred virgin into a postgraduate bordello catering to jaded connoisseurs. In time he just felt very uncomfortable and unhappy, as almost anyone in his position would. For in this sphere was where planning took place to separate the general citizenry from their money. But it all shows in another way just how unperceptive his father was —the battle-hardened field marshal of narrow vision. No doubt the father had private talks with the son. But these could not have been very revelatory. Nor did they serve to motivate the young man along either business or Standard Oil lines.

Young Rockefeller soon was complaining that as a director he was required to assent to various group decisions for which he didn't feel able to accept personal responsibility, thereby showing he misread the function of a company director. In that post one's jurisdiction is narrow and specialized: one chooses and appraises the officers, keeps a close eye on the balance sheet, and questions the officers only if the balance sheet turns sour or the company encounters, or seems likely to encounter, an unusual volume of public flak. It is once again like the pilot flying a plane by instruments. One watches only the indicators and does not worry about the effect of the plane's exhaust on the environment or question the validity of ferrying groups of nitwits at high cost from here to there. If the hands way down below are suffering, one doesn't directly know it. Anyhow, it's not one's concern. Can one make an omelet without breaking any eggs?

Junior resigned from the National City Bank board in 1902 on the ground of inability to accept responsibility for blank-check decisions and by 1910 had gradually relinquished all directorships except, fatally, one—the Colorado Fuel and Iron Company. He was not emotionally equipped for the savage cut and thrust of the higher business world.

Young Rockefeller in time felt in far more congenial company with the top personnel of the universities, institutes, foundations, and other philanthropic boards, but here too his ego was further unnecessarily depressed. For his associates now, although more genteel than the business gentry, were top scientists, educators, and wide-ranging social thinkers, all dealing with really high-level stuff. Whereas the father had always kept himself defensively surrounded by Baptist clergy, Junior from now on was to surround himself with university presidents and the like. Yet the young man was in this quarter also out of his depth for a long time, and his self-esteem could not have been bolstered by his close association with such expert operators. In this quarter it was as though he were in a continuous postgraduate seminar on the major problems of mankind and the world, enough to leave any groundling breathless.

All of young Rockefeller's corporate and institutional experience from 1897 to 1913, it should be noticed, was gained amid the rising public clamor against Standard Oil, his father, and the trusts in general. Thrust suddenly into an arena he did not understand, without any special coaching from his doting but insensitive father to armor him, he found himself in a public battle-royal of the passions. And a battle, it soon turned out, his side was losing. And, furthermore, one in which the watchwords of the opponents were the very ones he had been taught by his mother and the Bible. Right, it appeared—at least from court decisions, pronouncements of writers, independent clergymen, and editors, findings of government agencies, and the thunderings of the then president of the United States—was all on the other side. No doubt all the public outcry had much to do with young Rockefeller's abrupt resignation of his corporate directorships—except the fatal one.

Whether young Rockefeller read Henry Demarest Lloyd or Ida Tarbell is not known. Fosdick mentions neither, nor does he mention the verbally fiery President Theodore Roosevelt. But as the newspapers of the day were full of the stuff, Junior had to be deaf, dumb, and blind not to get some idea of the complaints. Despite old man Rockefeller's calm public demeanor through it all, the clamor unquestionably must have been very disturbing to the Rockefeller household. Very.

The neat precepts Junior had absorbed from his mother and assorted clergymen were certainly not a good guide for the roughhouse world he found himself in. And the fact that his father had done nothing adequate to prepare him for it certainly showed the narrowness of the father's perception. In Baptist circles, it was apparently the same with "business" affairs as it was with the subject of sex: nothing was ever said about it. One had to find out the hard way. But young Rockefeller never altered his high opinion of his father, which was always (on the record) the standard one of a boy of about five —that his father is the greatest man in the world. And Junior would never accept from anyone the least disparaging word about the elder. Fosdick vouches for the story that hard-bitten James Stillman, president of the National City Bank, on a visit to 26 Broadway early in young Rockefeller's career, passed some unflattering remark about the elder Rockefeller. "Mr. Stillman," JDR Jr. exclaimed excitedly, jumping up, "you can say those things to my father, but you can't say them to his son. Good day!" To the younger Rockefeller his father was always a perfect hero. The emotional bond between the machinelike father and his hypersensitive son, although they rarely broached intimacies, was extremely strong.

The father posed no objection to his son's withdrawal from the hard-nosed corporate world, told him to do whatever he thought right, although Archbold and other officers of Standard Oil were perturbed. Possibly the old man was also. Archbold and the others wanted to use young Rockefeller, as he saw it, as a convenient screen for their own murky operations, allowing him to take the blame or put up the defense for anything that went amiss. JDR Jr. virtuously would not allow himself to be so used, apparently failing to see that the operations of the others were also for his own ultimate financial benefit. While those men might indeed be lice, they were going to be, through the beneficent operation of the laws of inheritance, *his* very own lice. As it seems to me, if he was going to take the money they schemed to make in devious ways, he owed them commendation. There seems to have been some confusion here.

But young Rockefeller, in seeking to retain his self-image of towering rectitude, kept the one directorship he should have divorced himself from, Colorado Fuel and Iron. And it was possibly out of deference to Gates that he did so.

Old man Rockefeller had long been a major stockholder in the company (40 percent) but the chairman of the board was L. M. Bowers, an uncle of Gates; the president was J. F. Welborn; and the superintendent, E. H. Weitzel. These hard-boiled types ran the company as they pleased, as a private fiefdom. The board had really little to do with managing the company, and young Rockefeller anyhow was only a dummy director, the son of Mr. Big, as he had been all along in all the other companies. He never visited the company properties and knew nothing about conditions on them. In fact, sheltered by his family, he knew little about the blood-and-guts world. For the benefit of the uninformed, if any such have strayed this far, it is entirely possible to be a director of a company and know little or nothing about it. It often so happens in many companies and organizations that certain directors and sponsors are present only as figureheads, dummies.

But on September 23, 1913, about nine thousand desperate miners in the southern Colorado coalfields went on strike over the issue of being allowed to join the United Mine Workers of America, a union. They had lost a strike over the same question in 1903-04. This latest walkout was to last for fifteen months, steeped in blood, and Colorado Fuel and Iron was the major company in the area.

The company management, practically autonomous as far as any outside direction was concerned, amoral as corporate operators usually are, was adamantly opposed to the objective of the strikers. Working conditions were bad, wages low and hours of labor long, as indeed they were throughout most of American industry contrary to all doctored reports of the Unit-

ed States being a high-wage country. It never was this except
in certain special areas, and for limited times, after World War
II.

At Colorado Fuel, as at many other companies, degraded
workers lived in shabby company houses, leased subject to
three-day eviction notices. Purchases had to be made at company stores, where prices were suitably high, quality low.
Moreover, advances against meager wages were paid in scrip
good only at the store. Workers were housed in fenced-off
camps to which entry could be had only through heavily
guarded gates; "undesirables," naturally, were kept out, and
the term referred especially to union organizers and uncontrolled journalists. Armed guards patrolled all about, the
workers' ranks were infiltrated by company spies who reported any sentiments of disaffection, churches and schools were
controlled by the company and independent expression by
them was forbidden. In brief, the whole affair distantly but
distinctly resembled a latter-day Soviet labor camp—all under
the sacred Constitution and the Stars and Stripes! Dissenters
or union members, when detected, were simply expelled,
sometimes after being beaten.

At first young Rockefeller, knowing little or nothing about
the situation, supported the company officers and opposed the
strike. All he knew was what his mentors fed him. And, his
father's men, he trusted them.

On October 17, 1913, an armored car driven by company
deputies drove through a tent camp set up by strikers (they
had had to leave their company houses), shot it up, and killed
several men. The pretext was that men in the camp had directed gunfire at some of the guards. On October 29, the governor
of the state sent in the militia, ostensibly to keep order but
actually to strengthen the hand of the company. Arrests of
workers and union organizers were thereupon freely made,
and many were thrown into jail forthwith without trial or
hearing and held several months incommunicado, Soviet style
or, if one prefers, Gestapo style. The Colorado State Federa-
tion of Labor appealed to Congress to unleash an
investigation.

JDR Jr. was unceremoniously summoned before a congressional investigating committee. There he said that all he could do was to keep in touch with the company officers and trust them to do the right thing. "The moment we believe that their policies are not wise policies, it will be then our next and immediate duty to take the matter up with them." Duty!—one of his favorite words. He naively told the committee he believed 90 percent of the men did not want a strike, favored the company. Blame for the whole affair was placed on "union agitators."

That the management of Colorado Fuel was not acting out of harmony with the elder Rockefeller's thinking is shown by a letter the elder sent to the conspicuously brutal Henry Clay Frick at the time of the Homestead steel strike in 1894. After the Homestead workers were shot down in the suppression of the strike, Rockefeller Senior, as John T. Flynn reports, expressed to Frick approval of his action and pledged his solidarity.

The magnates had a rationale for their low-wage policy. If the men were paid more, they said, they would only waste more of their wages on whiskey, beer, tobacco, gambling, and painted ladies. However, the men worked for their money, so it was morally theirs to do with as they pleased. In the long run, recognizing this, the business community reluctantly conceded a more generous wage policy but now, by means of advertising, cheap goods with built-in obsolescence, and plenty of paid-admission distractions, managed to keep most of the populace poor by another happier route: consumerism. So much for the Affluent Society, smeared with huge slums. Actually, the capitalists go farther than this in accommodation: they charge high interest so that workers can buy ahead of their income on the installment plan. The workers, with nobody to guide them, embrace this salutary method of remaining poor.

"On April 20, 1914," writes Louis Adamic, "either a striker shot a non-union miner or a soldier fired at a striker near the camp outside of Ludlow, whereupon a battle started and soon spread over an area of three miles. About 500 miners were opposed by approximately 200 militia, but the soldiers, many of whom were but recently sworn-in gunmen, were equipped with machine-guns and other superior weapons, which made the strikers' numbers count for nothing.

"Machine-gun bullets riddled the tents; then the camp took fire. 'In the holes which had been dug for their protection against the rifles' fire,' says one contemporary account of the battle, 'the women and children died like trapped rats when the flames swept over them.'

"Thirty-three people were either shot or burned to death. More than half of these were women and children. Over a hundred others were wounded or badly burned."

The Ludlow battle lasted fourteen hours, after which the camp was abandoned and most of the women and children, dead and alive, were taken to Trinidad, while the strikers began to organize into military companies, taking up positions on the hills. Several mine-shafts were attacked and burned. More battles occurred.

The Denver *Express,* not a labor paper though favoring the strike, printed a vivid characterization of the Ludlow slaughter:

> Mothers and babies were crucified on the cross of human liberty. Their crucifixion was effected by the operators' paid gunmen who have worn militia uniforms less than a week. The dead will go down in history as the hero victims of the burned offering laid on the altar of Rockefeller's Great God Greed."[3]

This miniature domestic preview of Vietnam is what is known as "The Ludlow Massacre," which was far worse than the often celebrated so-called "Boston Massacre" of 1775 in which five rioters, palpable hoodlums and layabouts, were killed. John Adams, no less, defended the accused British officer, who was acquitted by a local jury. There was in fact no "massacre" at Boston; the designation was a canard dreamed up by Paul Revere. (And many of the alleged grievances of the

---

3. Louis Adamic, *Dynamite: The Story of Class Violence in America,* pp. 259-60.

colonists against Great Britain were of the same tenuous order. The sole solid issue of the American Revolution was who was to manipulate the populace, absentee Britons or ambitious American politicos and major native property owners.)

As to Ludlow, a congressional investigating committee found that the attacks on the workers were "unjustifiable." As a matter of simple fact, Americans have experienced an astronomically greater percentage of indignities and violence from their own bipartisan officialdom, *mutatis mutandis,* than they ever experienced at the hands of British officialdom, which is something for patriots to ponder over long and deeply.

President Wilson now ordered in federal troops but before they arrived, a dozen more miners were killed, raising the death toll to forty-five, a figure that does not include those killed on October 17, 1913. The troops disarmed miners and militia. No guards, militia, or troops were killed. It would seem that the miners were exceptionally poor shots. Or did they shoot at all? Who fired first? was one of the boobish questions widely debated. As to this, the intelligent person needs only one guess.

In the United States literally thousands of wageworkers were killed in the struggle for unionization between the Civil War and the first inauguration of Franklin D. Roosevelt, to say nothing of those killed later. Almost none of this had any connection with the Rockefellers. Actually, on the industrial front the country, with the Republican party in the saddle, was in a sporadic state of low-grade civil war throughout that period. So much for freedom of association under the ever-sacred banner of liberty.

But, even in passing, more remains to be said. For with all this antiunion violence as justification, many of the newly risen latter-day unions, especially including the United Mine Workers of America, have comported themselves as high-handedly as did the industrial tycoons and their servitors in office. Power, it is evident, is a heady mixture. In many cases there is little to choose between the industrial tycoons and the present-day labor tycoons, a number of whom are regularly found guilty by dirt-level juries of crimes ranging up to murder. Most of the big unions are totalitarian affairs, the officers installed for life, exactly like Soviet commissars. So-called democracy is nowhere in sight, a pure fantasy of witless ideologues.

The national furor after Ludlow was great; the name of Rockefeller was again lustily denounced from coast to coast. Hostile parades unrolled in New York. The Standard Oil office and the Rockefeller homes in the city and at Pocantico Hills were picketed. Threats of violence against young Rockefeller were freely uttered. A time bomb, apparently intended for young Rockefeller's house, exploded in a tenement, killing four members of the Industrial Workers of the World (IWW) and injuring seven others.

After much stalling and backing and filling, young Rockefeller, or his mentors, made a sudden belated about-face. A special investigator Rockefeller sent to Colorado turned in a report that contradicted management reports. On the recommendation of President Charles W. Eliot of Harvard, a young man named Mackenzie King, later the distinguished prime minister of Canada and always thereafter a standby Rockefeller advisor, was chosen to untangle the situation. King, thoroughly schooled, was a specialist in "industrial relations"— that is, the management of labor.

At King's suggestion a board was set up, composed half of miners' elected representatives, half of company men. Miners' grievances would now be referred to this board, although the company representatives had full veto power. Had it been suggested that such a board would also hear company plans for the business as well as those of the workers, thereby giving the workers' representatives veto power over business proposals, the operators and top stockholders would have died laughing. The miners voted to terminate the strike in December, 1914.

So that was that.

But young Rockefeller, far from admitting the true inwardness of the situation, clung to his high moral stance. During the strike, Rockefeller before a subcommittee of the House of Representatives, maintained that he could not accede to unionization because "our interest in labor is so profound and we believe so sincerely that that interest demands that the camps be open camps, that we expect to stand by the officers at any cost." If Rockefeller believed this was his motivation, then, as people commonly do, he lied to himself.

A little later, to an offer of the union simply to call off the strike and waive unionization in favor of negotiating about improving conditions, Rockefeller replied: "We cannot enter into negotiations of any character with the officers and agents of the United Mine Workers of America, who alone are responsible for the terrible reign of disorder and bloodshed, which has disgraced this State. Instead of it being our duty to do so, we conceive it to be the duty of the U. M. W. of A., who called the strike, to now call it off."

Labor, it appears, has many friends in the crunch: employers, union officials, and radicals of the left deployed in libraries and underground printshops, awaiting D-Day. Labor's true position, at all times and places, is that of a bone over which a pack of dogs is fighting. No matter how the fight turns out, one of the dogs is going to be left gnawing the bone. If I am wrong in this observation, let someone show me the jurisdiction, worldwide, where labor is either top dog or even-Steven. Labor fared badly under the thumbs of the industrialists. But American labor does not fare much better under union officials who, among other things, regularly now, among other misdeeds, mismanage and rifle union pension funds. Further left looms the Soviet alternative: the Gulag Archipelago. Everything appears to be very far this side of Paradise.

The experience was a firsthand eye-opener for young Rockefeller, rousing him from the dreamworld of theoretical morality in which he lived. Upon King's advice he made a trip to the Colorado region, fraternized with the miners and their families, visited their homes, attended dances with them. He was, naturally, a big hit, as anyone at all from on high would have been. The lower classes are always enchanted by visits of higher-ups and would welcome Hitler, Genghis Khan, Stalin, Nero, and Caligula equally with Jesus, Buddha, Mohammed, or Jerry Ford, Calvin Coolidge, Chester Arthur, or Lydia Pinkham. Anything for a diversion in a drab existence.

Young Rockefeller, now in his forties, was to be thereafter guided between King and Gates. Aging Gates, however, did not approve of Rockefeller's conciliatory attitude before congressional committees, during which he was raked over the coals but kept his composure. Young Rockefeller now became a public advocate of better treatment of industrial workers, via company unions, much to the disgust of old-line industrialists.

Was young Rockefeller's new attitude purely a facade? I don't think so even though it didn't extend so far, wasn't so "radical," as to concede the right to independent unionization. Fosdick convinces me at least that Junior genuinely but helplessly sympathized with the lower elements who tried, under difficult conditions, to keep their heads above water in a troubled world. But he was much in the position vis-à-vis the lower orders of a thoroughly healthy person making a tour of a hospital for terminally ill cases. What could he do except bring flowers and candy and empty words of sympathy? Or set up a new first-aid station?

He certainly could not, alone, alter the attitudes of other inheritors of great wealth or of the voracious newcomers among preening "self-made" men. Nor could he alter the attitudes of politicos or ambitious brass-knuckle labor leaders. Above all, he had no cure for the incurable diseases of inherent weakness, inability to acquire a skill, ignorance, gullibility, fanaticism, and situation-induced dementia. No doubt he looked into various schemes for bootstrap salvation and found them wanting, as indeed all of them are. Not at least until the second coming of Christ will everything be OK for everybody. The simple reason for this is that the human condition is laced with too many skewed variables. All those offering surefire solutions are simple quacks.

But Colorado Fuel was not his only trouble on the labor front. There was a strike at the Bayonne, New Jersey, refinery of the Standard Oil Company of New Jersey in 1915, hastily settled by Junior and King. King was then turned loose on all the Rockefeller companies, Standard Oil and various others. His remedy was always—a company union. The twelve-hour day, seven-day week had long been conventional in Standard

Oil as well as other industrial companies, and was to remain in force into the 1920s.

As recently as 1922 Robert S. Lynd, the sociologist who was later to attain fame with his *Middletown* study (which the Rockefellers financed) wrote in *The Survey Graphic* about bad conditions at the Elk Hills, Wyoming, property of Standard Oil of Indiana, where the twelve-hour day, seven-day week prevailed. Junior, now sager, wrote to Lynd, agreeing with him. In 1924 young Rockefeller wrote to his father that the conditions at Vacuum Oil Company were also "distinctly bad." The men at Vacuum had just walked out. Junior's agents also reported that conditions at Consolidation Coal, International Harvester, Western Maryland Railroad, and other companies in which the Rockefellers had important minority interests also needed attention, lest there be more trouble. In other words, labor conditions had not been as great at Standard Oil as many writers report.

In the end Junior caused to be formed Industrial Relations Counselors, Inc., designed to educate management in the handling of labor. By this time Junior was committed to the view that capital and labor were partners—but not, in the event, equal partners. Fosdick lavishes great praise on Rockefeller Jr. for his greatly changed attitude. But his new accommodating mood was not gained autonomously, by excogitation. It was gained, by him as well as other large industrialists, only because it had now been demonstrated that the workers would no longer put up with whatever was offered, which was never very much. If labor was going to be treated in the old way, it was now clear, it would have to be at the point of the bayonet. And that would not look very tidy.

5.

In the meantime the elder Rockefeller, who was seventy-one in 1910, had been conveying stocks and bonds regularly to his son, a policy he began soon after the son finished college. By 1924 most of the fortune had apparently been transferred to the younger man. For in that year, according to general tax figures made public in 1925 by act of Congress, the younger Rockefeller paid no less than $6,279,669 in income taxes and the older man paid only $124,266. What they owned in tax-exempt stuff, God alone knew. At his death in 1937 the father would have in his name only $26-plus million, a comparative pauper.

The anguished outcries of the wealthy at having the amazing proportions of their opulent incomes disclosed—not that very many citizens took note of the disclosures or were unduly perturbed—led Congress to close off this source of eye-opening information after two years. The disclosures, it was complained, made the wealthy the targets for all sorts of annoying crackpot solicitations. This just wouldn't do.

There can be no doubt, though, that young Rockefeller, within the conditions brought to him by inheritance, was trying to be a good citizen. But in so trying he was forced to attempt the roles, simultaneously, of Croesus and Francis of Assisi. His problem boiled down to this: how to "give away" wealth, or divorce himself from it, and yet remain wealthy. How he solved this problem we shall come to anon.

In all these years there was often gleefully quoted against the Rockefellers the biblical verse, *Matthew,* 19:24, that "It is easier for a camel to go through the eye of a needle, than for a rich man to enter into the kingdom of God." It is at least difficult, everything considered, for a rich man to enjoy the confidence and friendship of the generality of his fellow men. But the Good Book, like Supreme Court decisions, is filled with quotations that point in divergent directions. For in line with evidence adduced in Congress *in re* the nomination of Nelson Rockefeller, *Proverbs,* 14:20, truly states: "The poor is hated even of his own neighbor: but the rich hath many friends."

And, as opined by blues singer Sophie Tucker, perhaps as nifty a proverb propounder as Holy Testament geezers, "I've been rich, and I've been poor, and believe me, rich is better."

The younger Rockefeller obviously yearned to be respected by the fickle public, and in his later years he was, by and large, at least by the middle classes who absorb facile newspaper interpretations as a sponge does water. Even the elder Rockefeller, believe it or not, wanted to be loved by everybody, respected. His twisted personality, though, as we have seen, made him go about soliciting this affection in bizarre ways.

JDR Jr. finally had his finger in too many pies, most of them loosely characterized as philanthropic, to review here in their entirety. A question that must arise, however, in considering the Rockefeller philanthropic thrust is: why should anyone harbor this professed great love of humanity? Considering the uneven performance of mankind through the ages, might not such love, accepting it as advertised, be somewhat misplaced? Or futile? Or, a darker question, might there not be something involved other than love?

By the 1920s, however, young Rockefeller, many times seared by fire along the way, ambushed by fate, and intensively coached by Gates, Mackenzie King, and others, finally began to feel more at home in his enlarging role of piloting the family fortune to a safe harbor. Actually this was a much more difficult feat than his father had performed in constructing it; it required far more finesse. Most of the elder Rockefeller's effort had been put forth in anonymity and secrecy. For a long time, up into the late 1880s, he was hardly noticed; he was just another plodding old-fashioned businessman. Young Rockefeller, from the start, had to operate in a goldfish bowl. People, catlike, watched Junior's every move—criticized him, denounced him, crossexamined him, insulted him, derided his most innocent actions and mannerisms. The corporate sins of his barracuda father were literally flung into his face.

Many years ago, a taxi driver in New York out of the blue volunteered to me this anecdote, which he told with a great deal of self-satisfaction. He said he had just driven JDR Jr., whom he recognized from news photos, from the midtown area to Pennsylvania Station. "Did he give you a good tip?" I asked encouragingly. Pausing a moment, the cabbie said, "He didn't have the chance. He offered me some money and I said, 'Keep it, Jack, you need it more than I do,' and I drove away."

Junior was fifty years old in 1924, and it was in the years to come that he was, for the first time, to undertake anything really original with him, to make his own mark. No doubt in the earlier years he had some behind-the-scenes guidance from his father, but, according to family intimates, the old man was quite taciturn even with his son. Yet as the father did turn over to him a great deal of unearned wealth, John Sr. earns the stellar position in family annals. His ghost broods over all that his descendants do, for better or for worse.

Junior's first big independent exploit came in the later 1920s with his financing of the costly reconstruction and endowment of Williamsburg, the old colonial capital of Virginia. While this job was concededly attention-arresting, a question might be raised, as with other Rockefeller philanthropies, about its priority. Granting that it should have been done, isn't it a fact that a great many other things were more in need of doing in the United States then and later?

For many years the Reverend Dr. William A. R. Goodwin, chairman of the endowment fund of the time-hallowed College of William and Mary (where Jefferson among other early patriotics had gone to school), had had the vision of reconstructing colonial Williamsburg, once a fine old town that stood to a top-notch modern housing development about as a Stradivarius fiddle does to a machine-made ukelele. The place had quiet class written all over it. But Goodwin was making little progress, and there were enormous problems about acquiring run-down privately owned properties and unsightly business structures that had sprung up with the advent of Progress.

It wasn't until he met JDR Jr. in 1924, and again in 1926, that he made headway. After many consultations and much staff analysis, Rockefeller agreed to back the project, which in view of its reception by the ultrapatriotic element among old-established families, turned out to be a huge success in institutionalized nostalgia. It has since become a standard tourist attraction. Rockefeller and his wife took on the site a modest mansion, Bassett Hall, where they subsequently passed much pleasant time. As photographs show, it is a vine-embraced storybook dream house.

As of 1956, Fosdick reports, 720 latter-day buildings were

moved or torn down, 82 eighteenth-century structures were restored, 404 were reconstructed on their original foundations, and 83 acres of eighteenth-century gardens reinstalled. The cost of the whole affair was up around $100 million.

Apparently this venture whetted Rockefeller's appetite for more construction because soon after he conceived the idea for mammoth Rockefeller Center, his first independent venture on a large scale into the stormy seas of profit making. Before continuing, however, one should note that in addition to being organizers, and good ones, the Rockefellers are also builders, sometimes *manqué.*

The old tycoon had liked to lay out walks and buildings on his Cleveland estate. He gave full rein to this proclivity in constructing Pocantico, going so far as having a railroad line moved at great expense eastward, buying out a college on the location, and thereafter laying out walks, drives, groves, gardens, and planning and locating buildings. Junior at an early age took over the chore, which he enjoyed, of superintending these intrafamily operations, even designing some of the newer family houses, and right after leaving college was pretty much the family factotum. So Junior was continuing, while expanding, this intrafamily activity.

Nelson while at Dartmouth College became interested in architecture, thought of becoming an architect, and as governor of New York State gave full rein to his ambitions in the way of construction by having erected a large number of enormously expensive (to the taxpayers) and grandiloquent public buildings, roads, and other structures—so much so that some acidulous observers likened him to a modern pharaoh. Nelson's father, though, had financed other enterprises in the building line: the Cloisters, a massive reproduction of a medieval monastery that functions as a museum on upper Manhattan; the huge United Nations Library in Geneva, Switzerland; the Palestine Archaeological Museum in Palestine—the rebuilding of the ever-memorable Stoa in Athens; and so on. Laurance, Nelson's brother, is an indefatigable builder of far-flung luxury hotels, resorts, and apartment complexes.

As I am only touching the high spots in this disquisition, it would be disproportionate to list all the libraries, universities, colleges, museums, and medical institutes to which JDR Jr. conveyed heavy money all over the world. The list ranges pretty much from A to Z. In addition he funded International Houses for students at American and European universities, deeded enormous tracts of land for a number of national parks, and put up $8.5 million for land along the East River for the United Nations—a gesture, made at Nelson's suggestion, that brought the UN to New York City (and its account to the Chase Bank). For details of these and many other instances of public largess, the reader should consult Fosdick. For their significance, see Chapter Five.

But Rockefeller Center was unquestionably his *chef d'oeuvre,* standing today at a conservative valuation of $1 billion gross and, as a switch from the nonprofit contributions, a big money-maker. It is unquestionably the most gigantic private real-estate development in the world.

6.

Rockefeller Center began as an idea for an opera center in 1928. It is a city within a city, now consisting of a giant collection of twenty-one huge contiguous buildings, most of them skyscrapers, with many similar non-Rockefeller structures now rising around it (thereby enhancing regional values all around). Because the old Metropolitan Opera House, built in 1883, was deemed obsolete, it was proposed that what is now Rockefeller Center be devoted to a new opera house and a vast public square.

Junior Rockefeller was definitely interested, but the plan had to be shelved owing to dissent among factions in the Metropolitan Opera Association. But Rockefeller's interest in the region had been fixed.

The tract in the very long block from Fifth to Sixth Avenues, and from Forty-seventh to Fifty-first Streets, was originally British crown land, conveyed to the city after the War for Independence. The city leased it in 1802 to Dr. David Hoosac for use as a "public Botanic garden." The doctor was the man who attended the dying ultrapatriotic Alexander Hamilton after his duel with Aaron Burr, vice-president of the United States (a predecessor of Nelson Rockefeller), the most attention-getting man-to-man gun-battle in American history. In 1811 Dr. Hoosac, financially squeezed, sold his interest to the state of New York for $75,000. Three years later the state conveyed the property to Columbia College by way of giving aid to education. In 1823 Columbia received in rent for the tract $125 and taxes, and in 1826 received $500. But a hundred years later the college, now a university, received in rents more than $3 million a year even though it had by then sold the Fifth Avenue frontages at high prices. All the increment came from the growth of the city, the input of anonymous people whose value-input was captured.

Most of the region was now filled with old four-story brownstone buildings that harbored stores, shops, delicatessens, lunchrooms, speakeasies, and apartments, many of them desirable in the eyes of semi-affluent bohemian elements.

In late 1928 Rockefeller decided to buy or lease all of this with a view to providing a new home for the opera. When the opera project collapsed, Rockefeller decided to go ahead on his own. As the Great Depression was gathering ominous impetus, he seemed shortsighted to proceed in that unpropitious time, but, as the years were to demonstrate, he was just the reverse—or lucky. For everything was now cheaper and, for Rockefeller, capital was abundant as breadlines proliferated over the land. From the start, however, he was derided as foolish.

Architects and builders were mobilized, prospective big tenants were sought out, and a committee of art and architectural experts was assembled. The three initial tenants were the Radio Corporation of America, the National Broadcasting Company, and the Radio-Keith-Orpheum Corporation. The latter went under in the Depression and so had to be counted out. The lease for the university land required $3 million annually, other land was bought, enormous expenses were incurred in demolition and construction costs. It is said that

225,000 persons were employed, directly and indirectly, in erecting the first barrage of mammoth structures, thus bringing manna to as many deserving God-fearing families.

The place included two opulent theaters. One, the Music Hall, is the largest indoor theater in the world. It could have been the home of the opera but has instead been devoted to showing leading films along with a stage show accompanied by a large orchestra. It has always until recently been heavily patronized by a diversion-addicted public. The other, the much-smaller Center Theater, for some years featured excellent minor opera companies, ballets, and musical shows but was discontinued. Its space is now filled with offices and boutiques. There is also a very small film theater.

In order to develop new tenants, the Center created the British, French, Italian, International, and other special buildings, and brought in many corporations and banks to take office space and even whole buildings. While many of the structures have stores facing the street, below them all is an interconnected maze of shops, stores, and restaurants. The Center contains just about everything, including doctors, dentists, barbers, beauticians, except a hotel; but many leading hotels, some of which the Rockefellers helped finance, are close by. Connected with it underground is the massive New York Hilton, in which the Rockefellers initially had a participation. A nightclub, the Rainbow Room, is on a top floor of the soaring RCA Building, a "must visit" place in New York.

As the Center in its first or chrysalis phase was finished in 1934, the depth of the Depression, there was doubt about getting tenants; but Rockefeller ingenuity was equal to the task. Tenants were lured from other buildings with tempting lease offers plus agreements to assume their old leases. Competing landlords complained, filed suits, as they lost people. Many luxury shopkeepers were afraid to venture into the new place at high rents so the Rockefellers made agreements to take a percentage of their gross in lieu of fixed rents. Nelson Rockefeller, recently out of college, was the go-getter renting agent. Rockefeller family headquarters were shifted from 26 Broadway to several upper floors at 30 Rockefeller Plaza.

For a number of years the venture ran at a loss, but at some point the corner turned and from a commercial point of view has been very profitable—in fact, a golden anthill. And since then the Center has greatly expanded, with more buildings added, strung along west of Sixth Avenue (Avenue of the Americas).

But, like all Rockefeller projects, this cathedral of profit ran into criticisms. With the Rockefellers around, those of a critical bent always have something safe to sink their teeth into, thus guaranteeing their claims to critical stature but at the same time avoiding dangerous matters of greater priority such as the antique laws of inheritance by which vast and usually dubiously acquired hoards of wealth are absurdly transferred from people who never did a serious stroke of work in their lives to people who will also never do a stroke of work. At the same time Americans fatuously boast that the United States has abolished titles of nobility; it has merely retained the plenary *substance* of such titles, discarding the words. Still, the Rockefellers, powerful inheritors though they are, amount to only one plutocratic current in the American stream. And, influential though they are, they are only one element in steering the boiling course of American affairs. Let us not forget that there are also the Du Ponts, Mellons, Fords, Pews, and hundreds of other wealthy inheritors. They aren't midgets.

No doubt ornaments of the Establishment, the Rockefellers also serve it, although unwillingly, as a fixed lightning rod. Without someone like the Rockefellers to focus on as scapegoats, people might have to focus on the system itself, an exercise that would bring many cherished myths tumbling about their ears. And people notoriously don't like to see their myths crumbling.

Rockefeller Center (which Junior didn't even want to name after the family) came in for its share of criticism. It was denounced as a tardy example of "1929 elephantiasis," an attempt to surpass the Empire State Building of the Du Ponts. Walter Lippmann called the Music Hall a pedestal to sustain a peanut. *The New Yorker* scoffed at the whole thing by word and cartoon. Lewis Mumford, an anointed architectural critic, referred to the "graceless bulk" of the RCA Building, and so on. Both the *New York Times* and the *Herald Tribune* had many disparaging things to say. "Radio City is ugly. Its exterior is revoltingly dull and dreary" said the *Herald Tribune.* (The first designation of the place was Radio City). "Never can such universal condemnation have been visited upon a great artistic project as that which has been the lot of the suggested buildings for Radio City," pontificated the *Times,* then still in its Ultra-Ponderous Period. "A magnificent and unparallelled opportunity for a great architectural development has not been seized as it should have been. . . .From every source of intelligent appreciation . . . has come a perfect stream of objection, protest, and, one may say, wondering malediction." The editorial also dwelt upon "architectural aberrations and monstrosities."

Considering the totally lackluster structures in which both these newspapers were themselves housed, and the rest of the city, these were indeed weird tidings. But, once again, the Rockefellers weren't asking anybody; like the Politburo, or the pharaohs, they were telling them. And the message was: Rockefeller Center. It is now, *faute de mieux,* generally accepted as a distinctive part of the city, something for people to feel pleased about and to make a hub of their activities. New York revolves around Rockefeller Center.

For the central plaza someone along the line, no doubt an artistic advisor, chose just the symbol of maximum impressiveness. For it is dominated by a giant gilded statue by Paul Manship of Prometheus, light-bringer to the world. In front of the International Building, facing Fifth Avenue, is a huge statue of his brother, Atlas, the ancient god who carried the continent of Atlantis on his shoulders. Whatever one thinks of the symbolism, it is intensely interesting as a self-conception. Not many builders would be able to arrive at the heady notion, either by themselves or through advisors (for they just don't have such high-geared advisors), of constructing their mundane project around the statue of the ancient Greek god of light.

The Center itself, and these decorative touches, brought an

interesting interplay and clash of symbolisms into the region. For across the street stands St. Patrick's Roman Catholic cathedral, dwarfed to the proportions of a wayside chapel by the massive expression of secularism and paganism facing it. Over the main entrance to St. Patrick's, in relatively small enplaqued bronze figures, are Christ and the Twelve Apostles. True, for neither of the represented institutions do the respective symbols have integral significance. The symbols in both cases play the role of figures stuck on a wedding cake.

As soon as one enters Rockefeller Center one is very conscious of being amid Rockefeller order, cleanliness, exactness, symmetry, utility, efficiency. It is Standard Oil all over again, this time in soaring stone and steel. One is now under the eyes of the Rockefeller security force, so that the Center happens to be one of the safest places to walk in the city. In this and many other respects it contrasts sharply with nearby Times Square, a block to the west, awash with rootless, slapdash wanderers, brimming with movie grind-houses, "massage parlors," clip joints, sin dens, half-hour hotels, narcotic depots, fast-food emporiums, low bars, sleazy bookshops, dance halls—pimp-infested, prostitute-ridden, thief-embedded, germ-laden, a Mecca of sordid politically protected profit, very much an un-Rockefellerish affair. In this paradise of the untrammeled democratic id, one can be mugged or stabbed in broad daylight, as the newspapers regularly report. At night, of course, the id, in all its shapes, reigns supreme under garish lights and shadows.

Comparatively Rockefeller Center seems like Paradise.

7.

Eliot of Harvard in 1926 wrote to Gates that the younger Rockefeller "seemed always anxious and troubled." He was, disclaimers by himself and Fosdick to the contrary notwithstanding, indeed always anxious, wondering if he was properly doing his "duty" and accepting his "responsibility" for making the world a better place. Wealth, the Rockefellers all claim, is a "burden." They are merely stewards, servants of humanity.

At any rate, some of them have felt burdened by something. But isn't there at least a touch of inverted megalomania here? For why should, and how can, any individual, no matter how wealthy, assume the unrealistic mission of being responsible for world betterment? The notion itself is neurotic, whether the true or false self-perception of an individual or the program of a political party. The world is too complicated a mechanism, too filled with interlaced variables, to be susceptible to such laid-on "improvement."

Shortly before he died in 1929, Gates wrote of the younger Rockefeller: "I have known no man who entered life more absolutely dominated by his sense of duty, more diligent in the quest of the right path, more eager to follow it at any sacrifice."

Fosdick, in giving a eulogistic summary of Junior's life, frequently uses words like duty, responsibility, indefatigable worker, conscience, perfectionism, absorption in detail, tenacity, humility, modesty, self-deprecation, sensitivity, "this reluctant acceptance of his own worth," reserve, natural reticence, formality, love of privacy. By Fosdick's account, he was a Baptist saint, self-tortured on an invisible rack.

People frequently ask, "Are the rich happy? Are they happier than the nonrich?" "I have always been happy," JDR Jr. asseverated in later life. To his mother he wrote on his fortieth birthday: "It seems to me that no one has ever lived a richer, happier life than I have." He was correct about the richer in its monetary sense, anyhow.

The son of the oil magnate was indeed happy in the same sense that his father was, in the sense of someone who looks over all the common indicators and decides that he *must* be happy because the indicators for happiness all seem to point to 100. But every known psychiatrist would dispute that someone beset by ever-present anxiety can be simultaneously happy. A man as driven as all testimony shows Junior was, driven much as his father was by invisible signals, certainly is not happy in the carefree or contented sense that most people understand the term. That he had his moments of euphoria is undoubtedly true. But a happy person, for one thing, doesn't feel impelled to isolate himself from informal contact with people as the younger Rockefeller did.

So afraid was he of encounters with new people that he restricted his ebullient wife in making contacts. As she wrote home to the children when she and her husband were away on a trip: "Your father is afraid that I shall become intimate with too many people and will want to talk to them, so we generally eat in what I call the old people's dining-room where he feels I am safer"—that is, where he felt safer. But she balanced this observation, like a good wife, with the self-deprecatory reminder that "my enthusiasm for all sorts of people is likely to carry me away."[4]

So she, too, was—shall we say?—somewhat restricted, sheltered.

8.

But the younger Rockefeller, as he grew older, escaped the tight bind that held his father as in a vise. And he, unlike the sire, was at least conscious that something was amiss with him, although he knew not what. For his deliverance from some part of his upbringing, or partial deliverance, he had his wife to thank. The best thing that ever happened to Junior was Abby Aldrich—no doubt about it.

Soon after their marriage, he carefully and gravely explained to her the Rockefeller system of keeping account of all expenditures and suggested that she do this for her household and personal expenditures. To this attempt to bind the gazelle with Rockefeller shackles, she promptly responded: "I won't."[5] Here was probably the first breath of fresh air in his life.

She startled him a few days later by serving notice out of the

---

4. Mary Ellen Chase, *Abby Aldrich Rockefeller*, p. 33.

5. Ibid., p. 28.

blue that if he should ever strike her—the last thing Junior would have ever done—she'd leave him.

Her defiance of his suggestion that she keep accounts just about set the tone of their marriage in the sense that he might suggest but she would not necessarily concur. She was, after all, just as familiar with wealth as he was. And she was far more sophisticated, and easy in her own mind.

Stiff and rule bound as he was, needing to rationalize every move with some elaborate web of principles, his liking for her from the beginning focused on her "unexpectedness," her unpredictable reactions to what he said. She was, in brief, merely spontaneous, not afraid of herself. One can divine that what he experienced, deep in the dungeon of Davison-Spelman conditioning, was a heady glimpse of freedom, which she exemplified. And while he was never completely free of invisible fetters, in time he became more free, happier at least rather than happy. No doubt he saw in his wife something of what Eliza Davison had seen in Wild Bill Rockefeller until he became much too much for her.

Abby Aldrich came from a paternal household of broad interests. Her father, although a devoted corporation man in politics (in the course of which he amassed a substantial fortune trafficking in public franchises) was widely read and intensely interested in art and travel—in brief, in enjoying and expanding himself. He discoursed of books at home and often took his children to Europe to tour the museums and galleries, far from his beginnings as a common grocer and far from the culturally backward United States. The Aldrich household in Providence was filled with gaiety and rollicking spirits, very different from the Rockefeller household; in this difference lay one of its secret attractions for Junior.

Abby brought all her own interests to the Rockefeller menage, which she gradually transformed, passing on many of those interests to her children. The Museum of Modern Art in New York City developed under her special sponsorship.

By Abby, JDR Jr. sired six children, five of them boys. Of the latter, three today more or less rule the Rockefeller roost— David, Laurance, and Nelson.

Except for John D. III, the second born, who is in temperament and personality much like his father, quite a bit of a recluse, none of the children who has come under public scrutiny adheres to the inner Rockefeller pattern however much each may outwardly, on ceremonial occasions, conform to it. The simple reason for this is that they are more like Aldriches than Rockefellers.

The world in looking at the Rockefellers follows the doings of the men. And, outwardly, the Rockefeller story is an all-male show. Inwardly, though, the story is an all-female extravaganza, beginning with Eliza Davison who largely made John D. I what he was, and Laura Celestia Spelman who made John D. II largely what he was. And so it is with the third generation, where the lighter and more deft hand of Abby Aldrich shows very clearly. As far as formative influences are concerned, the family would be better named the Davison-Spelman-Aldrich family.

Four

The Clan Today

The original John D. Rockefeller, as we have seen, had four children. Of these Junior became the main line of descent for the largest of some ten big Standard Oil fortunes. The founder's brother William, head of the Standard Oil Company of New York, sired four surviving children. These came to make the estate region of Greenwich, Connecticut, their home terrain. John's descendants, as we know, clustered on the vast family *hacienda* at Pocantico Hills, New York, some twenty-five miles or so to the northwest.

JDR Jr. had six children of whom one, Winthrop, twice governor of Arkansas, twice divorced, father of only one child, died of cancer at age sixty in 1973 at his posh winter home in Palm Springs, California.

The six children of Junior in turn have to date had twenty-four children of whom Michael, Nelson's son, apparently drowned during a postcollege archaeological safari in New Guinea in 1967. Junior's grandchildren refer to themselves as "The Cousins" and have established a Cousins Fund (funds being strictly *de rigueur* at all stages in the family). Cousinage, of course, began (in relation to old John D.) with the

201

children of the founder and his siblings: William, Frank, and
two sisters. The descendants of these first cousins or cousins
german by civil law reckoning are all first cousins of the first,
second, or third removes. These third, fourth, and fifth generations are now on stage as the rhetorical dervishes dance in
maddened cadences. And The Cousins of the Pocantico Hills
or Chase Bank Rockefellers (distinguishing them from the
Greenwich or First National City Bank branch) are first cousins twice removed in relation to the never-to-be-forgotten
founder of universal renown.

If one believes a popular song, "You're nobody till somebody loves you;" but in the Rockefeller stratosphere you're
nobody unless you are integrally connected with one of the
very big money-market banks. Such umbilical connection is
the very *sine qua non* and *ne plus ultra,* the without which
nothing and no more beyond—the top of the top, the summit
of the summit. The Rockefellers, both branches, are so connected, as we have seen—first to Chase Manhattan Bank and
First National City Bank and also to Chemical Bank of New
York and First National Bank of Chicago. They are, in their
latter-day manifestation, big bank freaks.

Owing to Nelson's sudden official elevation through the
laying on of hands by President Gerald Ford and the mighty
oaths sworn by both men before the always awesome black-
robed chief justice of the United States Supreme Court, interest centers on the Pocantico Hills branch which is, anyhow,
the one that is always most to the fore and most heavily endowed. The National City Bank branch, however, should never be overlooked where money is concerned.

While all the Pocantico Hills Rockefellers function separately, even in finances, they also function in concert, as a
formal corporate entity, through arrangements they themselves have made and trust funds set up by their parents and
grandparents. There is also, through many marriages, heavy
outside money in both branches of the family, a fact seldom
noted.

The current head of the Pocantico branch as well as of the
more extensive Rockefeller Syndicate is David, the youngest

of Junior's children. He is chairman of the board of the ultra-powerful Chase bank, as close to God as anyone can get, certainly at least as close as the pope or the archbishop of Canterbury, and has several times been offered by three presidents the post of secretary of the treasury. Informants I consider thoroughly reliable tell me he was last offered the Hamiltonian post by Gerald Ford before Nelson was offered the vice-presidency. Only upon his refusal, I am told, was Nelson named.

This is not to say that David is boss or "godfather" of the family. But he is the *primus inter pares* by general consent, arbiter and censor, the person with final say on family matters as they relate to the outside world—prime minister or viceroy. To many of The Cousins, as I have ascertained through sources close to family members, he appears as an aloof *éminence grise*, the intrafamily personage whose veto or disapproval is most to be heeded. Some of the cousins feel distinctly uneasy in his very presence. The brothers defer to his judgment in a way they do not defer to anyone else. None, however, is anything but voluntarily subordinate to him and each, with plenty of money in his own control, could go his own way. Winthrop did just this in more ways than one.

Each of the brothers nurtures his own affairs and special interests, but there is also very definitely a division of labor with respect to family projects or projects with which the family name or money is associated. These last may become matters of some delicacy owing to the ever-present possibility of public flak, which is of course undesired; the family feels it has already endured its full quota of such flak.

On the whole, the family operations proceed smoothly and efficiently, no sweat, except now and then for tempests in teapots, mainly occasioned in later years by Nelson's political career, in earlier years by Winthrop's escapades.

Just as two of the boys were voted by their percipient college classmates as the graduates "most likely to succeed," so the family on its present course, barring the unforeseen, appears to be the American family most likely to succeed in the future. No knowledgeable person expects the Rockefellers to be other than highly solvent and right in the main stream of things fifty or a hundred years from now, barring the fairly remote possibility that the concentration-camp ideologues have taken over. It will be a long time before anyone sees a Rockefeller walking the streets of London barefoot (other than in jest). And, should the People's Directory with its labor camps someday triumph, it is my guess there would be a Rockefeller or Rockefeller agent sitting on it (no doubt as a Girondist).

There is much outside speculation about who does precisely what in the group, and particularly about what any of the joint meetings of the brothers are about. For there are professional Rockefeller-watchers, just as there are Kremlin-watchers.

What does it portend for mankind, some people ask themselves, if one of the brothers makes some obscure allusion in a speech?

Such speculation ignores the fact that the Rockefellers operate through personal and general staffs of hired experts and specialists, much like a tightly knit government. What each brother says from moment to moment is not especially significant. As for ideas, most of them unquestionably originate with one of the hundreds of staff people tangentially out of conferences with the staffs—the one at the Rockefeller family offices at Room 5600, which is actually the entrance for three large floors; the one at Chase National Bank, or Nelson's political entourage. New members for the staffs are carefully selected, and staff changes year to year are few.

The family staffs have readily accessible to them the professional staffs of the various Rockefeller foundations, Rockefeller Syndicate companies, associated banks, many universities, and, for that matter, ready entree to the staffs of the State Department, Treasury Department, United States Commerce Department, etc. The Rockefellers in fact are and have long been an adjunct to the government—or the government to the Rockefellers! Government and the Rockefeller institutions readily interchange personnel on the highest level, as has been demonstrated many times. The brothers themselves have all been in the innermost governmental councils, officially, with full warrant. It is certain the Rockefellers are not just another wealthy family. They are distinctive, *sui generis*, a modern version of the Medici—or an American version of the Mitsui.

Nor is this all.

In a pinch they always have available to them as special advisors even prime ministers of foreign governments, such as Mackenzie King of Canada. In the early 1930s, when Junior was looking around for someone to do the biography of his father that Allan Nevins was finally selected to do, his first choice is reported to have been Winston Churchill, author of the five-volume *Marlborough* and other books. Churchill turned him down, mainly because the Nazis were beginning to induce static on his antenna. That Churchill was a name that came to mind for this purpose shows that the Rockefellers think in large perspectives.

And beyond all this are the batteries of computers at their disposal.

The diatribes composed in underground printshops and on backroom mimeograph machines rain against all this like volleys of spitballs against the sides of a battleship. "Agitators of the world, lie down; put on your chains!" is the slogan for these termites of the established order to heed.

One of the little noticed features of the brothers is the ready entree they have to all high-level quarters, foreign and domestic. A telephone call from David at Chase can unlock practically as many tightly shut top-level doors all over the world as a call from the president of the United States, perhaps more. This is power. And anyone the Rockefellers cannot reach directly, they can quickly gain introductions to from intermediaries. Do they want an audience with the pope, the head man in the Kremlin, Fidel Castro, the emperor of Japan, the shah of Iran, the Dalai Lama, Chou En-lai? They can get it, on short notice. Scores of precisely such power-people have been guests at Pocantico Hills.

While it is the possession of properties with an undulating high money value that serves most positively to focus popular attention on the Rockefellers, money is only the beginning, and it is not the be-all and end-all. The Rockefellers are too well heeled to be concerned much in one way or the other about money other than in terms of large capital sums.

What is basically distinctive about the Rockefellers, what sets them apart in the world, is not the way they preserve money but the way they use it to collect and mobilize specialized and well-placed people. The essence of the Rockefeller story is not money—that is, not money *only*—but people. And it is in the character of their people-collecting that the Rockefellers are most different from any other rich family in the United States or, for that matter, in the world. There is, too, an intelligent self-serving system about all this, first put into operation by old John D. and his aides. Whether he foresaw in advance all the implications and nuances of his system one doesn't, of course, know. Probably not. But the system is nevertheless there. And it works very much in favor of the Rockefellers, generates for them constant warm waves of gratifying commendation.

Not only do the Rockefellers collect people, but they probably have more genuine friends, close personal friends, and always ones who are important, influential, or both, than any other family in the world. According to conventional wisdom, money has nothing to do with friendship, is if anything a contaminating influence. One cannot buy friends, as it is commonly said. And although it is true that one cannot buy friends like fish over the counter, reliable friends, one certainly can gain friends, valuable ones, by funding their projects and even by funding the friends themselves.

There is no known reason why a friend won through the placement of money should not be as good a friend as one won through some more intangible means. Saving someone's life is usually thought of as a way of making a friend. But if one saves or bolsters someone's life, reputation, project, or career by advancing them money, does this not amount to the same thing?

True, money attracts shallow and unreliable people, but many other magnets also attract such specimens. Where people are concerned, they must be individually evaluated, whatever has attracted them. This sort of thing falls under the heading of patronage.

As a result of their funding operations, the Rockefellers possess thousands of staunch friends concentrated in the upper functional and strategic levels of society—in science, scholarship, religion, education, politics, technology, journalism, law, trades unions, social and civil services, business, etc. These funding operations are generally called philanthropies although many of them, such as endless campaign contributions, personal gifts and loans, subventions to achieve specialized technical objectives, the underwriting of junkets, embellishments to foreign relations hardly classify by any criteria as philanthropies. Most of the Rockefeller supporters —and there is very definitely an influential pro-Rockefeller claque—pay little attention to critical sneers and catcalls. Let all who will, embrace the demagogues and whirling dervishes of instant salvation; the entourage itself is content to follow the golden Rockefeller line. Along that way lies heavenly peace of mind and rich dividends.

To list all the boards the brothers and their subordinates are on or have been on, all the corporation directorships, all the offices they have held or now hold, all the hundreds of foreign and domestic awards and decorations they have received, all their high-level acquaintances, connections, and interlocking subordinates would require the space of a good-sized telephone book. As such encyclopedic lists make for dull, repetitious reading, I forgo composing them. One gathers the impression, as one studies the record, that the Rockefellers are omnipresent through surrogates.

Manifestly no individual or even group of four or five could attend to all this personally. And that is true.

How, then, do they handle it all on busy daily schedules?

The answer to this is: fine-tuned staff work.

They are invariably heavily briefed, and by people—allowing for a certain point of view—who know whereof they speak. Speeches are written for them, even books, schedules compiled, arrangements made.

David, a Ph.D. in economics, at an earlier stage wrote two books by himself, and John D. 3 has written a book of which he is proud, titled—of all things—*The Second American Revolution* (1973). We are now, he wrote, right in this glorious revolution, as expressed by black's, women's, and youth's protests against being shunted about, and it will take decades to work out. John D. 3 wants moderates to assert themselves in this "revolution" and bring to the fore humanistic values in a humanistic politics—all straight, beautiful fantasy in a world of sharks, most of them former poor boys "on the make." Reviews of the book were mixed and languid, with the observation common that the ideas were plainly derivative, old, and the writing stiff. As to Nelson, no realist believes he wrote any of the books credited to him.

Like monarchs and presidents, the Rockefellers often deliver prepared speeches—prepared by someone else. Until they scan such a speech before "going on," they don't always know what, precisely, they are going to say although they know it will be on the family "line." In the upshot, the speech is seldom startling and doesn't either galvanize an audience or stir up large waves. David's speeches are particularly unstartling, and many of them, indeed, would not be at all out of character for Calvin Coolidge, Andrew Mellon, or Herbert Hoover. They are definitely never of Hamiltonian caliber. Sometimes they are far out of harmony with the occasion, as in a suggestion to a bemused Canadian audience of a common market for the United States and Canada, a proposed common endeavor of the beady-eyed American eagle and the gentle Canada goose. The next step would surely be lopsided *anschluss*, with the jurisdiction of the FBI greatly widened. To this idea the Canadians were understandably cool.

Nelson, as a politician, usually appears to be saying more than David but, except for the fancy trimmings, or the false cues, what he says boils down to the dicta of a hard-liner. Yet Nelson has a very smooth, persuasive delivery, the work of a finished con artist who could sell refrigerators to Eskimos. His manner is frank and forthright although he has been known to speak with a forked tongue, as on his promise to

bring down New York taxes (which he later increased astronomically). Naturally, like all the politicians today, he is
"dedicated." And, naturally, he is foursquare in favor of
home, motherhood, the family, religion, prosperity, a dandy
job for everyone (someday), equality all around, no discrimination against anyone by reason of race, religion, sex, age, or
present condition of ineptitude, a fair day's work for a fair
day's pay, peace, health, education, welfare—the usual soothing pap dear to political rallies. Now and then, to give him
his due, Nelson may deviate somewhat from bogus political
truisms, and whenever he does, as one might expect, he is in
trouble with some highly vocal and joyously vituperative
splinter group.

What the brothers really believe one can't always tell from
their formal public remarks owing to the ghost-factor, which
haunts their very presence. One can't even be sure that this is
what the ghosts believe. But one may be sure, whatever they
say, that they believe it is the politic or necessary thing to say
at the moment. Nelson particularly is as much of a consciously prefabricated image-projector as anyone in politics, perhaps even more so. Like many politicians he is an actor. He
invariably puts on a rousing show.

While most of the public utterances of the brothers are
plainly designed to gain them public acceptance, at times one
of them will, as I have indicated, advocate some measure,
such as birth control or abortion, that contravenes Neander-
thal mass prejudices. Then the returning growls and even
howls of the benighted devotees of unrestricted concupis-
cence are unmistakable, and the offending advocate is accused of planning genocide against future precious progeny
of Slobania.

What is the fundamental cultural orientation of the Rockefellers? They are certainly "progressives," modernists, ration-
alists, children of the Enlightenment, anything but
obscurantists (leaving aside economics and politics). But they
are progressives strictly within the ambience of a murky status quo, subject at most to slow and bit-by-bit change. They do
believe in slow change because they believe change to be

inevitable, but the emphasis is on *slow*. Whatever people find irksome about the status quo the Rockefellers believe is fully amenable to reform—eventually. Although mild progressive reformers, believing in treatment of symptoms, not causes, they are far from being broad-front political liberals in the terms laid down by many post-Rooseveltians: a legally guaranteed high-rise life for every out-of-step *descamisado* and *sans-culotte* at the expense of working taxpayers in the labor force.

Formally they are eastern corporate Republicans, neither mid-western Republicans of the La Follette school nor right-wing Republicans of southwestern spur-and-boots stripe, but actually they are bipartisan, have as many friends in high Democratic councils as in the Republican. The idea of Nelson being "socialistic," as fevered right-wing critics have accused, is ridiculous. Even more ridiculous is the central thesis of *Rockefeller "Internationalist"* (1952) by Emanuel M. Josephson that the Rockefellers are the hidden driving force behind every communist movement in the world. Patching up and shoring up they all do believe in, unquestionably, but revamping or reconstructing the system is not their mission. They will, though, adjust to any new current.

In a nutshell they are very much like intelligent British Conservatives, Tories, Establishmentarians, and if they lived in England they would unquestionably belong to the Conservative party and the Anglican Church without being deeply hostile to the Labour party. In France during the past thirty years they'd be Gaullists, which is about as far right as they would care to go in any context. They are not in any sense radicals or obscurantists of the Right nor, by any present signs, protofascists or analogues of the German industrialists who gave Hitler a leg up. Where they would stand if options became fewer, if push came to shove, I just don't pretend to know.

Another way of putting it is that they zigzag in a fairly narrow range down a right-centrist line, thereby incurring the wrath of outright rightists and leftists who, in the United States at least, are not—at least, not yet—very numerous. Rightist Republicans like Sen. Barry Goldwater and Sen.

Jesse A. Helms of North Carolina conspicuously voted against Nelson's confirmation whereas most liberals in both houses of Congress voted for him, many of these no doubt in anticipation of a final reckoning the other way in the election of 1976. Had there been Communists, Socialists, or Syndicalists present they would have no doubt voted against him. But the Rockefellers have friends in these quarters, too.

Laurance, with staff assistance, is the new-investment scout of the family. He describes himself as a "venture capitalist." Both he and David probably do more in-and-out investing, for their own account and risk, than do other members of the family.

Nelson, four times elected governor of New York, resigning after fifteen years, and now vice-president, on the threshold of the presidency, is obviously the big political ace of the family. The deceased Winthrop was the most deviant member of the family, widely described as a swinger. Many in benighted Arkansas considered him an ultra-leftist, but then anyone endorsing Lincoln's Emancipation Proclamation is apt to be so considered in that region.

John D. 3, the oldest, has confined himself more than any of his brothers to the Rockefeller institutions and to largely cultural projects in New York City (except for his special guidance of Asiatic institutional-cultural links in close harmony with the State Department). He lives like a wistful monarch-in-exile waiting to be recalled to a distant throne, chopping wood in his spare time.

The sister, Abby Mauzé, operates within the surviving quintet as a silent partner, seldom appearing in the public limelight.

In examining the Rockefeller affairs one cannot always be sure at what precise point there is a division between private, public, and technical governmental affairs. It all tends to blur together.

But, the most overlooked point of all about the brothers, is that they are all very different even though of common genesis, even though they operate within a scenario laid out by old John D. How does one account for the differences?

Brief rundowns of each of this group by priority of birth

will perhaps convey the situation better than any further de-
lineation of them all together.

2.

A relevant detour at this point, though, concerns the Greenwich branch of the family.

William Rockefeller (1841-1922), brother of gilt-edged John
D., married one Almira Geraldine Goodsell in 1864. William
for many years held one-eighth of Standard Oil stock, was the
New York representative of the company, and eventually became president of the Standard Oil Company of New York,
which transformed itself into Socony, then Socony-Vacuum,
and finally Mobil Oil Company.

William was personally a far more genial man than John but
always very much under John's influence, and in latter years
was strongly influenced by John's freebooting Standard Oil
associates. He and they became Wall Street market
manipulators.

The surviving children of this marriage were Emma
(1868-1934), William Goodsell Rockefeller (1870-1922), Percy
Avery Rockefeller (1878-1934) and Ethel Geraldine
(1882-1973). Both John D. and William bought substantial interests in curmudgeonly James Stillman's National City Bank
of New York. It was, in fact, the lush Standard Oil account
that enabled the hitherto routine bank to become an outstanding institution.

Upon relinquishing his holding after many years, John D.
took a position in the stock of the Chase National Bank, now
the Chase Manhattan complex. This position the family has
expanded and placed in charge of its youngest son, David. For
many years Junior's brother-in-law Winthrop Aldrich ran this
roost. The William Rockefeller branch continued to make National City its headquarters. That bank is now First National
City Bank (Citicorp) by reason of its absorption of the First
National Bank of New York, one of the biggest corporation
banks of its day.

William Goodsell Rockefeller married S. Elsie Stillman, and Percy Avery married Isabel G. Stillman, thereby forging a double Rockefeller-Stillman link. It seems to me impossible to look upon these marriages as other than consciously dynastic arrangements.

In 1907 Ethel Geraldine Rockefeller married Marcellus Hartley Dodge, son of the founder of the Remington Arms Company and himself a corporate operator. They had a son, Marcellus Hartley Dodge, Jr. Remington Arms now joined the group. Her son, in his 20s, was killed in an automobile accident.

Emma married Dr. David Hunter McAlpin, son of a very wealthy corporation magnate and himself a physician, company director, and owner of the big McAlpin Hotel, New York. Their children, all heirs to two fortunes and top Social Registerites, were David Hunter McAlpin, Geraldine Rockefeller McAlpin, William Rockefeller McAlpin, and Elaine Rockefeller McAlpin. Elaine married Henry Clinch Tate and Geraldine married Jerome Pierce Webster.

Just what further interrelationships and corporate connections all these grandchildren entered into would be interesting to explore but would carry us deep into a thicket of additional dynastic detail and corporate interweavings, would bring to light no known wizards.

In all, John's and William's children fused in marriages with five outside fortunes: Stillman, Dodge, McAlpin, McCormick, and Aldrich. Such plutocratic alliances have long been common on the American scene, resulting in the formation of a small, closely knit, biologically and financially interlocked plutocratic class—just what many degree-flaunting and grant-laden pundits absurdly deny exists in the great American pseudocommonwealth.

William Rockefeller, founder of this family line, had prudently but apparently not wisely reduced his Standard Oil holdings prior to the dissolution decree of 1911, but he branched out into a multiplicity of other corporate holdings—as, indeed, his brother John to some extent did also—and became an active and successful stock-market manipulator. He was a director of some thirty-five corporations, in all of which he no doubt had an ownership stake.

His son, William Goodsell, Yale '92, became treasurer of the original Standard Oil Company, a member of leading clubs, and vice-president and/or director of a long string of corporations, including the Inspiration Consolidated Copper Company—a genuine big-league operator. Percy Avery, also a graduate of Yale, '00, became a big-money operator in oil, banking, railroad, nitrate, copper, match, land, industrial alcohol, and steel companies. He also belonged to many of the leading clubs and, as a hobby, went in for breeding prize dogs and horses.

Differences between the William Rockefeller and John D. Rockefeller branches of the family are that the former is entrenched in the First National City Bank, always sends its sons to St. Paul's School and Yale, and its members are associated as directors and, presumably, investors in many more companies while its members also belong to many more of the leading clubs than do the Pocantico Hills Rockefellers. A further difference is that the William Rockefeller branch has always maintained a low public profile, does not profess to be concerned with improving the world.

The most prominent of the grandchildren of William Rockefeller were James Stillman Rockefeller and William Rockefeller III, sons of William Goodsell Rockefeller, and Avery Rockefeller, son of Percy Avery. Other children of William Goodsell were Godfrey Stillman Rockefeller, Yale, '21, John Sterling Rockefeller, and Almira Goodsell Rockefeller. Percy Avery also had four daughters—Isabel (Mrs. Frederic W. Lincoln), Winifred (Mrs. Brooks Enemy), Faith, and Gladys.

James Stillman Rockefeller, Yale, B.S., Phi Beta Kappa, '24, married Nancy Carnegie, niece of Andrew Carnegie, the steel king. Here we get a Rockefeller-Stillman-Carnegie fusion. Their children, all heavily endowed, are James Stillman Rockefeller, Jr., Nancy R. McFadden, Andrew Rockefeller, and Georgia Rose Rockefeller.

James Stillman Rockefeller started out on the corporate circuit with the investment banking firm of Brown Brothers and

Co., later Brown Brothers Harriman, 1925-29; joined the family's National City Bank in 1930; became vice-president for the period 1940-48; senior vice-president for 1948-52; executive vice-president in 1952; from 1952 to 1958 was president and director; and from 1959 to 1967 was chairman of the board, opposite number to David at Chase Manhattan. He was also a director of many leading corporations, including Pan American Airways and National Cash Register, a trustee of many boards, and a member of many leading clubs.

William Rockefeller III, born in 1918, St. Paul's School, '36, Yale, A.B., '40, Columbia, LL.B., '47, is a corporation lawyer. Admitted to the bar in 1948, he has been with the big Wall Street law firm of Shearman and Sterling since 1955. He holds various company directorships and trusteeships, was a lieutenant commander in the United States Naval Reserve, 1941-46, was awarded the Bronze Star, and belongs to fifteen leading clubs. He has three daughters.

Avery Jr., son of Avery and Anna Mark Rockefeller, St. Paul's, '43, Yale, B.A. '49, has long been with the influential investment banking firm of Dominick and Dominick, is a company director and a member of the board of the New York Stock Exchange. He was in the air force from 1943 to 1945. He is a member of many clubs and the father of three children.

The males of this William Rockefeller line, as is readily seen, are for the most part corporation operators and general investors, their fingers in many pies domestic and foreign, with the central sun of their particular constellation the First National City Bank of New York (Citicorp). Yet there are many interlocking corporate connections between this branch of the family and the branch centered in the Chase Manhattan Bank.

4.

The first child of JDR Jr. and his wife Abby was a daughter, Abby, born in 1903. She attended the socially elite Miss

Chapin's School and Brearley School in New York City. In 1925 she married David Meriwether Milton, a childhood chum from Pocantico Hills and Seal Harbor, Maine, a descendant of Meriwether Lewis, the American explorer (Lewis and Clark expeditions), a lawyer, and later a real estate and investment operator. Their children were Abby Rockefeller Milton and Marilyn Ellen Rockefeller Milton. Abby divorced her husband in 1943. She then married Dr. Irving Hotchkiss Pardee, president of the New York Neurological Society and clinical professor of neurology at Columbia University, but was soon left a widow. She later married Jean Mauzé, a banker, and is now again widowed. As she plays no public role in Rockefeller affairs we may leave her out of any further account.

The first of the five sons of Junior and Abby was John D. 3, born in 1906. In temperament and personality a somewhat blurred replica of his father, he is physically very different as, indeed, are all his brothers. In physique he takes more after his mother, and in one way or the other, all the brothers hark back in looks and build more to the Aldriches than to John D. or Junior.

Whereas Junior was stocky, John 3 (he prefers the numeral in Arabic) turned out tall, like all his brothers, and of spare frame like his mother. And whereas Junior had a broad face, this son had rather thin, finely chiseled features, giving him in later years an ascetic appearance. Observers with an eye for such things pronounce him conspicuously handsome.

Like all his brothers, he has been a member of scores of boards, frequently decorated by many governments, and the recipient of many awards. Enough praise has been heaped on him by people in his own crowd to sink a battleship. For many years he followed exactly the course his father put him upon.

First educated at the Browning School of Rockefeller origin, then the Loomis School in Windsor, Connecticut, he took a B.S. in economics at Princeton University in 1929. During his postsophomore summer at Princeton, he bicycled through France with Nelson. The following summer he served as an assistant in the information section of the League of Nations in Geneva, where the organization's huge library building was a Rockefeller donation. In the summer of 1929 he went on a trip around the world as secretary to the chairman of the Foreign Policy Association, a private organization that generates much background material on American foreign policy and with which the Rockefellers have long been intimately associated, notably as funders.

Asia had the greatest impact on John 3. In Japan he attended a meeting of the Institute of Pacific Relations, funded by the Rockefeller Foundation and certainly not by any stretch a charitable organization.

"Wherever we went, we met topside people," Rockefeller said in an interview with *The New Yorker* in 1973. "These focused my interest on the international area."

Obviously all this was an experience remote from anything encountered by the usual college graduate. And it was the experience that was to lead to John's becoming the behind-the-scenes family specialist in international affairs, supervising the development of the top personnel for this sphere in the Rockefeller institutions. They are seedbeds of future government personnel.

At the end of 1929 he took a desk in his father's office, then in the Standard Oil Building at 26 Broadway, later moved uptown to Rockefeller Plaza. In short order Number Three was placed on fifteen Rockefeller boards, there to watch and pick up the Rockefeller knack in financial legerdemain. He was right in his father's footsteps. He joined the Rockefeller Foundation in 1931 but did not become chairman until 1952, when he replaced John Foster Dulles as the latter moved on to become secretary of state and the occasion for the coining of a new word in diplomacy: brinkmanship. As Dulles left he was soon followed by Dean Rusk as president of the foundation. Rusk was to succeed Dulles as secretary of state but not before Christian Herter, married to a Standard Oil Pratt, briefly held the office. After Rusk the office was held for a time by William Rogers, but it was then to be taken up by Henry Kissinger, who for a number of years had been groomed by the Rockefellers after Nelson had spotted him up at Harvard for work on one of the many Rockefeller "studies." As to Kissinger one can say this: he's every bit a match for Gromyko. Most of the time since World War II, Rockefeller people have run the State Department and managed United States foreign policy.

Number Three served obscurely on the Rockefeller boards for many years and might indeed still be doing just this had it not been for the intervention of World War II. As an old friend is quoted as saying, "Up to the Second World War, John had not done much of anything. He was just sitting around in his family's office. The best thing that happened to him was Blanchette"—a reference to Blanchette Ferry Hooker, daughter of the founder of Hooker Chemical Company, whom he married in 1932. She, it was reported, spurred him on to make waves, not just be a wallflower.

After Pearl Harbor he joined the US Navy, haven of many Rockefellers, as a lieutenant, eventually emerging as a lieutenant commander. Here he worked in Washington with the Combined Civil Affairs Committee and the State-War-Navy Coordinating Committee, no doubt gaining considerable inner-governmental know-how. As a consequence he was made special assistant to the undersecretary of the navy, serving from October into December, 1945.

His extrafoundation activities became significantly more telling when he was made a consultant to the Dulles Mission to Japan to negotiate the peace treaty. Dulles, of course, now with the rank of special ambassador, was an old familiar, one might say an employee, chairman of the Rockefeller Foundation, since 1911 a partner of the big corporate law firm of Sullivan and Cromwell that handled much Rockefeller business, and long involved in State Department affairs as a member of the Foreign Policy Association. Dulles had also been chairman of the Rockefeller General Education Board and of the Carnegie Endowment for International Peace—the word which in Orwellian Newspeak means war. A precisely accurate name for the Carnegie outfit would be Endowment for International Affairs—that is, foreign policy.

"John's four years in the service pushed him out into the

world," an associate reports. "He learned a lot how you get things done. He gained confidence. He'd been pretty isolated, sitting up in that fifty-sixth-floor cocoon." And, overprotected very much as his father had been, shepherded about from here to there, confidence in himself was something he needed. He now has it, pretty much.

His association with the peace conference focused his mind more strongly than ever on Japan and Asia. Soon he was engaged in joint State Department-Rockefeller endeavors on behalf of creating better relations between the two hemispheres although China, alas, an old love of the Rockefellers, had now joined the votaries of the concentration camp.

According to a *New Yorker* profile by Geoffrey T. Hellman[1], Number Three "was a very shy, sensitive and rather unaggressive boy. . . . He has an anxious, inquiring, sometimes tormented, often sweet expression. Besides being polite, serious, gentle, diffident, non-circulating, naturally withdrawn, and less cautious than he used to be, he is shy, modest. . . patient, tactful, earnest, conscientious, orderly, idealistic, persistent, constrained but graceful, deliberate, frugal, courtly, stubborn, Calvinistic, and Puritan-ethic-ridden (Baptist division) to a point where spontaneous pleasure is not his thing."

Although informative in a superficial way, this profile does not go very deep or get into "sensitive" matters. In general, it presents Number Three as a sad-eyed semirecluse, vibrating with sympathy for suffering humanity—a beautiful exercise in public relations projections. (The Rockefellers, incidentally, never cooperate with any interviewers unless they know they are going to come out in a favorable light. Why should they?)

As one of my secret agents reports, Number Three is the most liked of the brothers among The Cousins. Yet, despite his gentle attitude, many persons report that he can be very stubborn and unyielding, and some find him to be like a monarch without royal authority. "He can't understand people

---

1. Geoffrey T. Hellman, "Out of the Cocoon on the Fifty-Sixth Floor," *The New Yorker*, November 4, 1972.

with a few million dollars, or none," says another. Yet still another says he is really, despite it all, a very warm person.

Reports of much surface phenomena about the Rockefellers are made by many people, and in time one gets the impression one is hearing statements about a prepared bath—very warm, cold, tepid. Thus one person says that Laurance is very warm; another says he's very cold, the coldest, shrewdest of the lot. No doubt the Rockefellers are, like everyone else, affected by their interlocutors, reveal momentary attitudes provoked by another. Does it really matter much whether they are warm, cold, sweet, or chummy? What really does matter, it seems to me, is where the chips go down, how, and why.

His wife thinks Johnny (as his brothers call him) was a very serious child who suffered from being outstripped in adventure and naughtiness by his more boisterous younger brothers. Not only as the eldest son was he crowned with The Name that is magic to some, anathema to others, but he was very influenced by his father, and all reports about him show that he is much more of an obsessive-compulsive than any of his brothers. He is certainly the most inhibited of the lot, saddled with a puritanical superego. By all signs he was the one Rockefeller brother who was in the beginning singled out for the full treatment of overcare, oversupervision. Some of this may have come about, too, because of childhood health problems.

In private he leads the life of a gentleman-farmer on his portion of the Pocantico estate, raising blooded cattle and chopping wood.

He is, at any rate, very different from his harder hitting brothers—Nelson, Laurance, and David—or from his deceased brother Winthrop, who, although sufficiently aggressive, was never able to get fully organized.

Rockefeller 3, although on the Japanese Mission as a consultant, was obviously something more: an important big-money observer to keep a wary eye on officials. He was therefore asked by the State Department—that is, by one of his own people in the State Department—to bring into being some of the suggestions he had made as a "consultant." He thereupon went back to Tokyo with Donald H. McLean, Jr., a lawyer then associated with him and later president of the Lahey Clinic Foundation in Boston.

There was soon formed a Cultural Center Preparatory Committee which, after being turned down for money by the Ford Foundation, applied to the Rockefeller Foundation. Not surprisingly, the foundation came up with $500,000. The Japanese put up a comparable sum, other money was siphoned in, three acres were acquired in Tokyo, and in 1956 International House, Tokyo, was opened. It contained a reference library on western culture, a lecture hall and conference rooms, a dining room, and living quarters for fifty Japanese scholars and teachers and visiting grant-laden American academicians—*la dolce vita* on the academic circuit.

In the United States there already existed the moribund Japan Society, founded in 1907 by the lawyer Lindsay Russell who had earlier set up the Pilgrims Society in New York and London. When the Japan Society was incorporated, its chief incorporators were the bankers Jacob Schiff (Kuhn Loeb), August Belmont (Rothschild), Henry Clews (banker-author of *Fifty Years in Wall Street*), and Isaac N. Seligman, (banker). Henry W. Taft was the society's president on the day the Pacific fleet, guardian of the western sea frontier, was caught snoozing and sunk by Japanese bombers. Here was a huge waste of taxpayers' money!

In 1952, after being accepted without question for membership in the society, Rockefeller was at once made president and John Foster Dulles chairman of the board. Dulles resigned soon after when he was made Eisenhower's secretary of state. The Eisenhower campaign, like all Republican campaigns, was heavily funded by the Rockefellers. The society was broke, but with the pecunious new president at the helm, things soon began to hum; offices were rented, committees appointed, and a dinner was staged at the Plaza Hotel for the first postwar Japanese ambassador.

Japan House, an ornate structure near the United Nations, was projected. The report for the year said that "a benefactor" (guess who) had provided $1,350,000 to acquire the land for the four-story black concrete building designed by Junzo

Yoshimura. Here the society mounts exhibits of Japanese art, stages Japanese spectacles and dance recitals, makes grants to Japanese scholars, poets, artists, and dancers, sponsors discussions on Japanese problems, and in general carries on in a way so as to blot out all memory of Pearl Harbor.

Rockefeller sank a lot of money from his own account into the society, but gradually other donors, wealthy individuals and corporations, have been roped into the act so that Rockefeller, at last report, sustains only a small percentage of the budget. By reason of this and other operations, John 3 has become known as a skillful fund-raiser for projects in which he and his brothers develop an interest. A word from him to a carefully indexed file of people brings in a flood of cash—for the simple reason that there is *moneybund* prestige to be had in having one's name listed as a donor to one of the Rockefeller projects.

So successful was the Japan Society that, perhaps with a nudge from the State Department, Rockefeller went on to found the Asia Society. This started with a seven-story glassy structure designed by Philip Johnson on the posh Upper East Side and was also the gift of "a benefactor" (guess who). Asia House was pretty much a reprise of Japan House except that it concerned all of Asia and has cost Rockefeller more than $6 million, with other elements, including the Rockefeller Foundation and the Rockefeller Brothers Fund, coming in heavily. In 1975 he also gave it a valuable art collection, tax deductible.

In both these projects as well as many others, culture is the capsule, business and political affairs the infrastructure, profit and good feelings all around the result, as history unfolds in its new, always erratic patterns.

In the 1950s Number Three also became interested in population problems—that is *over*population problems—and founded the Population Council, which has a staff of 250. This was launched out of a big conference called at the Rockefellers' Williamsburg, sponsored by the National Academy of Science of which Dr. Detlev Bronk was president. Bronk had previously been head of Rockefeller University, and in effect the conference was a 100 percent Rockefeller constellation. It would be difficult, indeed, to call a high-level conference on almost any subject without finding it heavily weighted with Rockefeller beneficiaries for the simple reason that the Rockefellers have at one time funded practically everybody who is anybody.

Now, in tackling overpopulation—that is, more people than there are resources natural and man-made to sustain them—Rockefeller took up something very real and very serious. But it was also something that the Rockefellers with their urge to intervene in large matters in the name of humanity had helped create. One can make a considerable list of such Rockefeller-created problems, wherein the solution to the initial problem has created a larger new problem.

For it was the Rockefeller Institute, in concert with such affairs as the Koch Institute of Berlin and the Pasteur Institute of Paris, that set to work to find the cause and cure of many diseases that were killing people worldwide like flies. These institutes were to an impressive degree successful, spectacularly so. But birthrates throughout most of the world remained the same as they had while people were dying prematurely in hordes. For religious and other reasons, many cultures declined to have anything to do with birth control, which they regarded as an impious interference with the life cycle. In the meantime governments, applying the new scientific findings, had instituted successful public-health measures, often funded by the Rockefellers.

Had the institutes merely done their work, letting whoever wished to apply it, there would be little ground to criticize. But the Rockefellers were particularly aggressive in pressing the lifesaving formulas on distant cultures, even financing implementation in the field. Hence much of the "population explosion."

Rockefeller's Population Council has not had as joyful a reception anywhere as he would have liked, has not been embraced as joyously as brother Laurance's conservation organizations. The fact is that most people the world over look with suspicion, for religious and other reasons , on birth control, abortion, and even sexual continence. Indeed, many religions prescribe coitus, early and often, with throttles wide open, and this is undoubtedly one of the many reasons religion is popular among the uncultivated. The consequence, as death rates are reduced by public-health authorities applying techniques developed by the Rockefeller, Koch, and Pasteur Institutes, and exported particularly by the Rockefellers, is that populations increase alarmingly. Irrationality is clearly in the saddle, with prospects ever brighter for large-scale famine, absolutely certain for permanent poverty.

Resultant poverty is blamed by the ever-nimble Soviets on capitalism and imperialism. Private capitalism, the Soviet state-capitalist pundits intone, is responsible for poverty (which long antedates capitalism), and in its foreign propaganda the Soviets decry all birth control, abortion, and preachments of continence. What is needed, say they, is an end to private capitalism and an embrace of the Soviet system of state capitalism, which will be able by means yet undisclosed (but no doubt relying heavily on penal labor camps) to support populations infinite in number.

At any rate, the pressure of rising world population is a distinct plus on the side of the Soviets because it fosters civil disorder outside the Soviet realm, increasingly makes it impossible to cater to human needs by means of any sort of system. Obviously, what with vagaries of weather, limitations of soil and other resources, tens of millions are slated to die of starvation. They are doing so right now. All this could, of course, boomerang in a big way on the scheming Soviets.

One can point to many other big short circuits induced by Rockefeller beneficence, philanthropy. The Anti-Saloon League and Women's Christian Temperance Union in the United States were for many years heavily financed by the Rockefellers, father and son. Old man Rockefeller, taught by his mother Eliza, believed that liquor was the devil's own instrument. He could see how it undermined the health of workmen, made it impossible for many to report for work on Monday after weekend sprees. He apparently never stopped to ask himself why they resorted to heavy drinking. Could it be that they felt hopeless, and this in the land of the free?

The league and the union were the backbone of the Methodist and Baptist forces in the United States that produced the Eighteenth Amendment to the United States Constitution, which forever banished vile alcoholic beverages from the United States. The widespread lawlessness of Prohibition ensued, with more people drinking than ever before.

To any apparent evil the puritan remedy is: forbid it. Many states, usually Baptist or Methodist in population, already had Prohibition, and it did not work there. But, it was felt, if one made it general, it would work. And this simplistic belief was entertained even though for centuries adultery, fornication, lechery, thievery, and suicide had been legally and canonically forbidden and yet had survived in great vitality

By 1932 Junior Rockefeller, prodded by Nelson, who took him on a trip through midtown New York to show him the many speakeasies, many on Rockefeller properties, was ready to accept the repeal of Prohibition. Here was another Rockefeller debacle.

The common law against monopoly, and a specific statute, had not led John D. Sr. to renounce his Standard Oil practices. Why should he believe people would give up liquor simply because the law said they should not imbibe?

It is for these and similar reasons that I believe the Rockefellers are obviously confused behind their pose of *savoir faire,* don't operate on the basis of a realistic or well-fashioned appraisal of the actual world. They may be more soundly grounded today, it is possible, with more and better educated people in the family, but there is still a large amount of fantasy and self-deception evident in their operations. Their biggest bit of self-deception is their apparent belief that they can forcefully and unilaterally privately intervene in fundamental historical and cultural trends and alter their courses according to some detached, rational, armchair blueprint.

Another area that has interested the Rockefellers is conflict and disharmony, of which there is much in the world. They would like to see much of it quelled, as indeed would most thinkers. But the Rockefellers believe also in *doing something about it.* Deep thinkers don't know what to do about it short of establishing Socialism. As much conflict and disharmony exists between different groups or religionists, the Rockefeller antidote for this has been interdenominational religion. Their Union Church at Pocantico Hills is interdenominational, and their big, cathedral-like structure the Riverside Church in New York, is also interdenominational—that is, usable by any denomination. So far, however, there has not been grass-roots response to this prepapal ecumenism on the part of the Rockefellers. And many grass-roots Catholics don't like the papal ecumenism.

There are many reasons for the lack of response, one of which is that religious people cherish their religious differences, don't think much of rival religions, often detest them as the work of the devil. It is part of the fun of being religious to feel that one is part of something exclusive. As it is, the interdenominational and ecumenical movements, despite their lack of spectacular success, have already brought together enough disparate elements to make astute observers look forward to the day of big explosions. Such a mingling of emotional dynamite, TNT, gasoline, and plutonium must some day produce some sort of a big bang.

The Population Council has succeeded in getting some thirty governments interested in implementing its program. Rockefeller put $250,000 into the council to begin with, supplied 50 percent of its funds for several years, but by 1972 is reported to have contributed only 3 percent of the budget, the balance coming from governments and other contributors.

As a result of his efforts, Number Three in 1968 was appointed by President Lyndon Johnson cochairman of the Committee on Population and Family Planning. The committee recommended the appointment of a Presidential Commission on Population Growth and the American Future. President Nixon, now in the saddle, appointed Rockefeller chairman. After much work by twenty-four commissioners and a staff of fifteen, the commission produced a report. It recommended brakes on population growth in the United States, increased sex education and child care, a halt to illegal immigration (there are reported to be about three million, perhaps more, illegal immigrants in the United States as of January, 1974), the extension of government suburban housing, and legalization of abortion and instruction in contraception.

The excellent report had a very favorable world press reception, but it did not reckon with Nixon, who specialized in sniffing around the garbage dumps and latrines of the human soul for prospective votes to bolster his shabby career. (I say this without any reference to Watergate, which was merely one of the accidental disclosures of what more or less analogous misbehavior that has gone on in Washington at least since the Civil War. Watergate merely lifted the curtain on a more or less standard behind-the-drapes performance, variations on a theme.) First ignoring the report and never saying anything in favor of any of its recommendations, the ineffable Nixon, endorsed in an electoral landslide in 1972 for his second term, finally came out strongly against abortion and contraceptive teachings to minors (over which spheres he had no jurisdiction anyhow). The report, of course, was entirely sensible in the light of domestic and world conditions. But Nixon knew in what benighted quarters several million votes lurked.

The antiabortion movement in the United States virtuously proclaims itself as opposed to the equivalent of murder, the taking of human life without due process of law. It wants instead every fetus conceived in a street-corner telephone booth or back alley to be born. But none of its members has demonstrated the slightest interest in caring for the children so produced by demoralized mothers who abandon them on garbage heaps, neglect and mistreat them. Such children, far from being rescued or assisted by the antiabortionists, are instead allowed to sicken and die under coarse institutional care or to develop hit-or-miss as psychic cripples, useless to self or to others. Instead of being aborted prenatally, they are brought into an aborted life. Disallowed the merciful prenatal *coup de grâce*, such children for the most part are instead set upon a road of inner torture. Indeed, many of the more articulate antiabortionists are notable for their opposition to governmentally funded social programs of child care because they burden now suddenly sacred taxpayers. Short on mercy, long on professions of extreme virtue, they are also niggardly— Nixon's people, literally and figuratively.

Naturally Rockefeller came under the fire of such, as did his

brother Nelson who as New York governor backed a successful bill legalizing abortion-on-demand in New York. However, soon after the permissive New York law was passed, the
United States Supreme Court held all state antiabortion laws
to be unconstitutional, clear violations of the personal rights
of women. Not quelled, the antiabortionists now cried for a
constitutional amendment.

An early project that, according to a former associate, "gave
John a damn good entrée into the District of Columbia," consists of his Rockefeller Public Service Awards. These are five
annual $10,000 tax-free gifts, administered by Princeton Uni-
versity and given to selected career federal-government workers. Through these awards he has "developed quite a
following among the senior public servants." While I don't,
like a dog in the manger, want to interfere even verbally with
anyone's reception of such manna, a serious question might
here be asked, to wit: Why should one citizen be in a position
to give out such benefits, tax free and possibly deductible to
the donor, tax exempt to the recipient, to already highly paid
public workers possessed of retirement and other benefits and
in turn become the recipient of their benign judgment? We
see here how money may be of great muted use to the cheerful
giver.

A very big project of Number Three's became the Lincoln
Center of the Performing Arts in New York City, an *omnium-
gatherum* of opera, symphony orchestras, libraries, ballets,
and theater in several ornate buildings spread over a large area
of what was once a run-down upper Broadway district verg-
ing on slum. It all started with Robert Moses, the demon pub-
lic-clearer and public-project arranger who is analyzed at
devastating length in *The Power Broker* by Robert Caro
(1973). The original idea had been to "rehabilitate" Lincoln
Square, at the intersection of Sixty-sixth Street and Broadway.
But soon the concept was greatly broadened to produce a
greater financial, lawyer-using, contract-yielding, material-
consuming, corporation-sustaining, and labor-employing
affair.

The Metropolitan Opera was now at last ready to move, to

make way for a lucrative office building on its site, and the Philharmonic Orchestra had been told Carnegie Hall was also to be razed (by the wonderful office-builders behind the opera removal). Owing to outraged public protest, Carnegie Hall was eventually saved from the wreckers and office builders as a public architectural monument. Somebody brought Rockefeller into the Lincoln Square discussions in 1955 as "a citizen at large," better described as "a wealthy patron" or *padrone.* Rockefeller was made chairman of the usual study committee, which produced the whole gaudy plan for a cultural bazaar of radiant financial benefit.

After thirteen years of much toil and moil, committee meetings, planning, contract letting, solicitation of funds (for much non-Rockefeller money is also in the project), Lincoln Center was brought to fruition, and Rockefeller now became referred to as "Mr. Lincoln Center" as well as "Mr. Japan," "Mr. Asia," and "Mr. Population." "Mr. State Department" should also not be overlooked.

Planned to cost $75 million, the whole thing ran to $184-plus million. Of this vast sum, for most people equivalent to all the money in the world, the Ford Foundation threw in $25 million, Mrs. V. Beaumont Allen put in $3 million (hence the Vivian Beaumont Theater of the center), $15 million came from the Rockefeller Foundation, $10 million from Rockefeller Junior, $9 million from the trust of Muriel (Rockefeller) McCormick Hubbard, and some $11 million or more from Number Three. A great many local tycoons and corporations had the arm put on them for the balance of the money, and some people say ligaments were freely twisted here and there in the dark canyons of Wall Street.

A good many architectural critics, as one might expect, were not satisfied with the externals of the various edifices. Here ensued a replay of the strictures thrown out nearly forty years before about Rockefeller Center. Some said it looked like something Mussolini had ordered over the telephone. Lincoln Center, although built on the basis of tax write-offs, is not admission free. The charges are stiff to the customers, who must all be at least affluent.

Who patronizes Lincoln Center? First, the limousine and Social Register set. Its members may roll in from as far as fifty miles away. Next, the local taxi set, and this includes well-heeled visitors to the city and much of the United Nations crowd. Among subway- and bus-riders, students and young married college graduates make up an irregular contingent. And then, finally, the gallery crowd—scattered opera, theater, music, and ballet buffs. Few who have to get up early to go to work can afford the hassle just to get there and back, much less the prices. To most people, even local yokels, the whole thing is as far out of range as the moon.

But it is undoubtedly a great thing for midtown Manhattan real-estate values. And here is, too, culture as a set piece, something apart from and divorced from life, something laid on, not integral to existence. One can take it or leave it.

Lincoln Center, indeed, is a resort for the affluent in the city jungle.

In this latest phase, now increasingly uninhibited with the advancing years, Number Three has become interested in youth and its tribulations. The instrument of this new interest, Geoffrey Hellman reports, was his daughter Alida. She had gone to Stanford University in California, where she ran into quite a bit of anti-Rockefeller flak from semiradicalized chums who knew far more about her family than she did. "Daddy, why do they hate us so?" she exclaimed tearfully to her father.

Alida, for a while picking up the beat of the tom-toms from her fellow students, denounced her parents to their faces. This shook them. In time, naturally, she was won around to see them in a better light and found she respected them more than ever before. So the Stanford camarilla was, fortunately, thwarted here.

But Alida's perturbations turned her father's attention to the wayward youth, its life expectancies screwed up to concert pitch through advertising, public relations blarney, and propaganda. Toward bewildered youth he is reported to be highly sympathetic.

John D. 3 has two other daughters, Sandra and Mrs. Hope

Spencer, and one son, John D. IV, who favors the Roman suffix. John IV was born in 1937, picked West Virginia as a state in which to plunge into Democratic politics (the first non-Republican Rockefeller), and is already, with Nelson not yet in the White House, freely talked about as a future president of the United States. Judging by his record to date, the prediction may be fulfilled.

But now, having presented the pleasant side of this most agreeable of the Rockefeller brothers, allow me to touch in passing the area where the chips go down with a smashing bang. More of this will come in the final chapter.

In 1969 when Congress, in response to much clamor, was once again engaged in covertly stacking the deck against the holy common man and impishly calling it tax reform, Number Three appeared to testify before the House Ways and Means Committee on behalf of a certain provision of the tax code. According to this provision, if anyone decided to devote for ten years 90 percent of his income to charity—that is, to a wide range of tax-deductible and tax-exempt projects such as Japan House, Asia House, Lincoln Center, the Population Council, art collections, awards for excellent public servants —he was absolved from paying any federal income taxes. Of this array I'd call only the Population Council unchallengeably philanthropic.

"Ninety percent of one's income to charity!" exclaims the average man. "That's a lot and fair enough." And that's exactly the way he has been preprogrammed by the media to react. For the word "charity" is the operative one here that breaks down all resistance.

Rockefeller testified that since 1961 he had been completely tax exempt but that he had nevertheless voluntarily paid to the Internal Revenue Service 5 to 10 percent of his gross adjusted income, amount unspecified.[2] Congresswoman M. W. Griffiths of Michigan called this arrangement "incredible."

Let us see how this works.

---

2. *New York Times,* March 1, 1969, 21:1

Suppose a man has an income of $5 million-plus a year, unearned of course and probably inherited. As we saw in the first chapter, Nelson's gross income generally amounts to this level each year so his brother's must also. Such a man is now theoretically in a bracket where, according to the tax schedules, he might conceivably be required to pay 70 percent— that is $3.5 million. "Goody, goody," cry the plain citizens gleefully. "Soak the rich." As we saw in the first chapter, Nelson for many years paid at an average of about 25 percent, down very close to the 14 percent rate for the least imbursed taxpayers.

Let us refocus now on our theoretical man, who could be Johnny R., and whose income could be taxable at 70 percent were it not for allowable special deductions. Such a man has been able instead to devote 90 percent or $4.5 million to projects of his own choosing, keeping only $500,000 for his personal use—in other words, far from starving. If he pays 5 or 10 percent on this sum, he pays $25,000 or $50,000. Actually one could bank the $500,000 and live on a 5 percent income from it and be then in the upper 5 percent of income receivers in the United States! In brief, the ordinary *interest* on $500,000 would keep a family of four in very good style.

"So what?" says the average man. "The guy has given 90 percent for his fancy projects or 20 percentage points more than maximum tax. No skin off my nose."

As to this, let us see.

While the tax laws have been in force, the politicians have been devising budgets, which now run at more than $350 billion per annum, including an inflationary deficit. In the various states and counties, too, there are also budgets for government expenditures, and what one pays in taxes in many states, especially New York, is keyed to what one pays federally. Nothing federally? Then nothing in the state.

The various governments—state, federal, and local—are nevertheless going to get from the general populace the moneys they budget, if necessary at the point of the bayonet. One could not be allowed to trifle with sovereignty, could one? No judge would stand for it.

Now, whatever one person does not pay to defray the budget, *other persons must pay.* And if some don't pay, those who do pay must pay *more.* And anyone who has agreed (as many have) to divert for ten years 90 percent of his income into tax-deductible projects, not necessarily charitable or especially philanthropic, is required to pay nothing into the tax pool. Nothing!

In the hypothetical case I have cited the tax-exempt citizen has avoided paying $3.5 million, and he is only one of many. Whatever these people don't pay to the tax office, the average man must pay.

So, as is evident, the average man who is also a big Johnson-Nixon man, has in fact made most of the monetary input into the project for which Mr. Donor is saluted on every hand as a great guy—saluted first by the myriads of average citizens and then more meaningfully by the direct recipients of his largess. Mr. Donor has contributed only 20 percent of his disposable income. I consider this a masterful trick, deserving of respectful obeisance. For here the tax avoider stands forth as a public hero. And the ones who really pay get a kick in the *derrière.*

Later in 1969, while Congress was wrangling over the pseudoreform bill on taxes (which produced very little reform), Number Three appeared to protest flatly against the momentarily proposed elimination of this 90 percent deduction, holding that it would stifle "charity."[3]

Congress, as one might expect, heeded his and others' warnings. By way of "reform" it allowed this provision of the tax law to remain through 1975. Thereafter only (!) half of one's income may be so deployed in tax-deductible, tax-exempt frequently self-serving projects. For all these projects, as can easily be shown, bolster personal Rockefeller interests.

While the Rockefellers have been quite profligate with many so-called beneficences, subject in breakdowns to quite other classifications, they have not been profligate in the pay-

---

3. *New York Times,* September 18, 1969, 21:1.

ment of taxes. And they have been, as John 3 showed, opposed
to elimination of tax loopholes. Old John D. was just as adamantly opposed to taxes. Through his chief counsel, Joseph
Choate, he and his moneyed peers successfully scuttled the
original income tax in 1895 by means of a scandal-wreathed
Supreme Court decision (*Pollock vs. Farmers' Loan and Trust
Co., 1895*).

My conclusion, to be set forth in greater detail in Chapter
Five: The Rockefellers want to keep their money and dispose
of it as they see fit, in self-serving ways. And that, in my
opinion, makes sense. Any other interpretation is nonsense
from start to finish.[4]

5.

Between the birth of John 3 and Nelson, who was born in
1908, something unusual happened in the Rockefeller household, we know not what, because from Nelson onward the
children were all reared differently, according to new methods. As a consequence all the later children of Junior and
Abby are very different from any previously produced by
Rockefeller households since before the days of Eliza Davison. They aren't, for one thing, obsessives, are less uptight
than their predecessors.

While John 3 had in early years unquestionably been subjected to training similar to that of his father, the clear evidence in their personalities shows that Nelson, Laurance,
Winthrop, and David were given far more relaxed handling.
Whether greater relaxation came about because their parents,

---

4. Readers interested in a full and incisive analysis of the inequitable federal tax code
should turn to Philip M. Stern, *The Rape of the Taxpayer*. Nor is it only the federal
tax situation that is at fault. In every city of the United States there is a very large
volume of local real estate that is tax exempt on the ground that it is not used for
profit. Many, perhaps most, of such nonprofit enterprises are warrantably subject to
more critical stricture than the majority of profit-making enterprises, believe it or not.
There is no inherent merit in nonprofit.

in close touch with the newest writings, teachings, and teachers, had consciously adopted a new course, or because different child supervisors had been hired, one doesn't know. Both factors probably came into play.

While Abby was everything that could be prescribed in a responsible mother, she was far from being the anxiously hovering and aggressively elevating type of her husband's mother. Both she and her husband were able to leave the children in other hands while they went on trips, and as the children were growing up, the family would often be divided, some going in one direction while the parents took the younger ones in another. The closely ingrown character of the household was terminated.

Some writers attribute the difference in the later children, who are far more spontaneous and self-directed than were John the First, Junior, and the latter's oldest son, to the fact that they were sent to "progressive" schools—Horace Mann and the Lincoln School at Teachers College, Columbia University. But as character and personality are largely solidified in preschool years, at most modified later, the schools don't account for the basic differences. But the new type of schools certainly show that a new kind of thinking about children had taken hold *chez* Rockefeller.

Whatever the cause, the children from Nelson onward were given a different, more relaxed handling so that they are far more autonomous than any Rockefeller ever was since Wild Bill. Some observers feel it might have been to Nelson's advantage to have acquired a bit more restraint. They find him too brash, too impetuous.

But although the younger boys are free of the Rockefeller automatism, they have, with some variations, found it useful to adhere pretty closely to the Rockefeller scenario. And it is this scenario, rather than personal quirks and foibles, with which we are concerned. The scenario, the work of John I and his advisors, will be analyzed and expounded in the final chapter. It is a gem, which has baffled even highly critical observers.

6.

The current central public figure among the Rockefellers is obviously Nelson Aldrich, vice-president of the United States and ready at any moment to become what Nicholas von Hoffman rightly calls our god-president, ruler of the cosmos and all points west.

Nelson's specialty is government in general and, if anything, he's inherently more of a god than Eisenhower, Kennedy, Johnson, Nixon, or Ford ever were.

He was educated at Horace Mann School and Lincoln School of Teachers College, Columbia University, both free-and-easy progressive institutions operating according to the ideas of the philosopher John Dewey. He finished at Dartmouth College, AB, Phi Beta Kappa, class of 1930. Despite the Phi Beta Kappa, he is no scholar.

He has been married twice, first to Mary Todhunter Clark, granddaughter of a president of the Pennsylvania Railroad, and then to heiress Margaretta Fitler ("Happy") Murphy, also of the Philadelphia "Main Line." His children by his first marriage are Rodman, a businessman now in his forties who is in charge of the all-Rockefeller International Basic Economic Corporation and is a coming Rockefeller business-affairs manager; Mrs. Ann R. Pierson-Coste; Steven, a clergyman and teacher at Middlebury College; Michael (deceased); and Mary (first Mrs. William J. Strawbridge, Philadelphia department store, and then Mrs. Thomas Morgan). By his second marriage (1963) he has two small sons, Nelson A. and Mark F.

Upon his marriage soon after leaving college, he and his bride embarked on a prolonged honeymoon trip around the world, consorting by prearrangement with various top government people and rulers in many countries. When he returned he was made managing rental agent for the newly risen Rockefeller Center, of which he was a director from 1931 to 1958.

He was president of the Center, 1938-1945 and 1948-1951, and chairman of the board, 1945-1953 and 1956-1958.

His formal plunge into government came in 1940 when he was designated by President Roosevelt coordinator of inter-American affairs, dealing mainly with wartime Latin America; he held this post until 1944. At the time, on the eve of American entry into World War II, Roosevelt invited many Republicans into the executive branch, including the cabinet, thus forming an American version of a coalition government. As Roosevelt then said, "The New Deal is out the window." While the New Deal was operative, Roosevelt had been under unremitting but largely unsuccessful Republican attack.

In 1944-1945, now moving onward and upward thanks to Hitler and Tojo, Nelson was assistant secretary of state, a stop worth noting. Number Three held a similar post in the Navy Department.

The end of the war sent Nelson scurrying back to Rockefeller Center, but in 1950 he was named by President Truman chairman of the Development Advisory Board (Point Four program), where he served until the next year. This operation was designed to help friendly "underdeveloped" foreign nations with economic and other problems. Out of the insights gained, Nelson set up a Rockefeller variation on the program in the proprofit International Basic Economy Corporation and nonprofit American International Association for Economic and Social Development.

Terminated at DAB, he was out of government until after the election of President Eisenhower, but in 1953 he was made undersecretary of Health, Education and Welfare, where he was very liberal. To get him out the next year he was appointed a special assistant to El Presidente, serving until 1956.

In 1958 he narrowly defeated unforceful Democratic Gov. Averell Harriman, a very rich but New Dealish man who was former ambassador to Moscow, for the chief executive office of New York State, itself about as large territorially as Czechoslovakia, in population close to Romania. He rewon this office three times against weak candidates, serving until the beginning of 1974, when he resigned to head a heavily funded Rockefeller study group on American problems, which are numerous, perhaps infinite. His electoral majorities increased in each election. This study group was widely regarded as a disguised precampaign ploy aimed at the White House in 1976 and designed to get around a restrictive new campaign funding law. The Rockefeller family expended about $20 million visible money on Nelson's New York campaigns.

Owing to his repeated reelection in New York, Nelson became, finally, the acknowledged spokesman for the Republican party in the northeastern quarter of the country, east of the Mississippi and north of the Mason-Dixon line. Nearly all the party people here have enjoyed Rockefeller patronage in one way or the other.

Nelson has also been a director/trustee of various Rockefeller institutions and chairman of the Human Resources Committee of the Governors' Conference; member of the President's Advisory Committee on Intergovernmental Relations, 1965-1969; trustee of the Rockefeller Brothers Fund, Inc.; chairman of the President's Advisory Committee on Government Organization, 1953-1958; and, not to be forgotten, for five years a member of the Foreign Intelligence Advisory Board under President Nixon. Here he participated in the supervision of the Central Intelligence Agency of international renown. In short, he has been on the inside of the government at the very top for a long time, and in the most "sensitive" areas.

He has been frequently decorated by foreign governments and given many domestic awards. Like John and Winthrop, he lists himself as a Baptist; Laurance and David do not. One would not, however, describe him as a pious man. He belongs to three clubs, none of them in later years elite, and like his brothers has homes and apartments in various places—Maine, Pocantico Hills, New York City, Washington, Paris, Venezuela (seventeen-thousand-acre ranch), etc. He claims authorship of three books which observant journalists say were ghosted.

What is Nelson's political orientation and that of the Rockefellers?

In a nutshell the politics of Nelson and the family since 1940 have been right on the policy line of the United States government. There is no phase of United States policy, including the most controversial, that has found the Rockefellers in serious dissent. And that policy also is, by and large, Rockefeller policy.

Nelson is what is known as a hard-liner and, if anything, he leans to the right of certain basic government policies. He was, first, an enthusiastic supporter of the "cold war." Naturally, he is anticommunist and antisocialist to the core although he has done a good deal of hobnobbing with Soviet emissaries in the United States even as his brother David has been a guest in the Kremlin. There is no telling what these disparate parties may be up to in concert, *sub rosa,* and construction projects within the Soviet bloc have been planned in which the Rockefellers have been mentioned as playing leading financial roles. Up on this level of affairs there is no Left and Right, only *realpolitik.* But nobody plays ball with the Soviets without giving them a leg up somewhere.

In his early years as New York governor, Nelson actively promoted the building of atomic fallout shelters by everybody and, indeed, quite a number of suburban New York residents did follow his lead and build such hideaways. But this campaign on behalf of the construction industry and material suppliers largely came to naught. His peers wouldn't buy it, no doubt feeling that if matters came to that pass, survival was itself intolerable. The national cost of such a program would have been $24 billion.

But even as hullabaloo was maintained about possible atomic warfare and defense budgets were beefed up to unnecessary astronomical levels, wealthy elements—including the Rockefellers—were briskly constructing with tax-free and low-tax money office buildings and hotels all over, especially along the Atlantic Coast, and at the same time were resorting to every visible device in the trickily written law to avoid paying the sort of taxes the public thought rich people paid. As an atomic war would knock down all the profitable new structures built with tax-favored funds, one is led to wonder how seriously anyone among the wealthy expected such a war. The cost of the beefed-up defense establishment, of course, was largely borne by always patriotic taxpayers in the labor force. These usually respond like Pavlov's dogs to appropriate cues, by conditioned reflex.

Nelson was strongly opposed to the Test-Ban Treaty of 1963, which was passed by heavy votes in both houses of Congress. It was one of the few instances in which he was seriously out of step with government thinking, well to the right of it. Under this treaty atmospheric tests of atomic weapons by the United States and the Soviet Union were barred and underground tests limited.

Promising to lower taxes in New York State in his first campaign and to stop the flight of industry from the state, Rockefeller instead repeatedly came up with proposals that greatly increased the New York taxpayers' burden—in fact, stepped it up to the highest level in the nation and in the history of the state.

In 1958 total New York indebtedness was $2,074,703,000, of which $53,603,000 was short term. In the same year California, a state with slightly lower population then, slightly higher now, had total debt of $1,455,496,000. Per capita New York State debt was $128.48 compared with $104.43 for California.

In 1973, as Rockefeller was ending his governorship, New York State indebtedness was $11,800,574,000 of which $2,-187,255,000 was short term. In the same year California had total debt of $6,039,292,000. Per capita debt of New York was now $646.08 compared with $293.14 for California. The average for the fifty states was $282.49 compared with $128.47 in 1958. (Source: *State Government Finances*, 1958, 1973, US Department of Commerce.)

In the same period New York taxes rose disproportionately in relation to the other states. Per capita taxes in New York State in 1958 were $92.97 compared with $120.45 for California, a national state average of $88.03 and a national median of $84.20. In 1973 per capita New York State taxes were $447.30 compared with $355.49 for California, a state average of $325.53 and a state median of $303.96.

Individual per capita income taxes in New York in 1958

were $31.80 compared with $10.73 for California, a national average of $9.11 and a national median of $12.32. In 1973 per capita income taxes in New York were $175.85 compared with $91.57 in California, a state average of $74.54 and a state median of $57.37. And per capita, of course, means the total taxes have been divided by every man, woman, child, invalid, and derelict. The payments per taxpayer in all cases are much higher.

State and local taxes in New York took "a higher proportion of personal income than in any other state" in 1972-1973, according to computations done by the Citizens Public Expenditure Survey, a technical outfit. In 1972-1973 the tax take amounted to $169.52 for every $1,000 of income in the state compared with $157.83 for Wisconsin, $149.09 for California and $129.47 for the national average of state and local taxes. In addition to this, of course, there were federal taxes—unless one belonged to the gilt-edged loophole crowd.

In the same period, the indebtedness of New York local governments, many of their expenditures mandated by the state, also climbed steeply; the figure finally stood at about double that of state indebtedness. Much of this increase in local-government indebtedness was forced or encouraged by the state and its debt-creating governor, so that the local total cannot be looked upon as something separate and apart. It was all part of the free-wheeling Rockefeller Operation. As we have seen, the indebtedness of Albany County was increased by $1 billion in order to finance Rockefeller's Albany Mall. Although the state taxpayers must ultimately defray this, the debt is not charged to the state, does not seem on the records to have any connection with the governorship which inspired it.

Much of the local financial profligacy was stimulated, moreover, through Rockefeller's original concept of "revenue-sharing," whereby the state collects money in taxes and distributes part of it (59 per cent) to local governments. As many disclosures have shown, much—and perhaps most—of this money has been squandered on ill-considered projects and dissipated in various irregularities—just what realists expected to happen.

But the whole operation kept local politicos and their henchmen and hangers-on happy, and kept them singularly quiet and docile with respect to Rockefeller, the money-bringer. They are all, naturally, strongly pro-Rockefeller. The tab for it all, of course, must be picked up by the rank-and-file citizens, many of them now out of a job and on welfare or unemployment insurance—as long as it lasts.

Nor was all Rockefeller spending of public money accounted for by these rising debt totals and tax collections. He also set up what has been well described as "a second state government" in a series of semiautonomous state agencies, actually public corporations, called "Authorities." The state now has sixty-one of these. In doing this he copied a method worked out by Robert Moses for bridges, ports, and toll roads. Rockefeller set up the Metropolitan Transportation Authority, the Urban Development Corporation, the Housing Finance Agency, the State University Construction Fund, and others. And these entities borrowed and spent billions with almost no legislative supervision and usually without voter approval.

"The greatest system ever invented," said the governor with the satisfaction of the cat that swallowed the canary.

The debt total run up by these agencies upon the governor's resignation was $6.7 billion, double the former bonded debt. New York, however, was spending much more than this, of course, because it was also in receipt of federal funds.

The Metropolitan Transportation Authority took over the local passenger service of the Long Island Railroad, the New York Central and the New Haven Railroads, all of which were examples of glorious private enterprise that went smash by reason of joint juggling by management and politicians. The Urban Development Corporation had the objective of decorating city and suburbs with apartment buildings but was widely fought by many localities as a veiled attempt to spread the slums into employed middle-class communities.

The "Authorities" are supposed to be self-supporting out of their own revenues, with the state standing ready to make up any deficiencies.

As borrowing and spending by these agencies bypasses the

legislature and the electorate, so did arrangements the governor made to build the South Mall state office buildings in Albany, named Empire State Plaza.

As a consequence of the expenditures for a large variety of construction—massive buildings, plants, roads, bridges, colleges, campuses, twenty-nine state office structures in addition to the Albany affair—public money flowed like water. As a first result there was much fallout in the way of business for supplying corporations, commission-generating for banks in the issuance of securities and loans, contracts for private contractors, fees for lawyers and highly compensated employment in the construction trades.

It was in connection with all this activity that Rockefeller became known as a modern Pharaoh, a pyramid-builder. A great deal of it was called "Rocky's Follies." The Albany Mall was derisively named Instant Stonehenge and the Albany Pyramid.

Meanwhile, as debt and taxes quadrupled, the number of state employees was increased from 101,729 to 183,383 and the compensation of individual employees doubled. While rough on the general taxpayers, whose taxes were increased in eight of the fifteen Rockefeller years, the governor knew what he was doing because this army of state employees could be relied upon at the polls.

And while all this activity can be justified as constructive from various points of view, the cost, of course, is borne by the general taxpayer, who is in the main an employee subject to layoffs with downturns in the business cycle. Money expended in taxes over a period of years or, indeed, money expended for anything superfluous to mere maintenance, is not retained for the proverbial rainy day. On that day many now join the welfare hordes.

Plutocratic incomes in New York State are not excessively taxed, the top bracket being 15 percent of gross adjusted federal income. With most plutocrats the gross adjusted income is relatively low, owing to the many loophole deductions in the federal code. Even so, relatively few plutocrats maintain home residences in New York. Instead they favor New Jersey,

Connecticut, and more distant states that are without state income taxes. Most plutocrats with a New York address maintain it, usually an apartment or hotel suite, ancillary to a primary residence elsewhere out of which they pay cut-rate federal taxes and no state taxes. One could cite hundreds of cases.

The merely affluent and the lower orders pay by far most of the New York taxes. Nationally, the labor force pays the lion's share of tax money, much of it grossly squandered by the estate-building politicos as many bulletproof analyses show.

In any event, Rockefeller's promise to reduce expenditures was not kept, pretty much the usual political story. Nor was his promise to arrest the flight of industry to tax-lenient and cheap-labor states, reduce crime, and improve general conditions for the lower orders. Admittedly, all of this is too much to expect of any man. But he claimed to be able to deliver.

Bilious observers all along, and congressional investigators during the vice-presidential nomination hearings, showed themselves anxious to detect conflicts of interest on Rockefeller's part. Not that conflict of interest is unknown to legislators and other public officials. It is, in fact, endemic. In the case of Rockefeller, especially, it is hard to see how any move of his as governor, pro or con, could avoid affecting the vast Rockefeller domain in some financial way, especially in New York City and in Westchester County. The Rockefeller enterprises during his governorship prospered, naturally.

Rockefeller's entire term as governor was one of business-generating for banks and hundreds of corporations, with many of whom the Rockefellers are closely tied. Land values were affected by road proposals, especially at Pocantico Hills. And some of the proposals, notably for a value-enhancing Hudson River Expressway passing Pocantico Hills, were publicly fought and defeated.

A tremendously costly project which Rockefeller pushed, and on which he was defeated by public protest, was for a very long bridge to extend diagonally over Long Island Sound from Rye to Oyster Bay, New York. Such a structure, everything else apart, would be an eyesore, no matter who the designer. But it would be a tremendous traffic-generator for the outer environs of the city, no doubt of interest to banks and commercial estabishments with their many outlying branches. And it would call upon the steel and cement industries for tremendous quantities of material. The result: more bond issues, more contracts, more direct beneficiaries. Other results: more traffic, more use of petroleum, more air pollution, more eyesores. And more taxes.

All in all, during his long tenure, it is certainly true that Rockefeller was very good for business in New York State, especially big business. But costs were tremendously increased, especially for small business and the ordinary citizen, always the occasion for crocodile tears from politicians. In American politics any enterprise that is small is rhetorically sacred but in practice allowed to go down the drain.

By reason of his long tenure in office, though, Rockefeller had the privilege of appointing or nominating more public officials than any other governor in New York history, literally thousands. As a consequence, the number of Rockefeller appointees now holding life-time or long-term appointive office in New York State is enormous. Quite a few of these, moreover, are Democrats. The entourage of New York political appointees, naturally, should be added to the already large Rockefeller claque. For most of them, naturally, are pro-Rockefeller to the bone.

Rockefeller's administration was *relatively* (note the emphasis) free of scandal, and he is generally considered a good administrator. But although relatively scandal-free, there was the bribery incident independently managed by L. Judson Morhouse, chairman of the New York State Republican party and Rockefeller's chief political sponsor. Morhouse had been accused by other Republican gubernatorial aspirants of giving Rockefeller the inside track to the nomination in 1958. If he did, Morhouse knew what was good for Morhouse. In general, Republican leaders thought it a Democratic year and acquiesced in the belief that Rockefeller would finance his own campaign, which he did, much to the gratification of party workers. Morhouse was convicted in 1966 on two counts of bribery and sentenced to two to three years in prison. He had induced the State Liquor Authority chairman to accept $50,000 from the Playboy Club of Chicago and grant it a New York liquor license. He got $100,000 for himself in the deal—keeping money. As it transpired, the State Liquor Authority had long been corrupt, pre-Rockefeller, in the matter of granting liquor licenses, a bipartisan graft-encased plum.

Evidence presented by the Democratic prosecutors in New York City showed that Morhouse regularly took "fees" ranging up to $100,000 from corporations and others for making special arrangements in which they were interested, the usual political thing. Although losing appeals from court to court on a sentence that could have run to twenty years (if the original judge had not taken into account Morhouse's "unblemished" reputation and "good character"), the convict, though disbarred as a lawyer, never served a day in jail. His sentence was commuted by the governor. Not only that but, according to information brought out at the Rockefeller nomination hearings, the governor gave him prior to these disclosures of wrongdoing $101,900, nominally a "loan" but later made into a gift. According to further evidence uncovered by the *New York Post* (December 2, 1974), Rockefeller people found him a bargain real estate investment out on Long Island that returned him $408,100 in net gains. Other juicy real estate investments were found in the same region which, after juggling, paid him a substantial annual income. The interpretation placed by unpleasant realists on this favoritism to Morhouse (before he was unmasked) is that it was all a payoff for putting Rockefeller on the inside gubernatorial track, nothing unusual in American politics. In fact, with variations, it is pretty standard practice.

Rockefeller's excuse for making the phantom loan to Morhouse was that as state party chairman, the man had no income (apart from his secret gift!). His excuse for quashing the Morhouse sentence was that he was ill. But five years later Morhouse was still up and about, drawing investment income and well heeled in general, although reported to be physically shaky.

Politicians and corporate higher-ups infrequently convicted usually plead for leniency on the ground they are ill. And, in most cases, they really are. For the fact of the matter is that nearly everybody becomes ill after being put through the judicial meat grinder. A nuance, though, is that clear-cut offenders of lower social status do not usually get compassionate exemption from prison. They do "hard time." The higher-ups, however, are nevertheless stung in the ego as they are all men of lofty pretensions, now revealed to their wives and families not as wonder boys but as plain *gonifs* and ordinary slobs. The moment of truth finds them to be simple frauds who have for years been riding around in chauffered limousines, thumbing their noses at the common bus-riders, many of whom are completely honest.

From the moment he took office in Albany, Rockefeller's sights were obviously trained on the White House. Indeed, the word was out and around in the early 1950s that the family had bouncy Nelson earmarked for the presidency. And nearly all his major moves in the governorship were clearly designed to enhance his claim to consideration for the top office.

So it is always with the knowledge that one is watching a full-blown presidential aspirant that one traces Rockefeller's career as governor—a career during which he several times tripped himself up, as though carrying an unconscious death-wish. A mind doctor might argue that unconsciously Rockefeller is afraid of the office even as he strives to attain it.

At Rockefeller's resignation as governor, he was tearfully hailed by his successor to the $85,000-per-year post, Lieut. Gov. Malcolm Wilson, as a man of "total integrity." As there was nothing sad or even bathetic about the occasion, Wilson's were presumably tears of joy. "God bless the day we met and all the days we will meet," Wilson astoundingly exclaimed. The latter was defeated a year later in his attempt to capture the office by election—no animal appeal, said the analysts.

Rockefeller took office in the 1958 election after an overwhelming and expensive media display and a spectacular sidewalk campaign in which he pumped hands right and left and made a big splash by gorging on various folksy foods thrust at him—hot dogs, hamburgers, bratwurst, blinis, blintzes, pizzas, shish kebab, and shashlik. He was at once dubbed "Rocky," a plain man of the people.

Leading Democrats, many of whom were beneficiaries of his patronage, in summarizing his administration thought he did a generally good job (good for them, anyhow) and used patronage and power in ways that would have been envied by old-line Tammany bosses. Euphemists addicted to classier language called him a pragmatist, a word which in American politics means "anything goes if you can get away with it." He has himself applied the word to himself. First given wide currency by the philosopher Charles Peirce, the word is grossly misused in the political application. In its Peircian usage one tests the *truth* of a proposition pragmatically by an operation or process, such as an experiment. In the political sense, successful bank robbers are thoroughgoing pragmatists. In the abused sense of the term whatever works to one's desire is "pragmatic." Sheer nonsense, *shlock.*

Rockefeller's tenure is divided by chroniclers into the first ten years as liberal and the last five as conservative or reactionary. It was in the first ten that most of the spending was done; after that the belt was tightened and crackdowns were instituted all around—once again the Pavlovian short circuit. Naturally, many observers were confused.

What he did under the rubric of liberalism was as follows:

1. Greatly expanded the state university system, producing a near-replica of the California system. In this process the student body was increased from 36,000 on twenty-eight campuses in 1958 to 246,000 full-time students on seventy-one campuses. All this, of course, required a great deal of lucrative building at taxpayer expense. At the same time he expanded the community colleges from fourteen to thirty-eight; these two-year institutions for home residents are funded partly by the state, partly by the local county, and partly by towns and cities.

2. Caused the creation of the $1.5-billion Empire State Plaza in Albany, the South Mall, requiring at least the liberal outlay of money. But many liberals more or less liked it as it

gave much employment to the uniformly deserving working class from mine and quarry to the construction industry, at the same time generating lucrative contracts.

3. Led the way to the erection of twenty-nine additional state office buildings from eastern Long Island to Buffalo, with similar widespread beneficient job and contract fallout and much applause from local communities.

4. Brought into being two hundred water-treatment plants, thereby exciting the adulation of the antipollution element.

5. Brought into being via bond issues thirty thousand Urban Development Corporation residential units, sixty thousand units of the Housing Finance Agency, and three new model communities funded by UDC.

6. Pushed through 23 new state mental health facilities and had constructed or expanded 109 voluntary and municipal hospitals and nursing homes.

7. Pressed to completion the Long Island Expressway, long unfinished. He himself estimated that he had added four and one half miles per day of automobile roads, as the state groaned over mass transit shortages.

8. Increased state aid to local schools and private universities and colleges, and repeatedly led *banzai* charges to siphon public funds to the Catholic parochial school system. On these last efforts he was repeatedly frustrated on federal constitutional grounds by the courts which ruled: no dice.

9. Brought into being 235,000 scholarship awards of $100 to $600 a year for public and private college students and set up 75,000 Regents scholarships for in-state students ranging up to $1,000 per annum.

10. Formed the Metropolitan Transportation Authority to take over the mismanaged New York City subway system, the Long Island Railroad, and the commutation passenger services of the internally looted New York Central and long mismanaged New Haven Railroads. The latter, though, had been hurt by the building of the New England Thruway and all the railroads had been hurt by the politician-generated road-building and airplane subsidy programs. American railroads, although usually mismanaged from their inception, were real-

ly finally done in by the politicians, supported by a car-crazy, advertising-doped public. If the railroads are ever restored, we'll have to thank the Arabs.

11. Called into being, to deal with the illegal drug problem, a $1-billion narcotics-addiction medical program. Thousands of people were freaking out in the American paradise.

12. Created fifty-five new state parks and established the Adirondacks Park Agency to supervise and preserve a vast upstate area in something like its pristine condition.

13. Caused a reduction in the patient load at state mental hospitals from ninety-thousand to forty-nine thousand but, according to critics, only by dumping the inmates on inadequate community facilities. Some of the reduction was achieved, too, through the copious use of new tranquilizing drugs. Here again were more freak-outs in paradise.

14. Established the State Council on the Arts by which $15 million a year is siphoned to localities for soul-stimulating cultural events.

15. Inaugurated state revenue-sharing with local communities so that about 59 percent of the state budget goes to localities.

In the succeeding five-year conservative-reactionary phase he:

1. Tried to impose a residency test for welfare recipients that was rejected as unconstitutional by the courts. Under his earlier administrations, when he was presumably building up voter support for his presidential push, the number of state welfare recipients had increased from 513,681 to 1.8 million or one in each ten state inhabitants and one in five New York City residents. This, too, in a time of industrial boom.

2. Became tardily perturbed about soaring welfare costs and appointed a welfare inspector-general to ferret out ineligibles, of whom quite a few had latched on to the welfare rolls. Many of these were found to be drawing several welfare checks from different offices under different names, others were employed and enjoyed supplementary welfare income as though they were inheritors of independent means who had gone to Yale and made Skull and Bones. The whole welfare operation was found to be sloppy.

3. Appointed an inspector-general to smoke out any wasteful capers going on in the sprawling higher educational system.

4. Finding progress under the narcotics rehabilitation program too slow, at least unsatisfactory to many hard-line observers, pushed through draconic laws that required mandatory life sentences for drug peddlers. As part of this latter program, he established one hundred new narcotics judgeships, which were criticized as patronage posts, slush.

5. Placed two dozen Republican county chairmen in lucrative posts on the state payroll, more slush.

6. Appointed a Republican state chairman to be presiding judge of the sinecure State Court of Claims, induced him to resign in order to manage a political campaign, and then reappointed him. As a judge is not supposed to be involved in electoral affairs, although many judges surreptitiously are at state levels, these moves were obviously freewheeling evasions of the law.

7. Freely appointed Democrats who assisted in his various maneuvers or kept quiet from among men he had earlier stigmatized as "Tammany bosses," some of the appointments being tinged with nepotism. For example, he appointed as judges a son of Manhattan Democratic leader Frank G. Rossetti and a son-in-law of State Senate Democratic leader Joseph Zaretski. These, among many others, are Democrats who will never direct any flak at Rockefeller.

Among his politically self-wounding actions were the following:

1. His divorce in 1963 from the mother of his five children, wife for thirty-one years, and his prompt remarriage to a simultaneously divorced mother of five whose children elected in court custody proceedings to remain in the care of their father. An infant was awarded to the father by the judge in order not to break up the cohesive sibling group. Seasoned politicians all agree that the divorce and remarriage made him anathema to political managers at the Republican presidential convention of 1964, where his name was put forward, because a large grass-roots voting bloc throughout the country was alienated. The politicians thought he could not have won.

(Politicians are agreed, however, that had Rockefeller pushed aggressively for the nomination in 1960, he could have obtained it; Rockefeller himself says that he didn't because he did not yet have an experienced organization, did not know how precisely to proceed, what levers to pull—no doubt, too, which palms to grease. And had he obtained the nomination, politicians of both parties agree, he would have beaten John F. Kennedy decisively. So, 1960 was the golden Rockefeller year in which he could have made it.)

2. He hurt himself very much again with Republican stalwarts at the 1968 convention by his maneuvers in an illegal strike of New York City sanitation workers, predecessor of many squeezes on the city by civil employees. His conduct is attributed to a desire to embarrass Mayor John V. Lindsay, then regarded as having strong presidential potential. The mayor resolutely requested that the governor call out the National Guard as garbage piled up all over the city, a clear menace to public health and order. The governor counterproposed that the state take over garbage collection, a clear invasion of a local function, a slap at Lindsay; and that the illegal strikers be given a raise. They got it. It was the last that annoyed starchy Republicans. Even the usually docile legislature, full of pro-Rockefeller people fattening on patronage, refused to commend the governor. Then later, in his State of the State message, the governor unprecedentedly went out of his way to rebuke the mayor, a breach of decorum on a purely formal occasion and undeserved by Lindsay.

The sanitation workers' Rockefeller-assisted grab was the prelude to similar grabs by other New York City municipal workers—police, firemen, transportation personnel, office workers, and others—so that the city is now groaning over the payment of their high salaries, pensions, hospital, and other fringe benefits. A New York City policeman or fireman now makes $19,500 per year base salary plus about $7,000 in fringe benefits. The police work an average four-day week. Sanitation men get 10 percent less. All contracts contain automatic escalator clauses. The rates of pay, moreover, do not apply to a few but to some 370,000. And this in a city where a large number of citizens work at the national minimum of pay, live on welfare or social security, or depend upon unemployment insurance. The question is not whether the city workers deserve their good fortune, but who is going to keep paying for it in a city that some observers visualize becoming another Newark.

But in one of his most virulently criticized operations, the quelling of the Attica prison uprising of 1971, politicians in general believe Rockefeller helped himself nationally because a large section of voters endorse precisely such roughhouse tactics. Approval comes about not because the lowbrows are more than normally bloodthirsty, but because they feel frustrated by being caught in a constitutional system that was established quite consciously in order to frustrate various elements, especially the general populace. Out of the frustration rises a desire for abrupt direct action against anything or anyone disliked, especially by the employed classes.

At the Attica State Correctional Facility, the euphemistic bureaucratic name for a maximum security prison for dangerous habitual offenders, some twelve hundred inmates revolted, rioted, and took thirty-eight guards hostage, killing others initially and threatening to kill more unless pseudorevolutionary demands were met. After four days of inept parleys, at the governor's order, one thousand state and local police stormed the prison, indiscriminately shooting to death twenty-eight convicts and nine guards, wounding many others—a regular My Lai massacre at home.

A commission Rockefeller appointed to investigate the incident criticized him, and Rockefeller admitted at his nomination hearing that he had made a mistake in not acting resolutely at once. But he did not concede that his "final solution" was a mistake.

Analysis of the events shows that at every stage of the proceeding, including the finale, the affair could have been handled more adroitly. There was no need for any loss of life, especially by the guards. The rioters, always confined by walls, could have been brought to submission simply by cutting off water and food supplies and waiting them out. But that would not have been dramatic, not *macho*.

What many observers discerned about the finale was that it

was a deliberate, calculated effort to show muscle, always popular for the reasons stated above when done at the expense of unpopular people.

Some observers feel that the affair was purposely managed as it was from the very beginning to produce, quite cold-bloodedly, such a denouement, thereby making Rockefeller appear in the eyes of the mob as a giant-killer—anyhow, a killer. Such a *macho* image has political attraction in many quarters that feel anxiety if the government does not show itself as tough—toward others, of course.

Toward the end of his administration Rockefeller increasingly neglected the cities and was more in harmony with Nixon policies than ever before. He raised very big doubts in the minds of many liberal supporters by backing thuggish-looking, tough-talking Rep. Charles W. Sandman, Jr., for governor of New Jersey. Sandman, who lost out, was shunned even by New Jersey Republican leaders and was rejected by his constituents for reelection to Congress after his hard-boiled pro-Nixon performance on television during the House Judiciary Committee's impeachment hearings. Politically Sandman is a down-the-line, gravel-voiced Nixon man.

In 1973, as part of his later right-curving operation, Rockefeller backed Democrat Robert F. Wagner as a Republican-Liberal mayoralty candidate; Wagner didn't make it. But only eight years before, Rockefeller and Alex Rose, head of the Liberal party, had joined forces in order, as they said, to end twelve years of Wagnerian misrule in New York City. They backed Lindsay then.

Although much earlier a high-minded conspicuous detester of political bosses, in this latter phase Rockefeller entertained Brooklyn Democratic political boss Meade Esposito at his Fifth Avenue apartment and took down from the wall a work of art which he gave to the newly discovered Canarsie statesman.

As Rockefeller raised income taxes to the highest level of any state, from a maximum rate of 7 percent to 15 percent, he naturally came in for commendation from the low-income people out of range of the tax or subject to very little income tax. But many of the less noticed Rockefeller taxes were regressive, squarely hit the "little man," rhetorically beloved of all politicians. When he took office there was no state sales tax; when he left it was 4 percent. As New York City also had a 4 percent sales tax, the total sales tax in the city became 8 percent, clearly killing much city business, especially on big-ticket items. But low-income city dwellers were trapped. When Rockefeller took office the state cigarette tax was three cents per pack; when he left it was fifteen cents. The state gasoline tax was moved up from four cents per gallon to eight cents. Liquor taxes were also jacked up. Local real-estate taxes also rose in the free-spending atmosphere.

While food and prescription drugs are exempt from the sales taxes, taxes are levied on all restaurant charges and on proprietary drugs. In New York City now a tax of one cent is levied on every fifteen-cent cup of tea or coffee, two cents on a twenty-five-cent glass of milk. New Yorkers are deluged by taxes, and living costs in New York City are the highest in the nation except for remote Alaska and Hawaii.

So, if one argues that Rockefeller left the people something in the way of new facilities and services, it is a fact that the rank and file of the people, including the ever-bemoaned poor, are the ones required to pay for it all, directly and indirectly. The rich, meanwhile, cavort at their urban and exurban resorts, loaded with tax exemptions.

Rockefeller's formula throughout was to spend and spend, borrow and borrow, quite contrary to all sound Republican doctrine. The formula was taken from New Dealer Harry Hopkins, who once memorably said: "We'll spend and spend, and elect and elect." While the general public is usually likely to applaud government spending on the ground that it creates jobs for always deserving workers, it is apt to feel surly when it is clear it must pay for it all. Hence the jocular congressional slogan: Never vote against an appropriation bill and never vote for a tax bill. Hence, also, inflation, which is a secret indirect tax produced by the simple process of printing money; one does not need any conventional tax at all. The public would feel even more surly if it understood that the tax laws are so written that the big income receivers pay little or no taxes. The public does not know it is being taken for a glorious ride, always, without reference to any political party. Always. . . . Much of the public, too, does not want to know what goes on because the knowledge arouses painful anxiety. In other words, the more one knows the worse one feels. In brief, ignorance is bliss.

What Rockefeller didn't do and didn't say was also significant. Although he didn't hesitate to pronounce on national policies when so disposed, he never said a word against the Vietnam war or the way it was sneaked into being by a Democratic president, against the culprits or actions in the Nixon-Watergate imbroglio, against Nixon policies, against huge cost overruns and heavy budgeting by the Pentagon, against palpably inflationary moves by the government under Democrat Johnson as well as Republican Nixon, against gross inequities in the tax laws, against always-present monopolies and administered pricing, against widespread frauds on consumers, against CIA, FBI and Internal Revenue Service improprieties, or, indeed, against any gross federal ineptitude, lapse, or sin of commission.

The fact of the matter is that he favored the Vietnam war, favored the all-Republican Watergate element although he personally disliked Nixon, a man who had outmaneuvered him for the presidency, favored Nixon policies, favored the huge Pentagon defense budgets (many of his family companies are big Pentagon suppliers), favored the sweeping indirect tax of inflation, favored the tax laws which are immensely beneficial to himself and his family, and favored the whole monopoly system.

One couldn't say that Rockefeller as president would never bust a trust. But one can be sure that he will never launch a general assault on monopoly. Some one or two monopolies, possibly adverse to Rockefeller interests, might be singled out for unwelcome attention, a tactic useful, too, as window dressing. But one will never hear the crowd cheering "Rocky the trustbuster"—nor, for that matter, almost any other president. One will just as soon see the Kremlin denouncing the Communist party or the KGB.

And for all his frank and open manner on the hustings, newsmen found Rockefeller singularly unforthcoming in press interviews. There he showed himself a master at parry and thrust, evading all disclosure.

The public is a great believer in interviews. "Have you interviewed the subject of your writing?" is frequently asked. When the answer is "No," it is felt that a writer has done less than his duty, knows not whereof he writes. The fact, though, is that nobody ever got anything out of an interview without the willing cooperation of the subject. "Stonewalling" is an old protective tactic. People in public life use interviews for their own purposes, to conceal rather than to reveal. The person being interviewed completely controls the interview, especially a person who knows how to handle himself. The public is confused about the difference between an open interview and a cross-examination under *subpoena*. In a television interview, however, the interrogator has more power as he has the silent assistance of millions of observers, who can discern for themselves evasions, refusals, and pretensions. The subject, too, knows he is under critical outside observation and therefore conducts himself more openly. But even here there are various slick ways of evading proper answers. And few public figures submit to in-depth interviews.

Unless the interviewee is fully cooperative, newsmen do not get much out of official interviews, even out of press conferences, for they are under the constraint of their home offices. Unless their publisher is willing to back them to the hilt, which few publishers are, the newsmen must be circumspect, polite. If, on the other hand, a publisher is solidly in accord with his employee (which few are beyond a certain point), journalistic technique can accomplish much. There is, first, the "smoke 'em out" tactic; if the official won't talk, speculative or semispeculative material is published. If this produces no result then political enemies or secret "leaks" are interviewed, the results published. And now simple description of the Herculean efforts being made to get information of public concern is published and a "cover-up" is charged or implied.

A newspaper can, provided the publisher consents, bring almost any uncommunicative official to heel, make him talk to the point—or flee. But a private interviewer, or one obliged to preserve the synthetic amenities, cannot do so. A newspaper, of course, is itself subject to behind-the-scenes pressures, arm twistings. It is often pinned down as by adversary pieces in a chess game.

What did any of the Watergate investigative reporters ever get out of Nixon or his press secretary except evasions and packs of lies? Without the secret tapes, everything in the end would have been up in the air, ambiguous.

Men who are up to *sub rosa* operations in politics or corporate juggling will simply not yield anything informative via an interview. And most of them in those lines of endeavor have something to promote or to conceal—not all but most. "No comment" is the usual motto.

The New York Times, in editorializing about Rockefeller's resignation, praised his first-three terms as "progressive Republicanism" but found much fault with his latter three years. It dubbed him the "father" of revenue sharing with the localities, praised the financially shaky Urban Development Corporation and the expanded state university system, but characterized the Albany South Mall as "wildly extravagant." It had praise for his veto of the repeal of the abortion law voted by an intimidated legislature but reprehended Rockefeller for his support of Nixon and the New Jersey gubernatorial campaign of Charles W. Sandman. And it faulted him for resigning the governorship in the face of his duty to serve out a term of office he had sought.

Whatever luster he had acquired during the governorship was, therefore, somewhat dimmed as he departed to head his own heavily financed Committee on Critical Choices, a last springboard to the presidency.

On a number of objectives Rockefeller was frustrated during his governorship. The voters, for one thing, turned down two transportation bond issues he advocated that provided mainly for more new automobile roads. Not until a new package was fashioned giving more support to mass transit facilities was a bond issue passed.

He was frustrated on the attempt to build the Hudson River Expressway, an extension of Broadway from the city line northward to Ossining and beyond. He was flatly repulsed on the Rye-Oyster Bay Bridge project and did not get as far with some aspects of the state university system as he desired.

He made an attempt to capture the system of the City University of New York for the state system, which would indeed have been a big coup. But city forces defeated him here, mainly because under the state system some tuition is paid by students. The city system has from its inception been tuition-free. While this system worked very well in earlier days, under the new mass registration of students, many of them not especially motivated for study and many, indeed, not properly prepared for university work, the student-load is heavy and the cost is totally borne by the taxpayers. What the future will show remains to be seen.

Rockefeller also sought, according to reports, to develop within New York State the counterparts of Massachusetts Institute of Technology and California Institute of Technology and got at least the nucleus of such an affair established at Stony Brook, Long Island. The idea behind such triplication of facilities is that it would attract more savants to New York, raise the local tone—and also, incidentally, make much recondite expertise more readily available to local large-scale enterprises.

Now that Rocky has "gone national," someone else will have to realize such a vaulting dream—or else rely on Boston. After all, MIT is only forty-five minutes away by plane.

What Nelson accomplished for New York, always at the great expense of individual taxpayers, was to greatly improve the public infrastructure of the state, thereby providing, among other things, a much better climate for business. And while the tax load was greatly increased for individuals, it was significantly lightened for business for the claimed reason of stopping the drain of enterprises away to low-service, low-tax states. At the same time, much new business and industrial activity was stimulated by the expenditures of the state.

Simultaneously, by the use of official and personal patronage, Nelson greatly enhanced the ranks of Rockefeller supporters, people who felt beholden to him.

On the negative side of this ledger, however, New Yorkers have less income left to their discretionary disposal in view of the heavier tax bite. With the increased sums required for debt service and maintenance of all the new facilities, taxes must, if anything, be further increased.

And as to Nelson's administration being relatively scandal free, the emergence of the giant nursing-home scandal after he left office shows that much putrescent matter may have been swept under the rug, to be disclosed in the course of time. In 1973 Rockefeller himself appointed a Temporary State Commission on Living Costs and the Economy. As chairman he appointed Assemblyman Andrew Stein, the son of Jerry Finklestein, a favorite Rockefeller Democrat whom he had previously appointed to the lucrative post of board member of the Port Authority.

It was Stein who forced the scandal into view although he attempted to blame leading Democrats who had defended against Republicans the creation of the commission for conditions that were disclosed. At the same time he astonishingly cleared Rockefeller of any responsibility for conditions. The final report of the Commission, however, found Rockefeller chiefly responsible for all that was amiss.

For the State Health Department, stacked with Rockefeller appointees, had jurisdiction over the nursing homes and, despite many reports of bad conditions, all along was careful not to intervene.

The politics of the situation was given penetrating reportage by Geoffrey Stokes in the *Village Voice*, (February 3, 1975, pages 22 and 23.). Stokes points to Rockefeller as "The Big Enchilada" of the nursing home scandal, not certain Democrats Stein had pointed the finger at.

Adverse official findings, all swept under the rug, have been made about the nursing homes since 1960. Since that time heavy federal funding had come in to take care of the indigent aged, with the result that nursing homes proliferated, even took the form of chains and pyramids. In New York they get $1,550 per month per indigent patient, half from the federal government, one quarter from the state, and one quarter from the city.

As the Stein Commission has showed, in hundreds of places in and out of the city, little of the benefit reached the inmates, who were shown to be grossly neglected in illness, underfed, allowed to dehydrate, and left to lie for days in filth and bedsores. At the same time many nursing home operators, some of whom had piled up more than $30 million, overstated the value of their properties by many times—selling them back and forth to themselves at constantly rising prices—so as to show eligibility for proportionately greater net return. Other costs were similarly padded in the double ripoff—first on the public treasury, then on the patients. The operators shared with politicians under the guise of legal fees and insurance premiums. Even the legal costs of contesting government regulations were charged to operating costs.

The conditions disclosed were as savage as anything in *The Gulag Archipelago*.

While it was a Rockefeller-appointed commission that brought all this to national attention, it is a fact that the malpractices had been going on for a long time, unimpeded by state or city officials. Rockefeller admirers claim he was a great administrator. Yet, what was he and his appointees doing while all this went on?

It is not being suggested that Rockefeller profited monetarily from the nursing home ripoff, but, as a politician desiring to keep in the good graces of other politicos in the political racket, he merely kept quiet, didn't lift a finger. Were he the demon administrator his admirers claim, he would have been down their throats. But in the symbiotic political camarilla his name would then have been mud and his political career perhaps in ruins. The patriots in the backroom must always be served.

Astute observers, moreover, have said that the nursing home scandal is by no means confined to New York, is not chargeable to any one political party but is a national biparti-

san gouge for money at the expense of taxpayers and helpless
patients. Such observers claim that if the investigation, which
has now reached Congress, is not maneuvered out of sight, it
will eclipse Watergate, especially in its effect on the emotions
of the public.

It is a big time-bomb, in the opinion of such, ticking away
as the nation heads into the two-hundred-year anniversary of
its establishment, a genuine lalapalooza.

Toward the close of his hearings Chairman Stein, seeming
to concentrate on appointed officials to the exclusion of elected Democrats and Republicans, put the blame squarely on
Rockefeller's State Health Department officials under Dr.
Hollis Ingraham, health commissioner from 1963 through
1974. He said the Medicaid reimbursement formula worked
out for the nursing homes "is a license to steal." What is
needed, Stein said, is a new nonprofit system and the ousting
of the for-profit nursing home operators.

But the nursing home scandal was only one time bomb to
explode after Rockefeller left office.

Early in 1975 the Urban Development Corporation default-
ed on more than $100 million of construction notes due to
banks. Some eight thousand workers faced layoffs from many
large projects until the state and the banks worked out a new
corporation to be backed by tax funds—the taxpayer again.
But the default brought down the market for all UDC bonds
and with them the entire municipal bond market and the general bond market. Investors coast to coast, including banks
and insurance companies, were put into a dither.

The situation was this: Under Rockefeller the electorate had
twice voted down propositions to issue tax-guaranteed bonds
for needed low-income housing, perhaps recognizing it as an
attempt by the tax-avoiding Rockefellers and their friends to
shove the burden on to the labor force as they have already
shoved most of the tax burden. The housing, however, was
needed because private investors would not provide it for two
reasons: (1) New York politicians had for years exercised controls over rents and (2) the poor in need of housing were

extremely destructive toward their rented habitations, were not acculturated to city living. Most were recently arrived from the swamps and bayous in the South and the Caribbean. Rent control was instituted because there were more votes among tenants than among landlords, against whom it was applied rigorously as all other costs soared.

Rockefeller therefore bypassed the electorate, as he often did, and bypassed the legislature as well by having UDC issue with the advice of John Mitchell, later the Big Enchilada of Watergate, what were called "moral commitment" bonds. That is, the state was morally committed to pay principal and interest but was not legally bound to do it, and tax collections did not guarantee payment. Mitchell, however, then in private practice as a bond lawyer, walked out on Rockefeller when he began issuing "moral commitment" bonds not tied to specific projects but merely issued in general by the corporation. What bond buyers want, however, is backing by some specific property against which they can foreclose and resell to get their money in the event of default. As it is, UDC has outstanding hundreds of millions of bonds, many of them not tied to any specific property.

However, the way UDC is set up, although it is supposed to be self-supporting, in many cases its projects are not programmed to collect rents sufficient to defray costs. For costs to be met the rental units will have to be offered at least on the middle-income level, defeating the plan for decent housing for the poor.

No matter what solution is arrived at, the final bill will have to be defrayed by the state taxpayer—unless the federal government can be induced to pick up the loose end. Even if nothing is done and all the UDC obligations allowed to go down the drain, the state taxpayer will pay. For then the cost of new financing for New York State will be driven so high, and on such rigorous terms, that it will hit the state taxpayer as hard as if he picked up the tab for UDC directly. Whatever the decision, the taxpayer will pay—and pay and pay.

One thing that was evident in all this was a case of taxation without representation, which was the ostensible reason the American colonists chased out King George III. Many other Rockefeller projects, including the Albany Mall, similarly classify under nonrepresentational taxation. Where are the Minutemen of '76?

So if Rockefeller is on the Republican national ticket in 1976, either in the stellar spot or playing second fiddle, there is room for much national hullabaloo, provided the Democrats put up a plausible candidate. Another Harry Truman, with a knockout punch in either hand, could win for the Democrats simply by, like Al Smith, "looking at the record." But the Democrats may not be as anxious to unhorse Rockefeller and Ford as they say they are.

Something I haven't mentioned until now is that some very keen political observers in New York State think it very strange that the Democrats always opposed Rockefeller, three times, with weak contenders, people with no statewide image. Such observers suspect that the Rockefellers, through friends in the Democratic party, arranged it that way, didn't want Rocky to face a real heavyweight. All the campaigns against Rockefeller, truth to tell, were very mild, with none of the dubious Rockefeller maneuvers stressed. An Al Smith, Roosevelt, or even Herbert Lehman could have sent him packing.

Naturally if the national Democrats put up a dummy in 1976, Rockefeller is going to have an easier time capturing either of the top spots. Such things have been arranged in the past. Why not again?

In other words, everything wasn't wonderful as Mr. Wonderful resigned.

Until he was nominated for the vice-presidency by Gerald Ford, himself an unelected vice-president and president, Nelson Rockefeller's political future was regarded as quite clouded by the crystal-ball gazers. But with the nomination everything lit up in the Rockefeller empire like a Christmas tree. Happy days were here again as Nelson swung into his private jet plane—part of the RAF (Rockefeller Air Force)—for Washington.

7.

Laurance Rockefeller was born in 1910 and has been far less in the public eye than any of his brothers. He is nevertheless an important and active member of the sibling sextet.

While Nelson and David might well be described as the "front men" of the present Rockefeller group, Laurance and John 3 are more like "back office" or backup men although Laurance roams pretty far afield on specific building and promotional projects, mainly to the Caribbean, West Coast, and Hawaii. He is, too, a close confidential collaborator in the political career of Nelson as well as a corporate man, all made clear at the Washington nomination hearings.

Laurance describes himself as a "venture capitalist," and he is an investment-finder of the Rockefellers, especially in the sphere of new technology. In appearance he most resembles John 3. Nelson, Winthrop, and David turned out beefier.

The bare bones of his background are as follows:

After schooling at Horace Mann and Lincoln Schools of Teachers College, Laurance went to Princeton, A.B., 1932. He concentrated there on philosophy. Since then he has been the recipient of five honorary doctorates so that he, like brothers Winthrop and David, might well be called Dr. Rockefeller. Married to Mary French in 1934, he has four children: Laura (Mrs. Laura Case), Marion (Mrs. Warren T. Webber), Lucy (Mrs. Jeremy P. Waletsky), and Laurance. Of the last not much has been heard yet.

Like his brothers he was put through the mill in the various Rockefeller organizations and was chairman of Rockefeller Center, Inc., 1953-1956 and 1958-1966 and remains as a director; is chairman of the Rockefeller Brothers Fund; Caneel Bay Plantation, Inc., Rockresorts, Inc., Woodstock Resort Corporation, Grand Teton Lodge Company, Olahana Corporation, Citizens' Advisory Committee on Environmental Quality, New York Council of Parks and Outdoor Recreation; president of the American Conservation Association, Jackson Hole Preserve, Palisades Interstate Park Commission (governmental); chairman of the New York Zoological Society, the Outdoor Recreation Resources Review Commission, (established by Congress), 1958-1962, the Hudson River Valley Commission (governmental), 1965-1966, the White House Commission on Natural Beauty, 1965. Since 1973 he has been a director of mass-circulating *Readers' Digest,* a significant connection. Melvin Laird, President Ford's right bower, is a top executive there.

He is a trustee of Massachusetts Institute of Technology, 1965-1971, the YWCA, Princeton University, the Alfred P. Sloan Foundation, the Sealantic Fund, the Greenacre Foundation, the National Geographic Society, the New York Historic Trust and a past director of the International Nickel Company, Olin Mathieson Chemical Corporation, Cape of Good Hope Corporation, Filatures et Tissages Africains, etc. He is also chairman of the Memorial Sloan-Kettering Cancer Center, a director of the Community Blood Council of Greater New York, and the National Park Foundation. In other words, an authentic big shot.

During World War II he was a lieutenant in the United States Naval Reserve and rose to lieutenant commander, stationed in the Bureau of Aeronautics as liaison officer between the Navy Department and aircraft production plants—a key post and good learning place financially and industrially. At the time he was in his early thirties. He is a recipient of the Order of the British Empire and, like his brothers, has been lavishly decorated by foreign governments and given a large number of public awards at home. Were all the Rockefellers to appear in public wearing their decorations and insignia of award, they would be taken for field marshals in mufti. He is a member of eleven clubs, four of them top elite. Among his brothers he is the leading clubman. His two main places of residence are a Fifth Avenue apartment in New York City and Pocantico Hills, but he has others.

His wife, like the wife of John 3, plays a leading role in many organizations concerned with the arts, education, community services, and charities. To list them all for both women would yield another long catalogue. Suffice it here to say that they are into a spate of community and art-booming organizations.

He has been said to divide his time half to public organizations, half to investing in or financing specialized upcoming or limping companies believed to have potential for great profit. Until recent post-Nixonian periods of uncertainty, his investment success in new ventures, largely concentrated in advanced and military technology, was reported at 80 percent (*Fortune*, March, 1955). As far as such operations are concerned, the score, if true, is equivalent to perfect. As the ancient Babylonian adage has it, "You can't win them all."

Some few of the companies into which he has put "seed money" are known to be the following:

Wallace Aviation, up to 27 percent interest; Nuclear Development Associates, up to 17 percent; Reaction Motors (rocket engines), up to 21 percent; Marquardt Aircraft (ramjets), up to 20 percent; Flight Refueling, up to 30 percent; Airborne Instruments Laboratory, up to 24 percent; New York Airways, 3 percent; Piasecki Helicopter, 17 percent; Geophysics Corporation; J. S. McDonnell Aircraft Corporation, later McDonnell-Douglas and one of the ten largest Pentagon contractors; Itek Corporation, business machines; Thiokol Corporation; and various others. As early as 1938 he took a substantial position in North American Aviation in concert with Eddie Rickenbacker, the air ace, and this company became Eastern Airlines, the second largest airline in the country, operating along the Atlantic Coast down into the Caribbean region. There are, of course, many additional companies.

He has also been active in constructing luxury hotels, resort caravansaries, and apartment houses in the Caribbean (Puerto Rico and Virgin Islands), on the West Coast, and in Hawaii.

The main source of business of the new-technology companies has been government contracts, almost exclusively with the Pentagon. Laurance has been the activist here even as Nelson and John 3 have concentrated on the State Department and the Central Intelligence Agency. The technique of Laurance (and his brothers) with these companies has been described as follows:

". . . they put a small amount in a company; get it munitions business; have its stock sold to the public at ten to a hundred times the original cost; sell what they want, subject to only 25 percent capital gains tax, and keep enough stock to retain control, if they wish."

Laurance in the 1950s served on a panel that issued a policy report written by Henry Kissinger, *International Security— The Military Aspect.* It recommended successive increases of $3 billion per year in military spending until 1965; the government in fact spent more.

Although the Rockefellers are personally nonbellicose, adversaries of the United States in wars of this century have felt the Rockefeller sting. First, vast quantities of oil, gasoline, and kerosene were supplied by Standard Oil companies in both world wars. The same sort of thing was seen in the Korean and Vietnam wars where, in addition, aircraft of Rockefeller companies entered the fray. Helicopters from once-tiny Piasecki Helicopter, now a big operation, were first prominent in the Korean War, and Phantom and Banshee fighters got into both wars, supplied by J. S. McDonnell Aircraft. The Phantom is a Rockfeller weapon, reputed to be the best combat airplane in the world. Moreover, parts for various military instruments came from other Rockefeller companies.

None of this indicates that the Rockefellers are evolving into an American Krupp or a Du Pont, merely that they are diversifying in a military age. If military procurement continues to boom, no doubt their military positions will be extended to parallel resorts, hotels, office structures, apartment houses—and various energy fuels. If military procurement declines, they will turn elsewhere. For there is a wise old saying: a dollar is a dollar.

As to money making on the part of people hailed *ad nauseam* as conspicuous philanthropists, Laurance has said that he and his brothers must continue to make money lest the well run dry and they have nothing left to dish out in the "nonprofit" sphere. He here put the Rockefeller scenario into a nutshell. But why one should continue to strive to make money in order to give, if that is the game, is more than some people are able to understand. Why be acquisitive in order to be donative? Why not let other people acquire it for themselves while one watches in philosophic detachment from the sidelines? In brief, why take the initiative from others?

There's more to all this than is fathomed in the average man's simple philosophy.

Laurance has been the least written-about of the Rockefeller brothers in the general media, but he is given extensive reportage in specialized publications on forestry, geography, conservation, gadgetry, land development, resort-travel and financial projects. And his interest in conservation has brought him under fire from some who know about the family's long-term position in public utility companies like Consolidated Edison of New York, some of whose Hudson River projects have aroused the ire of conservationists. As to this sort of thing, however, there is really no basic contradiction. In an industrial age there must, manifestly, be a trade-off between some industrial requirements and conservation and pollution. The complete solution, producing maximum conservation and minimal pollution, would be to end industrialism with all its ugly structures. Even better for the American environment would it be if everybody left it, going back where they originated in Europe, Africa, and Asia. It is doubtful that much support could be raised for such objectives. The worst polluters and anticonservationists, anyhow, are the rank-and-file automobile drivers, the common man. And those who are most caustic against the maneuvers of Con Edison and the like are those who are first to howl when their supply of electricity is curtailed. Everybody denounces the oil companies; but the same people keep on burning oil, complain if they can't get enough gasoline for their cars. And so it goes.

It is the opinion of some observers to whom I, for one, give credence, that Laurance and David operate financially for their own accounts, taking risks and profits (when available) that Nelson and John 3 do not participate in. Because three of the brothers were not as interested in money making *per se*, it is thought that Laurance and David have greater independent net worth than Nelson or John 3. As I don't really know this, I merely throw in the thought and keep it as a hypothesis. Seems reasonable.

While most of Laurance's ventures are individually rather modest, except Eastern Airlines and McDonnell-Douglas, in the aggregate they add up to a diversified bundle. As yet none has turned into a Xerox or Polaroid. And when, as, and if one of them does, the aggregate of Rockefeller wealth will eclipse that of old John D. in his palmiest days. The potential is there, which is no doubt one of the reasons Laurance fools around with this stuff. Financially, anyhow, the big frontier today is technology. With the right tools Switzerland could rule the earth, an outcome devoutly to be wished.

Many of the things Laurance is into are unfamiliar to the public but nevertheless represent impressive outlays. Take Grand Teton Lodge Company. What is it?

Between 1927 and 1932 Junior bought thirty-three thousand acres inside the then-proposed Grand Teton National Park, Wyoming, on which the government was slow in moving. He deeded this land to the National Park Service after long delay in obtaining permission from Congress. Naturally, it gave him a tax write-off. It is all now a scenic national park available to long-distance automobilists who, incidentally, consume oceans of gasoline. As there were not sufficient accommodations there for people, who slept in their cars, the Rockefellers advanced $10 million to finance fireproof lodges —Jackson Lake Lodge and Jenny Lake Lodge. They also put up $2 million for an elaborate recreation complex at Colter Bay into which the government put only $1 million. Colter Bay has lodgings, stores, cafeteria, launderettes, baths, and 160 log cabins.

Grand Teton Lodge Company, which is profit making and tax paying, operates the lodges, a bus line, and the other facilities, all relatively moderate-priced.

Laurance has a philosophy about conservation. He is opposed, for one thing, to having the government take vast stretches of wilderness and hold them in a deep freeze for the indefinite future. He believes they should be both conserved and used by people now.

"Conservation is a job for a philosopher," he says. "It's a study in values. Bringing man and nature together harmoniously is an art. Fitness and outdoor recreation go hand in hand. Tension and stress are the causes of many ailments. If you can restore peace of mind and re-create a person, you've given him a new lease on life."

While operating in the Caribbean his attention was called to the island of St. John, Virgin Islands. Here, through Jackson Hole Preserve of Wyoming, he advanced $1,750,000, bought twelve thousand acres, and turned it over for the Virgin Islands National Park. At the same time nearby profit-making, tax-paying facilities were established for tourist accommodations. These were handled by Caneel Bay Plantation, Inc., which put in stuff similar to that found at Colter Bay.

The Rockefellers have also donated twenty-seven hundred acres of Mt. Desert Island, Maine, where they have long summered at Seal Harbor. The donation went to make Acadia National Park. The parks all serve to keep out land "developers"—that is, commercial vandals.

Laurance's ideal of a conservation project is Palisades Interstate Park, diagonally across the Hudson River from Pocantico Hills. This park is preserved wild land, state regulated, yet it is open throughout to public use and is heavily used. It is the consequence of a Rockfeller donation of $20 million many years ago; until then the region was being quarried for rocks and slowly chopped to pieces.

Laurance has a ranch on the southern edge of Grand Teton National Park where he has spent much time with his family. The fact is, one Rockefeller or another has a place abutting all these conserved areas, where they can keep an eye on things and enjoy the natural beauty. Like his brother John and his father, he likes to swing the ax in the great outdoors.

He was set on this conservation tack by his father, who first put up $60 million plus for the restoration of Williamsburg, Virginia, and $40 million plus to acquire the land for the Great Smoky National Park.

Laurance is also into the building of luxury hotels, for a profit. One of his most spectacular ventures in this direction was the Dorado Beach Hotel, Puerto Rico, into which $9 million was put. It boomed soon after its completion in 1958 when Castro thoughtfully drove all the tourists from Cuba. It has since been sold at a hefty profit. More recently he has completed a deluxe resort at Kawaihae, an isolated part of Hawaii. He also put one into the Virgin Islands. With his brother David he was a partner in The Embarcadero, a big office-apartment complex in San Francisco.

While Laurance and David aren't, as far as the record shows, raking in new money the way old John D. did with his secret railroad rebates, drawbacks, kickbacks, price wars, and secretly owned "independent" companies, both men appear to be plowing fresh ground in money making and to be doing good for themselves and their progeny. Bound to succeed.

In his personal life Laurance, like his brothers, lives unostentatiously on the top rung of luxury, everything the best. When at Pocantico Hills he often commutes to the city down the Hudson River in a fast speedboat. He has his own jet plane, with full crew, in which he darts all over the Western Hemisphere. Although he enjoys *la dolce vita,* he doesn't do so *fortissimo.* It is a *pianissimo* performance all the way. He is reputed to be the most coldly analytical of the brothers.

There is more to say about him, as there is about all the brothers, but what has been said will serve to place him in the constellation. There is enough material, though, to do a full-length book on each of the brothers.

8.

The limper or lame duck of the Rockefeller brothers was Winthrop, twice governor of Arkansas, who died in 1973 of cancer of the liver and pancreas. Widely regarded as the *shnook, shlemiel,* and *shlepper* of the family, by The Cousins as a black sheep, he developed this way quite by family accident. He is a difficult case for eugenists to account for.

What threw Winthrop off the track was neither constitutional defect nor parental fault but, as the evidence seems to show rather clearly, unmanageable early sibling rivalry. He was, quite simply, overwhelmed by slightly older brothers in childhood, with the parents helpless to deflect the primitive undercurrents, noticed probably too late. This sort of thing, of course, happens in many families.

Abby at one stage, no date given, wrote to her older sons (who were away on a trip or at school) as follows:

"I hope, when you boys come home, you will do nothing to disturb David's present friendly feelings with Winthrop. It seems cruel to me that you big boys should make Winthrop the goat all the time. I realize that he is often trying, but you know very well that the only way to help him is by being kind to him. Abuse only makes him angry and much worse, while for love and kind treatment he will do anything. Also, remember how young David is, take time to play with him, and be good to him."[5]

While this is only one small piece of evidence—others are found in her special efforts to give Winthrop personal support —it is evidently a late entry in a long line of parental interventions and admonitions, a final *cri de coeur.* Abby lost out here.

Winthrop, born in 1912, was obviously far behind the others, the "baby" in relation to them, and in the role of baby no doubt got special parental protection, which in turn aroused vindictive jealousy in the older ones, now a cohesive group—a typical family situation. John was six when Winthrop was born, Nelson four, and Laurance two. While Nelson could accept Laurance, and John could accept Nelson, the trio together as a body certainly had plenty of natural reason as capable older boys to look down on the less capable newcomer. Winthrop, therefore, was made to feel inept from the outset and was also given special protection by his parents, making matters worse all around. And he remained more or less inept the rest of his life, the odd man out of the family, the fumbler.

David escaped this effect because he was so very much younger that he did not need to keep up with the others, and

---

5. Mary Ellen Chase, *Abby Aldrich Rockefeller,* p. 43.

he was undoubtedly accepted as an obviously incompetent nonrival, a baby and no threat to the precedence of the elders. When David was born his older brothers were respectively nine, seven, and five, so far out of his range that he was safe. His father, moreover, took special individual care in the rearing of David, accounting for much of his self-contained difference from the others.

Winthrop, however, was repeatedly put down by his brothers, a habit pattern that developed and continued. By the time everybody had sufficiently matured, ready to accept Winthrop, it was too late. Now he really was a misfit, full of self-doubt. So the Rockefeller that grew up with the most scar tissue inside him, and who was the least organized, was Winthrop. He never came to full emotional maturity. If anyone wants to weep for a Rockefeller, weep for Winthrop, the victim of childhood family undercurrents that left him a loser all the way, internally crippled.

That Winthrop was increasingly far out of line with his brothers was shown to public view when he dropped out of Yale after being obliged to fall back from the class of '35 at age twenty-three to that of '36 owing to poor work. His brother David, born in 1915, was to graduate from Harvard in 1936. Unmotivated to study, apparently unmotivated for anything else, Winthrop was disorganized and adrift, a loser. By contrast, all his brothers at least finished college creditably.

"I just wasn't getting anywhere in college," he said later. "When I was asked why, I said that I couldn't seem to study properly and maybe my eyes were bothering me."

An eye doctor, however, turned thumbs down on this cop-out—blind people go through college—and asked him if he had ever tried opening a book. He was, obviously, emotionally blocked and unstructured, not too unusual. What he really needed at this point, and never got, was a routine psychoanalysis. Apparently such a bizarre notion never occurred to anyone among the Rockefellers. It would have saved much trouble.

In 1936, under a family cloud, Winthrop headed for Texas. It was vainly hoped, no doubt, as in many similar cases, that he would "straighten out." He had held a summer job in Texas in 1933 and got one now as an oil-field worker with the Humble Oil and Refining Company, subsidiary of Standard Oil of New Jersey (Exxon). He was soon accompanied by bodyguards and at one stage packed a gun himself owing to vague talk of a kidnaping. He was the first Rockefeller to have worked for pay with his hands. Not even Wild Bill did that.

After briefly having a go at the oil fields, he returned to New York, first to be a trainee with the Chase National Bank and a year later with the foreign trade department of Socony-Vacuum Oil Company (Mobil). He then became an "industrial relations consultant" for Rockefeller Center, Inc., a nothing job with a title. In 1938 family influence made him executive vice-chairman of the Greater New York Fund, a body soliciting charitable donations, and in 1940 was made a director of the National Urban League, a body often funded by the Rockefellers to help Negroes with social problems. Nothing of all these padded tasks panned out for Winthrop. He was merely the medium for demonstrating the family presence.

In the meantime he attracted some public attention by nightclubbing and pub crawling, an incipient alcoholic, soon to be full blown. Here, like many other losers, he could appear as a kingfish. He was the first Rockefeller to make a splash in the bright-light belt, the first big boozer of the family in a century and a half.

But his own and his family's efforts to find a niche in which he could function failed. He was clearly a ship without a compass. No doubt after hearing many family admonitions to shape up, perhaps some sharp reproofs and even ultimata, Winthrop gave up and put himself out of family reach (as he no doubt thought) by enlisting in the army as a private ($21 per month and found) a year before Pearl Harbor. Here was a very un-Rockefellerish thing to do, a move that certainly caught the family off balance. The last Rockefeller to have done anything so rash was Frank, John D.'s youngest brother, who enlisted in Mr. Lincoln's army and became a veteran of many Civil War battles. Neither old John D. nor his brother William heeded Mr. Lincoln's call for recruits to save the

Union, sensibly preferring instead to make fortunes. John D. never had any intention of going in, at risk of life and limb, to clean up politicians' unholy messes. He much preferred buying these former poor boys on their way up. If he didn't surely know, he sensed that wars, for whatever advertised cause, are usually pure idiocy. And, he must have noticed that after wars are over, the politicians of both sides are again as thick as proverbial thieves, shaking hands, madly embracing, and even in some jurisdictions kissing each other passionately in public. Tributes now flow for those dunderheads who have indeed died in vain.

Pearl Harbor, of course, found Winthrop headed in the right direction to be killed. And perhaps he didn't care; perhaps he'd have liked nothing better. As it was, he was rapidly advanced in rank, with or without family intervention. His gilt-edge name, certainly, didn't make him a leper to the professional killers of the War Department. He quickly moved up to sergeant in the First Division, and in early 1942 after attending officers' training school at Fort Benning, was made a second lieutenant. Soon he was a first lieutenant in command of "H" Company, 305th Infantry, 77th Division. He had become a major in the supply section when his outfit shoved off for the Pacific theater—very swift promotion, especially for a *shlepper.*

In the Pacific he was involved in various island operations and in the landing on Guam in 1944, opposing the wicked Japanese whom his brother John would soon be fraternizing with. Available accounts show him to have been highly popular with his men, relationships no doubt lubricated with the customary Rockefeller largess.

It was in April, 1945, during the invasion of Okinawa, that Winthrop nearly became the first Rockefeller to die in battle, and not in any charge or last-ditch stand. The headquarters ship he was on, caught like a sitting duck, was dive-bombed, hit hard. Winthrop received burns on his hands that put him aboard a hospital ship and brought him the Purple Heart. He also got the Bronze Star with oak leaf cluster. Upon his recovery he came down with jaundice and was shipped back to the United States for further hospitalization.

After the war, the War Department, one of his brothers ensconced as assistant secretary of state (1944-45), another as special assistant to the undersecretary at the Navy Department (October-December, 1945), singled him out for a cushy job of touring the country to find out how veterans were adjusting to civilian life. He did this for about six months, duly filed a report, which was duly pigeonholed, and duly returned to the production department of Socony, where he stayed until 1951. He then went to Ibec Housing Corporation and Rockefeller Brothers, Inc., under the family eye. His rank upon separation from the armed forces was lieutenant-colonel, and he was freely addressed by *maîtres d'hôtel* thereafter as Colonel Rockefeller until he became Governor and Dr. Rockefeller. In other days he'd have been Duke Rockefeller, drunk or sober.

But in 1948 Winthrop hit the headlines in a bigger way than any Rockefeller had done since, perhaps, the Ludlow massacre. For he had run into the dynamite blonde that *macho* young males are believed by the credulous Hugh Hefner and his readers of *Playboy* to dream of and drool over and in circumstances that drive tabloid news editors into delirium.

To the naive city rooms of the newspapers, here was one of the endless miraculous variations on the fabulous American Dream: rich boy, wounded war hero, meets and falls in love with beautiful poor girl, marries her, and both live happily ever after in a palace built of spun sugar, neon lighted, air conditioned. It was also a validation of the democratic credo in the variation that a poor girl can marry a rich boy (or vice versa) and thereupon ascend to the seventh heaven of infinite bliss while spectators swoon. One newspaper called the lady in the case the "Cinderella Girl." The previous journalistic Cinderella had been Heavyweight Champion James J. Braddock, "The Cinderella Man."

The lady was Mrs. Barbara "Bobo" Sears, a creamy dish of ripe ingredients. She and Winthrop were married on St. Valentine's Day, February 14, in the usual posh affair at the Palm Beach home of Social Registerite polo-player Winston Guest. Certified Triple-A "society" turned out in force, including the Duke and Duchess of Windsor and assorted Astors and Vanderbilts. A brilliant affair although, paradoxically, no really brilliant people were present, the usual thing. Money was the password.

And while the newspapers went into their usual conniption fits, Winthrop was heading into another of his all-thumbs losing ventures.

Who was Barbara Sears, or Bobo?

As the newspapers reported, when Winthrop met her at a New York shindig, she was living with a sister in an old red-brick walk-up flat facing the Third Avenue Elevated at East Fifty-fourth Street (the original Rockefeller street!). The description sounded a bit grim unless one knew that it was an intermediate high-rent neighborhood spotted with the affluent and semibohemians, part of the fun belt. Expensive restaurants and bistros were all around, and Bobo's flat was a comfortable hideaway, a place to which the Duke and Duchess of Windsor might have been amused to come. She was, moreover, living rent-free in a building owned by her ex-husband's socially faultless family and she had been adequately provided for.

Actually, as the newspapers did not stress, in marrying Winthrop she was marrying down socially although up financially. For she had been married before, in 1941, into top-drawer society, had remained married until December, 1947, and had surfaced pending a friendly divorce. In an eve-of-the-war romance she had, aged twenty-four, married a young scion of the Sears family of Boston, whose genealogical tree extended back to include Thomas Jefferson and beyond and embraced high diplomats, successful merchants, judges, and other proper lights among proper Bostonians. According to adepts in the delicate upper social nuances, the Sears family ranks several cuts socially and historically above the Rockefellers. Vintage Bostonians look upon the Rockefellers as newcomers and even as parvenus.

The Sears Bobo married was a young Harvard graduate who served in the navy and diplomatic service during the war, later (post-Bobo) became a banker. In the course of this marriage Bobo met and hobnobbed with just about everyone in the Searsian circle. When she met Winthrop she knew her way around socially much, much better than he did, was as much a virtuoso in protocol as anyone at the State Department. She knew who was who. And, having been through the mill, she had some knowledge of the law of marriage and divorce. She was nobody's patsy. Her nickname, affectionate in its overtones, had been given to her by her Boston father-in-law. She was definitely an "in" person, especially in Café Society and the jet set.

The newspapers, however, for the sake of effect on the ever-gullible *hoi polloi,* now stressed that she was the daughter of a coal miner. Bobo had probably never been near a coal mine in her life, and her father had long since given up digging for a living. What he actually was was a locomotive fireman, just a rung below the top elite of labor, the locomotive engineers. He was, too, long divorced from Bobo's mother. Bobo had been reared by her mother and a stepfather in Chicago, in the very South Side neighborhood where Mayor Daley has resided all his life, locally called "Bridgeport."

Bobo's entire background was unfolded in a fascinating article by magazine editor Laura Bergquist, a high-school chum.[6] It is one of the few sparkling writings the researcher will find in the entire Rockefeller canon.

Born in the United States as Jievute Paulekiute of Lithuanian parents, her years between three and six passed on a farm in Lithuania, she styled herself Eva Paul at Englewood High School, Chicago, where she was graduated in 1933. She came from a region north of a very extensive school district, near the stockyards but not "back of the yards" as some erroneously reported. If anything, it was in front of the yards, to the east. But the region as a whole was strictly mixed employed middle class and highly skilled working class and was earnestly committed, despite the usual backsliding around the edges at all social levels, to the higher values, to St. Augustine's domain of light. Local homeownership was common, the Bible was

---

6. Laura Bergquist, "Bobo As Seen By Her Oldest Friend," *Life,* March 15, 1954.

respected—but not much read. Eliza Davison and Celestia Spelman would both have felt perfectly at home there in their younger years. I happen to know this firsthand as I am myself an alumnus of Englewood High, although preceding Bobo in my claim to this unusual distinction by thirteen years. Born and raised there, I know the territory very well as it once was, is no more.

Bobo at the time, according to the Bergquist vignette, was an energetic, intelligent, self-reliant, well-organized, and purposeful person, one who was to increase her self-organization until when she met Winthrop, she was fully as well organized as Exxon. Winthrop, on the other hand, although not a bad fellow, was disorganized mush like some of the early befuddled competitors of John D. I., even when he wasn't falling-down drunk, and it is my surmise that this disparity, among others, led to the rapid contretemps. That, one might say, was foreordained. Bobo, I surmise, didn't realize she was marrying a first-class problem-child.

In Chicago Bobo lived in a four-story walk-up. Her mother, who was now married to a local carpenter, worked as a seamstress with the Englander Mattress Company. Bobo later thought it ironic that she should meet the Englander family socially; one gathers she was not a bit impressed. To get spending money Bobo did baby-sitting, house-cleaning and gave dancing and acrobatic lessons at a quarter apiece. While the young Rockefellers were doing contrived chores at home for money, playing at being common people, protected from the outside barbarians, Bobo was out in the big league, the real world, where the barbarians played for keeps.

No doubt she developed her aspirations through reading. For she was an omnivorous reader, which the Rockefellers had never been; reading was one of the few roads of personal elevation in her milieu. Her earliest ambition was to be a ballet dancer. As she matured, she raised her sights. She was, moreover, friendly and gregarious, got along easily in any company, awed by nobody. Winthrop, however, was shy—that is, afraid of people, sensitive to criticism (of which he had probably endured much).

At high school Bobo was the most popular girl in her class, expert in dancing and athletics, and while in school she won the high-jumping championship of the Chicago public park system. In the same period she entered local beauty contests, winning them all in a blaze of animal spirits.

In 1934 she entered such a contest at the Chicago World's Fair and was crowned Miss Lithuania, a triumph for the local Central European ethnics. She lunched there with a Japanese princess, her foretaste of high society, and was invited to Texas Guinan's nightclub where she got the usual big hand. After high school graduation she had studied modeling and gone to night classes at the in-town division of Northwestern University. At age nineteen she set out for New York even as the Great Depression held the wonderful Republic in its fond embrace.

Following a blurred beginning in New York, when she accepted modest employments, she found her way into the theater, where she was neither a star nor a flop. Her name was changed to Barbara because there was another actress named Eva Paul. She played leads in various road companies—*You Can't Take It With You, School for Brides,* etc.—and in 1945 played a lead in a Hollywood western. She met her first husband while playing in Boston, won a commendation from director-actor Walter Huston, and hobnobbed in Hollywood with such eminents as Michael Arlen (*The Green Hat*) and the usual assortment of writers, producers, and actors. As the wife of a naval officer-diplomat, during which role she always tried to keep up with her ambitions in self-fulfillment, she sojourned in Boston, San Francisco, Jacksonville (here she wrote an unpublished novel, working mornings), Washington, New York, and Paris.

At thirty-two when she married Winthrop, she was a mighty self-reliant little lady, oozing *savoir faire.* And Winthrop behind his thin pose of rakish man-about-town was an insecure, all-thumbs misfit, no doubt also considerably spoiled at home in compensation for his intangible disabilities. Bobo, as I read the evidence, could have made it with flying colors on the Rockefeller circuit. Even if she were present only as a close student of the dollar, she would not have been out of place.

But it was Winthrop, limber imbiber of strong waters and a heavy-footed swinger, who couldn't make it on the Bobo circuit. He had flunked out all along the line except with the army. He flunked, too, with Bobo, who had snatched him from under the noses of predatory debutantes and their mothers. For Winthrop was regarded as a prize catch, at least under the standards of Dun and Bradstreet.

Their son, Winthrop Paul, was born September 17, 1948, and very soon thereafter the marriage went on the rocks. Among Winthrop's hobbies at the time was reported to be a $1 million collection of pornography. Reports had it, too, that Bobo felt offended at being offered a view of this esoteric material. No doubt Winthrop had reckoned too heavily on Bobo's ebullient manner and appearance, little realizing she was much more like Eliza Davison than a priestess of the fleshpots.

Bobo herself supplied the perspective when she said to her friend Laura Bergquist: "My mother was a strict, old-fashioned European. She wasn't too different from the correct Bostonians I hobnobbed with during my first marriage."

Winthrop, the runaway Rockefeller, was really up against it in this combination. Barracks-room dreams of playboy meeting playgirl were clearly out the window. Winthrop had chosen as a wife probably the most exacting critic he had ever faced. Money or not, he couldn't make the grade.

After five years of separation and sparring between batteries of high-priced counsel (Bobo had some of the best), it was agreed that Bobo was to seek a Reno divorce and receive a settlement of $2 million cash, $3.5 million in trust, and allowances for the support of herself and her son. It was reported to be the largest divorce settlement on record. She was awarded custody of the child in the 1954 settlement, with Winthrop to have him for half of each summer and on alternate holidays.

Young Winthrop Paul at an early age, while living with his mother on his maternal grandmother's farm in Indiana pending the divorce, learned to speak Lithuanian fluently, an accomplishment he probably retains. But his mother, a stickler for form, saw to it that he became a true Rockefeller. He attended the Rockefeller-inspired Browning School in New York, the ultra-ultra Le Rosey School in Switzerland, Herringswell Manor in England, the American College in Switzerland, and Oxford University in 1969-70. He failed his first year's Oxford examination, was suspended and did not finish the course of studies.

Drawing closer to his father as he matured, young Winthrop finally made his address at the father's Arkansas plantation. In preparation for eventually taking over that project, he attended a southern agricultural college. Upon the death of his father in 1973 he became the principal heir and, as the only child of one of The Brothers, became the richest individual among The Cousins, each of whom must share assets with numerous siblings. Money-wise young Winthrop is Numero Uno in the fourth generation. He gets Winthrop's one-sixth share which, less taxes, should leave him not far behind the brothers.

At Oxford he met, and married, Deborah Cluett Sage, granddaughter of the late George Bywater Cluett II of Cluett, Peabody and Company, manufacturing clothiers, and Mrs. Cadwallader Washburn Kelsey of Guilford, Connecticut, Mrs. George Skinner of New York, and the late Donald Henry Sage of New York, Arlington, Virginia, and Tucson, Arizona. She was educated at the Chapin School, New York, and Lady Eden's and Queen's Gate School in London—Social Register all the way. The groom's grandfathers, of course, were John D. Junior and the ex-coal miner-locomotive fireman, Jievute Paulekiute. Two of his great-grandfathers were John D. I and Sen. Nelson Aldrich. In forebears he is provided, I conclude, as well as any of the Rockefellers.

The Cousins, according to reports reaching me, have met and fully approved young Winnie. As far as the Rockefellers are concerned, he is "in," one of the clan.

As for Bobo, she maintains apartments in New York City and Paris and keeps herself out of the public eye as much as possible. She never married again although newspapers from time to time have tried to concoct romantic scripts for her to follow. She signs herself "Barbara Rockefeller," an impressive name where she came from and especially impressive to doormen, *maîtres d'hôtel,* chambermaids, and other below-stairs gentry.

In late 1953, his marriage in ruins and his wife's lawyers holding out for big money, Winthrop departed more or less to exile in Arkansas to join an old army buddy—a deluxe version of a remittance man. He started out by buying one thousand acres on a mountain with a view to building a cattle ranch. He was to seek redemption and find it partially in the state of his adoption, where he remained the rest of his life except for occasional trips out.

Through the years, drawing on the capacious family funds put into his hands, he expanded his hacienda by fifty times, bringing in all possible technical improvements and install-ing an elaborate system for piping water to the mountaintop where he had the usual elaborate house and supplementary buildings.

It was in 1955 that then Gov. Orval Faubus, an Arkansas-style negrophobe, appointed Winthrop to head the new State Industrial Development Commission, a political mistake for Faubus. In this role Rockefeller was instrumental in bringing many new industries into what had been almost exclusively a lowdown, backsliding agricultural state. Two years later, when Faubus used the state's National Guard to bar Negroes from Little Rock's Central High School, thereby provoking Eisenhower's riposte with elite paratroopers, Rockefeller publicly objected to the Faubus ploy in line with his family's tradition of multiracial and multireligious tolerance.

By 1961 Winthrop began, Rockefeller-style, pouring money into the state's moribund Republican party, became the par-ty's national committeeman and sent paid agents into every Arkansas county to establish local party organizations. In 1964, running as a Republican, Rockefeller challenged for the governorship, but Faubus won his sixth two-year term with 57 percent of the vote.

Rockefeller now brought in more aides, had compiled a computer-produced profile of Arkansas voters, and launched a full-scale registration drive among the depressed blacks.

Faubus, discerning the handwriting on the wall in pure Standard Oil script, announced his retirement, and the Democrats nominated State Supreme Court Justice James D. Johnson, a segregationist firebrand. Johnson launched a fierce assault on Rockefeller's bedraggled personal life and habits, his family, and his civil rights associations. But Rockefeller won with 54 percent of the vote because he had formed a coalition of blacks, liberals, moderate Democrats, urban workers, and mountain Republicans. He was the state's first Republican governor in a century, a new-style carpetbagger— one bringing ever-welcome money. He won again in 1968.

Although he single-handedly (with paid aides) captured the Republican party and the governorship, Rockefeller could not, however, make the yokel legislature see things his way. He wanted the state to spend much more than it did on education and social services, but the legislature voted down his tax proposals three times by resounding majorities.

He claimed, however, to have forced through the state's first minimum-wage law, reformed state insurance laws, and the prison and parole system. He appointed some five hundred Negroes to state offices, unheard of for Arkansas, and declared a moratorium on executions soon after taking office. Opposed to the death penalty, he commuted the death sentences of fifteen inmates on Death Row.

He brought in an outside penologist to run the state prison system but finally bowed to the hostile reaction of the sounder citizenry. The new man found that the state's prison farms were run for profit precisely like Soviet labor camps of the Gulag Archipelago, with recalcitrant inmates simply killed and buried on the spot without notice to the outside, even without grave markers. As the new man in charge caused body after mysterious body to be uncovered, his term was ended through the pressure of the prison camarilla and local planters who profited from cheap prison labor. The lid was finally clamped on the prisons so that the world never did get a full body count on all those executed without benefit of due process of law, as positively guaranteed by the United States Constitution.

At the same time the new governor, undismayed by the local yokels, oafs, louts, boobs, and knaves, turned to the Rockefeller scenario for cues to further action. He gave money to schools, colleges, and hospitals around the state, put up $1.25 million to build a model school in Morrilton, adjoining his property, which had now grown to fifty thousand acres (some of it south near Texas) and was a working scientific agricultural showplace visited by farm experts from far away. In addition to cattle, his acres produced rice, soybeans, small grains, and other stuff, all very profitable and in line with the new trend toward agri-business.

He contributed heavily to the Arkansas Art Center in Little Rock, toured the state to raise more funds by subscription, and personally funded a medical clinic for a county that had no health facilities.

In 1956 he was married a second time, to Mrs. Jeanette Edris, daughter of a wealthy theater-chain owner and real estate nabob. They had no children and were divorced soon after his attempt at a third term for the governorship, when he was defeated by Dale Bumpers. His continued heavy drinking was widely blamed for his defeat.

Never a facile campaigner, his drinking habits did not help him. He was reputed to have addressed the legislature in a falling-down drunk condition, not especially unusual behavior for governors in the central south where legislators are often in the same boat. Huey Long of Louisiana comes to mind at once, also many members of Congress. He mixed metaphors freely, often ludicrously, in his speeches. An unhappy man who never attained his native potential.

Winthrop was heavily eulogized at his funeral, held at Winrock Farm on Petit Jean Mountain near Morrilton. Among the many eminentissimi who sent condolences were Queen Elizabeth II of Great Britain. In attendance were his two ex-wives, his son, his son's wife, and a grandchild, his brothers, and thousands of Arkansans who felt he had vivified the state with his repeated transfusions of money and attempts at uplift.

What was Winthrop's basic accomplishment? When he first took office Arkansas was nearer culturally to Afghanistan than to New York, Wisconsin, California, and quite a few other states. Among the states it held practically the lowest place on the totem pole, only Mississippi nosing it out for bottom honor. Through his efforts the state advanced a notch until it stood closer, perhaps, to Albania. No doubt this was quite an achievement in itself, one that deserves to be saluted. No political pro would have attempted it.

Prior to going to Yale, Winthrop had attended Lincoln School, Teachers College, and the Loomis School, Connecticut. But at his death he held seven honorary doctorates, one from the College of William and Mary and another from the University of San Francis Xavier, Sucre, Bolivia. He was entitled to be addressed as colonel, doctor, or governor.

At his death he was a trustee of the Rockefeller Brothers Fund, a director of Rockefeller Brothers, Inc., and Rockefeller Center, Inc., chairman of the board of Colonial Williamsburg, Inc. and the Williamsburg Restoration, and a past trustee of the National Urban League, 1940-1964. He belonged to four clubs, the most outstanding being The Links.

Winthrop, at any rate, was proof of one homely adage: money isn't everything.

8.

What Leonid Brezhnev is to the Politburo and Central Committee of the Communist Party, USSR, David Rockefeller is to the Rockefeller family and the Rockefeller Syndicate —not the only power, but the pivotal one.

As I pointed out in Chapter One, ownership is not the only consideration in evaluating the Rockefellers. There is also the question of control, which extends far beyond personal ownership stakes, and beyond this the question of influence, which is vast though often impalpable. The Rockefellers in concert with the components of the Rockefeller Syndicate undoubtedly comprise the most influential, tightly organized little group in the United States. In view of the importance of the United States, they are consequently of world importance.

They make their presence felt, though, very delicately for the most part, pianissimo, with a finger unobtrusively raised rather than with a crashing fist on the table. One might well call them masters of the light touch. And the soft-spoken always courteous David is the wielder of that light touch, the Chopin at the keyboard.

The youngest of the brothers, he was especially taken in hand by his father and carefully groomed as the future family mentor. Born in 1915, he came into the world too late to be squelched as was Winthrop by older brothers he was unable to keep pace with. In many ways he was raised as an only child. His nearest competitor was Winthrop who, never able to get organized, his attention fixed on his older brothers, was really never any competition. As a practical matter, the late-coming David luckily had the field pretty completely to himself, virtually ignored by the well-advanced others because of his obvious babyhood.

David, in other words, was able to mature at his own pace, and it shows in his complete self-possession. And although not brilliant by any discernible manifestation, he is steady, rational, systematic, hard-working and thoroughgoing, the German of the family. Both in Wall Street and in his family, he is looked upon as the family intellectual, its mastermind, the man capable of arriving at far-ranging analytical conclusions if necessary under his own steam, without ghostly helpers. Among the brothers he is apparently the one with the fewest illusions, the guy who knows what the score really is at most times, the brother least likely to be snared by his own rhetoric and fantasies. He it is, one gathers, who is most skeptical, the least inclined of the brothers to be carried away by fugitive enthusiasms. A sound, sound man.

After Nelson the politician, David has received the most notice from the press by reason of his position at the head of the mighty Chase Manhattan Bank. On this throne his financial and economic authority, necessarily also political, is far greater than that of his much-touted and roundly damned grandfather ever was, or that of his shrinking father. He is the real inheritor and enhancer of the Rockefeller power. Under Junior, the Rockefellers were in a holding action. Under David, they are moving forward again, slowly, up the slopes of the golden mountain toward ineffability. David is unquestionably the only Rockefeller old John D. would have deferred to.

Given the usual Rockefeller upbringing—chores for money at home, family prayers, earnest injunctions, residence on Fifty-fourth Street in New York, and at Pocantico Hills and Seal Harbor, Maine, ample education, sojourns on ranches in the mountains of the West, travel—he attended Horace Mann and Lincoln Schools, took a B.S., at Harvard, '36, studied two years more at Harvard and the University of London School of Economics, and then took a Ph.D. at the University of Chicago, 1940. He was a solid, serious student all the way, steeped in the worldly philosophers.

After his undergraduate years at Harvard, during which he maintained a low profile, David took a trip up to Ottawa to visit his father's long-time theoretical mentor, W. L. Mackenzie King, prime minister of Canada. He was undecided on his future course. King, himself a graduate of the University of Chicago, advised him to get a doctorate in economics, which would be useful whether he opted to go into government, business, banking, or investment management. It was the course of study King had himself followed.

After another year at Harvard, mulling over his talk with King, he went to London for a year and then turned to the University of Chicago. While in London he spent a few hours each week learning the ropes at the branch of the Chase Bank, of which his uncle Winthrop Aldrich was head man. Aldrich for many years held down this post for the Rockefeller interests, later being rewarded with the retirement bonus of ambassador to the Court of St. James's.

David's doctoral dissertation was published under the title *Unused Resources and Economic Waste* (1940). Twenty-four years later he published another nonstartling book, *Creative Management in Banking.*

What gives David his long reach is his chairmanship of the Chase Manhattan Bank, which rests most remotely on a charter granted in 1799 through the crafty work of Aaron Burr for the Manhattan Company.

Originally supposed to be a water company, it quickly

emerged as the Bank of Manhattan. This was the outcome of a legal trick played by Burr to set up a rival to the monopoly Bank of New York, which had been openly chartered earlier though the agency of Alexander Hamilton. It was one of the many points of bitterness between Burr and Hamilton that eventuated in their famous duel. And it was one of the points from which derived Burr's reputation as an unusually sneaky operator, a legend which gullible pro-Hamilton American historians have carried down to the present. Burr was not unusually treacherous, he merely played par for his course which, to be sure, called for marginal behavior. Like many other politicos he was an artful dodger, cards held close to his vest.

The Chase National Bank and the Bank of Manhattan were merged in 1955 and are now held by the Chase Manhattan Corporation, a holding company in possession of seventeen minor subsidiaries in addition to the giant bank. The assets of the latter, as we saw in Chapter One, stood at $42.453 billion as of June 30, 1974, a figure which projects but a small portion of its power and influence. By reason of trust fund holdings, leverages, and affiliations, the financial reach of Chase and its affiliated members of the Rockefeller Syndicate easily tops $200 billion—repeat: $200 billion. It could be up to $500 billion. That sum represents solid assets, a voice in corporate influence if not control, not evanescent flow-through money for spending. As Archimedes said, with a lever long enough, one man can lift the world. The setup that David heads is a mighty long lever, one that policy-makers all over pay attention to.

Cash holdings of Chase at the above date were $11.7556 billion, loans and mortgages came to $24.955 billion and deposits amounted to $35.1562 billion of which $14.7062 billion consisted of foreign deposits. Capital, surplus and undivided profits of the institution were $1,820,181,000 in addition to which it held $2.1185 billion of federal funds.

For 1973 net income amounted to $163,095,000.

But Chase was only the third largest bank, topped by Bank of America of California and First National City Bank of New

York, owned by Citicorp. For 1973 First National City, under the tutelage of the William Rockefeller family, reported net income of $252,019,000 on total assets of $44.019 billion. Although rivals, First National City and Chase Manhattan, as we know, are friendly rivals, sharing interlocking directors with Chemical Bank of New York and the First National Bank of Chicago. Combined, the two Rockefeller banks top the field.

Most people think of banks as places where people and corporations deposit money that the banks lend at a profit, and this is a true view, although oversimple, for the big money-market institutions. The cutting edge of the big money-market banks consists of their pool of nonbanking technical experts. Chase Bank employs more than sixteen thousand persons and many of these are experts in fields far removed from banking. The reason such are needed is that the big money-market banks make loans across the entire economic spectrum, and specialists are needed to evaluate the circumstances bearing on borrowing entities. For this job one needs economists, sociologists, linguists, political scientists steeped in the data of particular regions, engineers, journalists, lawyers, statisticians, physical scientists, anthropologists, geologists, mathematicians, agronomists, urbanists, psychologists—people with deep theoretical as well as practical backgrounds. The big money-market banks, therefore, are really talent pools. And make no mistake, it is genuine talent, the best or nearly the best, highly paid.

In addition there are batteries of the most advanced computers and memory systems to be used for all manner of purposes.

Chase Manhattan, like Citicorp, casts a worldwide net. It has 178 branches in New York State and 95 abroad. It has some two hundred vice-presidents, more or less. Where it doesn't have branches, it has representatives. Chase branches are spread throughout the Caribbean area, three are in London, and it also has branches in Paris, Lyon, Dusseldorf, Frankfurt-am-Main, Hamburg, Munich, Stuttgart, Athens, Bahrein, Milan, Rome, Bari, Tokyo, Osaka, Seoul, Beirut, Singapore, Taipei, etc. One of its representatives is now in Moscow. It has scores of subsidiaries at home and is affiliated in Great Britain with the Standard and Chartered Banking Group, Ltd., made up of the Standard Bank, Ltd., and the Chartered Bank, Ltd. This group has scores of offices that blanket sub-Sahara Africa and are scattered throughout Europe, the Middle East, and Asia.*

All this should serve to give a skeletal idea of the array David presides over. Naturally, as the man at the apex of this pyramid, David is in a position to get exact information quickly about any minute spot on earth. The branches, representatives, and affiliated chains, of course, are in intimate contact with the local governments so that they are usually well posted. They not only know what is happening but what is likely to happen.

As Chairman David said to E. J. Kahn, Jr. for a *New Yorker* two-part profile ("Resources and Responsibilities," by E. J. Kahn, Jr., *The New Yorker,* January 9 and 16, 1965), "I can't imagine a more interesting job than mine. . . . The bank has dealings with everyone. There is no field of activity it isn't involved in. It's a springboard for whatever interests one may have in any direction—a very good platform from which to participate in the economic advancement [a Marxist theologian would say "exploitation"] of the world." And highly profitable too!

The domain presided over by David is, as a matter of course, affected by every government decision in the world, pro and con.

Until the advent of the New Deal, J. P. Morgan and Company was regarded by Wall Streeters as the principal spokesman

---

*The Federal Reserve Board has ordered Chase to divest itself by June 15, 1975, of its 12 percent interest in the Standard & Chartered Banking Group, the $10.7-billion London organization. The participation sold for $122.32 million. The reason for the order was that Standard & Chartered operates in the United States and American banks are not permitted by law to hold ownership portions of competing banks. Chase, with only one office of its own in Africa against Standard & Chartered's nine hundred (fourteen hundred worldwide), and a joint office in Cairo, will now have to establish its own African offices in order to participate in the redemption of the Dark Continent. It has at this writing already received permission to open in Nigeria and Sudan.

and arbiter for the Street. Morgan's, while still important, no longer holds the premier position, which has definitely shifted to the Rockefeller Syndicate.

"Placid and kindly," as Kahn found him, he never deprecates anyone verbally, is never deprecated by anyone among his peers—a useful stance for a man in his position. Inclined to corpulence as a child, he has a continuous weight problem, which he works at successfully by eating only one full meal a day. He stands at nearly six feet.

He gets his weight problem because he is a gourmet, a *feinschmecker* who keeps a cellar of choice wines he is proud of. He is also, like Nelson, a connoisseur of modern art which he has spread through the Chase Manhattan Bank's main building and Rockefeller University, toning up those nonartistic environs considerably. And he is an internationally noted collector of beetles. You read it right: *beetles.* He rates as an amateur part-time entomologist. Several varieties of beetle he has "discovered" are named after him.

He is able to speak French, Spanish, and German acceptably if not fluently, being one up there against Nelson's French and Spanish. A visitor to every leading city in the world, in each of which he has peer-group acquaintances native and foreign, he is a large personal investor in various places. He owns hefty chunks of acreage in western Australia, given over to sheep ranching, and Chase International Investment Corporation is also heavily into northern and western Australian land.

Big crowds nearly always turn out when he planes in abroad, as though he were a head of state. And in every country he visits he has a scheduled meeting with the head of state, as though he were a roving ambassador or potentate. And he is the latter, an American sheik. At home he entertains just about every head of state or high official at his Pocantico Hills home, sometimes putting them up overnight or for several days.

He is much in demand as a speaker by organizations of all kinds and as a guest at functions, not because of any inspiring or entertaining remarks he may make, because he is, personally, rather flat, apt to be noncommittal or routine on just about everything. But his name lends "tone" to any occasion. And hostesses know that if they can be guaranteed David Rockefeller as a guest, they can be sure to get just about anybody from A to Z. Thousands want to meet him, get their names on his list of known people. And an invitation to Pocantico Hills is, for many influential people, equivalent to a command. Who would turn it down?

His chief office is in the new Chase Manhattan Bank Building, at Nassau, Pine, and Liberty Streets, just north of Wall Street on ground renamed Chase Manhattan Plaza. He also has offices at 30 Rockefeller Plaza on the celebrated fifty-sixth floor (plus two). In his spare time he golfs, and sails in his own and Nelson's fleet of vessels at Seal Harbor, Mt. Desert Island, Maine. He is a skilled sailor, which dovetails neatly with his ability as an organizer. In this last role he follows in the footsteps of his famous/infamous grandfather.

All of his time is scheduled by a cluster of executive secretaries who make up his personal staff. Each of the brothers has his own staff and they jointly share a special staff for family enterprises. David's staff has at its disposal a personal card file of more than twenty thousand people scattered all around the world, sort of an international *Who's Who* of business, finance, and politics.

Whenever he makes one of his international trips, his staff prepares for him a book-size script that shows who he is to meet, when and where, and fills in general background of what is to be asked and what told. He carefully checks this script at each stage of his travels.

He plays host at Pocantico Hills every two years in three to finance ministers and other high officials of dozens of countries at the annual sessions of the World Bank and Monetary Fund, which holds two out of three of its annual meetings in Washington; attends annual sessions of the Bilderberg Conference of world figures and entertains the Bilderbergers; and from time to time entertains the staff of the United Nations, for which Chase Manhattan is the banker.

His staff, like all the Rockefeller staffs, continually gets begging letters from far and wide, from individuals and organizations. After all, why not? The Rockefellers themselves have encouraged the idea that they are donors, that recipients can get something for nothing—a notion which conservative economists tirelessly point out is impossible. "There is no free lunch," "There is no Santa Claus," as Establishment Prof. Milton Friedman of the University of Chicago tirelessly quips. People nevertheless persist in believing that Santa Claus exists and is alive and well on the upper floors at 30 Rockefeller Plaza. There is, incidentally, no free lunch at Rockefeller Center, where all the restaurants lean toward the expensive.

David, finished with schooling, now a full-fledged Ph.D., the first member of the family to have risen that far on the educational ladder, started out in 1940 as an unpaid secretary to Mayor Fiorello La Guardia of New York City. He served here for a year and undoubtedly picked up much information on what makes the inner works of New York City tick. Not without a tucked-away sense of humor, he soon took to answering the phone with "Rockefeller speaking," until La Guardia stopped this, no doubt because it projected a thought-provoking political image.

The next year he enlisted in the army and was quickly made assistant regional director of the Office of Defense, Health and Welfare Services. In 1942 he was made a captain in military intelligence, went to North Africa with the army and then to Europe, winding up in Paris where he checked on local Rockefeller properties. With the end of the war, he made his decision, at the urging of Winthrop Aldrich, to follow the family money into Chase. A second vice-president in 1948-49, he quickly moved up the rungs through vice-president, senior vice-president (at age thirty-six), executive vice-president, vice-chairman of the board of directors, president and chairman of the executive committee and, in 1969, chairman of the board and chief executive officer—an upper-strata Horatio Alger story all the way.

In the meantime he has picked up directorships of Chase Manhattan Investment Corporation (also the chairmanship thereof), Rockefeller Center, Inc., the Chase International Investment Corporation (also chairman), and the Downtown Lower Manhattan Association.

Much earlier he had been made a trustee, soon chairman of the board, of Rockefeller University, one of his major interests; trustee and vice-chairman of Rockefeller Brothers Fund; trustee of the Rockefeller Family Fund; life trustee of the University of Chicago; trustee and chairman of the board of the Museum of Modern Art; and member of the board of overseers of Harvard University (1954-1968).

Like his brothers, he holds numerous decorations and awards—the Legion of Honor (France), the Legion of Merit, and so on. He could have more if he wanted them, bushel baskets full. He holds eight honorary doctorates, including one each from Columbia University and Harvard, and belongs to four clubs, one of which is The Links, a keystone of the intercorporate club world. He also belongs to the Philosophical Society of Philadelphia, founded by Benjamin Franklin.

Married to Margaret McGrath, he is sire to six children, like most of the Rockefellers not a practitioner of the preachments of Brother John's Population Council. The children are: David, Abby A., Neva (Mrs. Walter J. Kaiser), Margaret D., Richard G., and Eileen M.

He is, further, a director of the International Executive Service, a businessman's version of the Peace Corps, of the Center of Inter-American Relations and of the Council on Foreign Relations. He has been a director of the latter since 1949 and was chairman from 1951 to 1970—nineteen crucial years.

As a member and leading spirit of this council, he belongs to the inner circle of perhaps the most influential body in the country with respect to foreign policy. While everybody is more or less interested in foreign relations, the interests of most citizens are largely theoretical, vague, and often fantastic. As all literate persons know, relations with foreign nations are important, often spelling the difference between peace and war, prosperity and slump, high prices and low, employment and unemployment, dearth and plenitude. The price and quantity of oil, as everyone knows, depends on foreign relations, as does the price, quantity, and quality of many other articles of consumption.

And to guard foreign relations there is the State Department and the Defense Department with its authority over army, navy, and air force.

But members of the Council on Foreign Relations have a closer and more specific connection with foreign relations. For it is, largely, *their* properties, branches, and affiliations abroad that are guarded by the State Department and the army, navy, and air force.

Were the sea-lanes not fully guarded by the ships of the navy and its submarines and strategic airfields, there might be an interruption in the flow of oil and other materials to the United States. Then many citizens might find themselves without heat and electricity, without gasoline, perhaps without coffee, tea, spices, and Scotch whiskey. There would ensue a terrible public flap, with irate questions raised about what the government was doing about the horrible situation.

But propertied members of the Council on Foreign Relations would be raising such questions much sooner than the cold, lightless, and Scotchless resident. For it is their ships and properties that the navy and the State Department is *specifically* concerned about. Interference with those properties instantly puts the State Department into action. Backing the State Department, giving it "credibility"—which means "You better believe it, brother"—are the armed forces, the *Wehrmacht* and *Luftwaffe* of the American eagle.

Could not one depend on the general goodwill of the world to keep everything going smoothly? Judging by the experience of history, the answer to this question must, unfortunately, be "No." What happens if one is not armed or is lightly armed? For an answer near home, one should ask the question of the American Indians. One is, quite simply, dispossessed, denuded. For, despite all reassurances from anyone, this is a world where people have a propensity to grab.

The Council on Foreign Relations, then, composed of corporate bigwigs, bankers, and top corporation lawyers for the most part, with here and there a scattering of academics, is the main external adjunct of the State and Defense Departments and supplies these departments with top policy-makers and much advice.

Of all unofficial "in" groups, it is probably the most important of the Establishment.

The people associated with the Council on Foreign Relations include just about all who have a direct ownership stake in the external economic and financial instrumentalities that service the American market. They know long before the average citizen does when these instrumentalities are being threatened or interfered with. The maintenance of peace, of course, is important. But there come times when one may have to fight for one's vital interests. The American Indians learned that but, underarmed, disorganized, lost a continent.

Put another way, the *personal* financial interests of the Rockefellers and much of the membership of the Council on Foreign Relations are closely interwoven with the vital interests of the American nation as they are institutionally structured. Strike one and you strike the other. When they bleed, the rest of us hemorrhage.

None of this is to suggest that American foreign relations are always well managed. Indeed, there is much evidence to suggest that they are often handled in such a way as not to serve the interests of the country or even that of the prime beneficiaries. The Vietnam involvement is a case in point. Somebody certainly goofed on that one, all along the line after Eisenhower, and appears to be determined to keep on goofing. The Vietnam operation seems to have been a mere display of muscle that might better have been reserved for more vulnerable and more strategic points. Vietnam weakened the country internally and externally at a cost of some $150 billion and fifty-five thousand American lives, thereby playing right into the hands of the happy Kremlin.

Criminal stupidity in the handling of foreign relations, deserving nothing short of summary hanging for all concerned, is shown in the repeated appointment of boobish big political party money-donors, some of them alcoholics, to ambassadorships. Americans hold up their hands in horror at the one-time

European custom of selling military commissions to incompetents, little realizing that in a parlous era we do the same thing quite openly with our diplomatic corps.

Although leading members of the Council on Foreign Relations, including David Rockefeller and his brothers, backed United States involvement in Vietnam, the council as such did not formally do so, and many of its members did not. Rather than hand out a line of policy, the council is a pro and con discussion group, with lines of dominant national policy emerging through top key people after discussion, analysis, and argument. Nor is the membership of uniform ideological perspective although when policy lines emerge, ideological deviants and dissidents are few and ineffective. The top people represent the inner core, what one might call the caucus of the group or the inner circle.

As of August 31, 1973, the council had 1,551 members, grouped as follows:

Scholars (in foreign policy) and academic administrators (mainly university presidents), 373; business executives (mostly top officials and top stockholders of leading corporations and banks), 468; United States government officials, including many United States senators and representatives and State Department personnel, 195; lawyers (mainly from leading corporation law firms), 127; media people (newspaper publishers and editors, TV and radio executives, Washington correspondents and TV commentators), 135; administrators of nonprofit institutions (mainly endowed foundations, another arm of the corporate crowd), 187; and miscellaneous, 66. In response to a recent ruling, 28 women now belong.

The membership list reads like an Establishment *Who's Who*, with very, very few Establishment critics in the assemblage. Although it takes in Democrats, is "bipartisan," the CFR is dominantly Republican and Wall Street. For many years now, most of the policy-level positions in the State Department, including the secretary of state, have been filled from the upper ranks of the Council on Foreign Relations (scholars and journalists constitute the lower ranks). Franklin D. Roosevelt kept foreign policy in his own hands through

Secretary of State Cordell Hull of Tennessee, a nonmember of CFR. Roosevelt distrusted Wall Street. Roosevelt's James F. Byrnes, George C. Marshall, Dean Acheson, and E. R. Stettinius were also nonmembers, although Stettinius was a son of a former J. P. Morgan partner, and Morgan partners have always been sprinkled in among the CFR membership. But beginning with John Foster Dulles, and preceding the Roosevelt administration in the years after 1921, all the secretaries of state have been CFR members except William P. Rogers, 1969-1973. The CFR is to the State Department what a "farm club" is to a major league baseball club, a training and selection ground. Dulles, Herter, Rusk, and Kissinger were all Rockefeller people long prior to their appointments.

The Council on Foreign Relations was founded in 1921 as a reflex to the postwar position of the United States as a major creditor nation. As it slowly gathered headway, it was nourished with funds from J. P. Morgan and Company, the Rockefellers, the Carnegie Endowment, and other major Wall Street banking interests. What it does specifically is maintain a headquarters and library in New York, publish the high-toned quarterly *Foreign Affairs,* hold meetings almost weekly except in the summer, at which speakers present positions that are discussed, throw luncheons and dinners, award study fellowships to scholars, promote regional meetings out through the country, publish books and pamphlets, stage roundtable seminars, and provide a special corporation service to 115 companies at $1,000 or more annually. Its expenses for fiscal 1973 were $2,942,200, a low-budget operation. It nevertheless has great impact.

In some respects the Council on Foreign Relations overlaps with the Foreign Policy Association, has some common members and common interests. The FPA was formed in 1918 and its main task is educational—that is, to stir up general interest in foreign policy. It is, however, more theoretical, less heavily funded, and less directly involved in shaping foreign policy than is the CFR. It grew out of a meeting of nineteen writers, editors, educators, and such with a view to selling Wilsonian policies and the League of Nations to the public. The CFR, one might say, is more directly and personally involved than is the FPA, wields more muscle.

While, considering the nature of the world, every country needs a coherent foreign policy and armed forces, the United States, increasingly since World War II, has openly taken on a very broadened commitment throughout the world. Few of its citizens notice this. And much of this commitment to protect "interests" gives protection to many affairs that have nothing to do with supplying the American people. Both corporate and bank investments abroad, wholly external, have greatly increased. These increased private investments, naturally, must be protected. The protection is given by the State Department and the Pentagon; these function pretty much like a local police department in a business district or the sheriff and his deputies in a tough frontier town.

Many people cry "The United States should not be a world policeman." Yet American corporations and banks have, without any popular plebiscite, established positions abroad that require protection. Indeed, so expansive have American private interests become—a constant temptation to distant interlopers—that a local riot in almost any quarter of the world is of concern to the State Department. The consequence is that alarm bells ring in the State Department and Pentagon when almost anything out of the routine happens anywhere—a fact few Americans, glued to the TV tube, are aware of. At almost any moment the balloon is liable to go up, the bugles sounding their clarion call, summoning all good men to great deeds of distant defense on, perhaps, the Himalaya Line.

Most Americans believe that the armed forces are in being to protect Des Moines, Iowa, Peoria, Illinois, and perhaps Walla Walla, Washington, all of which are clearly expendable and would hardly be given much defense in the event of any conceivable attack. Americans who think these are defense points are 100 percent wrong. Places of far greater concern in the "defense"-thinking of American officialdom are the Eastern Mediterranean, Western Europe, the Indian Ocean, the Persian Gulf, Southeast Asia, Japan, the Adriatic, and sea-lanes of the Atlantic and Pacific Oceans. These are where the "vital interests" of the United States lie that foreign-policy students talk about. Nobody is aiming at Walla Walla, Washington, or any similar places. Nobody of consequence, in fact, wants them, even as a gift, the average citizen will no doubt be astounded to learn.

Naturally, the United States has friends throughout the world, friendly countries. And it is one of the aims of foreign policy to retain that friendship, born of a common fear. For the United States also has enemies, conspicuously humane and self-sacrificing countries like Soviet Russia and its forced satellites that wish to rescue the people of the earth from the onerous American shackles—the better to swallow them up at a single gulp like eastern Europe. The last, as it turns out, is the inner meaning of Moscow socialism, which is actually an instrument of Soviet foreign policy. As socialism it is a travesty.

Of course, the Council on Foreign Relations is opposed to such an outcome, wants everybody to trade goods and services freely, and the American people are committed through their government to seeing that such a Soviet coup does not take place, that the Soviet is "contained." In the meantime, mutually profitable international trade goes on, with the Soviet and its dupes interested in blocking and intercepting the profits, a mission the State Department and Pentagon are committed to thwarting. Peace, as it turns out, is a nonshooting war, a covert contest of intrigue and implicit threat.

But, to come now to the most beautiful part of all this valuable protection, to the payoff, one asks: Who pays for all this? "Defense," the State Department, and foreign aid amount to approximately a third of the $300-plus billion national budget. This budget is largely defrayed by the general nonrich taxpayer, the bus rider and jalopy driver, in taxes directly and by means of governmentally-induced inflation. The beneficiary members of the CFR, however, either are liable to no taxes at all—like John 3, a member—or benefit from a long array of obscurely phrased tax exemptions, tax discounts, and tax preferences. Beautiful, beautiful, beautiful—worthy indeed of the craftsmen in the Kremlin.

John 3, as we saw, is liable to no taxes for 1961-1975 on income of around $5 million. Instead of paying taxes, he funds various nonprofit enterprises that are termed charitable —sundry such as the Japan Society, Lincoln Center, and Asia Society, cultural adjuncts of foreign policy. Nelson is also, on the record, a notable tax economizer.

And now, the most ethereally beautiful part of it all, after having avoided proportionate taxes for all the foreign protection provided by the government, John 3 and others like him, his peers, are celebrated in press and open forums as gigantic big-hearted donors for the benefit of humankind. Awards, certificates of merit, and medals are showered upon him and others from every hand. Large numbers of taxpayers, the ones who are really directly and unmistakably paying for it all, join in the general celebration to largesse that passeth all understanding even as they get no credit for comparable donations. For they have made none. They have only paid taxes. We are here at the acme of the absurd.

As I contemplate this vast hoax, I laugh and laugh and laugh—all the way to the cemetery that awaits us all. The immortal bard was certainly right on target when he wrote: "What fools these mortals be."

Am I overstating the case when I suggest that the general citizenry are dunderheads? Could this be termed an unbalanced judgment? Is it "radical"?

In all this David Rockefeller and his brothers play big, albeit tax-economizing roles, along with many peers, as the general citizenry goes about its mundane affairs, whatever they are, and pays disproportionate taxes while enduring government-induced inflation that shrinks the value of their bank accounts and pensions.

David and his brothers, as loyal establishmentarians, were 100 percent behind the Vietnam War. Winthrop endorsed it openly, as did David, while Nelson, governor of a state in which many opposed the war, merely called upon everybody to stand behind Presidents Johnson and Nixon, which amounted to the same thing. Laurance and John did not disagree.

Neither the CFR nor the Rockefellers conducted the war,

which was carried on under the direction of those presidents, who took the flak. What was lacking about the American conduct of the war was the boldness and finesse with which the people-loving Soviets buttoned down Czechoslovakia. There, before one could say boo, the operation was all over, hardly any shooting, a really neat rip-off.

Why did the United States get into Vietnam? Secretary Rusk said it was to avoid another Munich, which sounded a bit simple. And why did the United States continue to finance the Saigon government?

As nobody has been able to point to any concrete material interest in the region, other than the possibility of untapped offshore oil being the stake, a tenuous suggestion, one must conclude that the war was fought because the whole of Southeast Asia, holding a corner between India and China, was the stake. It was, then, a war for a position bearing on other positions. United States policy apparently was that if the status quo existing when the French left could not be maintained, then at least the Soviet, backing the Hanoi government, should not be allowed to consolidate itself in the region. Was the cost to the taxpayers worth it? Many experts say "No."

A look at the map explains much. Whatever superpower controls this region—if it can establish control—is obviously in a position to influence India, possibly Japan and China and a large part of the offshore Pacific and Indian Ocean region. If the Soviet controls or has influence, it has leverage against China and India. If the United States controls, the Soviet is denied this influence and the United States has it. While those who opposed the war, grounded their opposition largely on its being an immoral war, overlooking the fact that all wars are inherently immoral (because they violate well-established, agreed-upon moral tenets), what was wrong about it from the point of view of *realpolitik* is that it was incompetently managed on the American side. As there are no moral wars, to call Vietnam an immoral war is a simple tautology.

As supporters of the war, the Rockefellers were *realpolitiker,* perhaps mistaken ones. They can hardly be blamed because President Johnson was maladroit in his practice of *schrecklichkeit.* The flaw in the conduct of the Vietnam War is that Lyndon Johnson, trying to keep it on the level of a secret minor operation, was always too late with too little. The result was that it became full-scale regional carnage.

The United States was at a disadvantage from the beginning because the "side" it favored consisted only of a paper government most of whose supporters, many of them refugees from the north, cannily wanted to avoid fighting at all costs. All along, the United States, claiming to be supporting a free government, was backing a straw man. In the world as constituted, where God is on the side with the heaviest artillery as always, merely being a free government confers no privilege, wins no battles. And then again, just how "free" was the Saigon government?

But David Rockefeller, although backing the Vietnam War, has since the middle 1950s been in favor of American rapprochement with China. Here he lines up with many American liberals. He was for that long ago when Richard Nixon was huffing and puffing against the devilish Chinese Reds. And it was finally a Rockefeller man, Kissinger, who brought the thoroughly mixed-up president around to a sensible point of view, for which (naturally) Nixon claimed full credit.

As former chairman and a director of the prestigious Council on Foreign Relations, David Rockefeller is quite obviously a power in the realm, is much more than a kooky beetle-collector. There's a lot more to the CFR story and the interested citizen is urged to look into it.

As a leading spirit of the Lower Manhattan Downtown Association, David Rockefeller has made his impress felt in a big way on New York. He was, first, a strong voice in his bank to have it put up its ornate new big building. And he was the original pusher to have built the huge two-towered World Trade Center, financed through the Port of New York Authority, one of the state's independent debt-creating bodies. His idea in both cases was to revivify the Wall Street area, which was losing corporate tenants to the midtown and suburban areas, thereby jeopardizing valuable real estate holdings.

The World Trade Center was projected for one of those

sideline marginal regions that consisted largely of old buildings—warehouses, lofts, run-down stores, and tenement
dwellings. Whenever the Rockefellers or anyone else schedules such places for a ground-up revamping, there is aroused a
great outcry against dislodging the down-at-heel bedraggled
elements who have found shelter there. So there was in this
case. If the denizens to be dislodged were really being given
consideration, substitute new facilities would first be provided elsewhere. But they never are. Those being evicted, as
mere leaseless tenants, are simply ejected with much futile
public weeping over their plight.

The World Trade Center cost $700-plus million, consists of
two 110-story structures that will house fifty thousand office
mechanics. Its funding is tax-exempt and it pays no taxes itself. When it opened, it was found there was no rush to lease
space; the Port Authority had a losing proposition on its
hands. However, Nelson Rockefeller as governor helped out
by taking many floors in the place for New York State offices.
As it was later disclosed, the state in many places went on
paying office rent in formerly occupied buildings so the state
paid rent in two places at once—an instance of one Rockefeller washing the hands of another at public expense. Had the
state not taken this space, David would have been left with
more egg on his face than is the case. The Trade Center,
though, is still not fully rented and has had an adverse effect
on the whole Wall Street rental situation by reason of its
competition.

The Port of New York Authority, moreover, was then in
charge of its new director, William J. Ronan, former executive
right bower to Governor Rockefeller and one of the prime
beneficiaries of his personal largesse as shown in Chapter
One. So expansive, indeed, is the domain of the Rockefellers
that very few of their dealings are arm's-length affairs with
strangers or outsiders. Many of them are inside dealings within their own owned, controlled, or influenced public-private
domain.

There is a price to progress as to anything else. The World
Trade Center represents progress, as defined in Wall Street.

But the price is not paid by the Rockefellers but by others—by those dispossessed, by the owners of buildings that have lost tenants to the Center, and by the taxpayers. Nor does the capital for the place come out of the pockets of the Rockefellers; the capital is supplied by the general investment market but is guaranteed in its earnings by the people of the State of New York, the taxpayers.

David had much experience when it came to launching Chase Manhattan Plaza and the World Trade Center. He had been blooded with Morningside Gardens, which he took up in 1946. This project displaced thousands. As I have earlier remarked, one can't make an omelet without breaking a few eggs.

Morningside Gardens is located just north of Columbia University. At the time David directed his attention to the region, adjoining which he had attended school at Teachers' College, it consisted of ten acres of run-down buildings, formerly good apartment houses that had, however, been overused through being overcrowded in multifamily occupancy by landlords reaching for more rent. The overpopulation, bringing with it hordes of children, many of them playfully destructive, naturally gave the structures extra intensive wear and tear; at the same time the landlords saved money by failing to maintain the buildings in good condition. The region had become a slum or near-slum, a private-enterprise nuisance to nearby Columbia University and similar institutions such as Union Theological Seminary, Jewish Theological Seminary, Julliard School of Music, etc.

David himself refers to the region as the Acropolis of New York. And bad things were happening to the Acropolis. For the barbarians were in increasing command.

He first brought in a sociologist from the University of Chicago to make a survey which he could have got from the local cop on the beat. But having the name of a sociologist attached to it is more impressive. He then recommended that the nine leading institutions of the locality establish an organization called Morningside Heights, Inc. There was then obtained the backing of City Hall, where David had once been ensconced, and a federal grant of money (which is taxpayers' money, not government money; for the government, not at all oddly, has no money at all, at any time, of its own, not even printing-press money).

With the money-grant, Morningside Heights, Inc.—that is, David Rockefeller—acquired the ten acres of land, ousted the uncivil tenants against much outcry, and razed the buildings, all sturdily constructed several decades before. There was then erected a complex of apartment buildings at a cost of $16 million to rent to one thousand middle-income families. The new project, housing more decorous elements, was called Morningside Gardens. When his work was finished, David received an honorary degree from Columbia University, making him a multiple doctor.

No doubt inspired by the success of the Morningside Gardens construction David in 1967, with brothers Winthrop and Laurance as partners, engaged in a similar operation in San Francisco. Plans were drawn up for a $150-plus million project called Embarcadero Center, near the waterfront. The place was ripe for "development." Against the usual criticisms from outside architects and city planners, there was laid out a whole new neighborhood consisting of a sixty-story office building, a forty-five-story office building, a twenty-five-story two-block office building, a sixteen-story hotel of eight hundred rooms, three theaters, shops and boutiques, bistros and restaurants, a wine museum and wine library. Local wits dubbed it Rockefeller Center West.

As the plans violated local building codes right and left, there ensued the usual flap, but David appeared before the city-county Board of Supervisors and convinced it the whole thing represented progress. As he said, the outdoor areas, which would embrace half the ground space, would be decorated with a million dollars worth of sculpture and other art works. He had the backing of local financial interests and of organized labor, which feels the gainer whether stuff is being torn down or built up: jobs in an overpopulated, job-short world.

One of the major objections to the plan, overruled, was that the structure would cut off the view of San Francisco Bay for a large part of the city. The project, however, was something of a bellwether for many similar construction projects in San Francisco, enhancing values of central-city landholdings all around. Slums and run-down city areas, it should be noticed, are all potentially valuable. And that is the reason real-estate operators hover over them like buzzards and often deliberately create them.

The running-down transition of neighborhoods like that north of Columbia University to heavier occupancy at higher total rents, in all such cases is managed, under the rubric of equal rights for everybody, by renting to unacculturated or semicultured elements—undesirables, as they are freely called. Many of these are not housebroken to city living, are fresh from rural enclaves where garbage was simply thrown out for animals and poultry to devour; the tenants continue to dispose of garbage in much the same way, only now there are no animals to eat it. Against the equal-rights slogan, the older residents, conditioned in the schools, cannot stand up; those that nevertheless protest are accused of racism or some other form of bigotry. For the newcomers are generally Negroes, Puerto Ricans, Chicanos; in an earlier day they were Russian Jews, Irish, and eastern and southern Europeans.

Those who try to protest the influx despite the equal-rights slogan are pushed aside, cried down, buffeted in the courts. In the upshot they simply all flee, leaving the area clear for the lower-class, higher-paying, more profitable newcomers— higher paying because they constitute more families per flat.

In the Soviet Union when the government decides to move many people from one site to another, it simply issues a crisp order, a decree. Everybody moves. Neat! That's dictatorship and, most Americans feel, very bad. In the United States when private real-estate operators, tightly allied in every case with monetarily participating politicians and banks, want to move old residents from an area, sending them further out to buy high-priced housing on original low-cost (to the operators) land and to move in higher-paying unacculturated elements, they simply raise the equal-rights slogan and start moving in the bogeymen. Those who move out have a point: they don't want to be living near people who believe that public hallways are latrines, that streets are battlegrounds. So the old-time residents respond like Pavlov's dogs to the ringing of the bell and flee.

They leave the solidly built housing and the old neighborhoods with built-up facilities such as schools, churches, stores, hospitals, libraries, parks, and playgrounds and move into more expensive but flimsily built, nonmasonry housing farther out, often entailing a long train, bus, or auto ride to work. In the new suburban neighborhood, moreover, there are few ancillary public facilities. Many of the new suburbs are bleak havens, especially in inclement weather. The outward-bound refugees don't generally realize it, but they have lost something, have been subtly jobbed. So have the incoming refugees.

And whenever the operators want to reverse the process, they can do it by the same methods.

There is profit at every stage of the process. There is, first, more profit in renting to more people at higher rents—several families per flat being able to pay the higher rent. There is profit again in undermaintaining a building, allowing it to run down. There is profit again in the sale of the run-down building to a public authority or private builder, who now builds either with public funds or funds from a bank loan or bond issue. Naturally there is profit for the contractors in building the new structure, whether it is publicly or privately owned. And the new people in the new structure, best of all, pay higher rents per square foot than ever.

There is, of course, profit for the moving companies in moving people in and out.

And there is profit out in the suburbs in buying cheap farm land and selling it, plus jerry-built new buildings, at elevated prices. All this is managed by syndicates in which politicians have beneficial interests.

And, like Pavlov's dogs, the actors in the drama don't have the least idea they are being manipulated by banks, politicians, and real-estate syndicates, all in the name of equal rights and freedom.

David Rockefeller came into the Morningside Gardens picture at the moment when the area was run-down. He had had
nothing to do with the drama prior to then although the banks
in general had. But in a region like that, run-down, on the
verge of becoming a slum, it is clearly time to do something
especially when the area abuts an enterprise like Columbia
University. If the run-down area abuts nothing like that it can
be ignored and allowed to sink under the weight of its own
ineptitude and *schweinerei*. In such areas landlords in New
York simply allow the city to take over the land and dilapidat-
ed structures for unpaid taxes. Later, with public money (the
taxpayer again holding this basket) there is "urban-renewal"
construction of low-rent, tax-subsidized high-cost housing—
more profit to contractors and banks that handle the financing.

Banks, insurance companies, and building and loan associations have foreknowledge of the regions scheduled to get
this sort of profit-generating treatment and refuse to make
loans for property improvements. Too risky. They can see, for
example, that the city is beginning to move in welfare cases,
paying the rents for them. The low-class families with an
abundance of children are going to have an uncouth impact
on a neighborhood. They would quickly wreck Buckingham
Palace or even the Tower of London.

Real estate operators alertly spread the word around that
"undesirable elements" are coming in, thus stimulating resident property owners to sell to newcomers, often at elevated
prices. Owners of multiple dwellings simply rent at elevated
prices and allow the places to deteriorate. Spreading the word
around that undesirable elements are coming in is called in
the trade "block busting," because whole blocks of established residents move out as though fleeing the plague. Bro-
kerage fees proliferate.

Those who don't like to see the "undemocratic" flight call
the movers bigots. Yet they may merely be people who don't
want to live with public hallways used as latrines and fes-
tooned with garbage. Such places are periodically shown in
TV "exposés."

How one relocates large numbers of people in the Soviet
Union and in the United States, then, comes down to a matter

of different techniques. The American technique, slower, "democratic," is immensely profitable to the operators and manipulators. And, best of all, the general nonrich taxpayer pays.

For David Rockefeller, as for the rest of us, this is a world he never made. But David Rockefeller and his brothers have, obviously, made a better adjustment to it than most of us. They started, though, with more external advantages. However, despite all this, their minds and time simply have to be cluttered with a great deal of stuff the rest of us are free of. We, for our part, can fix our attention on larger matters, such as the tides of history or the evolution of thought. Whether we do or not, of course, depends on ourselves. Some people prefer navel-gazing. On the other hand, none of the Rockefellers needs to engage himself in purely time-killing activities, as many people do. Structuring time, as some pundits put it, is no problem to them. They have plenty on their plates to fully occupy their time.

One of the major steady nonprofit preoccupations of David is Rockefeller University (formerly Institute), of which he is chairman of the board of trustees. This is an unquestionably important institution, and he gives it serious attention, seldom if ever failing to attend meetings and make his influence felt. The place is one of the major stars in the Rockefeller constellation of nonprofit institutions. He is, as we have seen, also a life trustee of the Rockefeller-endowed University of Chicago and has been a member of the board of overseers of Harvard University.

Each of the Rockefeller brothers has as a major stint the job of supervising at least one of the major Rockefeller nonprofit institutions, whose crucial role in the system will be examined in Chapter Five. John 3, for example, was from the early 1930s a trustee of the huge Rockefeller Foundation and was chairman from 1952 to 1971. He is also a trustee emeritus of Princeton University. Laurance is president of Jackson Hole Preserve and a trustee of Massachusetts Institute of Technology and president of the board of trustees of Princeton University. Nelson since 1932 has been trustee, treasurer, president, and chairman of the Museum of Modern Art. Winthrop, from 1961 until his death, had as his chief stint along these lines the post of chairman of the big Colonial Williamsburg Foundation.

Each of these places is a pillar among the family institutions.

9.

In the fourth generation only Nelson's son, Rodman, and John 3's son, John D. IV, have yet had public notice.

Rodman is a businessman, developing his grasp with the International Basic Economy Corporation. He rarely figures in the news.

John D. IV, nicknamed Jay, born in 1937, has to date come into the most notice in his generation. After attending Phillips Exeter Academy, where he finished in 1954, he embarked on the study of Oriental languages, in this pursuing one of his father's avenues of interest. He was a student at the International Christian University in Tokyo in 1957 and, after graduating from Harvard in 1961, engaged in postgraduate studies at the Yale University Institute of Far Eastern Languages.

He seemed destined for something in the field of Eastern foreign affairs. In 1961, age twenty-four, under President Kennedy he was made a member of the advisory council of the Peace Corps, became special assistant to the director of the corps in 1962, was soon made operations officer in charge of the Philippines, where he remained until 1963, and then was made a desk officer for Indonesian affairs in the Bureau of Far Eastern Affairs at the State Department. In 1964, under Lyndon Johnson, he was made a consultant to the President's Commission on Juvenile Delinquency and Youth Crime and in the same year became a field worker in the Action for Appalachian Youth.

This last assignment brought him to West Virginia, like Arkansas one of the backward states. He soon went into local politics as a Democrat, the only Rockefeller so registered, and was first elected to the state's House of Delegates and then became secretary of state, holding this office until 1972. Defeated in a try for the governorship, in 1973 he became president of West Virginia Wesleyan College, where he remains at this writing. He campaigned as an environmentalist, conservationist, and opponent of strip-mining—a "good guy" against "The Interests." He is also a trustee of the University of Chicago and writes for the national magazines, the only Rockefeller to have engaged in this sort of activity.

In 1967 he married Sharon Percy, daughter of Senator Charles Percy of Illinois. They have one son, Jamie.

Owing to his having entered politics he was quickly singled out as a future logical aspirant to the presidency of the United States, an ambition he does not deny harboring. What with this, that, and the other, he could make it although it is still too early to tell. His defeat for the governorship somewhat blighted the premature presidential preboomlet, but political observers believe he is sure to try again for higher office and feel certain he will make it. His college presidency in the meantime keeps him in a ready position.

He clearly holds many firsts among the Rockefellers: first to learn a string of Oriental languages, first to become a state legislator, first to register as a Democrat, first to publish for money, and first to be a college president. He wasn't, however, the first to marry a senator's daughter; his grandfather, Junior, beat him out there. Nor was he the first to hold elective office. Nelson holds that ambiguous honor.

His father, of course, is very pleased by his obvious competence. In an interesting disclosure of a low-keyed rivalry among the brothers, he expressed annoyance that newspaper accounts referred to John IV as Nelson's nephew rather than as John 3's son.

Other sons of the brothers who haven't yet shown their mettle publicly are David's sons, David II and Richard, Laurance's son Laurance II, and Winthrop's son Winthrop Paul. Whether any of them will hit the long Rockefeller ball, *à la* David and Nelson, is something journalists are waiting to see. None of the women has yet made a bid to assume commanding posts.

Two of Nelson's sons, Nelson and Mark, progeny of his second marriage, are still children. Steven, the clergyman, came into most prominent notice by marrying a Norwegian maid in his father's home, another triumph for democracy that sent the tabloids into the usual tizzy. They are now divorced.

Although Nelson and Winthrop have been the only ones of the brothers to be divorced and remarried, divorce and remarriage has been quite frequent among the Cousins, especially on the numerous distaff side. Outside men don't appear to fit readily into the Rockefeller scenario.

Of such a numerous collection of people, there is, clearly, much more to be related, pro, con, and up the middle but from the critical-expository point of view of this dissertation enough is set down here to convey the scenario. For chitchat about the Rockefellers, of which there is much, the reader must turn to the popular magazines which deal with them much as European magazines deal with royalty. The Rockefellers, of course, are the nearest thing to a royal family the United States possesses. If not they, who else comes close to filling the role?

Five

Looking the Gift Horses
in the Mouth

The roseate aura that enfolds the Rockefellers in the perceptions of the *hoi polloi*, largely in its middle strata, has been generated entirely by their polyphonically orchestrated performances on the philanthropy-charity circuit, with warbling obbligatos by platoons of public relations men and Syndicate professors. The definitely sinister, charcoal-streaked aura perceived by a minority of fellow-citizens, sicklied o'er by a critical spirit, derives mostly from the sinuous operations of the Rockefellers in corporate affairs and politics. An intelligence test is posed by the situation. How account for two such contradictory, intensely surrealistic appearances other than by postulating a schizoid ebb and flow at work?

As to the original John D., the one and only, he fits into the Rockefeller scheme today as the mainspring because he developed the script, the scenario, according to which they all reverently function, as if in a trance. His descendants even take their cues piously from his early life, and faithfully reenact as nearly as they can (but amid luxurious surroundings) his meager early routines in the upbringing of their children: household chores, family prayers, pennies for errands, Sunday

School, work on the woodpile, solemn deference toward underlings—nobody uppity or Vanderbiltish, everybody humble. The handy chameleon script is always there, not the Imitation of Christ but the Imitation of John. In passing, just how many people in the world try to model their deportment on their grandfathers or great-grandfathers?

This scenario in all its elaborated details arose quite obviously from the obsessive-compulsive syndrome of the founder, as we saw in Chapter Two, a combination of signs and symptoms that involved a life of endless fixed rituals, ever-orderly organization, and incessant wide-ranging activity, "work," designed at bottom to ward off ever-welling anxiety and, incidentally, to pile up a lot of money. The accumulation of the money was itself a ritual, and a sacred one, the most sacred. At this point, let us pray.

Just how obsessive-compulsive his descendants may individually be is, of course, not as easy to ascertain as in the founder's case because the script they follow requires that they restlessly poke into everything, at least *act* compulsively. Their adherence to the script is itself compulsive. The family style as a whole, set by old John D. and followed like gospel, is itself definitely obsessive and compulsive as well as schizoid, every step of the way. Traces of the syndrome, though, are discernible, among other character traits, in John D., II and John D. 3. The others among the brothers are less conformably organized, although formally they adhere to the valuable script.

And following hard upon syndrome and scenario, erected upon each, is the Syndicate—the Rockefeller Syndicate we scanned in Chapter One, a many-splendored thing. There, of course, is the main operation, the powerhouse, far outside the ken of the Syndicate professors.

We get, then, the Rockefeller formula in a capsule of triple alliteration—syndrome, scenario, Syndicate, a fugal interplay all the way of many themes, an intricate tapestry of far-flung disparate elements baffling to the *hoi polloi*. And baffling all the way to rut-bound ideological critics of Left and Right who see the Rockefellers in their own fantasied scripts: the workers of the world rising and casting down their capitalist masters (and getting new and harsher masters) or the workers put in their proper place by bands of marching louts clad in distinctive colored shirts.

Leftists particularly, I am aware, don't like what they call psychologizing because it syncopates and loosens up their mechanical script, largely composed by Karl Marx and assisting dialecticians. But all systems and plans of systems are themselves the outgrowth of temperaments, not inherent in nature. Lenin, himself an obsessive-compulsive and paranoid to boot, wrought many variations in the Marxist script as, indeed, have others, bringing it closer to each heart's desire. He and Rockefeller, incidentally, would have found much to agree upon—such as the need for everyone to shape up better —although Lenin's vision embraced a much more extensive scene—all history, no less. Why be parsimonious, why not go all the way?

It is time, now, or past time, to take a good hard look at the total Rockefeller performance in order to arrive at some genuine understanding of what it may all signify. In doing so, one must go far beyond the usual shallow notions freely purveyed.

2.

The *bouleversement* in public opinion toward a more favorable view of the Rockefellers in the decade 1914 to 1924, interrupted now and then by renewals of earlier distempers, has often been remarked upon. Most writers simplistically attribute the change to John D.'s hiring of Ivy Lee, formerly with the Pennsylvania Railroad, as a public relations advisor, and Lee's gimmick of having him hand out new shiny dimes (they are always described as shiny) to everyone he encountered on the street. The conclusion suggested is that the dime-gimmick transformed once-villainous John D. in the public eye into a harmless old gaffer, probably gone soft in the noggin—a masterly stroke! No explanation of the change in national temper toward John D. could be more fatuous.

Hardly an old-timer is now alive who remembers how vigorously old John was hated. As John T. Flynn opened his biography, "For forty years—from 1872 to 1914—the name of John D. Rockefeller was the most execrated name in American life. It was associated with greed, rapacity, cruelty, hypocrisy, and corruption. Upon it was showered such odium as has stained the name of no other American. Theodore Roosevelt denounced Rockefeller as a law-breaker. William J. Bryan, his fellow Christian, went up and down the land demanding that he be put in jail. The attorney-generals of half a dozen states clamored for his imprisonment. La Follette called him the greatest criminal of the age. Tolstoi said no honest man should work for him. Ministers of the gospel called the money he showered upon churches and colleges tainted. For years no man spoke a good word for John D. Rockefeller, save the sycophant and the time-server."[1]

If it wasn't Lee's Houdini trick with dimes, what was it that muted all this rage and turned it all around, transformed Rockefeller for a large section of the public into a saint rather than a sinner? Why, in other words, did Americans cease actively hating John D. Rockefeller?

The real reason the hatred subsided and then stopped was simply that it blew itself out, exhausted itself by its own excess. For the hatred of Rockefeller was always, in the proportions it assumed, one of the most overdone things in the world, as indeed are most American hatreds. They fall under what Richard Hofstadter called *The Paranoid Style in American Politics* (1965), the title of his book on the subject. And the hatred was largely misplaced. But in becoming inadvertently a big American hate-object, a scapegoat for all ruthless capitalists, for all of a minority of acquisitors who stole a lot of money while most folks could hardly make enough to live on, and for all of the millions who had boxed the compass in their sinning, Rockefeller performed one of his greatest but involuntary public services. He gave lowdown folks during a period of historic slack something to feel passionately about, a

---

1. John T. Flynn, *God's Gold*, p. 3.

satanic manifestation to pursue, thereby injecting high drama into their essentially drab lives. Scotch the wicked monster!

The American people have always hated somebody, have always been easily roused to hatred. The penchant comes from the frustrations systematically built into the political system fastened upon a naturally lush country and from constantly having to adjust within a racially and religiously polyglot people wherein at least half the population from each individual point of view is regarded as mongrel or worse. This ever-seething, almost gaseous hostility, quick to spring into flame, is something discerned by very few. It was, however, noticed by one of the first realistic observers of the American scene, H. L. Mencken.

As Mencken noted in 1926, "The whole history of the country [the United States] has been a history of melodramatic pursuits of horrendous monsters, some of them imaginary: the red-coats, the Hessians, the monocrats, again the red-coats, the Bank, the Catholics, Simon Legree, the Slave Power, Jeff Davis, Mormonism, Wall Street, the rum demon, John Bull, the hell hounds of plutocracy, the trusts, General Weyler, Pancho Villa, German spies, hyphenates, the Kaiser, Bolshevism. The list might be lengthened indefinitely; a complete chronicle of the Republic could be written in terms of it, and without omitting a single important episode."[2]

Mencken wasn't talking through his hat when he said the list could be extended indefinitely, that the history of the country could be written in terms of its bubbling hatreds and unreasonable fears. There was also anarchism, the IWW, socialism, neocommunism on top of Bolshevism, free love, immigration of undesirable aliens, carpetbaggers, the Spanish fleet hovering over the horizon off New York, Emma Goldman, invaders from Mars, Soviet submarines and spy ships in the Atlantic, the Black Hand, the Mafia, Cosa Nostra, moonshine poison, the Japanese menace, syndicalism, the Chinese menace, the Yellow menace, the Black Panthers,

---

2. H. L. Mencken, *Notes on Democracy*, pp. 22-23.

atheism, speculators, Robert G. Ingersoll, Soviet warships in the eastern Mediterranean, Soviet warships in the Indian Ocean, Soviet warships anywhere, freethinkers, the Viet Cong, white slavery, godlessness, Soviet spies in the State Department, miscegenation, cheap foreign imports, Margargaret Sanger and birth control, subversive professors, commercialized pornography, Un-Americanism, rampaging students with long hair, uppity blacks, permissiveness, Martin Luther King, and on and on and on. And Rockefeller. Common hatreds play a far greater role in binding the nation together than love or mutual esteem. In the meantime, actual dangers were ignored, even denied.

Within a nation of many clashing orthodoxies this sort of thing is perhaps inevitable.

What damped down hatred of Rockefeller in combination with self-exhaustion was the appearance on the scene of a brand-new made-in-Wall-Street hate-object: the Kaiser and German militarism. These new twin menaces monopolized the stage from 1914 to 1918. But in swift succession there followed Lenin, Mussolini, Stalin, Hitler, Tojo, Trotsky, John L. Lewis, and many, many others. Rockefeller was now all but forgotten, golfing away ritualistically on his various private links until his death in 1937 at ninety-eight. At least Jehovah recognized in him a worthy servitor, granting him a long life, many descendants, and much wealth, eventually a chorus of hosannas, with only a few bouts of illness along the way.

Behind all these raging hatreds at inception is always an individual or a small group desirous of promoting self or some profitable project down to selling newspapers, books, or advertising space. The hullabaloo about the monocrats, the fantasied danger of a king taking over rather than (as we have) the CIA, IRS, PO, OASI, FBI, and Pentagon, was started and kept alive by Thomas Jefferson, practically its sole sponsor and major beneficiary. Groups seeking to stir up the mob for their own purposes, or the government itself (politicians) doing it, are behind all these hatreds, producing a turbulent backwash in a conglomerate society of half-baked heterogeneous and always manipulable outcasts largely from Europe

—the beloved "ethnics" of latter-day synthetic sentimentalists.

A reason for it in the political system itself is that in the United States, thanks to the Founding Fathers, it is very difficult to produce the least change, even a small change. The government can't even bring itself to establish control over the ready sale of firearms. If one feels it necessary or advisable to campaign for visible street numbers or an end to dry sweeping, one must elevate the undesirable condition to the status of a national menace and call for the mobilization of the armed forces, possibly the use of the hydrogen bomb. Such is the built-in inertia of the system that something approaching all-out war is often required to get a needed traffic signal installed. As the saying has it, one can't fight City Hall. Is Congress corrupt? Any correction to take effect requires full-scale revolution, nothing less, carnage over a wide area, scorched earth from Maine to Yuma, Arizona. A simple eradication of some specific evil is not the way to go about it because, as it turns out for seemingly mysterious reasons, one can't eradicate evils. They merely hang on and accumulate like barnacles.

Rockefeller, whose career we scanned in Chapter Two, was unlucky enough to fall afoul of this American proclivity for hatred and fear and felt its full force. Naturally, he and his Standard Oil associates should have been brought to heel early in the game by the law enforcement agencies. But as this was the United States, moves against him, of which there were many, were easily blocked by lawyers, sabotaged, or the agencies bought off. There was, really, no way of bringing him to book in any way except by staging the verbal lynching party that was finally let loose against him and against which Syndicate historians like Allan Nevins bleat in befuddled protest.

All that was needed back in the 1880s was a clean indictment, a trial, and a verdict. But invisible forces—money procured—were always ranged on his side, and the public hullabaloo was substituted for orderly procedures. In several instances, especially in Ohio, officials who tried to proceed against Standard Oil were simply driven out of politics.

Eventually at least, all the ruckus finally brought Standard Oil before the bar of justice, there to be dissolved into a multitude of parts before it could become master of the entire economic system, which was a possiblity distinctly achievable. Yet Rockefeller, due to the grandstand overreaching of Judge Landis, was never personally brought to book. The only way to get roast pig, it seemed, was to burn down the whole house.

3.

Heading toward the 1890s Rockefeller and his associates knew they were in trouble even as their wealth secretly piled up to levels not fully disclosed even today. They had worked themselves out on a golden limb. He had already been extensively investigated, as early as 1879 in New York by the so-called Hepburn Committee launched by the state legislature. It was headed by Alonzo Barton Hepburn, who did a very good job of bringing disagreeable facts to the record. He worked so well, in fact, that Rockefeller, never one to harbor hard feelings, later made him one of the trustees of the Rockefeller Foundation. Rockefeller and Standard Oil did this scores of times with effective adversary lawyers they encountered. Samuel C. T. Dodd, his chief attorney and developer of the trust, was originally an able adversary. All along the line it has been part of the Rockefeller technique to gather in able people, even opponents, and make them contented inhabitants of the Rockefeller plantation, first citizens. Doing this is part of the scenario. It still goes on today.

Court proceedings and official extended hearings bearing on Rockefeller and Standard Oil prior to 1890 are alone extensive. There was, first, *Commonwealth of Pennsylvania vs. John D. Rockefeller et al.* (all his associates), Court of Quarter Sessions for Clarion County, Pennsylvania, record in print, 1879; New York Legislative Assembly, *Report of the Special Committee on Railroads. . . .* (The Hepburn Committee). Five volumes, Albany, 1880; *The Standard Oil Company vs. William C. Scofield et al.*, Court of Common Pleas of Cuyahoga County, Ohio, record in print, 1880; *The Lake Shore and*

Michigan Southern Railway Company, plaintiff in error, vs. *Scofield, Shurmer and Teagle,* in error. . . . Supreme Court of the United States, October term, 1886. No. 1,290. Transcript; United States House of Representatives, Fiftieth Congress, First Session, 1887-88. *Report of the Committee on Manufacturers, on the Standard Oil Trust.* H. R. 3112. Washington, 1888; and *Report of the Committee on General Laws on the Investigation Relative to Trusts.* Transmitted to the (New York) Legislature, March 6, 1888, Albany, 1888. Thereafter there were two major proceedings in Ohio, four federal investigations by the United States Industrial Commission and the United States Commissioner of Corporations, and finally the court actions that led up to the United States Supreme Court in 1910 and 1911. Up to 1928 there were eighteen major investigations and trials concerning John D. Rockefeller and Standard Oil, enough for years and years of full-time reading. There were also many local proceedings, all derailed.

And, throughout, the influence of Standard Oil in reaching behind the scenes to determine the outcome is detectable. Nothing was left to chance, to the fall of the dice of justice.

But what began to get the general public steamed up was, first, a magazine article in the *Atlantic Monthly* in 1881 by Henry Demarest Lloyd and then Lloyd's book *Wealth Against Commonwealth,* which appeared in 1894. It created even more commotion than Henry George's *Progress and Poverty,* now a classic of analytical protest. Edward Everett Hale pronounced Lloyd's opus the most important book to appear in the United States since *Uncle Tom's Cabin.* Distinguished foreigners read it and were appalled. Nevins makes much ado of finding flaws in it, never allowing for the fact that it was the work of one man unraveling a gigantic clandestine maze put together and nurtured by many hands.

Rockefeller now was rapidly slipping into the stellar position of public whipping-boy once graced by George III, Benedict Arnold, Aaron Burr, and Jefferson Davis.

And just as the public was beginning to forget Lloyd's book, along came a series of magazine articles beginning in 1902 that eventually emerged as *The History of the Standard Oil*

Company by Ida Tarbell (1905). It was this heavily documented book, really, that broke up the Trust. Rage against Rockefeller was now unbounded, and the government, whether it wanted to or not, simply had to proceed against him. For Standard Oil in its true dimensions made government itself appear ludicruous.

Actually Rockefeller and Standard Oil had been attacked from the beginning in Pennsylvania oil region newspapers. Such attacks spread out gradually to other publications. A reason for the spreading animosity apart from successful Standard Oil sneak plays was that Rockefeller, Standard Oil, and the railroads represented something new: the spread of industry to national dimensions. Until the 1870s and 1880s, business had been largely localized. Production and distribution took place within largely self-sufficient regional areas, and each region had little traffic with other regions. The railroads gradually changed that, made it possible for business enterprises to transcend regional boundaries.

But newspapers, until later, were tied in with local regional enterprises, looked upon larger enterprises as invading foreigners who undercut the local businesses. Hence the outcry against the larger and enlarging entities, an outcry that focused more and more on Rockefeller as the most successful of the interlopers. Not until the larger entities established their own organs, or bought into or subverted with money the older ones, did they get any sort of public defense. Even back in the 1880s Standard Oil had taken steps to see that it got a good press and it soon converted the Oil City (Pa.) *Derrick,* one of the earliest Standard Oil scourges. The first criticisms of Rockefeller, it is well to note, came from the old-style business community. It was a long time before radicals and so-called muckrakers took a hand in the game. As to muckraking, anybody who attempts to write realistically about the American politico-economic scene is going to find that he is a muckraker. The lining of that scene was revealed by Watergate and its aftermaths. Any writer on the scene who is not a muckraker is a purveyor of fiction or a syndicate professor able to distill sweet music out of cacophony.

4.

As Rockefeller found himself in trouble through the 1880s, he began developing the philanthropic counterpoint that in the course of time began running through the scenario like the dominant theme in a Bach fugue. It was simply a diplomatic tactic that, however, fit in perfectly with his personal syndrome.

He had been made a vice-president of the Theological Union of Chicago in 1882, which focused his attention on the city as a leading Baptist layman. Various Baptists wanted to found a university, the only question being where it was to be located. In Chicago there already existed far on the southside the Morgan Park Theological Seminary, Baptist, founded in 1867, which was associated with the nearby University of Chicago, a jerkwater undergraduate school founded in 1856 by Stephen A. Douglas and others. An insurance company foreclosed on its buildings in 1886. In 1888 there was founded the American Baptist Education Society with the Rev. Frederick T. Gates of Minneapolis placed at its head. Gates was thus brought to Rockefeller's attention and soon became his philanthropic guide, later his investment manager. Gates became in this way the latest of the brilliant aides taken up by Rockefeller, who by means of careful testing uncovered competence in others.

After much discussion and argument among the Baptists, it was finally decided to place the new university in booming Chicago. Rockefeller put up an initial $600,000 with the stipulation that $400,000 be raised by his fellow sectarians. Ten acres of land worth $125,000 just north of the Midway Plaisance, a parkway, near the site of the coming World's Columbian Exposition, were thrown in by Marshall Field. Rockefeller later acquired additional land. The Midway connects two giant public parks.

The university was therefore sited where it now exists: on a long rectangular strip twelve blocks long and, irregularly, two very long blocks wide. It paralleled this broad parkway which is situated between two streets a block apart, running east and west, with a block-wide strip of grass and trees in between, a regular Champs Élysées. Rockefeller later acquired a similar parallel strip south of the Midway so that the university really straddles the Plaisance although it has not even yet fully occupied all its southerly land.

Rockefeller quickly made additional gifts of $1 million each and by December, 1902, had put up $10 million, most of it in Standard Oil securities and most of it for endowment. Other local people also put in heavy lesser sums, especially Martin Ryerson, the steel magnate. All in all through the years, Rockefeller was to pony up $40 million or more for the university. Others from time to time put in even more, and the endowment has constantly churned out more money.

In deciding to found a university Rockefeller actually was merely joining in a well-established trend among men of wealth. For centuries wealthy people in Europe and the United States had given sums large and small for the creation of universities, colleges, asylums, monasteries, and churches. Doing so was a mark of great respectability, always gained kudos.

In 1876 Johns Hopkins donated $3.5 million to establish Johns Hopkins University in Baltimore, which moved quickly into the first rank of such institutions and was soon mentioned in the same breath with long-established Harvard. Leland Stanford in 1885 announced the founding of Stanford University in California; it opened its doors in 1891. Jonas G. Clark in 1887 founded Clark University, which opened two years later as a graduate university. Cornell University, founded in 1865 as a land-grant college, was named after Ezra Cornell because he put up $500,000 for buildings. Colgate University, in existence since 1819 as a Baptist institution under another name, was renamed in 1890 after James Boorman Colgate, a Wall Street broker, who gave it $1 million. Pratt Institute had been founded in Brooklyn in 1885 with a gift of nearly $4 million from Charles Pratt, a Standard Oil associate. And so on.

There soon was heard the charge that the university was a cat's-paw for Rockefeller, subject to his whim. Nothing could have been farther from the truth. For Rockefeller, in all his benefactions, was strictly first class all the way, no hanky-panky. To be otherwise would have spoiled the script. The university quickly became as good as any in the world, strictly independent. There were a few instances, though, in which underlings, no doubt to demonstrate their orthodoxy beyond the demands of the pope, acted in ways that made it seem Rockefeller must be pulling the strings. He never did.

However, in many ways, Rockefeller through Gates left his impress on the institution. It showed, first, in the highly symmetrical layout of the place, a preview of Rockefeller Center and the Albany Mall, although in English Gothic limestone, copies of buildings at Oxford and Cambridge. Whereas most universities until then were laid out rather helter-skelter, having grown by accretions, the University of Chicago was laid out in a rigid rectangle, the bordering buildings enclosing parklike quadrangles and courts—straight Rockefeller, straight Standard Oil. Columbia University, also erected by a latter-day corporate crowd, was laid out similarly in smaller compass. In recent years additions to the two institutions have deviated somewhat from the original pattern although at Chicago deviations are minor. What it symbolizes most strongly is: order, regularity, tradition.

That Rockefeller was not entirely unmindful of what went on at the university, even though he did not interfere with its intellectual operations, is shown too by his displeasure at the way without consulting him the administration hastened into an alliance with Rush Medical College. Gates had by then already convinced Rockefeller that he ought to back a medical research institute on the European model, and Rockefeller planned to give it to the University of Chicago. But the university forestalled him by hastily connecting with Rush Medical, and the result was that New York City got Rockefeller Institute, now Rockefeller University, a wholly graduate specialized institution, an intellectual hothouse with today three faculty members to each of about one hundred students.

The new University of Chicago opened its doors in 1892, the institute was launched on a small initial scale in 1901 with an initial pledge of $200,000. The General Education Board, incorporated under a special act of Congress, began in 1903. The Rockefeller Foundation, proposed to Congress in 1909 but rejected, was established by act of the New York legislature in 1913 and in 1918 came the Laura Spelman Rockefeller Memorial.

For these various institutions Rockefeller's input consisted for the most part not of money but of something more valuable because income-producing: securities. And the major part of the securities consisted of stock in Standard Oil Company of New Jersey.

According to the best available sources, the initial amounts and the totals with more added later in some cases by Junior, came to $486,719,371.22.

This amount was later retotaled to somewhat more than $500 million.

It is often said that Rockefeller Senior donated $500 million in his lifetime, his son an equal amount. Actually the elder put up more than this in lifetime donations. The third generation is credited with donating about $250 million, making initial donations around $1.25 billion. This figure does not include income from the endowments, which about quadruple the total—about $5 billion.

Many questions arise because of this activity which Nevins puts down to simple generosity on Rockefeller's part, the easiest and most simpleminded explanation. Yet Rockefeller can hardly be described as a generous man. He was close-mouthed, secretive, conspiratorial, acquisitive, stealthy, endlessly calculating—hardly traits found in a generous man.

Yet he did, from an early age part with money and securities other than for personal expenditure or investment. The people who received it would have described it in most cases as a gift. As Nevins lists his donations from the famous Ledger A, wherein he kept track of everything down to the cent, we may note again he gave $2.77 in 1855 at the age of 16, $19.31 in 1856, $28.37 in 1857, and on upward to $1,012.35 in 1865, to $6,860.86 in 1871, to $32,865.64 in 1880, and gradually each year on up to $1,472,122.52 in 1893—this and the two previous years embracing money for the University of Chicago.

Rockefeller, the fact is, would have given something each

year had he remained a lowly bookkeeper. First, he was conditioned by his childhood religious upbringing to give regularly to the church as many people were conditioned in the
United States and Europe; second, the giving fit like a glove
into his obsessive-compulsive personality structure, became a
ritual. As we have seen, rituals, systems, are a mark of this
character type.

Until he began putting up the money for the University of
Chicago, most of Rockefeller's gifts had been to the Baptist
church or Baptist causes, much of it to Baptist foreign missions; some of it was made to individuals he met under
church auspices. But word that he was an easy touch had
spread so that he was besieged in the 1880s with many thousands of requests per month for money. Cranks far and wide
wrote him beseeching funds.

Yet his giving, unusual though the uncritical and sycophan-
tic Nevins finds it to be, was nowhere near the level of his
income. By 1885 Standard Oil had a monopoly of practically
the entire American oil industry and had lucrative outposts
worldwide. No comparable competitor was in sight anywhere. The money coming in was a problem, likely investment outlets few.

Gates, once he learned something of the dimensions of
Rockefeller's fortune, constantly urged him to give more and
more and more, lest he and his family be capsized simply by
the excessive sums in hand. There were others as well with
designs on Rockefeller's coffers, but it was Gates who urged
systematic, "scientific" giving—that is, giving in the institutionalized form it took under his supervision.

The sudden outburst of large-scale giving, however, even
though Rockefeller had been a giver all along, needs some
explanation. Not only did Rockefeller have the means to give
on a large scale, an ever-enlarging scale, but he was also distributing money in places far from the philanthropic circuit.
The full extent of such disbursements is not known, but it is
definitely known that he and Standard Oil and his associates
were putting money into (1) political campaigns, (2) newspapers, (3) lawyers representing the company, and (4) special

distributions where it was thought they would do the most good, especially to politicians. In other words, there was a general distribution of money going on all around. Rockefeller, in brief, was no starry-eyed giver, no woolly-minded do-gooder. His giving always had purpose, self-oriented purpose.

As this was a calculating man from start to finish, it would be odd if no sense of calculation entered into his philanthropies. Taciturn, he said nothing of his thoughts on this topic, left no record.

But even though he never made any avowal of self-serving intent, the idea of disbursing money "philanthropically" with the intent to do himself some good in the midst of public outcry against him was not overlooked by some of his money-mesmerized Baptist advisors. Thus Dr. Augustus Strong, head of the Rochester Theological Seminary, who was pushing for the establishment in New York City of what became the University of Chicago, said to Rockefeller in a letter in 1887 that "Very many people do not understand you and they very unjustly accuse you [which the United States Supreme Court, better versed in mundane law than the theologian, found in 1911 was not so]. Your friends love and admire you, but very many are not your friends. Your present gifts, to education and to the churches, do not stem the tide of aspersion as would the establishment of an institution for the public good, so great that it has manifestly cost a large self-sacrifice to build it. . . . You have the opportunity of turning the unfavorable judgments of the world at large into favorable judgments —and not only that—of going down to history as one of the world's greatest benefactors."[3]

There it is, in a nutshell.

So we know, despite all talk of generosity, that this is a perspective laid before Rockefeller. And no doubt others adverted to it because it was such an obvious way of counteracting public difficulties. And no doubt Rockefeller, acutely rational within his narrow vision, no fool, saw the protective

---

3. Allan Nevins, *John D. Rockefeller: The Heroic Age of American Enterprise*, p. 208.

value of engaging in philanthropic maneuvers in the face of the rising storm. What is more, he could afford the luxury.

As to this the obsequious Nevins, citing no evidence, re-marks *ex cathedra* that "It need not be said that Rockefeller had too much self-respect not to resent this intimation. In his opinion it was neither necessary nor right for him to use great money gifts to purchase the good opinion of the world." Asinine.

Rockefeller had gone to a lot of time, trouble, and effort to build Standard Oil and his own fortune with it. He felt, we may surmise, much like Winston Churchill at a later date when he said he did not feel that he had been called as the king's first minister to preside over the dissolution of the Brit-ish Empire. Rockefeller similarly must have felt, as his ac-tions showed, that he had not built his fortune in order to dismantle it by reckless or sentimental disbursement or to allow it to be dismantled by hostile outsiders, which was at the time a looming possibility.

Instead, with the inception of large-scale giving, he acted like the commander of a victorious army finally forced to re-treat. He began leaving some of his booty behind, there to be seized by others and admired, as he continued his retreat with the major portion of his captures, which he intended to keep and did in fact keep. As far as the wealth is concerned, this is the Rockefeller story in a nutshell. Any other interpretation fails to make sense, as the fortune is extant, intact. On this level Rockefeller won all the way, exited laughing.

Let us imagine that Rockefeller did not get into philanthro-pies. What would have happened then?

First, he would not have received the kudos from much of the press and gullible public that he actually did begin receiv-ing. Many people interpreted Rockefeller's giving as evidence of guilt and contrition, but Rockefeller never felt any guilt over anything he had ever done—indeed, he felt virtuous about everything. There isn't a shred of evidence of any kind that he felt a bit guilty or contrite.

Had he not set up his philanthropies, had he instead clutched every nickel he possessed, he would instead have been open to much more severe strictures and proceedings than he encountered in fact. And the final legal judgment on his affairs might have been much harsher. He might well have lost it all or gone to jail.

Second, by setting up highly approved philanthropic institutions, Rockefeller *created hostages* for the consideration of any future judges. The institutions he established were endowed with Standard Oil stock. If Standard Oil went down or was hit too hard, these institutions would also suffer—the University of Chicago, the Rockefeller Institute for Medical Research, the General Education Board, the Rockefeller Foundation. To strike them would be like striking the Holy Ghost. Any judge would be reluctant to do so.

What seemed to many to be light treatment in the dissolution decree of 1911 issued by the Supreme Court was just about the only resolution to the question the court could arrive at without injury to institutions that were without question highly constructive in their work. As to the last there has never been any contrary suggestion from any serious quarter. Rockefeller had indeed erected strong defensive bulwarks, a canny customer, a genuine Machiavellian.

There was also advantage to him in endowing the institutions with Standard Oil stock. For such stock could, at crucial moments, become part of the structure of company control, as became the case in the challenge to control of Standard Oil Company of Indiana in 1929. In that showdown, foundation and university stock voted on the Rockefeller side and will no doubt always do so in any comparable situation.

5.

Private universities and foundations are erected in the pattern of insurance companies. They perform a valid function and are backed by an income-producing investment fund. The fund, however, does not produce all the revenues for a university any more than for an insurance company. All the private universities charge tuition fees and the University of

Chicago from its inception charged tuition fees. There was no charity whatever involved vis-à-vis the student body, contrary to the belief of the uninformed. Similarly an insurance company sells its policies, hoping to make a profit or at least break even. In years of good profits an insurance company adds capital to its investment accounts; in bad years it tides itself over by drawing for claims and dividends upon investment income which otherwise is reinvested, increasing the reserves. It is a double-decked proposition, contrapuntal.

A private university, therefore, is selling something, like an insurance company and unlike a foundation; the latter relies wholly upon its investment income apart from any new donations.

While Chicago was a good place in which to establish a university, the institution was not a gift to the public in the sense of providing free tuition except in the grant of scholarships to stellar students, a small minority. The city of Chicago, in fact, for many years lacked nontuition higher education. It was not until 1914 that the city established its first junior college; it now has a system of these offering two years of tuition-free college instruction. The tuition-free state university was located some 160 miles to the south, in Champaign-Urbana, where it was costly for most Chicago-area students to live because they could not reside at home and the downstate region offered few part-time jobs to youngsters of the lower classes. The University of Chicago, then, did not provide a leg up toward the light for the lower orders except for some of unusual talent. It was not until after World War II that the University of Illinois established a large branch in the densely populated Chicago area, offering competition to fee-charging University of Chicago and Northwestern University, a tuition-charging institution under Methodist auspices on the northern border of Chicago. Meanwhile, New York City had had a full-course tuition-free liberal arts municipal college system long antedating the University of Chicago; it still retains it despite Nelson Rockefeller's attempt to incorporate it into the new state system and impose at least nominal tuition. In New York City today one can go from kindergarten through undergraduate university tuition-free—up to sixteen years of schooling. The taxpayers, of course, pay the freight.

At the point of meeting the ultimate consumer, something not generally understood, none of the Rockefeller philanthropies—schools, colleges, universities, museums—is free. The Rockefellers subscribe to Prof. Milton Friedman's dictum: there is no free lunch.* And on this point, anyhow, they are correct; the public pays for everything, everywhere, directly or indirectly, visibly or invisibly. There is, truth to tell, no "free" anything, anywhere, at any time except possibly for children; and they pay the price by having to tolerate their parents, who are rarely what the children would have ordered had they been able to make rational choices.

One thing from which Rockefeller derived no advantage initially through his philanthropic capers, however, was in the area of taxes. For the tax structure then was such that he paid no taxes at all except locally imposed ones, mainly on real estate. Here and there light business taxes were levied, but on the whole he, like other fortune builders of the nineteenth and early twentieth centuries, paid hardly any taxes. As we have noticed, through his chief counsel the Supreme Court was argued in 1895 into holding an income tax unconstitutional even though such a tax had been levied during and after the Civil War. Rockefeller liked neither the income tax nor the inheritance tax. Nor the gift tax, for that matter.

But with the adoption of the Sixteenth Amendment to the Constitution in 1913, all the Rockefeller endowments encountered a big slice of serendipity, as they were now tax exempt under the tax laws that gave exemption for charitable contributions. This meant that the voting powers in the endowments could not be reduced by means of taxation, might instead be increased through retained income, which they were. The door was also opened to future offsets to income by means of well-timed further tax-exempt philanthropic contributions.

---

*Friedman likes the idea so much he has written a book titled *There Is No Free Lunch,* a salutary reminder.

It has always been a proclaimed aim of the Rockefellers in their philanthropies and quasi-public assistance programs to set an example to others of their plutocratic class to go and do likewise. In the establishment of foundations, surely, they set an example, although it took some time before others of the wealthy could understand the self-serving, self-reinforcing character of such operations—*mostly* self-serving in many cases of record.

According to *The Foundation Directory* (Columbia University Press, 1971, pp. vii-viii), before 1900 there were only eighteen foundations, and only one of these amounted to more than $10 million while fourteen were worth from $1 to $10 million each. In the period 1910-1919 there were seventy-five foundations, twenty-two of which had assets of $10 million or more and thirty-six of $1 to $10 million.

Today, however, there are more than twenty-six thousand foundations, 90 percent of which were established since 1940, clearly a reflex to the crazy tax laws. Only 5,454 of these have assets of $500,000 or more; and only 2,179 foundations had assets of more than $1 million.

The largest of all, as we have noted, was the Ford Foundation with assets of $2.902 billion, originally set up to avoid inheritance taxes and keep control of the Ford Motor Company in the hands of the Ford family. Next came the Lilly Endowment with assets of $778 million and then the Rockefeller Foundation with $757 million.

What produced this efflorescence of foundations? The opportunity for tax juggling and general chicanery was virtually unlimited, as disclosed in an extensive investigation by a congressional committee under Chairman Wright Patman (*Tax-Exempt Foundations and Charitable Trusts: Their Impact on Our Economy,* Second Installment, Select Committee on Small Business, House of Representatives, October 16, 1963). The foundation in general was found to be a useful tool for much high-level racketeering.

The Rockefeller foundations and other major ones are far from rackets but they are, in addition to their philanthropic missions, useful instruments in (1) maintaining corporate control, (2) influencing public policy and social trends, (3) garnering public kudos for the donors, and (4) cutting corners on the tax laws. The public does not realize it is itself paying a large part of the freight. For gifts to the foundations reduce the taxability of estates and offset taxable income. And whatever anyone does not pay in taxes that he would otherwise be liable to pay under law, causes the faceless taxpayer to pay more. Tax exemptions, in other words, for whatever purpose, laudable or damnable, raise the tax costs of others who are unable or unwilling to be donative. So the taxpaying public, which is not saluted in the newspapers as philanthropic, makes an input to the foundations and endowments.

That foundations and other endowments are instruments of corporate control is currently often cited by writers as something first observed by foreign savants. No such foreign commentators that I have thus far read antedate my own analysis to the same conclusion as of 1937.[4] It took no remarkable insight on my part to detect this utility of foundations. For I had seen with my own eyes the exercise of such voting control acted out step by step at the stockholders' meeting of the Standard Oil Company of Indiana in 1929. Whatever is, is.

In what is the major concern of the trustees of foundations and endowments? It is management of the funds: investments, sale and purchase of investments, voting of the company proxies to which the investments are entitled. The working affairs of the endowment itself are entrusted to professional administrators. Do the trustees interfere in any way with the operation of the institution being supported, whatever it is? Perhaps sometimes; but rarely. In the case of a large private university they usually leave the faculty sedulously alone, or to the administrators, as long as the faculty sticks to its formal task within each discipline. If, however, members of the faculty begin playing some sort of active role with respect to public policy (which most faculty people hardly ever do as they are trained to specialize) then there may be repercus-

---

4. Ferdinand Lundberg, *America's Sixty Families*, pp. 320-73.

sions. Usually there are not unless the subject under question is emotion-kindling and highly controversial. At an earlier date faculty used to be more directly interfered with than at present. Quite a number of distinguished profs, in fact, were cashiered here and there. But as most of the faculty people have been chosen because they are "safe" and "sound" anyhow, believe in the donors, there is rarely occasion for interference. Sophisticated trustees know, anyhow, that whatever is being agitated will soon blow over, to be succeeded by some different phenomenon.

Actually the trustees are not too interested, except at strictly jerkwater institutions, in what the faculty people do and say provided they stay within the law. At major institutions today they tolerate even Marxists and Zen Buddhists. Only the paranoids are disturbed by this.

But faculty are not all innocent bystanders by any means. The reader will recall that I have introduced the concepts of syndicate professors and counter-savants. A syndicate professor is one who functions as an apologist for one of the big financial syndicates, with which such are directly connected, churning out books and speeches in support of syndicate theses. The public accepts them as products of pure learning.

The counter-savants, however, as I have said, argue a demonstrably false thesis, one that can be shown false in open-and-shut fashion. It is sin disguised as virtue, learning turned on its head, usually on behalf of some special-interest group. The late Adolf A. Berle, Jr., was one of these counter-savants, a persistent as well as important one—indeed, indefatigable.

Sometimes one professor, strictly on the up-and-up, nails one of these counter-savants right in public in the process of clarifying some important matter, a beautiful sight.

Thus Stanley S. Surrey, professor of law at the Harvard Law School, former assistant secretary for tax policy at the Treasury Department, and author of *Pathways to Tax Reform,* in the *New York Times Magazine* for April 13, 1975, addressed himself to Prof. Irving Kristol of New York University. Kristol had written that those who use the terms "tax expenditure" and "tax subsidy" to refer to tax benefits "are implicitly assert-

ing that all income covered by the general provisions of the
tax laws belongs of right to the government, and that what the
government decides, by exemption or qualification, not to collect in taxes constitutes a subsidy. Whereas a subsidy used to
mean a governmental expenditure for a certain purpose, it
now acquires quite another meaning—i.e., a generous decision by government not to take your money."

"But these statements," said well-grounded Surrey, "are
simply wrong. The concept of tax expenditures does not imply that all income belongs to the Government and any decision to tax less than all that income is an act of government
generosity. Rather, it is based on the idea that a proper income
tax includes in its tax base all sources of income and allows
deductions for all the expenses incurred in obtaining that income. If a special provision excludes some types of income,
allows deductions for personal expenses associated with consumption spending rather than the earning of income, or allows special business deductions not reflected under proper
accounting standards, then it becomes something engrafted
onto the income tax for a special purpose—that of a subsidy or
assistance."

As Professor Surrey pointed out, some $80 to $90 billions of
actual income in the United States is tax exempt. It constitutes
subsidies largely to business and investment categories
which, of course, include the rich and the super-rich.

Just how many syndicate professors and academic counter-
savants are there around the country? At a guess I'd say several hundred, perhaps up to a thousand, perhaps more. Some of
them like the late Professor Berle carry a great deal of weight
for a long time because they are not opportunely challenged.
They spread much befuddlement.

However, much of the work of many endowments, university and other, is highly useful and profitable to the corporate
elements. If one traced merely the discoveries and alumni of
the departments of chemistry of the universities, public and
private, to their ultimate corporate roosting places, one would
see the multibillion dollar value of the institutions to the corporations. Take now the entire scientific product of the uni-

versities, throw in the uneven output of the other divisions, and one can see that the universities are foundations of the profit enterprise system (as well as of many other things, for universities are multifaceted). Think of all the money made in publishing alone out of all the people who have been trained in the universities to write. A university, indeed, is a Protean affair.

6.

As to the difference between profit and nonprofit operations *per se*, there really is none. One can have results bad or criticizable, good or laudable, under either dispensation. A workman who makes deposits in a savings bank expects to be paid interest, perhaps 5 or 6 percent; that is his profit. Profit, basically, is a return for the use—by someone—of one's capital or its product. It has become a bit of cant, no doubt influenced by socialist ideas, to look upon profit as *per se* evil. *Per contra,* as profit is taken as bad by many persons (rather than the abuse of profit) so nonprofit is taken *per se* as good. The capitalist who wishes to gain public esteem has only to do something nonprofitable to earn cheers from liberal nitwits.

But one could write a long book listing thousands of nonprofit enterprises that the finest-honed experts agree are harmful, beginning with jails. Soviet Russia, for example, is a nation erected on the principle of nonprofit. For making a profit on any activity in Russia a person can be thrown into jail for long spells. But would anyone in his right mind, given a choice, live in Russia in preference to Sweden, Switzerland, France, Australia, or any number of places in which profit is permitted?

The point: merely because something is set up on a nonprofit basis does not transmute it into something to be venerated, whether it exists in connection with other profit-making enterprises or not. What the enterprise does, and *how much* profit it makes, is what counts. So here arises the question of *fair* profit. What is a fair profit—5 percent, 10 percent, 15 percent, 50 percent, 300 percent?

Let us agree, just to have a figure to work with, that 17 percent is the outer limit of a fair profit for allowing one's capital to be used. What then about an enterprise that is making only 5 percent on invested capital but is purveying a product that is deleterious to public health, as many products are regularly found to be by the biological laboratories? Profit, in other words, or nonprofit, is not the prime consideration in making evaluations.

Granted that the profit motive lends itself to unlimited greed, which is what has called it into question. But the non-profit motive in its political extension in the modern world has analogously lent itself to unlimited cruelty. Just because they have come out against profit, many modern politicos, such as Lenin and Stalin, feel they are morally justified in doing anything. One may therefore apparently make one's choice of which is to be ascendant, greed or cruelty. Neither, of course, is *necessarily* linked to profit or nonprofit.

Let us, in any event, not be carried away by some enterprise merely because it doesn't make a profit. Everything needs to be examined so as to ascertain its true inwardness *in all respects.*

7.

The Rockefeller philanthropies aroused cheers far and wide by what they accomplished. The University of Chicago, of course, was devoted to education and high-level research. The Rockefeller Institute researched successfully into the causes and cures of many diseases. The General Education Board, by funding appropriate programs, raised the level of both black and white education in the South, making a considerable dent in a swamp of ignorance and ineptitude. The Rockefeller Foundation founded the International Health Commission to export without charge known methods of coping with epidemic diseases, thereby helping to fuel the later "population explosion," and the China Medical Board to establish Western-type medical colleges and hospitals in China; launched public health programs and concentrated heavily on medical education through the Division of Medical Sciences. In the latter area it did heavy funding of psychiatric programs, very much needed in a world that drives people bonkers, programs in the field of experimental biology, and finally it began putting money into the social sciences, so-called, and humanities.

The Laura Spelman Rockefeller Memorial was used to develop university centers of research in Europe and throughout America and to fund research councils and conferences by means of fellowships. It spread a good deal of money far and wide.

In 1928 the Foundation absorbed the Laura Spelman Rockefeller Memorial, the natural-science program of the General Education Board, and the humanities program of the General Education Board, which entity was later allowed to liquidate itself in various projects. The foundation thus became a bigger affair than ever, worth nearly a billion.

All these opportunities for activity were made possible owing to the backwardness of the government in stepping into the breach. What kept the South backward for so long was the dual-sovereignty interpretation of the Constitution, preventing the federal government from lending needed assistance. The South was literally dying, economically and culturally, under the "states rights" doctrine. Dual sovereignty itself was later allowed to die; the notion was never any good once the industrial age dawned. Now the federal government—the lowly taxpayer, that is—freely funds such programs, including programs in science.

What the Rockefeller philanthropies came down to was paternalism, which in turn stemmed from feudalism. The worthy *padrone*, well heeled, looked about and saw what his people needed and graciously allocated some of his tax-exempt funds, as thousands cheered. He was, thus, far more than an ordinary citizen. He was a power in the land.

To go into each of these and other later major Rockefeller philanthropic activities would require a large book and, in fact, all of these institutions have been written up in at least one book, some in many books, devoted to them alone.

Rockefeller Junior stepped into the philanthropic breach in 1917 and during his lifetime ponied up $474 million, including $111.5 million to existent Rockefeller philanthropic funds, $60 million to Colonial Williamsburg, and $6 million to Rockefeller Institute. At his death half his estate ($75 million) remaining after these distributions and trust-fund transfers to his children was paid into the Rockefeller Brothers Fund. His widow left her estate to various funds.

New funds he established were Jackson Hole Preserve, around $25 million, for the conservation of wild and scenic areas open to the public; Sealantic Fund, about $32 million, for building and supporting programs of needed enlightenment at schools of theology in the United States and carrying on local charities at Seal Harbor, Maine, and Pocantico Hills, latter work which was taken over by the Rockefeller Family Fund in 1968; $134 million paid into the Rockefeller Brothers Fund by Junior and $13.4 million by his wife; Martha Baird Rockefeller Fund for Music established with a $5 million donation by Junior's wife.

Assets of the Rockefeller Brothers Fund set up for supervision by the boys stood at $238 million by the end of 1971 but the Protean uses to which such funds are amenable is shown by some of its more far-out programs. In addition to contribution to civic projects, especially in the field of conservation and theater arts, and to health, educational, religious, and welfare organizations, this fund has also put up money in support of studies relating to military weaponry and the state of the performing arts. After all, many subjects are susceptible to study, not all of them generally recognized as charitable or philanthropic. Nor is everything designated as educational in conformity with traditional conceptions of education. The science departments of the universities are often adjuncts to military programs; various other university programs are adjuncts to corporate profit-seeking. I don't especially knock it as many do, but it just shows what such words as philanthropy and education may relate to. There is not only the question of science and education but *science and education for what.* The trend now is to deploy much of this money *politically* in the form of studies about this and that. What comes out on the bottom line is what needs to be examined.

The general public, when it hears or sees words like philan-

thropy, science, and education, naturally thinks of something
benign. But, oddly, these words may, upon detailed analysis,
also relate to something ominous and destructive—or at least
something questionable. It takes a good deal of education, for
example, to enable one to build the arsenal of modern weaponry. The task cannot be performed by journeymen mechanics. Is what is now built something to ecstasize over?

Smaller special funds, always susceptible to expansion,
have been established by the brothers and their sister—the
Rockwin Fund with $1.8 million from Winthrop; the Ameri-
can Conservation Association with $1.8 million to 1970 by
Laurance, Nelson, the Rockefeller Brothers Fund, and Jack-
son Hole Preserve; the JDR 3rd Fund with $4.6 million from
John 3; the Greenacre Foundation with $3.5 million from
Abby Rockefeller Mauzé. And so on.

All this reaches up in the vicinity of $1.25 billion (without
considering income received and expended down through the
years, easily quadrupling the sum—a lot of impact).

Not only is all this paternalistic, allowing the disposition of
a great deal of power and influence over a wide area at home
and abroad (for many benefactions have been bestowed
abroad), but it will be observed that all of it is deployed to
shore up and cushion the existing system, not to support any
fundamental restructuring or rearrangement of the system.
One could draw up a long list of entirely valid projects the
Rockefellers don't go near, such as (for example) funding a
highly constructive operator like Ralph Nader. Interested in
producing better doctors, scientists, teachers, and the like, the
Rockefellers thus far have not seemed interested in producing
better politicians or in eliminating obvious cracks in the political system. They haven't thrown any weight that one can
discern into improving the Constitution or the legal system,
both of which could stand much improvement. As to politics,
as Nelson's career shows, they seem content to play the sordid
game as it has developed over the years.

In other words, they could do better—much better. As Nelson Rockefeller himself has put it, the aim of the Rockefellers

is to make the existing system work. And good luck to them with this goal.

But it will be noticed, as observed by many, the existing system is subject to periodic and avoidable breakdowns, and when it is working at its best, much is going on that people find deplorable in later revelations—such as, now, the secret use for many years of government agencies like the CIA, FBI, the post office, and the Internal Revenue Service secretly and illegally to disrupt the lives of people carrying on lawful but ideologically disliked activity. Not merely to conduct surveillance but to disrupt by underhanded means.

Whenever the system breaks down, millions of people, most of them flag-wavers and yea-sayers over the years, are subjected to discomfort and hardship while the media put out waves of reassurances that improvement is in sight, that there is light showing at the end of the long dark tunnel. All of this is unnecessary and avoidable but obvious remedies and countermeasures are rejected as ideologically unhallowed, infringing upon a long-infringed-upon entity dubbed "private enterprise."

If a man owns an automobile that breaks down or misbehaves as frequently as the extant politico-economic system, he calls it a "lemon" and sues the manufacturer. What the big shots do when the politico-economic system breaks down or wobbles is—launch studies, make speeches.

Naturally the problems to be solved before one attains Nirvana, if one ever does, are complex. But problems even more complex and baffling are solved every year in science. If scientists can unravel the mysteries of DNA, the mysteries of government should be a cinch—if they were allowed to tackle them.

Actually the remedies for many conditions are known, many of them the product of the leading universities. But the remedies are not applied, ostensibly on ideological grounds, really because they are disturbing to entrenched blood-sucking interests.

The philanthropies, then, have not been used to obtain fundamental adjustments and changes with a view to obtaining a more smoothly working social system. The problems that are attacked by the Rockefeller and other foundations are only those that can be solved without producing any major changes in public policy. In other words, stop cheering.

As a management consultant puts it, when any system wobbles somebody, somewhere, has to be responsible for a "down" statistic through some act of omission or commission. The system does not cause a "down" statistic unless someone, somewhere, is causing it to go down or is deliberately failing to anticipate or to block the "down" statistic. Those who tend a system are, obviously, the ones responsible, and those closest to the tenders.

In my view the big financial syndicates, their people strewn through government and the corporate structure, are the chiefly responsible elements because they are the ones uniquely in a position to take steps to avert "down" or skewed statistics. The fact is, they are willing to tolerate a certain number of "down" statistics such as unemployment, uncontrolled crime, irresponsible reproduction and so on. Unemployment is never necessary in the sense of being *required.* It is, like other evils, tolerated by the system guides because, up to a certain point, it is convenient—to them. That is to say, it is more convenient than taking required steps to eliminate it.

So much for systemic inevitability.

8.

Myer Kutz in *Rockefeller Power* (1974), an informative survey, rightly makes the point that much of the power of the family lies in its philanthropic arabesques and capers. It is that, for one thing, which gives it and its members high public status, impressive to professors, theologians, simpleminded journalists, editors, and press lords. And the high status is part of a citadel with a springboard into quite different waters, as shown in the cases of all the brothers. These, no geniuses, were born fully fledged and armed from the brow of trust funds. The philanthropic power, direct and indirect, is paralleled by power also exercised in much more specific and direct ways. Phantom jets, foreign policy, military studies, and political donations are something very different from works of art and medical institutes.

Between the philanthropies, with all the ambiguities shrouding them (such as Nelson's tax deductions for political trips abroad and political TV programs at home, Rockefeller Brothers Fund military studies, and personal gifts to political cronies) and the work of the financial Syndicate, there is developed a double-pronged all-pervasive pressure-power, virtually invisible but nevertheless present at all times. It acts like a gyroscope, a stabilizer, on the status quo.

And apropos of ambiguity about philanthropies, as I write this it is disclosed that the Rockefellers have funded John Gardner's fund-soliciting direct-mail reform political organization, Common Cause, which until the disclosure came was thought to be working the opposite side of town from the petroleum heirs. Common Cause had been regarded as opposed to most of the political enthusiasms of Nelson such as nuclear prowess, a wide-open CIA, an aggressive foreign policy, support of Johnson-Nixon-Ford, heavy tax-money for the Pentagon, rough stuff in the prisons, and political skulduggery and estate-building in Washington. Gardner himself had been touted as a possible good-guy presidential prospect.

Exactly where the Rockefellers' hands are at work in the chess game of public policy is often never readily fathomable. They unquestionably have lines into the left, right, and center, blandly infiltrating just about everything in defense of their position. That, of course, makes sense for people determined not to be unhorsed and sent to scramble for a living down among the masses, always the main consideration in my view. Any other interpretation simply fails to make sense, is quixotic.

An interesting aspect of all this is that actually the Rockefellers need not stir in any way to exert their power. For many strategically placed persons, aware of past patronage bestowed, see to it that they do nothing to rock the boat of affairs and thus earn the disapproval of the Rockefellers and others like them. The heads of money-short colleges and universities, for example, are not going to stand up in public and recommend that people read the heady works of Ralph Nader or Ida Tarbell—or *The Screwing of the Average Man* by David Hapgood. If they feel the need to recommend reading matter, they are far more likely to recommend the works of Henry Kissinger, Adoph A. Berle, Jr., Allan Nevins, or Lewis Carroll. And seekers after study-grants don't sign manifestos protesting against cost overruns by the Pentagon, the inequities of the tax system, the wobbling transportation system, massive uncontrolled crime, or anything like that. Nor do any of the potential recipients call attention to the star-spangled political mafia of thuggish elements generally in charge.

For anyone looking for massive physical evidence of Rockefeller power, he need look no further than New York City. Without the Rockefeller presence that premier city would be so different as to be unrecognizable by its denizens. An imaginative entrepreneur could develop a bus tour around Manhattan, requiring a full day, merely to look at the main evidences of the Rockefeller presence, the outward signs of their power. Its name: The Rockefeller Tour.

Let us fancy such a trip beginning at profitable, tax-paying ornate Rockefeller Center, which the bus merely circles; one has already spent a day exploring the environs. The bus now heads north, to the paid-admission Museum of Modern Art (not free, free, free) on nearby Fifty-fourth Street, site of the original Rockefeller residence. After a look at this tax-exempt, tax-deductible institution the bus again heads north to Sixty-fourth Street, where one contemplates modernistic tax-exempt Asia House, soon to be expanded.

After pausing here the bus turns east to Sixty-eighth Street and the East River where there extends southward the fiteen acres and many jammed together buildings of ultra-ultra Rockefeller University. So far everything viewed has been 100 percent Rockefeller. But just to the north of Rockefeller University is the New York Hospital-Cornell University medical complex of many buildings, including Memorial Hospital (specializing in cancer). To all of this the Rockefellers at various times have made substantial inputs of money. And the bestowal of money, one should always remember, is invariably accompanied by thunderous public hosannas, especially from taxpayers who don't know they are also contributing, willy-nilly, by paying higher taxes. For what one does not pay, others pay.

All the juices squeezed out of this scene, the bus moves south toward United Nations Plaza at Forty-second Street (land worth $8 million when donated by Junior, tax deductible). But before reaching it, there is the Fifty-ninth-Fifty-third Street area to consider. At Fifty-ninth Street one can glance out in the East River in passing at Welfare Island* where Nelson's faltering Urban Development Corporation, using public funds, tax-backed, is erecting a maze of low-income apartment buildings, a compressed, water-surrounded little city reached via the Queensborough Bridge. This, like other similar projects, generates bonds for the banks to sell, contracts for the building contractors, joy all around—again except for taxpayers. The whole affair is tax exempt. One need not be detained by locating the various chic apartments of family members in the Sutton Place and Beekman Place enclaves near by.

But the United Nations is worth a look, and also nearby Japan House, tax exempt. A variety of other structures and organizations in the vicinity have had at least an input of Rockefeller money, tax deductible.

The bus again heads south, toward Wall Street. As one passes Bellevue and University hospitals in the East Thirties, one is looking at places into which the family has made substantial inputs from time to time.

In the Wall Street region at the southern tip of elongated Manhattan, one is right in Rockefeller country. There one finds the towering and profitable new Chase Manhattan Building on Chase Manhattan Plaza and the First National

---

*Now renamed Roosevelt Island.

City Bank of the William Rockefeller branch as well as the
headquarters of the affiliated Chemical Bank of New York.
The bus worms its way down to 26 Broadway, old headquarters of Standard Oil of New Jersey, the company now relocat-
ed in Rockefeller Center (the Exxon building).

After the passengers get their breath in this locale, the bus
works northwesterly a few blocks so that the travelers can
gawk at the colossal twin towers of the World Trade Center,
masterminded by David, and preparations just to the south for
publicly financed Battery Park City, an idea of David's, which
will contain buildings with fourteen thousand apartments, a
twenty-two-hundred-room hotel, and two sixty-seven story
office towers—holding in all eighty to one hundred thousand
people, a small city within the major city. It is all part of a
latter-day Rockefeller idea to erect whole new neighborhoods
and whole new towns, of which they have several in the
works both publicly and privately financed, in and out of New
York City. For they are builders as well as organizers. The
public, of course, pays, the Rockefellers get the kudos. These
at times become extravagant.

Finished on the Lower West Side, the tour heads north although various institutions, churches, and hospitals along the
way, too many for the tour director to take note of, have had
tax-deductible input at various times from the Rockefellers:
New York University in the Washington Square area, the New
York Public Library further north, settlement houses, clinics
—you name it.

The first major stop of the bus now is the Lincoln Square
area between Fifty-ninth and Sixty-eighth Streets along
Broadway, on the West Side. There we find effulgent Lincoln
Center of the Performing Arts—opera, symphony, dance,
theater, mime—and a variety of related institutions that have
felt Rockefeller largess: the Julliard School of Music, Ford-
ham University, the music division of the New York Public
Library, assorted nearby structures. Tax deductible all the
way....

Amid fatuous "oohs" and "ahs," the passengers clamber
back into the bus, which again heads north, this time to Morn-

ingside Heights, straddling Broadway between 110th and 125th Streets. In this rather large area we find Riverside Church, a vast cathedral-like structure, planned and financed by the Rockefellers; the Interchurch Center, 100 percent Rockefeller; Morningside Gardens apartment complex, masterminded by David, financed by contiguous institutions; and a large number of institutions to which the Rockefellers have made significant inputs of funds—Columbia University, Barnard College, the Cathedral of St. John the Divine, Union Theological Seminary, Jewish Theological Seminary, Teachers College, etc. The Julliard School of Music used to be in the collection. As we have seen, it is now down at Lincoln Center. Everything, as usual, is tax deductible, tax exempt. The general public also pays. And pays and pays. There is no free lunch.

Before quitting the neighborhood, the bus might well take a quick detour to the east on 125th Street, into Harlem, for a brief glance at the towering State Office Building located where it is at the express decree of Governor Nelson Rockefeller and paid for by the taxpapers, one and all. It was put where it is to lend some tone to the crazy-quilt environs, raise contiguous bank-financed realty values. Throughout Harlem and along the Harlem River are various UDC and other housing projects which the tourists may or may not want to look at—tax backed, edifying.

The bus now drives for the northern tip of Manhattan, the Riverdale section heavily populated with the families of diplomats to the United Nations. There one finds the Cloisters, a multimillion-dollar replica of a medieval monastery that houses an impressive museum of medieval European artifacts and works of art—100 percent financed by the Rockefellers. It is set within fifty-six acre Fort Tryon Park, a gift to the city from Junior. Everything, as usual, is tax deductible, tax exempt.

Although the tour is not yet over, one may pause to notice that the Rockefellers have concentrated their major punches in seven or eight centers, whence radiate value-enhancing ripples into the surrounding region. *Wunderbar!* One might look at these centers as Rockefeller oases in an otherwise rather workaday city.

On the return southbound trip, the tour guide is able to point out various objects of Rockefeller supportive beneficence such as the Columbia-Presbyterian Hospital at 168th and Broadway. After this pause the bus heads for the Metropolitan Museum of Art just south of Eighty-sixth Street on Fifth Avenue, to which a large number of the wealthy have contributed over the years, getting tax deductions for their input (which means the taxpaying public is also unknowingly contributing, a never-to-be-forgotten, ever-to-be-repeated fact). The Rockefellers are among the Metropolitan supporters on many counts—paintings, tapestries, money, whatnot—but in 1957 Nelson began the Museum of Primitive Art, with himself as president. Later this collection was expanded and incorporated into the Metropolitan Museum, which has converted it into a separate department. Across Central Park stands the Museum of Natural History to which the Rockefellers have also made substantial inputs, tax deductible.

Museums, too, are good places on to which one can unload *objets d'art* at elevated tax-deductible values—money saving. *Formidable!*

While others of the rich have also erected monuments of one kind or the other in New York, all tax deductible, nobody at all has been nearly so lavish as the Rockefellers. They are the kingpins, the first citizens, in what many professors tell us is an egalitarian society, an egalitarian culture. Could professors with so many degrees be wrong? One wonders because taxes at least are not equitably imposed.

The tour is now over, a whole day spent, as the bus heads back to Rockefeller Center. But, alas, everything has not been visited, only the high spots. To poke into everything in detail would take at least a week.

The New York tour could be expanded into a national tour consuming weeks, stopping literally at hundreds of places 100 percent Rockefeller, places started by the Rockefellers with others sharing, places helped by the Rockefellers, places influenced by the Rockefellers—all tax deductible.

Of the major Rockefeller centers, either all or mostly theirs, there is Colonial Williamsburg, the University of Chicago, Palisades Interstate Park, Jackson Hole Preserve, Acadia National Park, Virgin Islands National Park, Grand Teton Lodge. Of places in which they have combined with others there is the Embarcadero in San Francisco and the whole new town of Columbia, Maryland, floated by David Rockefeller on behalf of Chase Manhattan and two insurance companies. Both of these are income-producing taxpayers.

Places in which they or one of their foundations have made substantial inputs include Grand Teton National Park, Shenandoah National Park, Yosemite National Park, and scores of colleges, universities, medical schools, laboratories, museums orchestras, settlement houses, developments, clinics, hospitals, and the like—north, south, east, and west. On many campuses, buildings, halls and towers are named after the Rockefellers, whose name is more prominent in academic circles than Shakespeare, Milton, Newton, Galileo, or Einstein. And Rockefeller tax-exempt and deductible grants galore keep the scholars purring happily. Here it is as in the Hollywood films where among the preliminary credits one finds it stated in very large letters "Produced by Joseph Katzenellenbogen" and then on through a great number of nondescript names until at the very end in microscopic script it states "based on an idea taken from William Shakespeare." The opus is offered as "Juliet and Romeo"—a Katzenellenbogen Special.

Now, whatever one may say of all this, call it good or call it something else, it is all evidence of *power,* the power of money and the power of individual private decision. Who ordered this? Who decreed the re-creation of Williamsburg, Virginia? Who asked for a national park in the Virgin Islands which 95 percent or more of Americans will never see? Much of this, obviously, is the outplay of individual whim. Was another church needed where Riverside Church stands? The Cathedral of St. John the Divine is only a few blocks away.

Whereas a writer may project his fantasies on reams of paper or a painter his on canvases, the Rockefellers using irregularly obtained money, project theirs over large stretches of landscape. One may decline to read the scribblings of the writer or to view the smears of the painter, but it is hard to avoid the concretized fantasies of the Rockefellers, like the World Trade Center, Rockefeller Center, or the Albany Mall.

As all this is concrete evidence of private power publicly exercised, for Nelson to sit before a congressional committee and decry the "myth" of his family's power becomes so much triple-plated double-talk. If he believes his own disclaimer, then he is so self-deceived as to be out of touch with reality, not an impossibility. If he doesn't believe it, then he is dissembling, putting forth reassuring miniwords for the record.

None of what we have surveyed is evidence of the power of ordinary egalitarian citizens. It reeks of Louis XIV and Frederick the Great. Let us assume for the moment it all betokens something favorable. But if so it is good in a paternalistic sense, some sense separate and apart from open due processes of government. It is something laid on by highly privileged people, deriving from original law-breaking. Perhaps one should feel grateful. But we are looking the gift horses in the teeth, realistically. As nothing in this world is really free, not even philanthropic gifts, what is the price one must pay for it? Is it high taxes, war, economic dislocation, sloppy government by stooges? Or merely sloppy thinking?

As a consequence of such exercise of power, perceived as entirely benign by many, blandly interpreted as benign by publications far and wide, a platform is created for the prime movers for continuing political, financial, and economic operations *in other directions,* unbenign. One effect of all this activity, defined arbitrarily as benign, is to disarm public vigilance against cryptic moves made in darker theaters. These being benign people, they have immunity. They have become godlike. There is therefore no reason to wonder what they may be up to in the far more important spheres of foreign and domestic policy, world policy. To question them is churlish, uncivil, bad taste. And if such people privately decree that some once "underdeveloped" country shall no longer remain "underdeveloped" (cheers from shallow sentimentalists), that it shall begin producing some kind of ore, large forces are unloosed in the world, forces over which the prime movers turn out to have no control. A large portion of the public, in fact, believes that the Rockefellers are only out to do good, despite a dark past. Nelson repeatedly alluded defensively to the family's philanthropies in his congressional hearings, invoked them as a halo. David does this too. They don't mention that it is all tax deductible—and power conferring. Nor that the fortune was acquired in highly dubious ways. And neither the Rockefellers nor any of their advisors have shown any evidence of having fundamental solutions for anything. What they offer is the mixture as before—more weaponry, no revamping of the tax structure, more prisons, more automobile roads.

If anyone believes I am unduly preoccupied about taxes—i.e., money—it is only because I am following the script. The story is about money, money, money. A little item in the *Wall Street Journal* of January 15, 1975, tells its own story. It is reproduced here in its entirety, as follows:

"*A Grave Matter?* Or a dead issue? Recently the Tax Court ruled that the John D. Rockefeller Cemetery Corp. could qualify as a tax-exempt cemetery company even though the burial ground was limited to the Rockefeller family. Now the Tax Court has decided the same concerning the du Pont de Nemours Cemetery Co. in Christiana Hundred, Del. Burial is limited to descendants of Pierre Samuel du Pont de Nemours, who was interred there in 1817."

What this shows at a minimum is that not a trick is missed in tax avoidance by the heavy money crowd, including the Rockefellers.

Nor is that, by any means, all there is to the tax-economizing of the Rockefellers even as they are accepted by a wide public as tremendous public benefactors. As Congresswoman Elizabeth Holtzman of New York, who voted against Nelson's confirmation, stated on the floor of the House of Representatives, "During the fifteen years Mr. Rockefeller was governor of the state, almost everybody's taxes went up. And yet, curiously enough, the taxes on Mr. Rockefeller's estate at Pocantico did not go up. Despite improvements, they went down."

In the local township of Mount Pleasant the political influence of the Rockefellers has long been practically absolute.

At least the hearings leading up to Nelson's confirmation as vice-president, and disclosures attendant thereupon, showed there is sound reason to take a good hard look at what they may be blithely up to behind the philanthropic facade. Naturally they aren't the only ones to be watched. So to suggest would be to commit the fallacy of misplaced emphasis. Actually everybody ought to be watched, scrutinized, questioned, criticized, including barefoot statesmen from Jug Hollow, before we find ourselves once again at Armageddon for the sake of evanescent stakes. As far as any autonomous personal achievement is concerned, the big donors are blanks.

In an earlier day big nations had within them noble principalities headed by grand dukes which governments had to give heed to at their peril. In our own day, devoid of such principalities and titles of nobility, we have operating in our midst, unbidden, influential with governments, analogies in the form of giant financial syndicates consisting of quasi-anonymous men in well-tailored suits, of which the Rockefeller Syndicate is one. It was a financial syndicate like this, headed by the Morgans, which more than anything else brought the United States into World War I, with enormous consequences for it and the world, few of them any good for anybody. The concentration of mundane power and quiet influence in any one of these syndicates is beyond anything that most people can imagine. They are the entities which, more than anything else, produce or permit the "down" statistics.

Whether any or all of this sort of thing we have looked at was planned by Old John D. is doubtful. Along the way, though, the Rockefellers have encountered a good deal of serendipity (as well as great public gullibility). Some of this serendipity, however, became shadowed, perhaps irretrievably tarnished, in the congressional confirmation hearings. Nelson emerged from them less of a god in the eyes of many people, no doubt a good thing and showing the value of such hearings.

The scenario nevertheless remains and no doubt will be

referred to again and again by the family. It "works." It is "pragmatic." There is a public that "buys" it.

9.

Another way of showing evidence of Rockefeller power is to take the Dilworth figure of $1 billion for the family fortune, which I think I showed convincingly was much too low. Anyhow, take it now as gospel. If this amount of money were placed in the bank at the current 5 1/4 percent New York savings bank rate, about the lowest available hereabouts, it would generate an annual income of $52,500,000. This is annual income, remember, not a separate fortune. And over a period of ten years that would amount to $525,000,000. At about the same rate of return, it could all be put into tax-exempt government bonds which, however, would yield no managerial power.

There are eighty-four members of the family, Mr. Dilworth said, and income within the family is not parceled out evenly. But if annual income were averaged through the family by individuals, it would amount to $625,000 per person, annually. Capitalizing such income at a low 5 percent one arrives at a fortune of $12,500,000 per person, including babes in arms.

Throughout the United States any person worth $12,-500,000 is looked upon as extremely wealthy, and such persons are very few.

Assume now that the family fortune is double Dilworth's figure, or triple or quadruple, under boom conditions, and one gets prospects positively mind boggling. What is done with the income of all this also turns out to be mind boggling. Remember now that this fortune and several hundred now wholly dissimilar thrive, not in some betel-nut, coconut, or banana republic but in the often-hailed greatest egalitarian society in the world. One then realizes that one is living within absurdity run riot. A really crazy scene larded over with Public Relations blarney.

10.

The TNEC report of 1940 said that the Rockefeller fortune then was concentrated 30 percent in philanthropic foundations, 30 percent in trust funds for the benefit of individual members of the family, and 40 percent in holdings by family individuals. At this rate, it is apparent that about one-third or $1 out of $3 was allocated by the founder and his descendants to philanthropies. Those philanthropies, although they deprived the family of capital funds for personal usages, have contributed much to the power of the family, have in that sense alone been self-serving, and have established the quiet authority of the family in many high-level areas. They have also shifted the burden of taxation to others, as in the case of most of the rich. Whenever anyone questions what the family may be doing in finance and politics and in corporate affairs, allusion is made to the tax-saving philanthropies as a saving grace. The bitter pill, it turns out, has a tax deductible sugar coating, tax payable by others. Neat!

John D.'s idea, expressed in so many words at the time when he was developing his scenario in a big way, was to make all the money one can and give all one can. This compulsive precept proves interesting under analysis. As to making all one can, the outcome depends to a large extent upon objective factors. The world and its people limit the satisfaction of one's appetite, limit the exercise of one's will-to-wealth, as John D. eventually discovered. But in giving all one can, one is limited only by subjective factors; one's will has full play. In Rockefeller's case "giving" was self-limited to about one-third. And the tax-exempt and tax-deductible bread thus cast on the waters returned in the form of greater boons: greater power and tax economies. And public applause from those paying the tax freight. This is the scenario, basically a comedy.

During his early lifetime John D. Rockefeller, after he became successful in the oil business, was heavily involved with Baptist clergy and theologians. At his home he was often surrounded by them. Later in life he and his son, most of the clergy now banished, were surrounded by scientists, educators, social thinkers, editors, publicists, welfare workers, university officials—all publicly haloed people. Outside of office hours he seldom met with corporate people or bankers.

Which was the real John D. Rockefeller? The man in the oil business or the man engaged in avoiding taxes by beveling the edges and sandpapering the rough sides of the present human condition by erecting monuments as millions of tax-dupes cheered?

And, although devoted philanthropists in appearance to the outside world, the vehicle for Rockefeller political expression throughout the years has been the Republican party, which was always adamantly opposed to having the government carry on analogous benign activity even with taxpayer consent. All government "intervention" in the fields of science, medicine, higher education, social uplift, art, individual amelioration has been fought openly or indirectly impeded by the Republican party. For government to do it on a large and effective scale is bad; for the Rockefellers and other Republicans to do it on a restricted tax-saving scale is good—so they say. For the latter is private—that is, sacred.

If one looks at the Rockefellers as philanthropists, how does one account for this seeming contradiction? How can tough politics be squared with philanthropic benignity? The point is: it isn't philanthropy and it is tax avoidance and power building.

To me there is no contradiction. By deploying philanthropic funds themselves, by private decision, they gained public credit and tax gains, screening their wealth holdings against public attack, and at the same time extended their control and influence over wider areas, gained allies, ideological and substantive. Had they merely supported political people visualizing something akin to the Swedish solution to prevalent social disharmony, they would not only have obtained less public credit but they would have undermined their personally retained holdings by being liable for higher taxes. They'd be poorer today but the country, with more social-minded men in office, and sooner, would be better off.

What the Rockefellers haven't done with their power tells as much about them as what they have done. Their vision has been limited, self-oriented. And as to this I don't presume to reprove them. All I say is: that's their bag, and goody-goody. What does interest me, however, is how they are perceived, accepted, and put to the fore in public affairs. As to this I say: they are playing their own game, are not Lords Bountiful, are not committed to transforming the country by enormous inches into a bigger and better Sweden.

That the Rockefellers, contrary to some of the counter-savants, have not been engaged in liquidating their fortune is shown also by the way they have shifted emphasis into finance, real estate operations, and advanced technology. In consequence they have far more say-so throughout the realm than they ever had in the palmiest days of old John D. If John D. was a master of the disguised advance, then his successors have been masters of disguised entrenchment. For they are entrenched, in strong positions. One of them is now Vice President of the United States.

11.

The panel of the Rockefeller Brothers Fund on *International Security: The Military Aspect,* calling pre-Kennedy for heavier military spending, in the "America at Mid-Century" studies (1958), was headed by Nelson A. Rockefeller. The prime objective of these "studies" was to project an image of Nelson Rockefeller as a formidable public figure of possibly presidential stature. Everything else about them was purely incidental. None of the "studies," for all the hullabaloo accompanying them, was anything but routine.

Other members of the directing panel were Adolf A. Berle, Jr., author of the Brobdingnagian canard that owners no longer control corporations; Chester Bowles, ad man and former ambassador to India and former governor of Connecticut; Arthur F. Burns, Columbia University professor who was then president of the National Bureau of Economic Research and is presently the Nixon-appointed chairman of the Federal Reserve Board; General Lucius D. Clay, chairman of the Continental Can Company and former commander-in-chief of US Forces in Europe as well as military governor of the US Zone, Germany.

And, John Cowles, president of the *Minneapolis Star and Tribune* and chairman of the *Des Moines Register and Tribune*; Justin W. Dart, president of Rexall Drug Company; Gordon E. Dean, former chairman of the Atomic Energy Commission and senior vice-president for nuclear energy of General Dynamics Corporation; John S. Dickey, president of Dartmouth College; John W. Gardner, president of the Carnegie Corporation of New York and creator of Common Cause; Lester B. Granger, executive director of the National Urban League; Caryl P. Haskins, president of the Carnegie Institution; Theodore M. Hesburgh, president of the University of Notre Dame; Margaret A. Hickey, public affairs editor of *Ladies Home Journal*; Oveta Culp Hobby, president and editor of the *Houston Post* and former secretary of health, education and welfare and director of the WACS.

And, Devereux C. Josephs, chairman of the New York Life Insurance Company; Milton Katz, director of International Legal Studies, Harvard University Law School, former ambassador and chief in Europe of the Marshall Plan; the late Henry R. Luce, slanting publisher of *Time, Life,* and *Fortune*; Thomas B. McCabe, president of the Scott Paper Company; Gen. James McCormack, vice-president of MIT and former director of research and development, U.S. Air Force; Prof. Richard P. McKeon, department of philosophy, University of Chicago; Lee W. Minton, president of the Glass Bottle Blowers Association; Charles H. Percy, then president of Bell & Howell, now U.S. senator and Rockefeller in-law; Jacob S. Potofsky, president, Amalgamated Clothing Workers of America; Anna M. Rosenberg, industrial relations consultant and former assistant secretary of defense; Dean Rusk, former assistant secretary of state, president of the Rockefeller Foundation, and future Kennedy and Johnson-appointed secretary of state and big Vietnam warhawk.

Also, David Sarnoff, chairman of the Radio Corporation of America; Charles M. Spofford, Wall Street corporation lawyer and former deputy representative to NATO; Edward Teller, professor of physics, University of California, associate director, University of California Radiation Laboratories, and "the father" of the hydrogen bomb; Frazar B. Wilde, president of Connecticut General Life Insurance Company; Robert B. Anderson, who resigned from the panel when he was appointed secretary of the treasury; James R. Killian Jr., president of the Massachusetts Institute of Technology who resigned from the panel when he was appointed special assistant to the president; and Henry A. Kissinger, director of the project, associate director of the Center for International Affairs, Harvard University, and future Nixon-appointed United States secretary of state.

Rosenberg, Kissinger, and Anderson were on Nelson Rockefeller's congressional loan or gift lists.

A second panel for the military study included some of these persons but also Frank Altschul, vice-president of the Council on Foreign Relations; Gen. Frederick I. Anderson, former deputy U.S. special representative in Europe; Karl R. Bendetsen, vice-president of Champion Paper and Fibre Company and former secretary of the army; Detlev W. Bronk, president of Rockefeller University and of the National Academy of Sciences; James B. Fisk, executive vice-president, Bell Telephone Laboratories and former director of research, Atomic Energy Commission; Bradley Gaylord, chairman of the Pennroad Corporation; Roswell L. Gilpatric, Wall Street corporation lawyer and former undersecretary of the air force; Townsend W. Hoopes of J. H. Whitney and Company; Ellis A. Johnson, director of the Operations Research Office, Johns Hopkins University; Col. George A. Lincoln, professor of social sciences at the U.S. Military Academy; the late Frank C. Nash, U.S. delegation to the General Assembly of the UN and presidential consultant; Laurance S. Rockefeller, president of Rockefeller Brothers, Inc.; Arthur Smithies, department of economics, Harvard University, former economic advisor, Office of Defense Mobilization; T. F. Walkowicz, aeronautical engineer; Carroll L. Wilson, president of Metals & Controls Corporation and former general manager, Atomic Energy Commission; and John F. Floberg, who served on the panel until his appointment as a member of the Atomic Energy Commission.

The panel on *Foreign Economic Policy for the Twentieth Century* included all on the first list and a second panel additionally included Harlan Cleveland, dean of the Maxwell Graduate School of Citizenship and Public Affairs, Syracuse University, and former assistant director for Europe, Mutual Security Agency; Frederick H. Harbison, director, Industrial Relations Section, and professor of economics, Princeton University; Stacy May, economist and statistician, former special representative of the War Department, head of the division of planning and statistics of the War Production Board, and economist with Rockefeller's IBEC and with the McGraw-Hill Publishing Company; David Rockefeller; Max Weston Thornburg, foreign industrial consultant; and Forrest D. Murden, of Ford International, special assistant to Henry Ford II and former economic advisor to the U.S. Delegation to the United Nations.

The panel for *The Challenge to America: Its Economic and Social Aspects* included most of the first panel and additionally included along with some repeated names William F. Butler, vice-president, economic research department, Chase Manhattan Bank; Lowell T. Coggeshall, dean of the division of biological sciences, University of Chicago, former special assistant of HEW, president of the American Medical Colleges, and president of the American Cancer Society; J. Norman Efferson, professor of agricultural economics and dean of the College of Agriculture, Louisiana State University; Dexter M. Keezer, vice-president of the McGraw-Hill Publishing Company; Franklin A. Lindsay, consultant, McKinsey & Company; Joseph A. Livingston, financial editor, the *Philadelphia Bulletin*, former economist with *Business Week* and the War Production Board; Roswell B. Perkins, Wall Street lawyer and former assistant secretary, HEW; Eugene Rostow, dean Yale University Law School; J. Cameron Thomson, chairman of the Northwest Bancorporation; and Bayless A. Manning, associate professor of law, Yale University.

The panel for *The Pursuit of Excellence: Education and the Future of America* included the original list and the following additional names on a second panel: J. Douglas Brown, dean, Princeton University and former member of the mobilization program advisory committee, Office of Defense Mobilization; Philip H. Coombs, secretary and director of research, the Ford Foundation's Fund for the Advancement of Education and former executive director, President's Materials Policy Commission; Dana L. Farnsworth, director of university health services, Harvard University and Radcliffe College and president of the Group for the Advancement of Psychiatry; Eli Ginzberg, professor of economics, Columbia University and director of staff studies, the National Manpower Council; David Riesman, professor of sociology, University of Chicago; J. E. Wallace Sterling, president of Stanford University; Howard E. Wilson, dean of the School of Education, University of California, Los Angeles; Dael Wolfle, executive officer, American Association for the Advancement of Science and former director of the Commission on Human Resources and Advanced Training; Fred M. Hechinger, associate publisher, the *Bridgeport Herald* and education editor, *Parents' Magazine*.

The Power of the Democratic Idea was a study guided by the first-named panel which was, however, chaired by Laurance S. Rockefeller.

The panel on *The Performing Arts: Problems and Prospects* consisted of an entirely new cast, as follows: Patricia M. Baillargeon, former assistant to Eleanor Roosevelt and board member of the Seattle Repertory Theater and the Seattle Youth Symphony; Walker L. Cisler, chairman of the board of the Detroit Edison Company and director of the Detroit Symphony Orchestra; Kenneth N. Dayton, vice-president of Dayton's (department store) and director and past president of the Minnesota Orchestral Association; T. Keith Glaennan, president of the Case Institute of Technology; Samuel B. Gould, president of the State University of New York; William B.

Hartsfield, former mayor of Atlanta and trustee of the Atlanta Symphony Orchestra and the Atlanta Music Festival Association.

And, August Heckscher, director of the Twentieth Century Fund, former special consultant to president Kennedy and trustee of the National Repertory Theater Foundation; Margaret Hickey, editor for public affairs, *Ladies Home Journal*; Norris Houghton, chairman, department of drama, Vassar College, later in the same capacity with the University of the State of New York at Purchase; Devereux C. Josephs, former chairman of the board of the New York Life Insurance Company, vice-chairman of the board, Lincoln Center for the Performing Arts, and trustee of the Metropolitan Museum of Art and the New York Public Library; Abbot Kaplan, director, University of California, Los Angeles and chairman of the board, Theatre Group, and the California Arts Commission; Dexter M. Keezer, McGraw-Hill, Inc.; Louis Kronenberger, professor of theatre arts, Brandeis University; Warner Lawson, dean, College of Fine Arts, Howard University, member advisory committee on the arts, State Department and the John F. Kennedy Center for the performing Arts.

And, John H. MacFadyen, architect and former executive director, New York State Council on the Arts; Stanley Marcus, president, Neiman-Marcus (department store) and director of the Community Arts Fund of Dallas, the Dallas Symphony Orchestra, and the Dallas Theatre Center; Henry Allen Moe, president and chairman of the board, New York State Historical Association, president of the American Philosophical Society; James F. Oates, Jr., chairman of the board, Equitable Life Assurance Society and trustee, American Museum of Natural History; Perry T. Rathbone, director of the Boston Museum of Fine Arts and trustee of the New England Conservatory of Music and Boston Arts Festival; Oliver Rea, managing director, Minnesota Theatre Company Foundation and president of the Theatre Communications Group, Inc.; Joseph Verner Reed, Sr., chairman of the board, American Shakespeare Festival Theater and Academy; John D. Rockefeller 3, chairman of the panel and chairman of the board,

Lincoln Center for the Performing Arts and the Rockefeller Foundation; Samuel R. Rosenbaum, trustee, Recording Industries Music Performance Trust Funds and director of the Philadelphia Orchestral Association.

And, Emile H. Serposs, director of the division of music, Chicago Public Schools and a director of the Music Educators National Conference; Charles M. Spofford, lawyer and director and chairman of the executive committee of the Metropolitan Opera Association and vice-chairman of the board, Lincoln Center for the Performing Arts; Frank Stanton, president of the Columbia Broadcasting System and a director of Lincoln Center for the Performing Arts; James A. Suffridge, international executive vice-president, American Symphony Orchestra League and member, National Music Council and National Council on the Arts and Government; Frazar B. Wilde, chairman of the board, Connecticut General Life Insurance Company; and Harold Lionel Zellerbach, chairman of the executive committee, Crown Zellerbach Corporation, president of the San Francisco Art Commission, and director, San Francisco Ballet Guild.

This panel was a convocation largely of managerial people, much as though one were to have a conference about literature consisting mainly of publishers, public-relations men, and printing executives. These, of course, are the people who determine what programs the passive public is going to get.

I have given these names partly to show the wide range of people the Rockefellers can mobilize, partly to show their connections, especially with the Eisenhower, Kennedy, Johnson, and Nixon administrations. Throughout I could have done similarly with corporate, banking, government, and scientific elements but forbore because such lists, especially if endlessly repeated, become tedious reading. But if one listed all the people the Rockefellers are connected with through the magic power of money, all the investments of their various philanthropic and personal funds, and all the agencies in receipt of supplementary revenues from them, one would get a book equivalent in size to a big-city telephone directory—nothing but lists, lists, lists. And it would show they are into all administrations.

One thing all these panelists have in common is this: none of them is going to be shot in any war engineered by Henry Kissinger and Nelson A. Rockefeller. On that one can bet one's head against a plugged nickel and come out a winner. These are all certainly among the people who "call the shots." And they are among the "they" alluded to when the average shnook in the street asks helplessly, "What are *they* going to do about it?" The lists include people, too, who are responsible for "down" statistics, for syncopations and breaks in the system, people such as Arthur Burns, the great syncopator of money rates.

Who is responsible for the elimination of railroad passenger trains, lack of gun control, extortionately priced housing, an inequitable tax structure, air pollution, high interest rates, high unemployment rates, etc., etc? One may be sure it isn't Bobby Seale, Angela Davis, the Black Panthers, Abbie Hoffman, the Weather Underground, the Socialist Workers party, the Mafia, ex-Nazis, the Kremlin or the first ten names on the FBI "most-wanted" list or anybody at all on Richard Nixon's enemies list. In fact, it is nobody who is publicly decried for any reason. But in a complete directory of the Rockefeller connections, one may be sure one would find many candidates for cynosure.

The public also finds roles for itself in the Rockefeller scenario. There is, first, that vast section of the yokelry which believes it is getting a free lunch, a separate story. These are all hearty admirers of the Rockefellers, regarded as the people giving handouts right and left. Everybody likes to get a handout. But the Rockefeller handouts, as we have seen, have a tax recoil to them.

There are, too, the Rockefeller-haters, more interesting because they are more dramatic, higher in blood pressure. The rightists who hate them out of envy or because they have been outmaneuvered through the operation of the scenario are pretty easy to understand. They just want to play a simple game of dominance whereas the Rockefellers insist upon dressing dominance up in fancy camouflage, hard to understand. Some of these, however, like hard-liner Emmanuel Josephson, have gone to great lengths in endeavoring to depict the Rockefellers as spreading communism, as linchpins of the world communist movement. His books are proportionately diverting. John Birchers at the Rockefeller nominating hearings likened Nelson's nomination to appointing Al Capone to guard a bank.

Leftists in general have gotten an endless amount of mileage out of the Rockefellers, whom they use as a fuse—one of many in their armory—to detonate the world capitalist order. It was a splinter group of leftists in Latin America that staged the destructive riots against Nelson on his visit there as President Nixon's representative. The hope entertained by the riot managers always is that such riots will build until they become *Der Tag,* the day of liberation from all the ills of man. O happy day! And, also, cushy jobs in a new government for the riot managers, a chauffered limousine for each, bodyguards and secret police.

Various leftist groups in the United States from time to time have used the Rockefellers to give point to the script against the amorphous structure known as capitalism but the currently most interesting one is the National Caucus of Labor Committees (NCLC), also grandiosely known as the U.S. Labor party. If it numbers more than two hundred people, the fact is unknown to outsiders. But what it lacks in numbers, it makes up in noise.

One of the main functions of this group appears to be to send wreckers and disrupters into the public meetings of other more decorous radical groups, with a view to breaking up the assembly. In this it often succeeds. The NCLC claims to be pure Marxist. Some consider it an FBI dirty-tricks operation.

According to Danny Foss in the *Village Voice,* March 10, 1975, the "NCLC is controlled by a middle-aged management consultant named Lyndon (Lyn Marcus) La Rouche, Jr., who has fashioned for his followers a comprehensive 'intellectual' explanation of the universe. The centerpiece of the doctrine is the axiom that there exists a titanic struggle for the control of humanity between La Rouche and Nelson Rockefeller. Any person or thing not controlled by one is controlled by the other. The doctrine is inculcated into the faithful by manipu-

lating fears of sexual impotence, homosexuality, and 'Rocky-
CIA brainwashing.' Anyone who questions any part of the
doctrine is called sexually impotent, a 'brainwashed zombie,'
or both—the leader himself is obsessed by phobias about eating excrement and homosexual rape. La Rouche's writings are
memorized as scripture. He instructs his followers to meditate
on Beethoven to strip away their ego, find the true self, and
experience the 'oceanic feeling.' They are expected to prefer
spiritual love to 'animal sex.' The NCLC utopia is a world
where 'negative entropy' prevails; it would make '1984' look
like total anarchy. I was not surprised to learn of a family in
which the brother became a prominent NCLC and the sister
an equally prominent Hare Krishna."

But more interesting to me among the spin-offs from the
Rockefeller phenomenon, and more significant culturally and
socially, are the large number of syndicate professors and syndicate commentators who look upon the Rockefellers much as
devout Muslims look upon direct descendants of Mohammed.
For these are the people who dispense soothing scripts to the
citizenry as it is deftly shorn by the tax collectors and ad men,
a very smoothly operating act. Here one gets the Pavlov effect
in full force: as the bell rings signaling great gifts from on
high one receives an electric shock in the form of extra taxes
and elevated prices. Or, as everything slowly gets better under
the gentle touch of philanthropy, the roof caves in under the
inflationary weight of Pentagon overruns. Muggers take over
the streets as our armed forces patrol the outer atmospheric
frontiers, alert for flying Bolsheviks. Defense is everywhere
except at home.

The rightists, devotees of the Pentagon, are especially
shocked by this tax-collecting act and lash out at—welfare
recipients!

13.

"At all times the life of the Rockefeller family was a simple
one," wrote Raymond Fosdick. "The aversion to display, so

deeply rooted in the elder Rockefeller, was carried through the next two generations. Mr. Rockefeller, Jr., lived comfortably but never ostentatiously. Always he was restrained by natural fastidiousness, an innate temperance of taste."[5]

Writers close to the Rockefellers like to use homespun words like "simple." Nevins uses words like "generous."

Now, one certain thing about all the mature Rockefellers from at least 1870 onward is that none led a simple life. It is not to be denied that they did simple things, may have liked simple things, like drinking a glass of milk or throwing a stick for a dog. But simple life, never.

Here again one finds a complete *bouleversement* from reality to fantasy. For the Rockefellers have always led extremely complicated lives, so complicated that they need schedules to guide them among meetings, conferences, seances, reunions, government hearings, court trials, parties, outings, confidential confabulations, public appearances, soirées, trips around the country, trips around the world, trips back and forth to Europe, Asia, Africa, South America, concerts, grand openings—you name it. And the family in the third and fourth generation has been beset by divorces, interviews, criticism, denunciation, praise, appeals, and the like. There is nothing simple whatever about the lives they lead. Many in the younger generation are in fact extremely confused by it all.

As to ambience, they are, except when in contrived outdoor resort surroundings, always cushioned in total luxury. Where they are different from much of the American wealthy is that they lead their lives hidden from public view, at Pocantico Hills, Seal Harbor, Maine, or at various of their metropolitan apartments, clubs, ranches, and distant places in the Caribbean, Hawaii, or Wyoming.

They jet about all over in their own planes, once traveled the country in private railway cars.

What is simple about any of this?

Pocantico Hills is a vast luxury estate. The home of John D.

---

5. Raymond Fosdick, *John D. Rockefeller, Jr.: A Portrait*, p. 428.

I and II is a palace, luxuriously furnished. The whole story is given away simply by the photograph, extant, of old John D.'s bed. It is a gigantic ornate four-poster, which would be acceptable to the Sun King himself. All their furnishings are topnotch, first-class, expensive, including works of art, tapestry, gadgets, antiques—you name it. Nelson owns a triplex apartment in the most posh section of Fifth Avenue, New York, facing westward over lower Central Park. It is the most expensive residential section of the city, one of the most expensive buildings. David has a townhouse nearby. John 3 is ensconced over in the Beekman Place area. Nelson also has a big house in Washington, a ranch in Venezuela.

Nelson as Vice President kept up the luxury pace. In the spring of 1975, it became known that he had just bought a water bed for $35,000. The contraption was even shown on TV. The price exceeded that of a Rolls-Royce. It, too, could be tax-deductible—if claimed to be necessary for his health.

Within this secluded, ultraluxurious, expensive ambience, they lead a quietly civilized life. While they ride horses up at Pocantico Hills, as well as do just about everything analogous thereto, they do not operate racing stables, herein differing from many others of the plutocracy. But they own ocean-going yachts, big cars, several jet planes, and anything they lack and want, they can instantly hire or purchase.

They do a great deal of entertaining—the third generation linking the entertaining with politics, philanthropy, finance, and the fourth generation, especially the women of the fourth generation, doing it mostly for pure fun. Guests at their dinner parties, which are numerous, report that food, service, and libations are strictly perfect. While the company of the third generation is apt to be more functional, more tied to projects afoot, that of the fourth generation is quietly lively. As one frequent guest told me, one sort of person they exclude is the bore. Most of the guests of the fourth generation are not Social Registerites or notably rich. But they are people who are doing things—in the arts, the theater, writing, music, dance, decoration, and so on. By all reports, an amiable assemblage.

The conversation is usually lively, sometimes sparkling,

seldom tendentious, mostly on a light level. But it is described
to me by informants as intelligent at all times, such as one
might expect of alert, educated people. While drinks are served
there are no drinking parties, no brawls or orgies, no nude or
lewd dancing on tables, or anywhere else in conformity with
popular fantasies of the good life among the higher-ups.

At times the parties of the fourth generation are joined by
members of the third generation. Guests gather the impression that John 3, the quiet one, is particularly liked by all—a
civilized man. The Cousins all regarded Winthrop as something of a black sheep although they were fond of him. David
has a bit of a chilling effect on most. Nelson becomes one of
the gang. "Hiya, fellah. Terrific!"

14.

The fourth generation doesn't often surface, but the women
are more in evidence, more in contact with outsiders, than the
men. John IV, of course, as a figure in West Virginia politics is
more known to the world and more visible than the others.
He, like Winthrop, has escaped from Pocantico Hills. Rodman, Nelson's son, as a businessman with many problems
tends to keep apart and to consort more with the third generation. But others of the fourth-generation males have not yet
had much public impact and are not reported to be seen frequently at the New York City dinner parties.

This more obscure generation of twenty-three members was
inventoried and interviewed as recently as 1969 by Bernard
Gavzer of the Associated Press (*New York Post*, March 8,
1969). Some of the attitudes he recorded are of interest. A
muted note of self-pity is noticeable.

"I think my first awareness of being a Rockefeller is associated with going to school in our Cadillac," said Lucy Rockefeller Hamlin, M.D., then interning at Harlem Hospital in
preparation for becoming a psychotherapist. She is one of
Laurance's daughters. "I used to slide down onto the floor
when we got near Brearley and stay hidden until the chauffeur

gave me the signal, and then I got out. I was very self-conscious about being a Rockefeller."

As to her meager internist's pay she said, "I find it difficult to explain the feeling or meaning but this is money I work very hard for. . . . In our society, one of the dominant forces is the need to make money. That is absent from us. We have more money than we can ever use. Therefore, it is necessary to replace that drive by achievement in other ways, or by creativity and imagination in the way we use our money for positive social good. I think my men cousins have worked very hard to do this and have found other forces—such as serving the society.

"I never studied American history because I didn't want to sit in a class and risk hearing my great-grandfather described as a robber baron."

Her notion that the family is serving society rather than taking bows at the taxpayers' expense shows that she has learned the family scenario

According to Hope Aldrich Rockefeller Spencer, daughter of John 3, "In many ways, in growing up as a Rockefeller I lived with a tag, just as a Jew or a Negro. I sensed what it was like to be discriminated against and have people ignore or accept you as part of a class or group rather than as an individual. I'm not suggesting by any means that I was discriminated against in the same way, but I think this is why I have an empathy for certain kinds of people. I felt often that when people heard the name Rockefeller they never saw the person named Hope."

"It was left to me to determine whether I wanted to be John D. Rockefeller IV," said Jay or John D. IV, age thirty-one at the time of the interview. He is the son of John D. 3. "When I turned twenty-one, I decided that I did."

"I have tremendous respect," he continued, "for the name and what it has stood for: concern, responsibility, considered judgment. I am proud of the family. My uncle, Laurance, contributed in the field of conservation. My uncle, David, is a progressive, creative banker. My uncle, Nelson, is Governor of New York, and my uncle, Winthrop, is Governor of Arkansas. My father made significant contributions in the area of population control, long before others. I am proud of a family that takes seriously the question of the quality of American life."

About his coming to West Virginia in 1965 as a community worker with Action for Appalachian Youth Community Development he said:

"I came here because at the age of 25 I realized I had spent a great deal of time in Europe and Japan but never had a quiet, concentrated experience in America. That didn't seem normal for a guy at 25. I wanted to be involved in something meaningful, at a grass-roots level. I thought first of working with Mexican-Americans and then learned of the plight of the West Virginians. I felt this was a state that was being ignored.

"I went into political life as a result of an analytic process. The question: How do you do something meaningful in this state? I thought that my work as part of the Appalachian project was useful but I could see that the real and effective way was through political action. It wasn't a difficult decision. The fact that it removes privacy isn't a big fat problem. I live with it very easily.

"I think people trust me even though I've inherited wealth. It is nonsense to argue that because one inherits wealth he is precluded from knowing about or understanding problems."

"I don't think there was a sudden moment of realization in which I discovered I was a Rockefeller and that I was different," said David Rockefeller, II, twenty-eight at the time, eldest son of Chairman David. He was employed then as arts administrator of the Boston Symphony Orchestra. A lawyer now, a graduate of Harvard College and Harvard Law School, he has most recently emerged as chairman of a national project, partly funded by the Rockefeller Brothers Fund, to inject more art into American school curricula. He is married and lives in Boston, where he sings bass with the Cantata Singers and was formerly chairman of the Associated Councils of the Arts.

"This generation has gone further to test itself and to see first hand," said Larry son of Laurance, who was twenty-four when interviewed. He had flown around the world in 1966 in a twin-engine Beechcraft Baron with a copilot who held a student's license. In his diary he wrote: "Calcutta is depressing. The crush of people—dead in spirit, incredibly poor, without hope, struggling to exist at all—unnerves us. It is July 29, my 22nd birthday—The next morning we are glad to be able to leave, sad to be leaving such misery unaltered."

"If I woke up tomorrow and there was no money, I think I'd stick to what I'm doing, a Vista worker in the Harlem ghetto. I figure that I could make a living. I could do it as a cowboy which I have done, or as an airline pilot."

Various things irritate these Rockefellers. Jay is irritated by being mentioned as a future presidential prospect—although he certainly is one. Steven was irritated by the kind of publicity that attended his marriage in 1959 to a Norwegian language student who was working as an *au pair* in his father Nelson's home; she was the daughter of a Norwegian businessman, strictly middle class. But the newspaper script called for her being a bone-deep maid so that the story could be "Rockefeller Marries Housemaid," a twist and an embroidery on the ever-inspiring American Dream. That story was as accurate as Bobo Paulekiute Sears being a coal miner's daughter, coal dust by implication filling every pore of her skin, when she married Winthrop. Steven and his wife, who has become a published writer, are now divorced with three children. No housemaid she.

Disagreement within the family, said Steven, was greatest during the Vietnam war. Steven, not knowing the score, pushed to have his father, seeking the presidency, come out against the war, but never succeeded. As a way out of his personal tangles, his wife writes, he has gone in for psychoanalysis.

Steven, a theologian with a cum laude from Union Theological Seminary and a doctorate, now teaching at Middlebury College, asserted that "Loyalty to one's own nation is a virtue, but blind patriotism and extreme nationalism are one of the evils that currently plague mankind. We are all members of one world and we have a responsibility to mankind as a whole

as well as to our own nation. While there are some very bellig-
erent Communist nations, our major enemy is no longer international communism. It is clearly poverty, ignorance, social
injustice, overpopulation, race hatred and international lawlessness." If he isn't careful someone will dub him a
Bolshevik.

He continued: "I think that if business does not learn how
to channel its resources into an effective redistribution of the
wealth then the free enterprise system will not last 50 years."
That this is not the aim of business was apparently not pointed out to him.

The subject of money came up, naturally. Said one Rockefeller who was not named, "It is not good to lend money to
friends. You do, and they almost automatically think because
you are a Rockefeller there is no need to pay it back. That
makes you wonder what sort of friend you have. So, our rule
was don't lend it to a friend."

This was pretty much what many people thought about
Nelson's lending, as disclosed before Congress, although Nelson said the loans were made out of friendship, had no strings
attached. Did the recipients expect to be dunned for
repayment?

"Consumption no longer has any meaning" to them, according to Nelson's son Rodman, president of the family's
International Basic Economy Corporation. "After the first
million, you learn you have all this money, and you buy what
you need, and then you know that you have to do something
with it."

"The profit motive," he said, drawing upon the Rockefeller
scenario, "is a tool we want to use to accomplish social ends."
As to redistributing wealth, Rodman said "the capitalistic system can meet the challenge. I still think we are not far from
getting unheard of commitments from the business sector."
The world is waiting.

"Our generation has all the elements of the new American
melting pot," said Hope Rockefeller Spencer. "There is diver-
sity and independence. And there is this very strong sense of
social equality. We're walking on the sidewalks—not riding in

Rolls-Royces. We're not going to skip any long roads because we have money."

Nelson, at least, is slumbering on a $35,000 water bed.

Others of the groups are Alida, youngest daughter of John 3; Nelson and Mark, very young children of Nelson by his second wife; Winthrop Paul, son of Winthrop and Bobo; Margaret, Richard, and Eileen, David's three youngest; and Abby Milton O'Neill and Marilyn, daughters of Abby Mauzé. Abby O'Neill busies herself with Colonial Williamsburg, and Marilyn is married to Egyptologist Prof. William Simpson of Yale.

Then there is Sandra, daughter of John 3, and Marion Weber, daughter of Laurance—both artists. Mary, daughter of Nelson, studies primitive art. Laura Case, daughter of Laurance, magna cum laude in art history from Bryn Mawr, also has a doctorate in political science from Harvard and is interested in the psychological underpinnings of politics. David's daughter Abby is a nonprofessional musician, was active in the antidraft movement. His other daughter, Neva Kaiser, is a magna cum laude from Radcliffe and into poetry.

One of this generation was already dead, Michael, a budding anthropologist lost on an expedition in New Guinea.

Larry, David, and Richard are still unknown quantities to the outside world, but Jay and Rodman seem well on the road to taking over for this generation. In order to fit into the scenario Steven will have to modulate his act, in which case he could function as a philanthropoid or a university president. His sort of talk does not lead either to the White House or into banking, might even get one on the F.B.I. "most wanted" list.

The younger generation appears confused by the pose of the Rockefellers about being "just plain folks," like everyone else. Like it or not, one can't be just plain folks and belong to a family worth several billion dollars and into matters political, corporate, financial, artistic, scientific, educational, environmental, and so on. It is like trying to be plain folks with names like Bourbon, Hohenzollern, Hapsburg, Romanoff, or Marlborough. For a family that has overreached nearly everybody else into the big money, and stayed there, to pretend that nothing much has happened borders on absurdity.

Apparently the older generation does not brief the younger generation or delegate any knowledgeable staffer to brief it on the family history and the way it is perceived by various outsiders. The family here comports itself, apparently, pretty much as middle-class American families once did, and probably still do, with respect to sex. Beyond a few gingerly references, they let the younger ones find out for themselves the hard way. After some of their encounters with outsiders, some of the younger Rockefellers no doubt feel like puppies who have been given a thrashing because their sire is a big fierce dog, the terror of the neighborhood. If they wish, however, they may console themselves with the thought that soon they too will be big dogs. They can then have the laugh when all the neighbor-bullies run at the sight of them or come crawling around as nice as pie.

But the fourth generation, adhering to the scenario, acts as a group, coming together after age twenty-one to discuss philanthropies, investments, politics, philosophy, art, theater, sports, and child rearing. They have launched a Cousins Fund, apparently designed to succeed the Rockefeller Brothers Fund in the course of time. Making money by remote control and disbursing it, with tax deductions through the courtesy of the United States Congress, appears fated to continue. The Cousins, in other words, are already institutionalized.

But adhering to the Rockefeller penchant for keeping a low personal profile while maintaining a high institutional profile, some of the women, says Bernard Gavzer, "dress as though they selected their entire wardrobe during a busy lunch hour in a bargain basement." This helps them escape notice while out on the sidewalks.

For as Bobo discovered, the mere mention of the name has a galvanic effect on everybody within earshot. It evokes thrills or shivers, part of the accompanying public syndrome.

Yet "What to do," Gavzer found, "occupies a considerable amount of energy and time on the part of the cousins and a corps of outsiders who are part of the army of experts—investment counsellors, accountants, public relations staff, etc.— available to these Rockefellers. The Rockefellers thus extend their own substantial intelligence and expertise by having access to intelligent people who can produce relevant information."

This, too, as we have seen, is part of the scenario, worked out long ago.

15.

The fourth generation appears to be more studious and reflective than either of the three preceding generations, although what if anything will come of this remains to be seen. None of the Rockefellers, thus far, at least of the first three generations, appears to have been widely read or given to generalized thinking. Even within the fourth generation today the parameters of their thinking about the position of the family in the world appear to have been derived straight from the public relations men. It is the image these have devised for the family that is the family's self-image, very probably sincerely and certainly self-deceivingly held. For their part, the public relations men have had to consider family susceptibilities.

Old John D. read nothing except business and church reports and newspapers. Junior and his wife, who was an enthusiastic reader, read discursively, unsystematically, and apparently largely for diversion. According to all reports, none of their sons has had much time for reading, all of them being in one way or the other organization men and activists. Winthrop was at about the farthest remove from being a reader. Nelson, afflicted with dyslexia, a reading disorder in which the words appear backward or upside-down, is also manifestly not a reader; he memorizes his speeches with the help of staff people. As to the others of the third generation, there is no question about ability to read. The point is only that they are not widely read, don't have the time for it. David, of course, is deeply read in economics and finance and in two instances of record has shown the ability to develop a thesis at book length.

But as for information filtering to the outside about any

particular reading interest of the family members, apart from David, there is none. Apart from the Bible, which was old John D.'s book of last resort, through the mediation of clergy and his wife, no central book or collection of books appears to be relied upon by the family for philosophic guidance. One could not, for example, say that they rested their faith on Adam Smith's *The Wealth of Nations*, which among other things is a polemic against monopoly. Naturally Karl Marx is out the window as a family guide. David Ricardo, too, must go with his outlandish theory that economic value is created by labor. As some of them term themselves pragmatists, it might seem that they draw support from Charles Peirce or William James, except there is so much in each pointed against them, including James's fury with "the bitch-goddess Success," that they can hardly claim pragmatism as a philosophic support.

In other words, what are they? Kantians? Freudians? Deweyans? Spinozists? Hegelians? Reasons abound in each case for denying any affinity.

As to politics, more particularly American politics, they seem to me to be Hamiltonians—at least Hamiltonians at bottom with some Jeffersonian rhetoric smeared over the whole as public relations frosting. Whether they have read into Hamilton, I don't know, but one can pick up the Hamiltonian line by being into the thick of the Republican party, as they have been right along.

Most of what the Rockefellers spout forth appears to be what they have heard, not read—heard from parents, from clergy, from better-read associates, from well-educated staff people, from public relations men and other sophists, the rhetoric drawn from the liberal vat, the concrete actions from the Hamiltonian. Little if any of this appears to have been modified by independent reading or research.

Although they have been into many things, it is interesting to notice, for all their claims to having a broad-gauged approach, that they have given no emphasis at all to anything at all critical of or opposed to the established order—civil liberties movements, legal-aid activities, critical analysis of the established order.

16.

I don't want to leave this subject without injecting a pleasant note about old John D. For many professors look with a jaundiced eye on any account that is not "balanced"—that is, full of on-the-other-hands. In their view everything must balance out, exactly, just why they do not say. Such professors, however, never tell one what to do in the case of characters like Hitler, Joseph Stalin, Ghengis Khan, and a few others. Old John D., of course, was never like any of these.

John D. Rockefeller, narrow though he was and with a certain peculiar personality formation, was very far from being a 100 percent dyed-in-the-wool rascal. Indeed, looked at from his side of the fence, he was a highly honorable and punctilious man, a man whose approval was worth a good deal. Schizoid perhaps, but not all antisocial.

In order to get this more pleasant view of John D., one must look at him always from the point of view of his own circle. Beyond this circle lay the enemy—competitors, the general public, hostile politicos, even the law and established political institutions. Although here one needs to make a nice distinction. While he saw nothing wrong with having his lieutenants intervene with money in legislatures, there is no record that he ever allowed anything similar to be done with the courts. Rockefeller and his associates, the fact appears to be, never attempted to bribe judges (which has not been an unheard-of thing in American industrial and financial history). As to the law itself, that was, as always, susceptible to interpretation, and Rockefeller had no scruples whatever about hiring legal casuists who could make an ironclad case out of just about any position. In this respect he apparently felt that if the law clearly pointed in some different direction, it was the duty of opposing casuists to carry the day.

Rockefeller was an in-group man, operating against out-groups—there was the infidel. He was, first, 100 percent for his family; nothing was too good for it and its members. He venerated his mother and was always respectful toward his father although he very much disapproved of some of his swindling sire's latter-day behavior. He harbored no hard feelings even against members of his family who had stung him deeply. He sent money late in life to his wayward father and also to his brother Frank who had hurt him most of all, not once but many times. Frank, a more autonomous free-floating character, had been a real thorn. No matter.

Next, he was loyal to his religious sect, the Baptists. Nothing was too good for them and anything he could do to keep the Baptists afloat, keep them making a good showing against their rivals the Methodists, he did. For the Methodists and others, however, until a much later date—nothing much.

Toward his business associates, too, Rockefeller was strictly on the up-and-up, straight. This was fairly unusual in American business, especially Big Business, where the knife in the back was not too rare. Andrew Carnegie tried to skin partners, would have skinned the tough Henry Clay Frick if Frick hadn't caught him at it and known how to take care of himself. Rockefeller was totally unlike people like Jim Fisk, Jay Gould, Commodore Vanderbilt, James Duke, Thomas Fortune Ryan, J. P. Morgan, and a whole crew who would take wherever the taking looked good, from anybody, friend or foe, rich or poor, saint or sinner. Rockefeller, within his narrow vision, was a moral man.

Nor did Rockefeller ever try to gyp anyone who became a stockholder of Standard Oil. Indeed, he beseeched all who sold out to Standard Oil to take stock rather than money, which most refused to do (and were proportionately sore about it later on; had they taken stock they'd have been his boosters later rather than among his knockers). Those who took stock or otherwise acquired it became as one of the family.

He never went in for stock-jobbing or manipulating the stock of Standard Oil—that is, talking it up and then selling, then talking it down and buying, profiting both ways. This was a common sneaky game of the robber-baron magnates of the day, and still is a common Wall Street game. Instead of painting rosy visions of the company's position, he kept its excellent position concealed; until a very late date, 1913, the stock never sold at anywhere near its true value. In brief, if one bought Standard Oil stock, one always bought something worth more. Standard Oil stock was a better buy than a United States or United Kingdom government bond, at all times, probably still is.

As to his playing square with his associates, it might be said that as he needed no more money, he had no need to play them false; but this applies as well to others, like Carnegie. They, too, needed no more money. Some acquisitors never draw the line on how they get money. It might also be said that some of his associates were dangerous men to play false and therefore he forebore; but Frick was as dangerous as anyone in the Standard Oil crowd and yet Carnegie tried to cheat him. No, all the evidence points to Rockefeller just being a square shooter within his own group. And this is one of the reasons the Rockefellers retain the loyalty of all the old Standard Oil families.

But he was better even than this. For when Standard Oil came under public and governmental attack, Rockefeller throughout took the brunt. All others, to this day, got off practically free of criticism. The company, it is true, was his creation, operated according to the signals he called and he was its dominant stockholder as well as titular head. But as the hue and cry against it intensified, he could easily have protested that there were others with leading roles in the company, that he was not the whole company. Yet he never did.

He never, as it were, turned state's evidence, not even in the company's darkest hour. Nor did any of his associates, who had no need to as Rockefeller was taking the whole blame. He was, of course, far from blameless; the company followed his blueprint. And where it didn't, where it followed some line suggested by others, Rockefeller of course was part of it because he accepted it, unquestionably knew of everything going on. But his associates were far more than his passive agents. Unquestionably many things were done that Rockefeller took care not to know of until after the fact although, once done, he accepted them, backed the man. Nobody was ever discharged from Standard Oil for being overzealous. If one sinned on behalf of Standard Oil, one was O.K. with Rockefeller.

And when with his vast surplus money, he decided to create and fund hostages for the sake of the company—which is what his early philanthropic institutions were—they were of high quality. Whatever the ulterior motive, it was not the act of a barbarian to found a university, a medical institute, a fund for invigorating education in benighted regions of the country. Rockefeller, in fact, could have made a much bigger sentimental hit than he ever made by establishing Christian orphanages, homes for unmarried mothers, shelters for derelicts and hospices for drunkards—money down the drain. He never did. He could have given big sums to the Salvation Army with which to serve Thanksgiving and Christmas dinners to the denizens of Skid Row. Had he done any of this, topping it off with homes for the aged and feebleminded, he'd have had the masses with him, probably imploring him to run for president. Rockefeller, the fact is, aimed much higher. And at higher mentalities.

One final word about the elder Rockefeller before I am carried away and rashly nominate him for canonization. Rockefeller never showed himself to be vindictive. He made a lot of enemies in his career, people who would have been happy to wring his neck and people who in retaliation for genuine or fancied wrongs gave him a lot of trouble and worry. Nowhere in the record does it show that Rockefeller thereupon engaged in counterretaliation. He could have done so, easily. He had the money for it. He could have made heads roll.

What he did about his retaliators was apparently to take their venom pretty much as if in a baseball game: he had had his innings, now they had their innings. Satisfied, he let matters rest there. His account books showed what the score was. He had won. He was the champ. Let the soreheads now do and say what they wished.

All that, too, is part of the scenario and, as I see it, applaudable. One thing Rockefeller, a Bible-reader, apparently believed and practiced: "A soft answer turneth away wrath." Percentage-wise, he was right. The retention of the fortune proves he was right.

17.

There remains to consider the political position of the Rockefellers.

Just as some persons on the Right claim the Rockefellers are partial to communism or socialism, so many persons on the Left claim they are pushing for the establishment of fascism.

Precisely why the Rockefellers should go in either of these unseemly un-American directions is not clear as they are closely interwoven in hundreds of ways with both political parties and the good old United States government, which thus far seems well able to take care of itself against would-be interlopers. Persons who claim the Rockefellers are wickedly trending either to the left or the right don't seem conversant with the nature of the United States government. Again, the Rockefellers are highly prosperous under the present dispensation.

Those, for example, who fear the establishment of a sinister one-party police state under the Rockefellers seem not aware of concrete official disclosures about the existent United States government—That for more than twenty years under Republican and Democratic administrations, the Federal Bureau of Investigation, all its agents also lawyers, has been surreptitiously intervening to disrupt the lives of unformidable people holding entirely legal but ideologically disliked political opinions; That the F. B. I. in a large number of political trials used secret *agents provocateurs* who themselves counseled and monitored the specific illegal acts that others were tried for and eventually acquitted of; That the FBI falsified evidence in such trials; That several presidents—at least Kennedy, Johnson, and Nixon—used the Internal Revenue Service to harass and spy on people holding political opinions adverse to them (people who wrote testily to congressmen or to newspapers; radio, television and other commentators; people who spoke out against the administration or its policies in public meetings); That the Central Intelligence Agency, restricted by law to operations abroad, developed dossiers on citizens conducting entirely legal political activity in this country, merely placing themselves in opposition to White House incumbents, and aided secret searches without warrants; That both the CIA and FBI pressed the Post Office into their service to open and read mail, wholesale, of politically passive people corresponding with friends and relatives abroad; That these agencies harnessed eager-beaver local police departments into cooperation with them in spying on, monitoring, reporting on, and harassing local residents conducting entirely legal activities such as questioning a wide range of official and sometimes unlawful activities; That these agencies, especially the FBI, spread damaging canards about many innocent citizens conducting entirely legal activities such as speaking up for civil rights and a wide range of other matters; That the FBI developed dossiers on independent congressmen, lawyers, and no doubt others; That the CIA spied on blameless American lawyers; That people were arrested on a large scale on trumped-up charges that fell apart under the scrutiny of the courts, the arduous legal process nevertheless subjecting them to expensive, undue, and disruptive harassment; That many such persons were deliberately "framed;" That under President Nixon the pace of such activities was increased so as to eventuate in everything connoted by the term Watergate, with most of the members of this criminal conspiracy—including several cabinet officers—winding up under jail sentences; That the most conspicuous conspirator, President Nixon, was hastily pardoned prior to any trial(!) by President Ford, whom Nixon had just appointed; That both political parties collected massive illegal funds; That under Presidents Kennedy, Johnson, and Nixon the armed forces were thrown into an undeclared, probably illegal, and unusually dirty war which an increasingly large proportion of the American people entirely rejected in its objectives, nature, and the manner of implementation; That absolutely crazy and inequitable tax laws hitting tens of millions have been a hallmark of this government for more than twenty-five years and that the government refuses to pass many salutary laws that a vast majority demand, such as gun control, and passes laws freely that vast majorities, as reflected in the polls, oppose. And so on.

The foregoing is by no means a full bill of ugly particulars. It could be greatly extended.

The government, in brief, has been conducting a covert reign of terror against any and all critics of its inept stooge officialdom, left, right, and center, and has been high handed in a wholesale police-state way so as to negate the sentiments of nearly every man who had anything whatever to do with writing the Constitution. What these latter-day administrations have proven is that the Constitution is readily subvertible by duly elected officials. In the meantime, civil disorder has been steadily increasing for twenty years, and has been spreading alarmingly.

Leading officials and politicos are assassinated—President Kennedy, Robert Kennedy, Martin Luther King. George Wallace is shot and crippled. Who is next? is the $64 question.

Closely locked into such a government, with how much worse in the way of a political formation could the Rockefellers be associated? In other words, if they went right or left, just where would they go that is very different? What, anyhow, is so unthinkable about a repressive one-party police state when we are, by all known tests, just about in it or close to it?

The final report of the Rockefeller Commission on CIA Activities in the United States, although backing away from tackling reports of planned political assassinations, confirmed that the CIA, always acting illegally, in defiance of statute and Constitution, developed "13,000 different files, including files on 7,200 American citizens." The documents in these files and related materials, said the report, "included the names of more than 300,000 persons and organizations, which were entered into a computerized index."

All the domestic information-gathering of the CIA, strictly illegal all the way, was done in response to "repeated Presidential requests." Law-breaking centered in the White House.

The CIA, in brief, was directed as though by a man who has a fierce watchdog to keep away external hostile intruders— entirely proper. But the man also, unknown to the neighbors, used the animal against members of his own family who by their opinions displeased him.

Government intelligence files—at IRS, FBI and CIA—, contrary to what many suppose, were not composed solely of the names of criminal or subversive characters, but included names such as Doris Day, Dean Martin, Frank Sinatra, John Wayne and former Ambassador to Great Britain, Walter Annenberg, a Nixon appointee. The point is: Just about everybody who manifested himself in any non-routine way went into the files—except, of course, the corporate "fat cats" and wing-ding operators.

By reason of woozy propaganda in schools, newspapers, and political rallies, Americans in general have only the vaguest idea of the actual thrust of American government. They are not aware of the full import of the founders' intent that this be a government that acts on *individuals.* The fact that the government is so organized as to act on isolated individuals makes it possible just as readily for *officials* to act surreptitiously on isolated individuals; for officials are the means through which the government operates. In brief, callous officials—executive, legislative, and judicial—exercise a great deal of person-to-person entirely illegal power and authority, masked in the case of the executive and legislative by a great deal of handshaking, joking, backslapping, and pseudocamaraderie vis-à-vis the electorate. The judiciary is much more aloof, and more reliable man for man, pound for pound, despite slips here and there. No doubt this will soon be taken care of. Nixon tried to load the bench with clinkers.

The excessively friendly outward demeanor of executive and legislator should not, however, deceive the intelligent. For it is meant, obviously, to disarm doubters and the fearful. Beware of politicians wreathed in affability is a good motto for the perplexed.

This being a government that acts on individuals, in any action of the government concerning citizens, the name of the citizen appears on the formal process. Thus in the case of legal proceedings the process reads: *United States of America versus George Q. Wrong,* which means that the entire United States government is arrayed against Mr. Wrong. In the case of secret dossiers it means that Mr. Wrong has been found guilty of some offense, *known only to officialdom,* of personal interest to officialdom, but has not been subjected to due process.

And the reason the citizen is not subjected to due process is that he has not committed any legally defined offense. Thinking and saying Presidents Kennedy, Johnson, Nixon, and Ford are *dummkopfs* or worse is not a legally defined offense. But saying it, and arguing it in any effective forum can be, as disclosures have shown, extremely dangerous to the individual. It brings the whole weight of government against him, secretly. What follows is straight police-state stuff.

As the school books and the Constitution say, the citizen is entitled to a speedy trial, which sounds good on paper. Let us suppose one quickly gets a trial—and wins. But the victory is usually pyrrhic. The defendant is shattered in purse and spirit. One may rejoice, however, in that one has defeated Leviathan. But at what cost?

The secret dossiers, however, permit no trial and no victory. These are merely passed around among officialdom, down to the grass-roots level. The community as a whole may not know one is a covertly convicted person but officialdom knows and, once it sees an opening, it will use the secret dossier to the citizen's civil disadvantage. And even if ascendant officialdom never sees an opening, it may, as it has done, use the contents of the dossier to disrupt one's personal relationships by *anonymously,* damagingly, and selectively conveying some of the contents to one's friends or relatives or to one's spouse. J. Edgar Hoover, the appointee of many presidents, did precisely this with some of the contents of his suspect dossier on Martin Luther King, seeing to it that the alleged information got to his wife. Her possible anguish meant nothing to him. And Hoover held office for more than fifty years.

The FBI in many cases anonymously passed on irrelevant gossip-type information and pseudo-information it had collected—to employers, wives, friends and neighbors. While what it had in such cases was not indicative of law-breaking it could, and did, make life miserable for many people, including the innocent connections of those that had drawn the ire of pettifogging White House staffs.

"But I'm not Martin Luther King," George Q. Wrong may bleat fatuously. As far as officialdom and the Constitution are concerned, he is no different, no better, no worse. If he's annoying, says politicians are crooks, he's doomed. Here we see the majesty of the law. What happened to Martin Luther King and others can well happen to still more, already has happened. In the case of tax harassment it has happened to thousands. And by harassment here I mean on the basis of no tax grounds whatever staging so-called "random" and grinding field audits of a taxpayer simply because he has expressed himself against puffed-up nobodies like John F. Kennedy, Lyndon B. Johnson, Richard Nixon, or any of a number of others or against their inane policies.

As the Rockefellers are thriving under this state of affairs, are major beneficiaries of it as recent disclosures before Congress showed, why should they go in any novel sinister political direction feared by either leftists or rightists? No Rockefeller has denounced any of this.

What, after all, is there to fear anew if we are already there, in the soup?

Americans have always boasted that they live under a political regime that permits freedom of speech and press, by constitutional fiat. The United States is not a country like Soviet Russia and others where one is forbidden to speak freely. But most Americans have never believed that what one says by way of expressing an opinion, if one says it in an effective forum, will be taken down, filed in computers, and may be used against one in some way, secretly, in the contexts of one's ordinary affairs. Things then start misfiring all along the line. The rule becomes: do not annoy officials, elected or appointed. And what transpires does so not at the behest of some local sheriff but perhaps by order of the president of the United States or his staff.

In view of the disclosures accidentally made, all this, some delirious optimists suppose, is now about to be changed. But is it? The same back-room types we have seen in the past now fill the pipeline of the Republican-Democratic party. In coming elections as in past the voters have a choice of two men for each office, both straight out of the pipeline, long trained. In 1960 for the presidency the choice was limited to Kennedy and Nixon, with Kennedy winning by a hair; in 1964 it was limited to Johnson and Goldwater, with Johnson winning by such a large majority that he claimed he had a mandate for just about anything; in 1968 it was limited to Nixon and Humphrey, with Nixon winning by a narrow margin; and in 1972 it was between Nixon and George McGovern. Although the total turnout now was very low, below half the electorate, Nixon won by such a large majority—thanks in part to dirty tricks—that he now claimed a mandate—a mandate from a majority of a minority!

With all the administrations established by these electoral victories, and with earlier administrations, the Rockefellers were closely intertwined. All these administrations were greatly liked by the corporate crowd, which passed over to their electoral managers heavy—and strictly illegal—sums of money in numerous instances.

As this is the so-called democratic system, as this is the way it works, why should the Rockefellers and their peers be contemplating moving off and supporting some supposedly horrifying other system with a detestable foreign name? The claim that they are so planning comes from those who stand on the unwarranted assumption that the present system is wonderful, wonderful, wonderful and should be blindly preserved in all its glory. Among other things, it guarantees free speech ... and plenty of trouble if one makes use of it.

Nelson Rockefeller has said it many times: the aim of the Rockefellers is to stay wholly and loyally within the present system. As to this assertion, I believe him without reservation. For him and his sheltered family, the system is wonderful.

18.

Spelling it all out, so that even flyweight professors can understand, the Rockefeller Operation boils down to the following:

A huge fortune, illicitly amassed, is doled out in part over a span of many years in a variety of projects appealing to different kinds of mentalities—a university; a medical research institute; foundations that make distributions seriatim to education, science, medical research, art museums and the like; a reconstructed historical site; national parks; opera and music halls; conservation programs and many other peripheral embellishments.

Two purposes of interest to the donor family are thereby served. First, a responsive sympathetic chord is struck with some part of the public for each project, appeasing discontent with the way the fortune was acquired. For in most cases (although not all) the projects are entirely valid. Secondly, specific managerial and entrepreneurial elements benefiting personally from each project naturally become Rockefeller boosters.

At the same time, all the outlay is tax-deductible so that the burden of taxation—for endless armaments, welfare, gaudy government operations and waste—is shoved over on to the precariously-employed taxpayer. He pays taxes from an insecure economic base; the Rockefellers avoid taxes on a Gibraltar-secure economic base.

The Rockefeller fortune is well into the 70 percent tax bracket, and was (until the rates were lowered) in the 90 percent estate-tax bracket. It never paid a significant amount of estate taxes. A large part of its income nevertheless was theoretically scheduled to be taken away in income taxes from personal disposition. So it was either a case of paying the money in taxes, and getting no public kudos for it, or devoting it to projects that produced hosannas of public joy and praise. Under close examination, however, some of the projects, such as Nelson's purely political exercises, were disallowed as tax-deductible.

A further gain in funding tax-deductible projects hailed as philanthropic is that one may choose the projects. One has, in brief, the privilege of legislating, decreeing, what shall and what shall not be created or supported. The involuntary contribution of taxpayers to such privately-decreed projects consists of that proportion of taxes avoided by the beneficent donors. The public, of course, does not realize that it is being forced to make a monetary input into the philanthropic projects.

At the same time, a vast fortune is retained through the generations and is so managed as to confer great financial and economic clout from one generation to the next, endlessly, without any need on the part of the fortune's owners to show any special proficiency. The fortune supports what is the equivalent of a noble family—that is, before nobility was ostensibly abolished, superseded by the glorious Stars and Stripes. Through the apt management of the fortune and attendant tax-exempt projects, an extensive family is, thus, sustained in a life of extreme luxury.

Finally, anyone who presumes to criticize this operation is countered by the techniques of serpentine public relations officers and the outcries of the immediate beneficiaries, the tax-exempt project administrators. As it turns out, the villain of the piece, the one who should go stand in the corner, face to the wall with a dunce-cap on his head, is—the critical analyst of the operation! There is the distempered churl, the bad guy, the disbeliever in star-spangled nonsense, who has proclaimed the nakedness of the emperor.

True, the Rockefeller Operation is not the only piece of legerdemain that holds the befuddled American public under an hypnotic spell. It is only one of many.

19.

In conclusion, there seems to be no better way to describe the Rockefellers than as the modern Medici. Theirs is a story of money and funding, all the way, and of intimate involvement in the very warp and woof of the established order at every level. Their dicta, whatever they are, have much impact. They are not ordinary Joes, even if some of them tread the sidewalks in bargain-basement clothes.

Bibliography

Abels, Jules. *The Rockefeller Billions: The Story of the World's Most Stupendous Fortune.* New York: The Macmillan Company, 1965.

Adamic, Louis. *Dynamite: The Story of Class Violence in America.* New York: The Viking Press, 1931.

Alexander, Franz, and Ross, Helen, eds. *Dynamic Psychiatry.* Chicago and London: University of Chicago Press, 1952.

Allen, William H. *Rockefeller: Giant, Dwarf, Symbol.* New York: Institute of Public Service, 1930.

Alsop, Stewart. *Nixon and Rockefeller: A Double Portrait.* Garden City, N.Y.: Doubleday, 1960.

American Handbook of Psychiatry. Vol. I. 2d ed. New York: Basic Books, 1974.

Attica Prison Report. *Attica: The Official Report of the New York State Commission on Attica.* New York: Praeger, 1972.

Bailey, Thomas Andrew. *Presidential Greatness: The Image and the Man from George Washington to the Present.* New York: Appleton-Century, 1966.

Bergquist, Laura. "Bobo as Seen by Her Oldest Friend." *Life,* 15 March 1954.

Berle, A. A., and Means, Gardiner C. *The Modern Corporation and Private Property.* New York: Commerce Clearing House, 1932.

Bigart, Homer. "The Men Who Made the World Move," (Laurance S. Rockefeller). *Saturday Review,* 22 April 1967.

Bryce, James. *The American Commonwealth.* 2 vols. London: Macmillan & Co., 1891.

Caro, Robert. *The Power-Broker: The Decline and Fall of New York.* New York: A. A. Knopf, 1974.

Carr, Albert Z. *John D. Rockefeller's Secret Weapon.* New York: McGraw-Hill, 1962.

Chase, Mary Ellen. *Abby Aldrich Rockefeller.* New York: Macmillan, 1950.

Connery, Robert H., ed. *Governing New York State: The Rockefeller Years.* Philadelphia: American Academy of Political Science, 1974.

Council on Foreign Relations. *Report of the Executive Director,* 1933-1974. New York.

Cousins, Norman. Review of Nevins's *John D. Rockefeller: The Heroic Age of American Enterprise. Saturday Review of Literature,* 26 October 1940.

Debate on the reliability of Henry Demarest Lloyd between Prof. Allan Nevins and Prof. Chester McArthur Destler, *American Historical Review,* October 1944, and April 1945. As put by Jules Abels, *The Rockefeller Billions,* p. 365, it shows "the extreme partisanship of Professor Nevins for Rockefeller."

Desmond, James. *Nelson Rockefeller: A Political Portrait.* New York: Macmillan and Company, 1964.

Dictionary of American Biography. New York: Charles Scribner's Sons.

Eaton, Merrill T., and Peterson, Margaret H. *Psychiatry.* New York: Medical Examination Publishing Co., 1969.

Flynn, John T. *God's Gold: The Story of Rockefeller and His Times.* New York: Harcourt, Brace and Co., 1932. (The premier biography to date with most extensive bibliography, lacking only the Rockefeller papers to which Nevins was given access.)

Fogel, Yvonne. "Laurance S. Rockefeller." *Parks & Recreation,* March 1970.

Foreign Policy Association. *Annual Reports.* New York.

———*Twenty-five Years of the Foreign Policy Association,* 1918-1948, New York, n.d.

Fortune. "Directory of the 500 Largest Industrial Corporations." May 1970. (This directory appears in the same month each year.)

Fosdick, Raymond. *Adventure in Giving, The Story of the General Education Board.* New York: Harper & Row, 1962.

—— *John D. Rockefeller, Jr., A Portrait.* New York: Harper and Bros., 1956.

——*The Story of the Rockefeller Foundation.* New York: Harper and Bros., 1952.

Goulden, Joseph C. *The Money-Givers: An Examination of the Myths and Realities of Foundation Philanthropy in America.* New York: Random House, 1971.

Hapgood, David. *The Screwing of the Average Man.* New York: Doubleday & Co., 1974.

Hellman, Geoffrey T. "Out of the Cocoon on the Fifty-Sixth Floor" (Profile of John D. Rockefeller III). *The New Yorker,* 4 November 1972.

Hoffman, William. *David* (David Rockefeller). New York: Lyle Stuart, 1971.

House of Representatives, Select Committee on Small Business. *Tax-Exempt Foundations and Charitable Trusts: Their Impact on Our Economy.* Washington, D. C.: Government Printing Office, 1963.

Hunt, E. Howard. *Undercover: Memoirs of an American Secret Agent.* New York: Berkley Publishing Corporation, 1974.

Josephson, Emanuel M. *The Federal Reserve Conspiracy and the Rockefellers: Their Gold Corner.* New York: Chedney Press, 1968.

——*Rockefeller "Internationalist."* New York: Chedney Press, 1952.

—— *The Truth About the Rockefellers: Public Enemy No. 1; Studies in Criminal Psychopathy.* New York: Chedney Press, 1964.

Josephson, Matthew. *The Politicos.* New York: Harcourt Brace and Co., 1938.

—— *The Robber Barons.* New York: Harcourt Brace and Co., 1934.

Kahn, E. J., Jr. "Profile"—David Rockefeller. *The New Yorker,* 9, 16 January 1965.

Knowles, James C. *The Rockefeller Financial Group.* Andover, Mass.: Warner Modular Publications, Inc., Module 343, 1973.

Kutz, Myer. *Rockefeller Power.* New York: Simon and Schuster, 1974. (An informative round-up on the philanthropies with a special bibliography relating thereto.)

Lindeman, Eduard C. *Wealth and Culture.* New York: Harcourt, Brace and Co., 1936.

Lloyd, Henry Demarest. *Wealth versus Commonwealth.* Washington, D. C.: National Home Library Foundation, 1936. Originally New York: Harper and Bros., 1892.

Lundberg, Ferdinand. *America's Sixty Families.* New York: Vanguard Press, 1937.

—— *Imperial Hearst, A Social Biography.* New York: Equinox Press, 1936; New York: Arno Press, 1970; and Westport: Greenwood Press, 1971.

—— *The Rich and the Super-Rich: A Study in the Power of Money Today.* New York: Lyle Stuart, Inc., 1968; New York: Bantam Books, 1969.

Manchester, William R. *A Rockefeller Family Portrait, from John D. to Nelson.* Boston: Little Brown and Company, 1959.

Manning, Thomas G. *The Standard Oil Company: The Rise of a National Monopoly.* New York: Holt, Rinehart and Winston, 1962.

Mencken, H. L. *Notes on Democracy.* New York: A. A. Knopf, 1926.

Morris, Joe Alex. *Those Rockefeller Brothers: An Informal Biography of Five Extraordinary Young Men.* New York: Harper and Bros., 1953.

—— *Nelson Rockefeller, A Biography.* New York: Harper and Bros., 1960.

Myers, Gustavus. *History of the Great American Fortunes.* 3 vols. Chicago: Kerr Publishing Company, 1910.

National Cyclopedia of American Biography. Ann Arbor: Xerox University Microfilms.

Neuhaus, Richard J. "The Best Reviews Money Can Buy." *The Christian Century,* 30 January 1974.

Nevins, Allan. *John D. Rockefeller: The Heroic Age of American Enterprise.* 2 vols. New York: Charles Scribner's Sons, 1940.

—— *Study in Power: John D. Rockefeller, Industrialist and Philanthropist.* 2 vols. New York: Charles Scribner's Sons, 1953.

New York Herald Tribune, 17 January, 8 March 1929, p. 1. Reports on assertion of Rockefeller control over the Standard Oil Company of Indiana.

New York Post, various dates, 1974. Hearings in Washington on the nomination of Nelson Rockefeller as vice-president of the United States.

New York Times, various dates, 1974. *New York Times Index,* 1974. Hearings in Washington on the nomination of Nelson Rockefeller as vice-president of the United States.

New York World, 2 September 1908.

Patman, Wright. *Chain Banking: Stockholder and Loan Links of 200 Largest Member Banks.* Washington, D. C.: U. S. Government Printing Office, 1963.

Paul, Randolph. *Taxation in the United States.* Boston: Little Brown and Company, 1954.

Pyle, Tom. *Pocantico; Fifty Years on the Rockefeller Domain.* New York: Duell, Sloan and Pearce, 1964.

Rasmussen, Anne-Marie. *There Was Once a Time: of Islands, Illusions, and Rockefellers.* New York, London: Harcourt Brace Jovanovich, 1975. (Life among the fourth-generation Rockefellers.)

Regier, Cornelius C. *The Era of the Muckrakers.* Chapel Hill: The University of North Carolina Press, 1932.

Reich, Wilhelm. *Character Analysis.* New York: Noonday Press, 1961 (1933).

Rockefeller Foundation. *Condensed Record of Activities from 1913 to 1963.* New York: Rockefeller Foundation, 1963.

Rockefeller, Nelson A. *Rockefeller Report on the Americas.* New York: Quadrangle, 1969.

Rockefeller Panel. *Prospect for Tomorrow: The Rockefeller Panel Reports.* Garden City, N. Y.: Doubleday, 1961.

Rodgers, William A. *Rockefeller's Follies: An Unauthorized View of Nelson A. Rockefeller.* New York: Stein and Day, 1966.

Securities and Exchange Commission, U.S. *Investigation of Concentration of Economic Power.* Monograph #29. 76th Congress, 3rd session. Temporary National Economic Committee, 1940-41.

Shapiro, David. *Neurotic Styles.* New York: Basic Books, Inc., 1965.

Smith, Richard Austin. "The Rockefeller Brothers, Grandsons of JDR." *Fortune,* February, March 1955.

Stern, Philip M. *The Rape of the Taxpayer.* New York: Random House, 1973.

Sutton, Horace. "The Mauna Kea Caper" (Laurance Rockefeller). *Saturday Review,* 21 August 1965.

Tarbell, Ida. *The History of the Standard Oil Company* (the masterwork on the original company). 2 vols. New York: Macmillan, 1905.

———— "John D. Rockefeller." *McClure's Magazine,* July-August 1905.

Tocqueville, Alexis de. *Democracy in America.* 2 vols. New York: A. A. Knopf, 1945.

United States Circuit Court of Appeals, 7th Circuit. Opinion of the court reversing judgment of the U. S. District Court in the case of the United States vs. the Standard Oil Company of Indiana, heard before Justice K. M. Landis. Chicago, 1908.

United States Circuit Court, 8th Circuit, Eastern Division of the Eastern Judicial District of Missouri. *U. S. of A., Petitioner, vs. Standard Oil Co. of New Jersey et al., defendants.* Brief of facts and arguments for petitioner. 2 vols. Washington, 1909.

U. S. News & World Report. "Rockefeller Brothers: From Riches to Success." 1 February 1960.

Index

401